THE POLITICS OF HERITAGE

How does a country's past become its 'national heritage'? And whose history is counted as part of this heritage? *The Politics of Heritage* brings together leading cultural critics, practitioners, policy makers and curators to explore the processes of heritage formation, focusing on issues of 'race' and ethnicity.

The book opens with a landmark article by Stuart Hall, arguing for the urgent need to re-imagine our national heritage in what he terms the 'post-nation'. It goes on to examine how different types of heritage – from football to stately homes, and from museum exhibits to history teaching – deal with the complex legacies of 'race'. Whether exploring the fallout of colonialism, the domination of England over the other nations of the 'United Kingdom', Holocaust memorials or the way British heritage is represented in former colonies, a recurring theme of the book is the need to accept that Britain has always been a site of shifting ethnicities, shaped by waves of migration, diaspora and globalisation. Analysing both theory and practice, the book is concerned with understanding how 'heritage' changes and develops, and with exploring problems and possibilities for the future.

COMEDIA
Series Editor: David Morley

Comedia titles available from Routledge:

TELEVISION, AUDIENCES AND CULTURAL STUDIES
David Morley

TELEVISION, ETHNICITY AND CULTURAL CHANGE
Marie Gillespie

TIMES OF THE TECHNOCULTURE
From the Information Society to the Virtual Life
Kevin Robins and Frank Webster

TO BE CONTINUED . . .
Soap Opera Around the World
Edited by Robert C. Allen

TRANSNATIONAL CONNECTIONS
Culture, People, Places
Ulf Hannerz

VIDEO PLAYTIME
The Gendering of a Leisure Technology
Ann Gray

THE POLITICS OF HERITAGE

The legacies of 'race'

Edited by Jo Littler and Roshi Naidoo

Routledge
Taylor & Francis Group

LONDON AND NEW YORK

First published 2005
by Routledge
2 Park Square, Milton Park, Abingdon, Oxon OX14 4RN

Simultaneously published in the USA and Canada
by Routledge
270 Madison Ave, New York, NY 10016

Routledge is an imprint of the Taylor & Francis Group

© 2005 Jo Littler and Roshi Naidoo

Typeset in Bembo by
RefineCatch Limited, Bungay, Suffolk
Printed and bound in Great Britain by
Cromwell Press, Trowbridge, Wiltshire

British Library Cataloguing in Publication Data
A catalogue record for this book is available from the British Library

Library of Congress Cataloging in Publication Data
The politics of heritage : the legacies of 'race' / edited by Jo Littler and
Roshi Naidoo.
p. cm. — (Comedia)
Includes bibliographical references and index.
1. Great Britain—Race relations. 2. Great Britain—Ethnic
relations. 3. Great Britain—Politics and government. I. Littler, Jo,
1972– II. Naidoo, Roshi, 1965– III. Series.
DA125.A1P647 2005
305.8'00941—dc22   2004013125

ISBN 0–415–32210–3 (hbk)
ISBN 0–415–32211–1 (hbk)

CONTENTS

CONTENTS

ILLUSTRATIONS

CONTRIBUTORS

Gill Branston is Director of Undergraduate Studies in the School of Journalism, Media and Cultural Studies at Cardiff University. She is the author of *Cinema and Cultural Modernity* (Open University Press, 2000) and co-author (with Roy Stafford) of *The Media Student's Book* (Routledge, 3rd edition, 2003) and co-editor (with Cynthia Carter and Stuart Allan) of *News, Gender and Power* (Routledge, 1998).

Elizabeth Crooke is a Lecturer in Museum and Heritage Studies at the University of Ulster. She has published *Politics, Archaeology and the Creation of a National Museum of Ireland* (Irish Academic Press, 2000) and is currently writing a book for the *Museum Meanings* series with Routledge on the subjects of museums, heritage and community.

Lynda Dyson is Senior Lecturer in Media and Cultural Studies at Middlesex University. Publications include 'The Return of the Repressed? Whiteness, femininity and colonialism in "The Piano"' in *Screen* (1995) 'The Construction and Reconstruction of Whiteness in New Zealand' in *British Review of New Zealand Studies* (1996) and 'The Role of Objects in the Mnemonic Landscape of Nation' in J. Harbord and J. Campbell (eds) *Temporalities, Autobiography and Everyday Life* (Manchester University Press, 2002).

Stuart Hall was until recently Professor of Sociology at the Open University and is now Emeritus Professor in the Media and Communications Department at Goldsmiths College. He has written extensively on cultural studies, new ethnicities and cultural politics.

John Hamer is an Education Consultant and Special Lecturer in the School of Education at the University of Nottingham. He was formerly an HMI, Subject Adviser in History and Political Education to Ofsted, and Education Policy Adviser to the Heritage Lottery Fund. He has written a number of history textbooks and articles on the teaching of history.

Siân Jones is a Senior Lecturer in Archaeology at the University of Manchester. She has published widely on the subject of archaeology and identity, and her books include *The Archaeology of Ethnicity* (Routledge, 1997). Recently she has been engaged in ethnographic and historiographical research focusing on monuments, memory and identity in Scotland.

Naseem Khan OBE was Head of Diversity for Arts Council England for seven years until she left recently to freelance. A writer and policy developer, her pioneering report, *The Arts Britain Ignores* (1976) triggered a reassessment of the role of diversity in contemporary society. It also established MAAS (Minorities' Arts Advisory Service) – the first national umbrella body for non-indigenous arts – of which she was the founding co-ordinator. She has written a weekly column on arts and culture for the *New Statesman*, was Theatre editor for *Time Out* and has worked as a Senior Consultant with Comedia on studies such as the social impact of the arts and the future of urban open space.

Jo Littler teaches Media and Cultural Studies at Middlesex University. She is a contributor to Tim Bewes and Jeremy Gilbert (eds) (2000) *Cultural Capitalism: Politics after New Labour*, Helen Brocklehurst and Robert Phillips (eds) (2004) *History, Nationhood and the Question of Britain*, and Simon Faulkner and Anandi Ramamurthy (eds) (2005) *Visual Culture in Britain at the End of Empire*.

S. I. Martin is a writer and researcher specialising in black British history and literature. He is the author of *Britain's Slave Trade* (Macmillan, 2000) which accompanied the recent Channel 4 series of the same name, and *Incomparable World* (Quartet Books, 1996). He is a consultant and educator for English Heritage, the Prison Service, the British Council, the Public Records Office, the BBC, the Museum of London and a number of local authorities. He also conducts the *500 Years of Black London* walking tours.

Sharon Macdonald is Reader in Social Anthropology and Sociology at the University of Sheffield. In 2000 and 2003 she held Humboldt fellowships at the University of Erlangen-Nuremberg, Germany, where she has been working on cultural policy in relation to the Nazi past. She is writing this up as a book provisionally entitled *Difficult Heritage: Dealing with the Nazi Past in Nuremberg*. Her published books include: *Reimagining Culture* (Berg, 1997), *The Politics of Display* (Routledge, 1998) and *Behind the Scenes at the Science Museum* (Berg, 2002).

Jim McGuigan is Professor of Cultural Analysis in the Department of Social Sciences, Loughborough University. He has worked for the Arts Council and the BBC. His publications include *Cultural Populism* (1992), *Studying Culture* (1993, 1997), *Culture and the Public Sphere* (1996), *Cultural Methodologies* (1997), *Modernity and Postmodern Culture* (1999), *Technocities* (1999) and *Rethinking Cultural Policy* (2004).

Roshi Naidoo has worked as a Lecturer in Media and Cultural Studies at

Middlesex University and in the heritage sector. Her publications include with J. Littler, 'White Past, Multicultural Present: Heritage and National Stories' in H. Brocklehurst and R. Phillips (eds) *History, Nationhood and the Question of Britain* (2004), 'Joan Riley and Remembrance' in J. Anim-Addo (ed.) *Centre of Remembrance: Memory and Caribbean Women's Literature* (2002), 'No Place Like Home' in J. Rutherford (ed.) *The Art of Life* (2000) and 'All in the Same Boat?' *Soundings* 1998. She has also contributed to the *Black Film Bulletin*.

Mark Perryman is a Research Fellow in sport and leisure culture at the University of Brighton. He is editor of *Going Oriental: Football after World Cup 2002* (Mainstream, 2002), *The Ingerland Factor: Home Truths from Football* (Mainstream, 1999) and *Altered States: Postmodernism, Politics, Culture* (Lawrence and Wishart 1994). Actively involved in the development of a positive England fan culture, he is one of the convenors of the London England Fans Group, co-organiser of the 'Raise the Flag' initiative at England matches and has worked closely with The British Council. Mark is also the co-founder of Philosophy Football.

Jonathan Rutherford is Reader in Cultural Studies at Middlesex University. He is author of *Forever England: Reflections on 'Race', Masculinity and Empire* (1997), *Men's Silences* (1992) and *I am No Longer Myself Without You* (1999). He is co-editor (with Rowena Chapman) of *Male Order: Unwrapping Masculinity* (1988) and editor of *Young Britain* (1998), *Identity, Community, Culture, Difference* (1990) and *The Art of Life* (2000).

Bill Schwarz teaches in the School of English and Drama at Queen Mary, University of London. His edited collection, *West Indian Intellectuals in Britain*, was published by Manchester University Press in 2003. He is on the editorial collectives of *History Workshop Journal*, *New Formations* and *Visual Culture in Britain*.

Carol Tulloch is a Senior Research Fellow at Chelsea College of Art. She has published several articles on the dress culture of the African diaspora and has curated exhibitions on women's history. Her most recent work is as editor of the book *Black Style* (2004) which supported the V&A exhibition *Black British Style* (2004–2005) which she co-curated.

ACKNOWLEDGEMENTS

This book emerged from our involvement with academic debates about heritage and 'race', and from work in the institutional heritage sector, and the various enthusiasms and frustrations arising from both. Like most collections it is a result of many conversations and encounters, and we hope most of these are apparent in the main body of the text. However, we would like to give particular thanks and acknowledgement to the following:

- All the contributors, who have made working on this book such a pleasure.
- Our colleagues in Media and Cultural Studies at Middlesex University – Jonathan Rutherford, Lynda Dyson, Helen Cunningham, Gary Hall and Clare Birchall – for their friendship and their support of this project. Thanks also to Middlesex University for providing us with the sabbatical and secondment opportunities enabling us to start, expand and finish this book.
- Helen Brocklehurst and the late Robert Phillips, who convened the wide-ranging BRISHIN conference *British Island Stories; History, Identity and Nationhood* in York (17–19 April 2002), where some of the chapters in this collection were given as papers. BRISHIN is a major research project funded under the ESRC's *Devolution and Constitutional Change Programme* exploring the relationship between history, nationhood and state-formation. We are extremely grateful to both Helen and Robert for their generous support of this collection, for their time, their permission to use the pieces and for the opportunity to present papers at their conference.
- Rebecca Barden, Lesley Riddle, Kate Ahl and Helen Faulkner at Routledge for their keen response to the project and for their support through the process of bringing it into being.
- David Morley, whose enthusiastic reception of the manuscript and careful editorial comments have been enormously encouraging and helpful to us.
- Jeremy Gilbert and Phillip Cole, who have weathered all sorts of mini-crises to motivate and support us throughout.

Roshi would also like to thank Carol Tulloch for the invitation to participate in

The Design History Society Conference, *Situated Knowledges: Consumption, Production and Identity in a Global Context* at the University of Wales Aberystwyth (3–5 September 2002). Special gratitude goes to Sheila Gopaulen, Alice Robotham and Carol Tulloch whose integrity and genuine commitment to black heritage through professionally difficult times was inspiring. Thanks as well to Paul Dash for his generosity in sharing his ideas and experiences, and, as always, to the good friends and family whose support is immeasurable.

Jo would like to thank MCS, Francis Mulhern and Miriam Rivett for their role in helping her get a sabbatical; Charlie Jeffrey for the invitation to participate in the 2002 British Council Seminar in Brussels, *Whose History is it Anyway?*; Janice Winship and Craig Clunas for their help on earlier pieces of work which have in turn fed into this book; Jos Pye and Graham Kendall for their help with scanning equipment; and her friends and family, for all their various and extra-curricular forms of support.

Stuart Hall's chapter 'Whose Heritage?' was first delivered as a keynote speech to the national conference *Whose Heritage?* on 2 November 1999 at G-Mex, Manchester and appeared in the conference proceedings published by the Arts Council of England, June 2000. After this it was published in *Third Text* no. 29 Winter 1999–2000. We are grateful to both *Third Text* and to the Arts Council of England for permission to reproduce the piece.

Jo Littler and Roshi Naidoo
2004

ABBREVIATIONS

AAVAA	African and Asian Visual Artists Archive
AC	Arts Council
ACE	Arts Council of England
AMBH	Archive and Museum of Black Heritage
ATS	Army Transport Service
BCA	Black Cultural Archives
BEN	Black Environment Network
BHAP	Butetown History and Arts Project
BNP	British National Party
CARD	Campaign Against Racial Discrimination
CBDC	Cardiff Bay Development Corporation
CRC	Community Relations Commission
CRE	Commission for Racial Equality
DCMS	Department of Culture, Media and Sport
EH	English Heritage
EU	European Union
FA	Football Association
HLF	Heritage Lottery Fund
HMI	Her Majesty's Inspectorate
INIVA	Institute of International Visual Arts
MAAS	Minority Arts Advisory Service
NCA	National Council on Archives
OFSTED	Office for Standards in Education
PRO	Public Record Office /National Archive
TRC	The Truth and Reconciliation Commission, South Africa
UNESCO	United Nations Educational, Scientific and Cultural Organisation
V&A	Victoria and Albert Museum

INTRODUCTION
British heritage and the legacies of 'race'

Jo Littler

British heritage is the heritage of a nation of nations, shaped through waves of migration and diaspora, wide-ranging imperial histories and contemporary flows of globalisation. Not that you would necessarily know this from a cursory glance at many of its key sites and symbols. The St George Cross, afternoon tea and stately homes have often been used as emblematic of 'British heritage': a process in which white (and often upper- or middle-class) Englishness is used to define the past. But, and particularly more recently, a range of initiatives, from exhibitions at Bradford Art Galleries on Sikh art, through the work of Cardiff's Butetown History and Arts Project, to Darcus Howe's televisual analysis of the *White Tribe* and Eddie Izzard's programme about English immigration, *Mongrel Nation*, have sought to question what, and who counts as being part of this past. Such revisions of British heritage have exposed both the aggressive self-aggrandisement of white Englishness and the complex histories of its flags, tea and houses in the process.

At *Whose Heritage?*, an Arts Council conference in 1999, Stuart Hall identified such activity as part of a 'deep slow-motion revolution' still in progress: an unsettling of British heritage from its smug position as bounded entity unquestioningly representing the interests of the white English upper- and middle-class great and the good. Equally, though, he argued, heritage will not just simply and inevitably improve with the passing of time. Hall's speech is reproduced in this collection and it raises several key concerns that this book seeks to carry forward. First, it foregrounds how we should think of 'heritage' not as an immutable entity, but as a discursive practice, shaped by specific circumstances – through histories, interests, patterns, collisions and politics. Second, it insists that rethinking national heritage does not only mean 'including' 'other' heritages by simply tacking them on to an official national story that is already sealed, but that it instead involves revising Britain's island stories to acknowledge their long and intertwined histories with complex patterns of migration and diaspora. Third, it indicates that changes to what is *understood* as

1

'heritage' work themselves through on a number of different spheres, areas including, but not restricted to, policy, popular culture, academia and a myriad of heritage institutions. Heritage formations, in other words, are about process and policy as much as practice.

This collection explores how we might locate and understand such challenges to what Hall termed 'the Heritage' and how we might interrogate the obstacles and opportunities for heritage practices to address 'race'. Whilst 'race' as a category is widely discredited, we live with the remnants, the husk and the fallout of its legacies. These legacies shape the way British heritage has been produced and consumed and what and who gets to count as being part of it. Taking as its premise that heritage and the legacies of 'race' is not a somewhat specialist topic concerning 'ethnic minorities', but a mainstream issue affecting us all, this book asks several questions. What has been assumed to be part of British heritage, and how has this been marked in terms of 'race', 'ethnicity' and nationality alongside gender and class? Who has decided what constitutes 'heritage'? And, most of all, what are the possibilities for radical heritage agendas that can imagine decentred, hybrid and culturally diverse narratives of British history and identity?

In asking these questions the collection draws from a number of different debates. A wealth of work has emerged over the last couple of decades on the heritage industry, on what 'Britishness' means in the contemporary context of multiculturalism and devolution, and on the colonial history of museums and galleries, and yet in comparison there has been relatively little work linking such discussions together. By attempting to draw out some of the connections between these debates, this book aims to provide a space to explore what the possibilities are for progressive practice and activating theory and to open up further discussion on how the legacies of 'race' continue to shape heritage.

The heritage of 'heritage'

It is useful to begin by exploring some of the complex historical meanings of 'heritage'. What is circumscribed as 'heritage' is historically specific, culturally contingent and philosophically debatable. Its parameters have changed through the way it is used, and by the particular meanings that have coalesced around it. In medieval times it was used in religious discourse to mark the elect, the 'people chosen by God' (Samuel 1994: 231). Later, through industrial modernity and capitalism, through imperialism and the nation-state, its particular association with blood, land, property and old, 'high' culture was formed. Heritage proclaimed the 'lineage' of particular groups – their worth and power – at the expense of others. Letting what was deemed important from the past stand as self-evident, as just being there, singular, 'natural' and not subject to question was one of the key ways in which 'the Heritage', to use Hall's definition, accumulated power. Equally, the groups who got to define it – who 'had' heritage, in other words – were mainly upper or upper middle-class white people, particularly men, and their use of heritage imbued them with a power which others were invited or compelled to appreciate.[1]

To acknowledge this dominant formation is not to say, however, that what was classified as being 'heritage' either did not change or was passively imbibed by a docile populace. Peter Mandler's work on the various booms in nine-teenth-century popular consumption of public histories provides us with one example of how these complexities might be explored (Mandler 1997). Nor does it mean that heritage was as 'fixed' as it appeared; as with Robert Young's description of English imperial identity, we can imagine it fissured by differ-ence and marked by longing for otherness, even whilst its fixed and stable nature was asserted (Young 1995: 2).[2] But these longer-standing élitist connota-tions, the associations of heritage with the blessed 'natural' rights of specific individuals, lineage and stock, do explain how it became available to become linked to racialised discourses.[3]

The conspicuous changes and challenges to dominant conceptions of heri-tage over the past few decades have, as Hall puts it, taken place in the context of the dismantling of the Enlightenment ideal of 'universal knowledge' – in which white Britons could claim to speak for other cultures – alongside the democratisation process in which 'ordinary' lives 'have slowly taken their sub-ordinate place alongside the hegemonic presence of the great and the good'. Such a democratic revitalisation of heritage owed a great deal to the practices of left historians concerned with excavating 'history from below', and with producing what John Urry calls a 'proliferation of alternative histories' (Urry 1990: 121) both inside and outside of the academy. These perspectives – for academics, most famously manifested on the pages of *History Workshop Journal* and through the work of Raphael Samuel – consciously sought to expand *whose* past could count as heritage (see Samuel 1994). It thus became more acceptable for 'heritage' to mean the past of the working as well as the upper classes, washtubs as well as gilt-edged paintings, back-to-back houses as well as stately homes.

But the 1980s heritage revival was also associated in various ways with new forms of reactionary conservatism, and the arguments around the extent of this 'democratisation' process, now anthologised in books such as *Culture and the Public Sphere* and *Representing the Nation*, became known in some quarters as 'the heritage debates' (McGuigan 1996: 116–34; Boswell and Evans 1999). The term had been invigorated by the rise of the right in the 1970s, as a predomin-antly conservative alliance of the 'great and the good' fought tooth and nail against Labour's attempt to introduce a Wealth Tax by annexing the fear of private aristocratic loss to nationalist sentiment (Hewison 1995: 191–3; Mandler 1997: 401–18). Later, culminating in the 1980 National Heritage Act, such revitalisation mutated into a Thatcherite version of heritage that was often used to *popularise* the idea of élitism, making prestige more available, something to be sought after and competed for rather than inherited(Wright 1985; Bird 1996).

3

Packaged in a variety of ways, used to sell goods, services, organisations, tourism and national identity, heritage became 'a key word in our national vocabulary; it is what Britain sells' (Morley and Robins 2001: 8). New, popular, category-melding kinds of heritage emerged, such as the heritage experience attraction (see Bennett 1995), and a Britain of floppy fringes, lavish interiors and costumed detail emerged on celluloid with the genre of heritage cinema (see Vincendau 2001). 'Heritage' could therefore encapsulate a range of practices and discourses, including money-spinning commodities to be 'mined' (or enterprisingly invented) whilst other kinds of mine were being closed down (Hewison 1987; Corner and Harvey 1991); as a populist challenge to official conservative history (Samuel 1998); or sophisticated disrupter of traditionally bourgeois modes of aesthetic display (Rojek 1993). Just as the core themes of 'enterprise' and 'heritage' came for many to define the political and cultural agenda of British life during the Thatcher era (Corner and Harvey 1991; Morley and Robins 2001: 5), so did the heritage debate function to a large extent as 'a critique of the Thatcher years' (Boswell and Evans 1999: 112).

As we have argued elsewhere, these debates had relatively little to say about the way heritage was racialised. They focused primarily on issues around class and simulacra rather than examining the interplays of gender or 'race' (Littler and Naidoo 2004). Such conceptions of simulacra – which might be traced from Plato through Debord and Baudrillard – often relied on a sterile binary opposition between 'real' or 'fake' representations of the past, and could easily be mobilised to implicitly mourn and validate a lost sense of authenticity, providing a sealed-off conceptual framework unable to account for complexity or processes of change. Many of these debates, therefore, came to circulate primarily over the question of whether these new histories were 'real' emancipatory histories-from-below, or Thatcherism in period dress, and often only gestured towards the rise of heritage in relation to the decline of empire. In part, this replicated the whiteness of many of the heritage displays under discussion themselves, and the relatively piecemeal and circumscribed effects of mainstreaming diversity in heritage institutions. However, this response was not uniform, with Patrick Wright, for example, insightfully both locating British fascination with heritage in the context of the decline of its world role and gesturing towards how heritage functioned in relation to racialised discourses at home (Wright 1985; Littler and Naidoo 2004).

Whilst these heritage debates were being discussed in and around cultural studies and cultural history, 'heritage' was also taking different resonances in different contexts. 'Heritage studies', for example, was emerging as a more vocationally orientated discipline, as an offspring and/or sibling of tourism studies, archaeology and museum studies.[4] In and around museums 'heritage' became a term used alongside archaeological remains and exhibitions as a way of gesturing towards the apparent expansion of ways of presenting the past, including the use of new technologies and modes of display. Its increasing invocation as an issue for governmental and policy attention helped consolidate

4

an area now regularly defined as 'the heritage sector', which has been urged to adopt pivotal new roles in terms of governmental strategies for social inclusion. Under New Labour, the meaning of heritage has mutated in interesting ways. In the early years of Blair, the Department of National Heritage became the Department of Culture, Media and Sport (DCMS), and the archaic and Thatcherite connotations of the word 'heritage' were dropped, as swinging New Labour claimed to represent thrusting hyper-modernity. On the one hand, then, the role of 'heritage' in New Labour discourse has become less conspicuous (even though, as Andrew Higson has pointed out, the young country of Cool Britannia that Blairism was promoting still offered a heritaged-up version of national identity, merely referencing a different era: the 1960s (Higson 2001: 259).On the other hand, the invocation of 'heritage' and 'the heritage sector' in policy documents, particularly around social inclusion, and as a means of selling Britishness, has increased, as discussed below. Looking for heritage policy therefore becomes a more complex business, as it is more diffuse and references to heritage are scattered across policy documents relating to museums, libraries and archives, the natural and built environment, the culture and media industries, lottery funding and tourism.

The complex legacies of heritage, a living term, are such that there are some very different heritage paradigms in circulation within disciplines, and some quite separate conversations and understandings of what constitutes 'legitimate' discussion around it, for example, in cultural studies, archaeology, history and business studies. In this book 'heritage' is used in a relative open sense, and the book aims to make connections between these varied uses. 'Heritage' here, therefore, includes walking tours, public spaces, films, commercial enterprises and national days, as well as exhibitions and statues, and the contributors range from archaeologists to curators, from policy officers to educational consultants to academics. Such openness, as Raphael Samuel once said in a slightly different context, does produce as many problems as it resolves (Samuel 1998: 36), and will inevitably and inescapably reflect our own backgrounds in cultural studies and the encounters and biases that brings with it. However, we hope it will also work to make productive connections when thinking about heritage's formation in relation to the legacies of 'race'.[5]

The legacies of 'race'

If the heritage debates did not devote too much space to the legacies of 'race', plenty of other areas did. The expansion of museum studies since the 1980s has resulted in a proliferation of work examining and theorising connections between museum display, imperialism and colonialism (Karp and Levine 1991; Coombes 1994; Clifford 1997; Hooper-Greenhill 1997; Barringer and Flynn 1998; Hallam and Street 2000; Simpson 2001). In addition, a broad array of *practical* projects across the institutional heritage sector, particularly in museums, have displayed interest in refashioning British heritage, some of which are discussed below. All this work was able to draw on an expansive body of historical enquiry that has demonstrated the multiple heritages of Britain (Visram 1986; Fryer 1984; Gilroy 1987; Ramadin 1999) and the interwoven globalised histories of empire (C. Hall 2000, Young 2001).

Here it is necessary to make a few preliminary points about terminology. Like 'race', national identity and ethnicity are social and cultural constructions, rather than being natural propensities of people born or living in particular places. There have been similarly deep-rooted beliefs in their essential 'characteristics' together with the common (con)fusion and conflation of the three terms. Partly because of its etymology, 'ethnicity' can be used both in an essentialised sense (as a marker of 'natural' difference in a similar way to the word 'race', only glossed with the meaning of 'a sense of place') (Gilroy 2000: 94) or as a tool to move away from such essentialised biological conceptions and cultural racisms to enable an interrogation of how particular social, geographical historical experiences can shape identity (Sollers 1986; Brah 1992; Hall 1992a; Hutchinson and Smith 1996).[6] Whether we choose to use the term 'ethnicity' or not, we require a sense of the history of the term – to ensure it is never reified, or taken as a given – and to ensure local complexities are always scrutinised, as cultural racism can all too easily slip in through the back door.

The historical slippage between ethnicity and 'race' does also mean that some interesting possibilities lie in integrating what could loosely be called 'four nations' and post-colonial perspectives, which as Siân Jones discusses in this volume, are often quite separate. Internal colonisation within Britain, for example, has often been understood in ethnic and racialised terms (see Young 1995: 71) and 'external' colonisation was often marked by and constructed through its relationship with Britain's three 'other' nations. As Raphael Samuel illustrates in *Island Stories*:

> St Andrew's Day was more fervently observed in Bombay and Calcutta, Otago and Queensland than it was in Edinburgh and Glasgow. It is indicative of the importance of these Empire connections, and of the imaginative hold they exercised, that the first Celtic nationalisms, emerging as they did in the high noon of Britain's colonial expansion, had an unashamedly imperial dimension. Indeed, it is possible to see the growth of Empire and the ethnic revival of the 1870s and 1880s as two sides of the same coin; each, after its own fashion, worshipped at the feet of race consciousness, that scientific version of natural selection theory which in the later nineteenth century intoxicated thinkers of all stripes.
>
> (Samuel 1998: 35)

The possibilities of fusing four nations and post-colonial histories are therefore hugely significant. Thinking about the legacies of 'race' in British heritage and how they have been mutually shaped by ideas about ethnicity means that we can start to think, for example, about the complexities of Scotland's role as both coloniser and colonised, and the role of the Celtic diaspora in imperial heritage. We can also consider how Northern Ireland's exclusion from stories of national heritage is often marked through ethnic difference. In turn, this opens up more possibilities of thinking more internationally, more diasporically. Clearly, 'British' heritage cannot just be confined to the practices that occur within the landmass marked politically as Britain. 'British heritage' is international, in its multilayered histories formed through colonialism, slavery and trade. To draw from the famous quote from Salman Rushdie, British heritage, like English history, 'happened overseas' (Rushdie 1988: 343; Bhabha 1994: 166–7).

In addition, how ideas about 'race' have structured heritage need to be considered alongside other kinds of exclusions, of which there are many. Artefacts and information relating to disabled people have, for example, notoriously languished in museum basements and footnotes (Delin 2002). The consideration of the gender of heritage has similarly been subject to little discussion (particularly surprisingly given the prominence of housewives, land-girls, Victorian servants and 'feminised' shopping spaces in the reconstructions of heritage experience attractions that emerged from the 1980s). The dominant mode of heritage found in British public spaces had been to enshrine masculine prowess and heroism; if women were depicted it was usually as abstract and mythically transcendent figures (Rutherford 1997; Aitchison 1996; Warner 1996).

How, then, can such a variety of heritage contexts and factors be theorised together? In their recent book *The Geography of Heritage* Graham *et al.* point out that 'heritage cannot exist as a universal absolute. Ultimately, because it is what and where we say it is (the pivotal variant being 'we') then one person's heritage is the disinheritance of another.' They coin the term 'heritage dissonance' to describe this 'profusion of messages reflecting different purposes' (Graham *et al.* 2000: 93). This goes some way to help think through the multiplicity of different heritages, but it is also a model that appears to suggest that heritage can only ever be imagined as a series of individualisms. We would argue instead for a framework which can understand heritage as a more open process, one which shows how various inheritances interconnect, and can be changed through encounters, rather than the constantly individualised model of elevating 'someone's heritage at the expense of someone else's'. To adopt such a model involves investigating how 'racialised' understandings took on particular characteristics according to their relationship to (or articulation with) such factors as gender, class, sexuality and age. It involves looking at the past and present of international and transnational heritage and its power relations alongside what took place and what is taking place within the borders of 'Britain'.

The past-in-the-present: international, national and
local heritages

A good example of such an exploration of the imperial and international histories through which British heritage has been built is recent work around the
grand eighteenth-century stately home in Leeds, Harewood House. Built and
sustained from money accrued by the Lascelles family from slave plantations,
this house, like many other British and American grand or stately homes, can
also be viewed as a form of plantation house (Said 1994; Kauffman 2003).
Recently, Harewood has begun investigating its intricate connections to the
transatlantic slave trade, unearthing documents in its basement detailing its
plantation histories, working with historians at the University of York and
acting as the venue for a heritage sector conference based around the project
(Interculture 2003). Tracing these complex stories produces better understandings of these interconnected relationships, of how, as James Walvin has pointed
out, 'Britain is steeped in a slave past in a way people don't recognise' (Walvin
2003), and has the potential – even if it is not yet fully realised – to integrate the
history of slavery into the centre of a national heritage story (Heywood 2003).

Clearly, in more conservative quarters, even acknowledging that slavery or
colonialism ever happened and that Britain was a part of it is still offensive. The
Daily Mail continues to be outraged by any whiff of the mention of slavery in
the National Maritime Museum; and the sanitised history of *Cadbury World* in
Birmingham bypasses slavery, let alone current economic imperialism, on its
journey through the history of chocolate (Ransom 2001: 116). This brings us
to the issue of how, if thinking the complexities of heritage involves rethinking
a series of relations that existed in the past, it also involves thinking through the
relationship of this heritage to the present in its implicit or explicit form. In this
collection Bill Schwarz suggests that comprehending the past in the present is
arguably the least developed aspect of post-colonial research. Barnor Hesse,
analysing the presentation of America's slave heritage in Stephen Spielberg's
film *Amistad*, has powerfully argued that in the film the 'memory of slavery is
haunted by the spectre of a de/colonial fantasy' which establishes the memory
of slavery as 'the memory of its heroic and inevitable abolition'. It treats
plantation slavery as a one-off act of barbarity that happened in the past and
which has no links to the present (Hesse 2002: 150, 157–8). Hesse argues
that an 'ethics of postcolonial memory' should involve remembering and
re-excavating the

> numerous interdependencies that obtained between Christianity and
> slavery, liberalism and imperialism, democracy and racism, each of
> which was mutually constitutive of Atlantic capitalism's framing of
> modernity. Through insisting on the naming of these political forma-
> tions we may 'remember' something quite distinctive, yet traditionally
> unarticulated. How the slavery plantation complex's formative relations

8

of exploitation, exoticism, racism, and violence produced the consumerist contours of Western culture, principally through customizing the transnational cultural production and consumption of mundane staples of the Western lifestyle, such as coffee, sugar, cotton and tobacco.

(Hesse 2002: 160)

In short, what it means to 'remember' now, he argues, involves 'refusing to efface through forgetfulness' the implications of colonialism and slavery and acting against their contemporary legacies (Hesse 2002: 165).

It is clearly possible to acknowledge the brutality of empire whilst not acknowledging its links to the neo-imperial present, to a world in which more than a billion people don't have access to clean drinking water. Whilst the newly opened Empire and Commonwealth Museum in Bristol makes serious progress, for a British museum, in delineating the brutality of empire and the rich mix of our interwoven pasts, for example, its attempts to tackle the issue of continuities in between the British empire and contemporary global imperialism is only very sporadically gestured towards. This is registered symbolically in the museum shop, in which only a very small proportion of the copious amounts of tea for sale on the shelves are fair trade.

Likewise, it is equally possible to acknowledge the brutality of earlier forms of imperialism whilst actively arguing for a newly invigorated version. Such practices mesh into the category of what Paul Gilroy, Martin J. Beck Matustík and others have discussed as corporate multiculturalism, when a diversity of employees or corporate image is used to sell products for capital gain which perpetuates private profit and global inequalities of wealth (Gilroy 2000; Matustík 1998). There is clearly a range of points on this spectrum, from US gung-ho neo-conservatives, through Niall Ferguson's *Empire*, to Nike's multicultural aspirational optimism offering images of diversity whilst perpetuating the global exploitation of labour, and think-tank DEMOS's suggestion that Britain should be packaged as a multicultural hub. In this context it is also instructive to note the continued use of heritage to add value to corporations and to legitimise their practice – a process that has built on the 1980s alliance between consumerism and heritage. For Nike managers, for example, 'every company has a history. But we have a little bit more than a history. We have a heritage, something that's still relevant today' (du Gay and Pryke 2002: 214).

Clearly then 'multicultural heritage' can be articulated in a number of ways. It can be promoted as a characteristic of an entrenched nation-state that imagines its present and past as multicultural, but which has simultaneously sealed off many of the routes for current and future immigration and asylum, a recognition which is, to borrow Matustík's terms, profoundly 'one-sided' (Matustík 1998: 109). There is much further scope for heritage projects to explore the connections between stories of past and present refugees, asylum-seekers and migrants. It is often easier for heritage projects to ignore rather than confront migration, asylum, racism and imperialism, but there are projects attempting to do this, such as the 2003 *Migrations* exhibition at Gallery Oldham (Futuresonic 2003) and the forthcoming Rich Mix Cultural Foundation in Tower Hamlets.[7] However, unlike America with its Museum of Immigration in New York, and Australia with its Migration Museum in Adelaide, Britain does not yet have a fully funded and resourced national museum of migration (Szekeres 2002). Our nearest equivalent, 19 Princelet Street, Spitalfields, London, which aspires to this role with its historically significant building and its exhibition on *Suitcases and Sanctuary*, is at the time of writing still struggling for funds just to keep open.[8]

Multicultural heritage, then, can be articulated to a range of ends, not all of them progressive. A decade after the murder of Stephen Lawrence, racism still clearly takes a range of subtle and unsubtle forms in British culture. The high-profile incorporation of symbols of 'the Commonwealth' and migrant communities into the Queen's 2003 Golden Jubilee festivities, for instance, might variously signify both progressive multiculturalism and the perpetuation of imperial discourses. Multicultural heritage can also be used to embed essentialised ideas of cultural difference, whether through exoticising 'other' cultures or homogenising and sentimentalising 'local' white English heritages. Whilst localised heritage – indicating what Kevin Robins termed 'the importance of place-making in placeless times' (Robins 1991: 38) takes varied forms, its more parochial and nostalgic incarnations often rotate around racialised exclusions. As David Morley puts it:

> The destabilisations of the postmodern period have certainly engendered a variety of defensive and reactionary responses: witness the rise of various forms of born-again nationalism, accompanied both by sentimentalised reconstructions of a variety of 'authentic' localised 'heritages' and by xenophobia directed at newcomers, foreigners or outsiders.
>
> (Morley 2000: 194)

Today's range of heritage practices activate the legacies of 'race' in a variety of ways other than the reactively insular, end-of-Empire English heritage identified by earlier commentators – although that is still on offer too. But clearly the reasons why heritage organisations and practices came to adopt particular positions in relation to the legacies of 'race' are not simply to do with their powers of analysis. It is also because of the politics, position and location of the institutions in question: about how they are affected by policies, how they build their power, and the processes through which change can happen. On a broader level it is about their insertion into the current cultural and political conjuncture.

Politics and policies

Recently, many more 'mainstream' heritage organisations have begun to include histories of non-white communities that were previously absent from their narratives,[9] due in part to governmental emphasis on heritage's role in mainstreaming diversity and combating social exclusion. How governmental policies and politics shape heritage is not exclusively a matter of cultural policy, partly because broader political agendas shape what gets demarcated as 'cultural policy' at any given time, and partly because the meanings of 'heritage' are not formed by policy alone. However, cultural policy is still obviously hugely significant for the formation of heritage. Recent years have by and large witnessed the continuity of the post-war, high culture-orientated trajectory of cultural policy, supplemented by an entrepreneurial populism and the impact of lottery funding (which has often functioned to get high profile flagship projects off the ground but not to keep them there – for a discussion of this see Worpole 2001: 237). For our purposes here, there are two distinctive areas of cultural policy that deserve particular consideration: 'social inclusion' and 'creative business'.

The work of the Social Exclusion Unit (SEU), particularly in its 1998 report *Bringing Britain Together: A National Strategy for Neighbourhood Renewal* set in motion much of the government's cultural policy recommendations affecting heritage and diversity. The tenth of its 18 'policy action teams' ('PAT 10') focused on how culture and sports could be used to fight against social exclusion, recommending changes to bodies that distribute exchequer and lottery funding and to related organisations (*Building on PAT 10* 2001a: 5).[10] The heritage sector has been forced to consider more thoroughly whom it is taking for granted and whom it is excluding, not only in terms of education and outreach, but also in terms of representation and recruitment policies. For example, the thoroughly researched recommendations of the Cultural Access Group in *Not for the Likes of You* tackled broadening access and changing practice, and *People and Places*, the 2002 DCMS report promoting social inclusion in the built and historic environment emphasised the importance of change in organisational cultures. Whilst in various ways such initiatives may be problematic, the emphasis in these documents on the capacity of culture to change attitudes, identities and lives is music to the ears of those already versed in these issues. They have promoted ideas of shared communities and equality and have clearly had effects (Sandell 2002: 17). At a broader level, the language of social inclusion, as The Parekh Report on *The Future of Multi-Ethnic Britain* points out, is down-to-earth and can therefore mobilise more and wider support than drier terms such as 'reducing inequality', and can encourage a holistic approach to deprivation (Runnymede Trust 2000: 78–9).

However, as many commentators have pointed out, the language of inclusion can also imply assimilation to a pre-existing set of national norms rather than a genuine diversity. As The Parekh Report put it, the terminology of inclusion 'inherently focuses on marginality and boundaries, and therefore fails to address problems at the core' (Runnymede Trust 2000: 79). It can imply that there is only one already sealed and written national story, with room at the most for a little non-threatening difference, and to which 'newcomers' need to conform to gain acceptance. The outlines of such a politics have been only too crudely visible in David Blunkett's pronouncements on desirable characteristics of British citizenship, characteristics on which all immigrants should be tested. Such a discourse is of course not seamlessly replicated throughout cultural policies and is at odds with the works of many progressive heritage organisations and practitioners. However, at the same time, it is a powerful discourse, and it is clear that certain deeper-rooted, vested establishment power interests, such as the monarchy, can remain unchallenged and even be shored up by gestures of cultural 'inclusion', as we have discussed elsewhere (see Littler and Naidoo 2004). What is more, the focus in many DCMS documents such as *Building on Pat 10* is also often problematically very one-way, as strategies of cultural inclusion are being used as a sop or plaster in cases of deprivation without the broader reasons for such deprivation being taken into account. In other words, attempts to use heritage to create social inclusion are often made without this being 'joined up' to the issues of the erosion of basic public services through lack of funding and marketisation.

In this context it is also very instructive to look at how heritage, social inclusion and cultural diversity are discussed in terms of how they can contribute to the creative economy and be used to generate economic growth.[11] From Culture Minister Chris Smith's pronouncements in *Creative Britain* to the British Tourist Authority's packaging of Britain as an excitingly mixed place to be, the idea of selling an image of Britain as vibrantly diverse in order to encourage economic growth has gathered pace. Recent DCMS heritage policy documents have demonstrated attempts to make more links between business sponsorship and social inclusion objectives. PAT 10 for example recommended 'a two pronged approach': more industry sponsorship to be used to promote disadvantaged areas and individuals, and for more inclusion in terms of audiences and workers in the creative industries (*PAT 10*: 49). Whilst cultural industries can be run along a number of different lines, from co-operative to capitalist (for some of the history of this in connection to cultural policy, see Bianchini 1987) the yoking together of inclusion with industry in this context primarily involves the integration of what Matuštík termed 'corporate multiculturalism' into the contemporary enterprise/heritage agenda. In effect, the use of images of diversity to sell creative business and to sell national heritage can be viewed as being another twist in the longstanding saga of what John Corner and Sylvia Harvey usefully termed the 'enterprise and heritage couplet' (Corner and Harvey 1991: 45).

'A welcome mat by a closed door': processes and practices

For heritage practices and organisations the challenge is how to work within or around such contexts.[12] For example, there is a need to interrogate how diversity policies translate in practice, to how public institutions and archives continue to make assumptions about what is considered 'important'. It is clear that pious words about diversity alone are not enough. Naseem Khan gives a vivid example in this volume of how Glyndebourne Opera House once fulfilled the 4 per cent 'ethnic minority' quota demanded of it by the Arts Council by staging a one-off production of *Porgy and Bess* with an all black cast, a classic case of how lip-service can be paid to diversity without it being mainstreamed through the organisation with any thoroughness or longevity. As Khan remarks dryly, '[n]o-one who has been to Glyndebourne recently would be able to see the continuing effects of that brush with diversity'. Similarly, policies that bolt-on access without reviewing and reworking the ideologies at work throughout an organisation, Khan argues, can simply offer 'a welcome mat by a closed door'. Whilst such examples illustrate the influence of policy on practice (in this case by encouraging tokenistic inclusion), it also indicates that policy alone is not the sole factor that needs to be explored, and that politics and policies need to be explored alongside process and practice. Heritage, in other words, is not only about policy and representation but also about the lived and affective experiences and entanglements between various types of institutions and policies and the interests and agendas of individuals and groups. What happens to people and processes behind the scenes at an institution is also crucial to the way meaning is created, change occurs and ideologies are produced.

A heritage practice is in itself a type of theory with its own epistemology, and some forms of practice might therefore be judged as more progressive or 'advanced' than theories of heritage. Equally, however, 'practice' need not be romanticised, but rather the opportunities to interrogate and learn from it grasped. There are a wide range of possibilities of bringing theory and practice together in new ways. We need to pay attention to how change happens and to the possibilities for and limitations on this. This does not merely mean that cultural analysis should always and merely be reduced to a technocratic capacity, to fit into or to tinker with pre-existing policy objectives; but rather that an ethical commitment to social change for a more equal society has to be accompanied by a strategic sense of what is possible to be done and when. To combine this with Hesse's formulation, what we might call 'a postcolonial ethics of heritage' might emphasise the art of the possible in its most capacious, imaginative sense in order to strategically pursue its ends.

Revising 'the heritage'

To explore these issues, this collection is split into two sections: one is themed around the relationship between policy, process and practice; and the other contextualises these issues by exploring how the international pasts and presents of various versions of 'British heritage' have negotiated the legacies of 'race'. Inevitably there are overlaps between these two sections, as their concerns seep into each other. Inevitably, also, there are many other areas and types of heritage that it would be useful for this book to discuss (such as, for example, Chinese heritage in Britain, British heritage in India, or inter-European heritage). However, the usual restrictions apply: word length, the need for the book to act as a space which brings issues together; the need to pose questions and open up debate rather than formalising an overarching archive. We have deliberately not split the book into sections such as 'multicultural', 'four nations' and 'white' heritage as we wanted to increase the traffic between the often polarised debates around these areas and to foreground their interwoven texture.

The first section, 'British heritage is international heritage', takes an expansive view of British heritage by examining how in many ways it has always been profoundly un-British. The contributors interrogate the international past of British heritage and explore the implications of this in a variety of ways. The section starts with Stuart Hall's keynote speech from the Arts Council's 1999 conference, *Whose Heritage?*, which is picked up on and discussed in other chapters, such as Naseem Khan's and S. I. Martin's. Passionate yet measured, sweeping yet strategic, Hall's is a characteristically acute diagnosis of what is to be done.

One point that Hall makes is that the process of democratising 'the Heritage' has 'so far stopped short at the frontier defined by that great unspoken British value – 'whiteness'. As Richard Dyer pointed out, some people (such as 'white English') have been regarded as 'more white' than others (such as Jews and 'white' Eastern Europeans) (Dyer 1997). Many of the contributions following Hall's consider the relationship between the formation of white heritage and the legacies of 'race'. Jonathan Rutherford explores why so much contemporary heritage still relates inappropriately to the past by tracing its connections to the formation during modernity of white male English subjectivities.

Like Jonathan Rutherford, Siân Jones questions the idea of a contained and homogenous 'majority-white-indigenous' culture and heritage. She seeks to unsettle the gulf between 'four nations' and 'multicultural' agendas in her chapter which creates an object-biography of the ninth-century AD Hilton of Cadboll stone. Elizabeth Crooke's chapter considers the presentation of heritage in Northern Ireland, focusing upon how alternative forms of heritage in Northern Ireland are beginning to come to the fore: 'the unofficial, unsafe, contested history of the conflict, which is seeking recognition'.

Sharon Macdonald discusses the significance of the recent upsurge in Holocaust commemoration across Europe and America, focusing in particular on the meanings generated around Holocaust Memorial Day in Britain. Examining how Holocaust Memorial Day constructs a national identity against a generalised enemy of racial purity-seeking evil, she also explores the possibilities that it might also allow Britain to extend a sense of wartime moral superiority, avoiding cultural reflection on its own past and present racism.

Roshi Naidoo examines how racism can exist in covert form in heritage projects that present themselves as progressive multicultural alternatives. Picking her way through a heritage climate replete with buzzwords around 'inclusion', 'multiculturalism' and 'diversity', she draws on a range of specific case studies to argue that we need to re-examine and challenge liberal myths about past and present.

Lynda Dyson's essay explores the representation of bicultural difference at New Zealand's Te Papa Tongawera museum and in doing so demonstrates that 'British heritage' is not confined to Britain. Her chapter describes how British heritage is simultaneously being displaced whilst its residual 'superiority' – transmuted into 'Pakeha pride' and homogenising representations of 'Maoris' – continues to be affirmed, and shows how this is connected to a number of factors including the commercial imperatives of a globalising neo-liberalism.

Whilst the first section predominantly focuses on theories and ideologies of the legacies of 'race' in British heritage, the second section, 'Policies, processes and practices' considers how these issues can be worked out in practice. The contributors deal with questions of how policy shapes heritage, how public institutions and archives make assumptions about what is considered 'important', and how cultural practitioners have produced what many consider to be 'progressive' versions of heritage.

Starting from the premise that we need to investigate policy, alongside recommendations and responses to it, in order to understand the contemporary heritage context, Jim McGuigan explores these issues of cultural racism in relation to the vitriolic media response to The Parekh Report on *The Future of Multi-Ethnic Britain*. This book was one of the most significant recent attempts to influence policies affecting British heritage, and its reception tells us much about the problems facing heritage that seeks to address the damage done by the idea of 'race'.

There are many autobiographical elements to this second half, as curators, policy advisors and archive researchers write about lessons learnt in their experience of trying to implement particular projects. For example, in 1976, *The Arts Britain Ignores* provided the first survey of arts practice emanating from ethnic minority communities in Britain and argued that this culture should be considered and funded as part of overall national arts provision. Here, its author, Naseem Khan, reflects on its genesis and upon the way terminologies, the terms of the debate and arts and heritage provision have changed since 1976. John Hamer reflects on his experience of the changing status of the word during his time as both 'responsible historian' and educational advisor to the Heritage Lottery Fund (HLF). As he points out, in relation to the legitimacy of 'history', 'heritage' remains for many a suspect concept, a word 'guaranteed to make the crustier sort of historians reach for their revolvers', and argues that heritage education is integral rather than inimical to the future of history.

Gill Branston and Carol Tulloch both discuss projects representing previously marginalised heritage. Gill Branston's work with the *Butetown History and Arts Project* (BHAP) in the Tiger Bay area of Cardiff, in the form of interviews on memories of local cinema-going from the 1930s to the 1950s, foregrounds heritage stories which cut against the grains of more white, patrician and work-oriented histories of Wales and which bring the longevity of Cardiff's diasporic connections to the fore. Carol Tulloch describes working as a curator with heritage institutions including the Black Cultural Archives, the V&A and several local hairdressing salons (which exhibited a small touring exhibition on hairdressing histories). Her account foregrounds the challenges of working with a variety of 'mainstream' and 'alternative' institutions, and the role of the curator as an 'agent of change'. S. I. Martin, novelist, researcher for the Channel 4 TV series *Britain's Slave Trade* and tour guide for the *500 Years of Black London* walk discusses how presenting previously obscured heritage is not simply a matter of popularising it, but is also a question of being able to access the research, which means thinking about how sources are valorised.

Mark Perryman, who has been involved with a variety of initiatives to re-imagine Englishness, considers one of the most populist contemporary incarnations of heritage by discussing the uses to which the English flag is put. He focuses in particular on its meanings in the context of devolution and the expansion of its popularity during the 2002 World Cup, and claims that it is both possible and preferable to reclaim the flag for a multicultural and post-colonial Englishness. 'We cannot ignore what is written in England's history books' he argues 'but nor should that history be used as an excuse for inaction. Engagement requires the seeking out of the variegated components of a historical narrative, and seeking out alternative narratives too.'

Both sections, then, address heritage as a form of past-in-the-present. They ask what varied forms of heritage – or various heritage*s* – have to say about the legacies of 'race', whether they say all that they should say, and if not, how they can be changed. There are many clear examples around us of how 'The' Heritage was racialised, gendered and classed: public statues erected to the leaders of colonial military battles, museums that represented white European cultures as civilised and everything else as 'other', pronouncements about national heritage that drew on discourses of blood, stock and belonging. In the final piece of the collection, Bill Schwarz asks what appropriate ways to remember the imperial past might be. Reminding us that 'memory can only work in conjunction with forgetting', he argues that the best types of memory-text create new passages between past and present, working through rather than acting out the past. Highlighting how heritage can exist around us in a myriad of forms, and addressing critiques of post-colonial understandings of heritage, he points out that questions about the multiple and extraordinary power of the past in the present are still only just beginning to be formulated.

Common heritage

In March 2003, when American and British forces were bombing Iraq, a small exhibition in London, *Our Life in Pieces: Objects and Stories from Iraqis in Exile* was drawing to a close. Here, you could walk around the tiny white light room, holding the rudimentarily printed guidebook in which statements and stories about the objects on display were provided by the people who had lent them to the gallery. The objects were described in terms of the significance they had for their owners, all exiled in London at various points over the past decades. A stone, a Kurdish headdress, a book, a bus pass, a stamp. These objects, these stories brought into being Iraqs that were very different from the Iraq of news bulletins and headline photos, all sand and militarism.

As the guidebook mediated to its visitors a diversity of voices talking about the objects, it slipped by turns between lyrical, prosaic and enigmatic descriptions, stories that enlivened and made specific these objects and wove other stories through them, showing how they had been part of peoples lives and how peoples lives had been part of them (Act Together 2003). It was a patchwork of different textures. In part the exhibition became about how global events and transnational occurrences have shaped the lives of these people and their flamboyant and mundane, extraordinary and prosaic objects. The exhibition was important because, at a time when Iraqi 'difference' was being both narrowly defined and demonised, it made possible not only a different view but an accessible range of different views.

It was reminiscent of Richard Sandell's description of how in an exhibition in Nottingham a memorial from one man to his deceased male lover, in the form of a ceramic bowl, together with text explaining it, did not provoke the degree of adverse comment that was expected. Sandell quotes Ivan Karp's discussion of how assertions of unbridgeable difference tend to exoticise objects and cultures as 'other' (Sandell 2002: 13–14). He puts the noticeable popularity of this exhibition partly down to its emphasis on 'sameness' alongside 'difference'.

Our Life in Pieces also encouraged a multiplicity of narratives to group around a theme. Both gesture to how heritage can exist as interwoven, genuinely diverse and, in Nima Poovaya-Smith's words, '*by* rather than *for*' a community (Poovaya-Smith 2003). Bringing different experiences together, ones that do not necessarily agree with each other, works to create what Chantal Mouffe terms agonistic pluralism: a model of democracy that does not work for a smooth final resolution but which recognises that any consensus will always be provisional and conflictual; which does not ignore the place of passion and feelings and seek to leave it 'outside' any debate, but a model of democracy that

17

JO LITTLER

can recognise passion and conflict and which seeks to mobilise it towards sharing equalities of power (Mouffe 2000). *Our Life in Pieces* evoked a range of
different Iraqi heritages existing in London, a range which became at the same
time a part of British heritage. Its title remains a stark commentary on what
happens if we do not pay attention to the legacies of imperialism and 'race' and
how they shape our heritage today.

Notes

1 One arch example being Kenneth Clark and his best-selling book and TV series
from the 1970s, *Civilisation*.
2 'Perhaps the fixidity of identity for which Englishness developed such a reputation
arose because it was in fact continually being contested, and was designed to mask its
uncertainty, its sense of being estranged from itself, sick with desire for the other'
(Young 1995: 2).
3 Raphael Samuel notes the marked upturn in the word's use from the beginning of
the twentieth century, and so it is interesting to speculate on this usage in the
context of British imperialism – on the rising currency of the word at a high point
of British imperialism. Samuel also argued strongly for a more participatory *genealogy*
of heritage, although what he provides of this is predominantly a twentieth-century
genealogy (Samuel 1994: 231). We might also consider such interpretations in relation to broader international concerns with historical methodology, such as the
work of Pierre Nora in France (Le Goff and Nora 1985).
4 *The International Journal of Heritage Studies* for example describes heritage in terms of
conservation, stating every issue that: 'Heritage varies from the aesthetic object conserved in a museum to wildlife conserved within a nature reserve.'
5 What might be extrapolated from the recent mutations in heritage's meanings is that
it is seems increasingly possible to trace a developed genealogy for heritage as meaning something that is *shared* – amongst and across generations – as well as being able
to trace a genealogy of heritage as the inheritance of *individuals*, which in the post-
industrial West became most commonly articulated to discourses of superior worth.
As Simon Critchley has pointed out, Derrida uses 'the heritage' to mean 'the
dominant Western tradition': '[h]e selects a concept from what he always describes as
'the heritage' – let's call it the dominant Western tradition – and then proceeds, via
an analysis that is at once historical, contextual and thematic, to bring out the logic
of that concept' (Critchley 2001: vii–ix), a usage which suggests both the specific
exclusivity of its white European patrilinear context, and which has the potential to
mean something less élite, something broader and more capacious.One of the more
optimistic aspects of heritage today is that it can be less predominantly charged with
a conservative version of Victoriana and more charged with a sense of collective
pasts, as, for instance, The Parekh Report showed by using 'mixed heritage' as a key
term where in the past the term 'mixed race' might have appeared (Runnymede
Trust 2000: 41).
6 This ambivalence relates to its etymology. Formed from 'ethnikos', mainly used to
refer to gentiles, and 'ethnos' (nation) 'ethnicity' has a long history of being used to
refer to 'foreigners' or 'others'. As 'race' became an awkward term after the Second
World War, the obsolete word was revived, as a means by which a distance from
biological essentialism could be suggested – although at the same time it could be
used to reinforce it. Stuart Hall acknowledged that the meaning of 'ethnicity' as a
term has been forged by its links to nationalism, imperialism, racism and the state,
but argued that it could be decoupled from such simple linkages and used to

18

examine the complexity of identities, in order 'to notice that we are all ethnically located and our ethnic identities are crucial to our subjective sense of who we are. . . . this precisely is the politics of ethnicity predicated on difference and diversity' (Hall 1992a: 258). See also Sollers 1986 and Hutchinson and Smith 1996.

7 See http://www.richmix.org.uk.

8 See http://www.19princeletstreet.org.uk.

9 As Moira Simpson has documented, there is a long if sporadic history of radical projects within the museum sector (Simpson 2001). However, as Siân Jones points out in this volume, drawing on Eileen Hooper-Greenhill, 'tellingly much of the commentary focuses on repeated references to a few temporary or travelling exhibitions which have achieved almost iconic status, such as the *Peopling of London* exhibition at the Museum of London, and *Warm and Rich and Fearless* [an exhibition of Sikh Art] displayed at Bradford and Walsall Museum and Art Gallery.' For accounts of these exhibitions, see Hooper-Greenhill 1997.

10 Its recommendations were split into different sections, which in turn led to or influenced follow-up reports, such as a cross-sector Libraries, Museums, Archives and Galleries policy review and the Arts Council's strategy for social inclusion.

11 The importance of tourism in the construction of heritage, and since the 1980s in particular, has long been noted (McGuigan 1996: 128–32; Walsh 1992; Boniface and Fowler 1993; Kirshenblatt-Gimblett 1998).

12 Organisational processes have until recently remained a relatively under-theorised subject in contrast to, say, the representational politics of a museum display, a finished film, or the effects of national cultural policies. Now, work such as, in media studies, the *Media Practice* series, or, in museum studies, the *Heritage–Conservation–Management* series, is busy interrogating and theorising the institutional processes through which cultural products are produced and interpreting their effects, and there remains a lot of scope for further work in these and adjacent areas.

Part I

BRITISH HERITAGE AS INTERNATIONAL HERITAGE

1

WHOSE HERITAGE? UN-SETTLING 'THE HERITAGE', RE-IMAGINING THE POST-NATION

Stuart Hall

This conference on 'Whose Heritage?' provides an opportunity to look critically at the whole concept of 'British Heritage' from the perspective of the multicultural Britain which has been emerging since the end of World War Two.[1] How is it being – and how should it be – transformed by the 'Black British' presence and the explosion of cultural diversity and difference which is everywhere our lived daily reality?

In preparing to say something useful on this topic, I was struck again – as many of you may have been – by the quaintness of the very term, 'Heritage'. It has slipped so innocently into everyday speech! I take it to refer to the whole complex of organisations, institutions and practices devoted to the preservation and presentation of culture and the arts – art galleries, specialist collections, public and private, museums of all kinds (general, survey or themed, historical or scientific, national or local) and sites of special historical interest.

What is curious in the British usage is the emphasis given to preservation and conservation: to keeping what already exists – as opposed to the production and circulation of new work in different media, which takes a very definite second place. The British have always seen 'culture' as a vaguely disquieting idea – as if to name it is to make self-conscious what well-bred folk absorb unconsciously with their mother's milk! Ministries of Culture are what those old, now discredited, Eastern European regimes used to have, which has altogether the wrong associations! Culture has therefore entered the nomenclature of modern British government only when sandwiched alongside the more acceptably populist terms, 'Media' and 'Sport'.

This gives the British idea of 'Heritage' a peculiar inflection. The works and artefacts so conserved appear to be 'of value' primarily in relation to the past. To be validated, they must take their place alongside what has been authorised as 'valuable' on already established grounds in relation to the unfolding of a 'national story' whose terms we already know. The Heritage thus becomes the material embodiment of the spirit of the nation, a collective representation of the British version of *tradition*, a concept pivotal to the lexicon of English virtues.

This retrospective, nation-alised and tradition-alised conception of culture will return to haunt our subsequent thoughts at different points. However, it may also serve as a warning that *my* emphasis does include the active production of culture and the arts as a living activity, alongside the conservation of the past.

We spend an increasing proportion of the national wealth – especially since the Lottery – on 'the Heritage'. But what is it *for*? Obviously, to preserve for posterity things of value, whether on aesthetic or historical criteria. But that is only a start. From its earliest history in western societies – in the heterogeneous assemblages of the 'cabinets of curiosity and wonder' – collections have adorned the position of people of power and influence – kings, princes, popes, landowners and merchants – whose wealth and status they amplified. They have always been related to the exercise of 'power' in another sense – the symbolic power to order knowledge, to rank, classify and arrange, and thus to give meaning to objects and things through the imposition of interpretative schemas, scholarship and the authority of connoisseurship. As Foucault observed, 'There is no power relation without the relative constitution of a field of knowledge nor any knowledge that does not presuppose and constitute . . . power relations' (Foucault 1977).

Since the eighteenth century, collections of cultural artefacts and works of art have also been closely associated with informal public education. They have become part, not simply of 'governing', but of the broader purposes of 'governmentality' – how the state indirectly and at a distance induces and solicits appropriate attitudes and forms of conduct from its citizens. The state is always, as Gramsci argued, 'educative'. (That is what New Labour means by 'culture change'). Through its power to preserve and represent culture, the state has assumed some responsibility for educating the citizenry in those forms of 'really useful knowledge', as the Victorians put it, which would refine the sensibilities of the vulgar and enhance the capacities of the masses. This was the true test of their 'belongingness': culture as social incorporation.

It is important to remember that the nation-state is both a political and territorial entity, *and* what Benedict Anderson has called 'an imagined community' (Anderson 1989). Though strangers to one another, we form an 'imagined community' because we share an *idea* of the nation and what it stands for, which we can 'imagine' in our mind's eye. A shared national identity thus depends on the cultural meanings, which bind each member individually into the large national story. Even so-called 'civic' states, like Britain, are deeply embedded in specific 'ethnic' or cultural meanings, which give the abstract idea of the nation its lived 'content'.

The National Heritage is a powerful source of such meanings. It follows that those who cannot see themselves reflected in its mirror cannot properly 'belong'. Even the museums and collections apparently devoted to surveying

24

the universal rather than national achievements of culture – like the British Museum, the Louvre, or the Metropolitan Museum in New York – are harnessed into the national story. Carol Duncan and Alan Wallach have argued that these institutions 'claim the heritage of the classical tradition for contemporary society and equate that tradition with the very notion of civilisation itself' (Duncan and Wallach 1980: 451). Much the same could be said about the museums of Modern or Contemporary Art in terms of the way they have colonised the very idea of 'the modern', 'modernity' and 'modernism' as exclusively 'western' inventions.

Heritage is bound into the meaning of the nation through a double inscription. What the nation means is essentialised: 'the English seem unaware that anything fundamental has changed since 1066' (Davies 1999b). Its essential meaning appears to have emerged at the very moment of its origin – a moment always lost in the myths, as well as the mists, of time – and then successively embodied as a distilled essence in the various arts and artefacts of the nation for which the Heritage provides the archive. In fact, what the nation 'means' is an on-going project, under constant reconstruction. We come to know its meaning partly *through* the objects and artefacts which have been made to stand for and symbolise its essential values. Its meaning is constructed *within*, not above or outside representation. It is through identifying with these representations that we come to be its 'subjects' – by 'subjecting' ourselves to its dominant meanings. What would 'England' *mean* without its cathedrals, churches, castles and country houses, its gardens, thatched cottages and hedgerowed landscapes, its Trafalgars, Dunkirks and Mafekings, its Nelsons and its Churchills, its Elgars and its Benjamin Brittens?

We should think of The Heritage as a discursive practice. It is one of the ways in which the nation slowly constructs for itself a sort of collective social memory. Just as individuals and families construct their identities by 'storying' the various random incidents and contingent turning points of their lives into a single, coherent, narrative, so nations construct identities by selectively binding their chosen high points and memorable achievements into an unfolding 'national story'. This story is what is called 'Tradition'. As the Jamaican anthropologist, David Scott, recently observed, 'A tradition . . . seeks to connect authoritatively, within the structure of its narrative, a relation among past, community, and identity'. He goes on to argue that,

A tradition therefore is never neutral with respect to the values it embodies. Rather a tradition operates in and through the stakes it constructs – what is to count and what is not to count among its satisfactions, what the goods and excellences and virtues are that ought to be valued . . . On this view . . . if tradition presupposes 'a common possession', it does not presuppose uniformity or plain consensus. Rather it depends upon a play of conflict and contention. It is

25

a space of dispute as much as of consensus, of discord as much as accord.

(Scott 1999)

The Heritage is a classic example of the operation of what Raymond Williams called the 'selective tradition':

Theoretically a period is recorded; in practice, this record is absorbed into a selective tradition; and both are different from the culture as lived . . . To some extent the selection begins within the period itself . . . though that does not mean that the values and emphases will later be confirmed.

(Williams 1963)

Like personal memory, social memory is highly selective. It highlights and foregrounds, imposes beginnings, middles and ends on the random and contingent. But equally, it foreshortens, silences, disavows, forgets and elides many episodes which – from another perspective – could be the start of a different narrative. This process of selective 'canonisation' confers authority and a material and institutional facticity on the 'selective tradition', making it extremely difficult to shift or revise. The institutions responsible for making the 'selective tradition' work develop a deep investment in their own 'truth'.

The Heritage inevitably reflects the governing assumptions of its time and context. It is always inflected by the power and authority of those who have colonised the past, whose versions of history matter. These assumptions and co-ordinates of power are inhabited as natural – given, timeless, true and inevitable. But it takes only the passage of time, the shift of circumstances, or the reversals of history to reveal those assumptions as time- and context-bound, historically specific, and thus open to contestation, re-negotiation, and revision.

This is therefore an appropriate moment to ask, then, who is the Heritage *for*? In the British case the answer is clear. It is intended for those who 'belong' – a society which is imagined as, in broad terms, culturally homogeneous and unified.

It is long past time to radically question this foundational assumption.

It is, of course, undeniable that Britain has been in recent times a relatively settled society and 'culture'. But as something approaching a nation-state, the United Kingdom of Great Britain and Ireland (subsequently 'and Northern Ireland') is in fact a relatively recent historical construct, largely a product of the eighteenth, nineteenth and twentieth centuries. Britain itself was formed out of a series of earlier invasions, conquests and settlements – Celts, Romans, Saxons, Vikings, Normans, Angevins – whose 'traces' are evident in the palimpsest of the national language. The Act of Union linked Scotland, England and Wales into a united kingdom, but never on terms of cultural equality – a fact constantly obscured by the covert oscillations and surreptitious substitutions between the terms 'Britishness' and 'Englishness' (Davies 1999a).

The Act of Settlement (1701) secured a Protestant ascendancy, drawing the critical symbolic boundary between the Celtic/Catholic and the Anglo-Saxon/Protestant definitions of the nation. Between 1801 (the date of the Act of Union which brokered Ireland into the Union) and Partition in 1922, the national story proved incapable of incorporating 'Irishness' into 'Britishness' or of integrating Irish Catholic migrants into an imagined Englishness. Their culture and presence remains marginalised today.

Though relatively stable, English society has always contained within it profound differences. There were always different ways of being 'English'. It was always fissured along class, gender and regional lines. What came to be known, misleadingly, as 'the British way of life' is really another name for a particular settlement of structured social inequalities. Many of the great achievements which have been retrospectively written into the national lexicon as primordial English virtues – the rule of law, free speech, a fully representative franchise, the rights of combination, the welfare state – were struggled for by some of the English and bitterly resisted by others. Where, one asks, is this deeply ruptured and fractured history, with its interweaving of stability and conflict, in the Heritage's version of the dominant national narrative?

The British Empire was the largest *imperium* of the modern world. The very notion of 'greatness' in Great Britain is inextricably bound up with its imperial destiny. For centuries, its wealth was underpinned, its urban development driven, its agriculture and industry revolutionised, its fortunes as a nation settled, its maritime and commercial hegemony secured, its thirst quenched, its teeth sweetened, its cloth spun, its food spiced, its carriages rubber-wheeled, its bodies adorned, through the imperial connection. Anyone who has been watching the Channel 4 series on *The Slave Trade* or the 'hidden history' of the West India Regiment or the BBC's *The Boer War* will not need reminding how deeply intertwined were the facts of colonisation, slavery and empire with the everyday daily life of all classes and conditions of English men and women. The emblems of Empire do, of course, fitfully appear in the Heritage. However, in general, 'Empire' is increasingly subject to a widespread selective amnesia and disavowal. And when it does appear, it is largely narrated from the viewpoint of the colonisers. Its master narrative is sustained in the scenes, images and the artefacts which testify to Britain's success in imposing its will, culture and institutions, and inscribing its civilising mission across the world. This formative strand in the national culture is now re-presented as an external appendage, extrinsic and inorganic to the domestic history and culture of the English social formation.

Despite all this, the idea of Heritage *has* had to respond to at least two major challenges. The first we may call the democratisation process. Increasingly, the lives, artefacts, houses, work-places, tools, customs and oral memories of ordinary everyday British folk have slowly taken their subordinate place alongside the hegemonic presence of the great and the good. The inclusion of domestic vernacular architecture and the agrarian and industrial revolutions, together with the explosion of interest in 'history from below', the spread of local and family history, of personal memorabilia and the collection of oral histories – activities witnessed to in, for example, Raphael Samuel's memorable celebration of the 'popular heritage', *Theatres of Memory* – have shifted and democratised our conception of value; of what is and is not worth preserving (Samuel 1994). A few courageous if controversial steps have been taken in our direction – the Liverpool Museum on the Slave Trade, the Maritime Museum's re-hang. However, by and large, this process has so far stopped short at the frontier defined by that great unspoken British value – 'whiteness'.

The second 'revolution' arises from the critique of the Enlightenment ideal of dispassionate universal knowledge, which drove and inspired so much of Heritage activity in the past. This has to be coupled with a rising cultural relativism which is part of the growing de-centring of the West and western-oriented or Eurocentric grand-narratives. From the *Magiciens de la Terre* exhibition at the Pompidou Centre in Paris in the 1980s, on through the *Te Maori* exhibition from New Zealand at the Metropolitan Museum of New York, the *Paradise* exhibition from New Guinea at the Museum of Mankind, *The Spirit Sings* exhibition of Canada's 'first peoples' at Calgary, the *Perspectives: Angles on African Art* at the Centre for African Art in New York, and on and on, the exhibiting of 'other cultures' – often performed with the best of liberal intentions – has proved controversial. The questions – 'Who should control the power to represent?', 'Who has the authority to re-present the culture of others?' – have resounded through the museum corridors of the world, provoking a crisis of authority.

These two developments mark a major transformation in our relation to the activity of constructing a 'Heritage'. They, in turn, reflect a number of conceptual shifts in what we might loosely call global intellectual culture. A list of these shifts would have to include a radical awareness by the marginalised of the symbolic power involved in the activity of representation; a growing sense of the centrality of culture and its relation to *identity*; the rise amongst the excluded of a 'politics of recognition' alongside the older politics of equality; a growing reflexivity about the constructed and thus contestable nature of the authority which some people acquire to 'write the culture' of others; a decline in the acceptance of the traditional authorities in authenticating the interpretative and analytic frameworks which classify, place, compare and evaluate culture; and the concomitant rise in the demand to re-appropriate control over the 'writing of one's own story' as part of a wider process of cultural liberation, or – as Frantz Fanon and Amilcar Cabral once put it – 'the decolonisation of the mind'. In short, a general relativisation of 'truth', 'reason' and other abstract Enlightenment values, and an increasingly perspectival and context-related conception of truth-as-interpretation – and of 'truth' as an aspect of what Michel Foucault calls the 'will to power'.

28

Each of these developments would take a whole lecture on their own to elaborate. But I take them here as together marking an unsettling and subversion of the foundational ground on which the process of Heritage-construction has until very recently proceeded. We see it reflected in different ways: in how the texts supporting art works and framing exhibits are written by museums; in the attempts to make explicit the 'perspective' which has governed the selection and the interpretive contextualisation, so as to make it more open to challenge and re-interpretation; in the exposing of underlying assumptions of value, meaning and connection as part of a more dialogic relationship between the cultural institutions and their audiences; and in the tentative efforts to involve the 'subjects' themselves in the exhibiting process which objectifies them. These are only some of the manifest signs of a deep slow-motion revolution in progress in the practices of cultural representation.

They have taken hold, but are certainly not yet extensively or ubiquitously deployed in the institutional complex of the British Heritage 'industry' as a whole. Their appearance is at best patchy, more honoured in the breach – in profession of good intentions – than actual practice. Nevertheless, the question, 'Whose Heritage?', posed in the context of the current 'drift' towards a more multicultural Britain, has to be mounted on the back of this emerging turn. I take the appearance of 'cultural diversity' as a key policy priority of the newly restructured Arts Council, its greater visibility in statements of intent by the Government and the Ministry of Culture, Media and Sport, the recent efforts by the British Council to project a more 'diverse' image of British culture abroad, and even the much-delayed declaration of a 'Year of Cultural Diversity' – two years after Amsterdam, but much to be welcomed nevertheless – as potential but uncertain harbingers of change.

Suppose this *were* to turn out to be a propitious moment. What would those new constituencies who feel themselves woefully inadequately represented in the mirror of culture which the Heritage holds up to British society want out of it?

It goes without saying that we would need more money specifically targeted at this objective. The corners of the government's mouth tend to droop significantly when the money and material resources required to meet objectives are mentioned, and the weary muttering about 'not simply throwing money at the problem' rises to a quiet crescendo. However, the idea that a major culture-change – nothing short of a cultural revolution – could take place in the way the nation represents the diversity of itself and its 'subject-citizens' without a major redirection of resources is to reveal oneself as vacantly trivial about the whole question.

In fact, however, money really *is* not enough. For if my arguments are correct, then an equally powerful obstacle to change is the deep institutional investment which the key organisations have in going on doing things in the ways in which they have always been done; and the operational inertia militating against key professionals re-examining their criteria of judgement and gate-keeping practices from scratch and trying to shift the habits of a professional lifetime. It will require a substantially enhanced programme of training and recruitment for curators, professionals and artists from the 'minority' communities, so that they can bring their knowledge and experience to bear on transforming dominant curatorial and exhibitionary habits. It will take the massive leverage of a state committed to producing, *in reality rather than in name*, a more culturally diverse, socially just, equal and inclusive society and culture, and *holding its cultural institutions to account*. There are some straws in the wind and a lot of wordage, but so far no consistent sign of this.

Nevertheless, it seems to me that *we* have here an opportunity to clarify our own minds and to refine our agendas so that we can seize every opportunity to challenge institutions, shift resources, change priorities, move practices strategically in the right direction. The rest of my talk is devoted to this task of clarification.

First, we need a better idea of who the 'we' are in whose name these changes are being articulated. Principally, we have in mind the so-called 'ethnic minority communities' from the Caribbean and Indian sub-continent whose presence in large numbers since the 1950s have transformed Britain into a multicultural society, together with the smaller groups of non-European minorities from Africa, the Middle East, China and the Far East and Latin America. Their impact on diversifying British society and culture has been immediate and significant. It may therefore surprise you to hear me say that it is really very complex to understand how appropriately these communities should now be culturally represented in mainstream British cultural and artistic institutions. Our picture of them is defined primarily by their 'otherness' – their *minority* relationship to something vaguely identified as 'the majority', their cultural difference from European norms, their non-whiteness, their 'marking' by ethnicity, religion and 'race'. This is a negative figuration, reductive and simplistic.

These are people who have formed communities in Britain which are both distinctively marked, culturally, and yet have never been separatist or exclusive. Some traditional cultural practices are maintained – in varied ways – and carry respect. At the same time, the degrees and forms of attachment are fluid and changing – constantly negotiated, especially between men and women, within and across groups, and above all, across the generations. Traditions coexist with the emergence of new, hybrid and crossover cultural forms of tremendous vitality and innovation. These communities are in touch with their differences, without being saturated by tradition; they are actively involved with every aspect of life around them, without the illusion of assimilation and identity. This is a new kind of difference – the difference which is not binary (either–or) but whose *'differances'* will not be erased, or traded (Derrida 1982).

Their lives and experiences have been shaped by traditions of thought, religious and moral values, very different from the Judeo-Christian and classical traditions whose 'traces' still shape 'western' culture; and by the historical experience of oppression and marginalisation. Many are in touch with cultures and languages which pre-date 'The West'. Nevertheless, colonisation long ago convened these cultural differences under the 'canopy' of a sort of imperial empty 'global' time, without ever effectively erasing the disjunctures and dis-locations of time, place and culture by its ruptural intrusion into their 'worlds'. This is the palimpsest of the postcolonial world. They are, as C. L. R. James once put it, 'in but not of Europe' (James 1990). Nevertheless, they have known 'Europe' for three or four centuries as what Ashis Nandy, in his unforgettable phrase, calls 'intimate enemies' (Nandy 1983). They are what David Scott has called 'conscripts of modernity'. They have dwelled for many years, and long before migration, in the double or triple time of colonisation, and now occupy the multiple frames, the in-between or 'third' spaces – the homes-away-from-homes – of the postcolonial metropolis.

No single programme or agenda could adequately represent this cultural complexity especially the 'impossible' desire to be treated and represented with justice (that is, as 'the same') simultaneously with the demand for the recognition of 'difference'. The agenda will itself have to be open and diverse, representing a situation which is already cross-cut by new and old lateral connections and reciprocal global influences and which refuses to stand still or stabilise. We ourselves should recognise that there will be many complementary but different ways of being represented, just as there are many different ways of 'being black'.

Without becoming too specific, what would be the basic elements or building blocks of such an agenda?

First, there is the demand that the majority, mainstream versions of the Heritage should revise their own self-conceptions and rewrite the margins into the centre, the outside into the inside. This is not so much a matter of repre-senting 'us' as of representing more adequately the degree to which 'their' history entails and has always implicated 'us', across the centuries, and vice versa. The African presence in Britain since the sixteenth century, the Asian since the seventeenth century and the Chinese, Jewish and Irish in the nine-teenth have long required to be made the subjects of their own dedicated heritage spaces as well as integrated into a much more 'global' version of 'our island story'. Across the great cities and ports, in the making of fortunes, in the construction of great houses and estates, across the lineages of families, across the plunder and display of the wealth of the world as an adjunct to the imperial enterprise, across the hidden histories of statued heroes, in the secrecy of pri-vate diaries, even at the centre of the great master-narratives of 'Englishness' like the two World Wars, falls the unscripted shadow of the forgotten 'Other'. The first task, then, is re-defining the nation, re-imagining 'Britishness' or 'Englishness' itself in a more profoundly inclusive manner. The Brits owe this, not to only us, but to themselves: for to prepare their own people for success in a global and de-centered world by continuing to misrepresent Britain as a closed, embattled, self-sufficient, defensive, 'tight little island' would be to fatally disable them.

This is not only a matter of history. London and other major cities have been, throughout this century, 'world cities', drawing to themselves the creative talents of nations far and wide, and standing at the centre of tremendously varied cross-cultural flows and lateral artistic influences. Many distinguished practitioners who chose to live and work in Britain – Ronald Moody, Aubrey Williams, Francis Souza, Avinash Chandra, Anwar Jala Shemza, David Medalla, Li Yuan Chia, Frank Bowling and many others – have been quietly written out of the record. Not British enough for the Tate, not International enough for Bankside, I guess. The ways in which the most 'modernist' impulse in western art drew inspiration from what it defined as 'primitive' is now an art-historical cliché. But the numbers of non-European artists who played a central part in European, and especially British, modernism, is far less widely acknowledged – what Rasheed Araeen called, in his historic retrospective, '*The (Largely Untold) Other Story*' (1989). The existence of major 'other modernisms', with their own indigenous roots elsewhere, passes without serious attention. The incontestable truth of the observation that 'The search for a new identity expressed in modern forms has been the common denominator of most contemporary art movements in Africa' is, for western curators and art historians, still a well-kept secret (Hassan 1999).

Then, second, there is the enormous, unprecedented, creative explosion by contemporary practitioners from so-called 'minority' communities in all the arts (painting, visual arts, photography, film, theatre, literature, dance, music, multimedia) which has marked the last three decades. Unless that work is funded and exhibited, young talent and promise will simply dribble away. And it needs to be said loud and clear that it is not work which is likely immediately to appeal to the new culture-heroes of the art world – the corporate sponsors – who are already in search of their next Monet outing at some prestigious venue. For a time the work of contemporary artists from the 'minority' communities was patronisingly secured within an 'ethnic' enclave, as if only non-European work reflected the cultural idioms in which they were composed – as if only 'we' had 'ethnicities'. However, the movement has long ago breached its boundaries and flooded – but only when permitted by the cultural gate-keepers – into the mainstream. Its visibility has depended largely on a few pioneering figures and the efforts of a whole fleet of small, local and community-based galleries.

Like the rainbow, this work comes and goes. Major practitioners surface and pass quietly from view into an early and undeserved obscurity. Their work occasionally surfaces in mainstream venues – and has an innovative vitality much 'indigenous' work lacks. But they cannot be properly 'heritaged'. The critical records, catalogues and memorabilia of this great tide of creative work in the visual arts since the 1970s, for example – from which, one day the histories and critical studies of black diaspora visual culture will be written –

existed for many years in boxes in a filing cabinet in Eddie Chambers' bed-room before they found a resting place – in AAVAA, the African and Asian Visual Artists Archive, courtesy of the University of East London. No proper archive, no regular exhibitions, no critical apparatus (apart from a few key journals like *Third Text* and the now-defunct *Ten 8*), no definitive histories, no reference books, no comparative materials, no developing scholarship, no passing-on of a tradition of work to younger practitioners and curators, no recognition of achievement amongst the relevant communities . . . Heritage-less.

Third, there is the record of the migrant experience itself. This is a precious record of the historical formation of a black diaspora in the heart of Europe – probably a once-in-a-lifetime event – still *just* within living memory of its participants. Anyone who watched the *Windrush* programmes, and listened to the moving and articulate interviews, or saw the images which Autograph (The Association of Black Photographers) helped to research and mount at the Pitshanger Gallery in Ealing or read the first-hand evidence of the political struggles of the period of 1940–90 being put together by the unfunded George Padmore series edited by a veteran figure – John LaRose, whose autobiography we await – will know the rich evidence in visual imagery and oral testimonies which is waiting to be consolidated into a major archive.

It needs, of course, to be supplemented by extensive oral histories, political memoirs and personal artefacts, from which, alone, 'the black experience' in Britain since the 1950s could be recreated. We know, from a few bold efforts to build the everyday concerns of migrants into 'daily life' local exhibitions (for example at the adventurous Walsall Museum and Art Gallery), of the rich and complex details – customs, cuisine, daily habits, family photographs and records, household and religious objects – which remain to be documented in these domestic settings, poised as they are on the edge of and constantly negotiating between different 'worlds'. There is no such systematic work in progress, though the Black Cultural Archives with its recent lottery grant *may* at last be able to make a small start on oral histories. Some selective attempts have been made to do this for some Afro-Caribbean communities. So far as I know, there is very little comparable work as yet on the Asian experience(s). Heritage? *Which Heritage?*

Fourth, there is the question of those 'traditions of origin', so often deployed to represent minority communities as immured in their 'ethnicity' or differen-tiated into another species altogether by their 'racialised difference'. These 'tra-ditions' are occasionally on view in performances by visiting companies, framed as an exotic entertainment. But in general terms, the public is deeply uninformed about them. The complexities of practice, interpretation and belief of Hinduism or Islam as world systems of religious belief are virtually a closed book, even to the intelligensia. The long, highly complex and refined traditions of Indian music or dance, the key texts, poets and novelists, of these great civilisations, the extraordinarily varied cultural history of the Indian sub-continent itself, are beyond the reach of even the well-educated. Equally obscure are complexities of tribe, language and ethnicity in sub-Saharan Africa.

These basic building blocks of the new global universe we inhabit confront a blank and uncomprehending provincial 'Englishness' as if fitfully glimpsed from outer space. Beyond sea, sun, sand, reggae and ganja, the fantastic intricacies of the 'transculturation' of European, African and Indian elements over centuries, which have produced the variety and vibrancy of Caribbean 'creole' cultures, is another Great Unknown. Latin America with its highly evolved Hispanic and Amerindian cultures may well be less familiar than the surface of Mars. The 'peculiarity' of Afro-Caribbeans – that they are simultaneously deeply familiar, because they have lived with the British for so long, and ineradicably different because they are black – is regarded by most of the British (who have never been asked by their 'Heritage' to spare it a thought) as culturally inexplicable. Here, the National Curriculum and the truncated remnant of History as a discipline which remains, with only its most simplistic relationship to notions of 'Heritage' intact, has done irreparable damage.

And yet many of the creative talents of these communities are still 'framed' within a familiarity with the practices of these richly traditional arts, so deeply are they interwoven with the textures of a lived culture itself; and even new and experimental work draws on their repertoires, idioms and languages of representation. Unless the younger generation has access to these cultural repertoires and can understand and practice them, to some extent at least, from the inside, they will lack the resources – the cultural capital – of their own 'heritage', as a base from which to engage other traditions. They will in effect be culturally 'monolingual' if not silenced – literally, deprived of the capacity to speak – in a world which requires us all to be or become culturally bi- if not multi-lingual.

There is no intrinsic contradiction between the preservation and presentation of 'other cultures' and – my fifth point – the engagement with the production of new diasporic forms. The popular culture of our society especially has been transformed by the rich profusion of contemporary hybrid or 'cross-over' cultural forms – in music, dance, street-style, fashion, film, multimedia – which mark the production of 'the new' and the transgressive alongside the traditional and the 'preservation of the past'. Here, 'modernity' (or post-modernity) is not waiting on some authority to 'permit' or sanction this exploration of creativity in contemporary media and form. This is the leading-edge cultural phenomenon of our time – the 'multi' in multicultural, the 'Cool' in 'Cool Britannia'. For a time, black Afro-Caribbeans were in the vanguard of these avant-garde cultural practices, like cultural navigators crossing without passports between ragga, jungle, scratch, rap and electro-funk. In recent years, they have been decisively joined by the 'disorienting rhythms' of Asian youth. Perhaps this aspect of cultural production needs no 'archive' or 'heritage'. But it is proceeding unrecorded and unanalysed, consigned to the ephemera of its day – expendable. Yet it represents one of the most important cultural developments of our time: the stakes which 'the margins' have in modernity, the local-in-the-global, the pioneering of a new cosmopolitan, vernacular, post-national, global sensibility.

What I have offered is a wholly inadequate sketch – leaving out whole tracts of activity and countless examples. The account is inevitably skewed by my own interests and preoccupations. The detail does not matter. What matters is some greater clarity about 'the big picture'. I have tried to suggest not only *what* but *why* the question of 'The Heritage' is of such timely and critical importance for our folks at this time. 'British' most of us were, at one time – but that was long ago and, besides, as Shakespeare said, 'the wench is dead'. 'English' we cannot be. But tied in our fates and fortunes with 'the others' – while steadfastly refusing to have to *become* 'other' to belong – we do, after all, have a stake, an investment – in this phase of globalisation – in what I might call 'the post-nation': but only if it can be re-imagined, re-invented to include us. That is the bet, the wager, the gamble we are here to discuss.

Notes

1 This is the text of a keynote speech given on 2 November 1999, at the national conference *Whose Heritage? The Impact of Cultural Diversity on Britain's Living Heritage* that took place at G-Mex, Manchester, England.

2

NEVER MIND THE BUZZWORDS

'Race', heritage and the liberal agenda

Roshi Naidoo

I suspect that most people who have picked up this book will have, at sometime or other, wandered around a heritage site whispering into the ear of a slightly irritated companion about the omissions and great acts of forgetting which are on display. At exhibitions, monuments and historic buildings around the world questions are raised about the peoples and events which are implicitly present but not explicitly referred to. Trips to British stately homes, for example, can often raise the following questions: where is the context for the artefacts on display? Why the reluctance to account for the colonial relations which led to their acquisition? Why is there no attempt to acknowledge the perniciousness of monarchy and the social inequalities it naturalises? Not just academics, curators or heritage professionals engage in this sort of critique – all sorts of people, particularly politicised 'minorities', are hungry for a more radical take on this nation's history and keen to see themselves written into the story of Britain. However, in a sense, these criticisms directed at the more traditional end of the heritage market are easy to make. What is harder is finding a way of expressing discomfort with heritage projects which *have* attempted to take on board critiques of the sector's exclusiveness, and which *have* made concerted efforts to include and 'speak' to racial and cultural minorities.

This chapter is an attempt to carve out some space to express this disquiet without simply dismissing all attempts at reforming the heritage sector as partial and therefore meaningless. To understand the need for continued criticism despite high-profile cultural shifts to 'include' and 'celebrate' a diverse and multi-ethnic Britain, we must examine the ideologies underpinning these shifts and pose some crucial questions. Are Britain's racial and cultural 'minorities' being written into stories of the nation in order to build a radical, new, democratic national culture? Is the primary objective to ensure that certain liberal values, such as universalism, tolerance and rationality, are bolstered rather than undermined in the public sphere? Are certain ongoing oppressive ideologies about 'race' and nation being repackaged and sold in new, more enlightened clothes? Are they being included in ways which question popular history, so that the story of 'minorities' simply becomes the story of Britain, rather than something hermetically sealed from 'traditional' history? And to what extent is there an awareness of the complexities of multiculturalism or of the problems evoked by the term 'ethnic minority communities'? (Hesse 2000).

Many would take issue with a volume such as this which could be seen to be 'carping' about 'race' at the very time when there are many initiatives to address the issue. One could point to, particularly in recent years, many exhibitions and museums which *have* taken on board critiques of colonialism (such as the Empire and Commonwealth Museum in Bristol) or which *have* attempted to represent the marginalised, as a necessary antidote to the average stately home. They would also be able to point to heritage projects aimed at and led by black and 'other' Britons which have extended the predictable heritage landscape. It is no doubt true that many national museums have moved from being repositories displaying their conquests to institutions aimed at regenerating communities and being part of a renewed public sphere, where New Labour discourses such as 'lifelong learning', 'inclusion' and a 'respect for diversity' can flourish. However, this transformation seems in many cases to involve marrying some of their traditional roles with their newer awareness of post-coloniality, post-modern identity and issues of class, gender, 'race', ethnicity, sexuality, disability and exclusion. As a result there is an attempt to stitch together often competing and diverse discourses and ideologies about their role as public institutions, about identity, about community and about the nation-state.

The approach to 'ethnic communities' is one example of how problematic this can be. Rather than simply letting out a sigh of relief because museums are now sensitive to those they have historically trammelled, we need to examine more closely and critically how 'ethnicity' and 'race' are mobilised, how communities are engaged with, and how a world view in tune with the neo-liberal nation can be shored up rather than undermined in these new, more 'sensitive' approaches. Obviously all such initiatives cannot be dismissed as partial and ultimately offensive, as there are different ways in which these changes in culture have been negotiated and a range of successes in how radical they have been. However, we need to delve behind the frenetically repeated buzzwords of 'inclusion' and 'diversity', behind the efforts to recruit those who can plug gaps in the heritage sector's understanding of 'race', to examine whether there are significant changes in how Britain is imagined and represented or if 'minorities' are being recruited to uphold a vision of a more traditional nation. I will be looking closely at two exhibitions which ran at the British Library, *Lie of the Land – The Secret Life of Maps*, and *Trading Places – The East India Company and Asia 1600–1834*, both of which reflect a more 'enlightened' approach to the age of exploration and colonialism. The British Library as a national repository of learning and scholarship remains to many a signifier of all that is 'best' about Britain and its education system and is therefore a well-placed institution to consider in relation to these issues. In the detail of exhibits are the clues to changes in ideologies of the nation and it is interesting that it is not only in those explicitly about 'race' or empire where battles between familiar museum narratives and newer more enlightened ones can be found.

Lie of the Land and *Trading Places*

The British Library's exhibition *Lie of the Land – The Secret Life of Maps* ran from July 2001 to April 2002 (Carlucci and Barber 2001). This exhibition – challenging in many important respects – presented a philosophy of science in an ambitious and imaginative way, its theme eloquently captured in its playful title. *Lie of the Land* was ostensibly a critique of maps and their status as 'factual', 'actual' and 'real' and instead presented them as representations informed by political ideas. This is an idea that is in active opposition to the sanctity of scientific and geographic knowledge – a cornerstone of the Enlightenment and one historically enshrined in Western museums. It is also, in one sense, something which raises questions about the relationship between knowledge and historical progress, an idea that lies at the heart of the project of modernity.

The exhibition began very impressively with the traditional and more familiar Mercator Map superimposed on to the Peter's Projection which depicts land masses according to different principles and which demonstrates, for example, how small Europe is in relation to Africa. Both maps, we are told by the exhibition panels, are 'distortions'. However the text continues in incredulous tone: 'It has even been suggested that the Mercator projection continues to be used in a deliberate attempt to deceive, by making Europe and North America bigger than the countries of the Third World'.[1] Leaving aside the implications of the reference to the 'Third World', there are a range of problems here. First, we are introduced to the notion that a map is a work of fiction – a discursive entity – but then the idea of agency behind the map-makers and their contexts is presented as totally bizarre. The next piece of text appears to back-pedal to tell us: 'different projections are appropriate for different purposes – fortunately at the last count there were over 100 to choose from'. Here then one gets the feeling that the exhibition narrative's flirtation with more radical ideas must be curtailed in order to preserve the sanctity of its intellectual omniscience. Similarly, a section of the exhibition entitled 'Whose World is it Anyway?' explains how individuals, societies, religious groups, etc., have their particular world views represented in their maps. This, we are told, is simply 'human nature', a natural impulse to locate one's status in the world. Elitist, hierarchical ideas are naturalised: maps may be ideological but they are located as 'natural' impulses in the same way that trading is naturalised in the story of colonialism in the British Galleries at the Victoria and Albert Museum (V&A) in London and at the Museum of Scotland in Edinburgh.

The place where it was most clear that attempts were being made to address racism while not disturbing the traditional liberal values of a public institution was the exhibit entitled 'The Politically Incorrect Map'. This was a 'Chart of religion, population and civilisation' from 1815. The narrative told us knowingly that the map contains graded levels of civilisation with 'Europe predictably at the top and Africa at the bottom'. On the one hand, one can applaud the critique of Eurocentrism, but the labelling of this as the 'Politically Incorrect Map' demonstrates how the issue of racism is boxed off and not allowed to impinge on the rest of the exhibition. This 'knowingness' also conveys the sense of linear progress in so far as the end of discriminatory practices goes. In effect, it is saying: 'Yes, everyone was racist in the olden days, but we all know better now and can laugh ironically at it'. What was also interesting about this map was that the ethnographic categories cited still have currency today. For example, is the notion of 'the Arab world' and the current confusion in the West between what are secular and Islamic states any less bizarre than this nineteenth-century map and its talk of 'Nubians' and 'Tartars'? The proof of how radical this line of argument is occurs in whether or not the 'lies' in maps are presented as an aberration from the past which historical progress will resolve or a continuing process through which political ideology translates itself. The 'Politically Incorrect Map' takes the former view.

Oppositional discourses are often boxed off in this way and confined to places where they can be acknowledged (grudgingly or otherwise) but not cause us to rethink the building-blocks and foundations of the rest of our knowledge. This is similar to the ways in which it is, for example, acceptable to mention in academic texts David Hume's contempt for 'Negroes' but not acceptable to re-evaluate his political theory and notions of subjectivity in light of it.[2] In such spaces concessions to 'minorities' are made. For example, the V&A puts on radical special events such as *A Day of Record – Nails, Weaves and Naturals: Black British Hairstyles and Nail Art* (7 May 2001) to explore the politics of black hairstyles and grooming, but the centrality of racial 'others' to the economy and culture of design history in Britain is still eclipsed in the story told in its British Galleries. It is in these moments where one can locate the battles between acknowledging the excluded and the economic structures and political systems that exclude them, and maintaining the sanctity of the liberal world view – that the political and economic divisions between peoples are, in the end, the result of the free choices of free individuals who must therefore bear the primary responsibility for where they happen to be in the global order, or who may, at the extreme, be victims of sheer bad luck.

The British Library exhibition entitled *Trading Places – The East India Company and Asia 1600–1834* (May–September 2002) was one which obviously would tackle Empire and economics more directly and like *Lie of the Land* made numerous radical points. At the entrance the panel explained that the East India Company was Britain's 'first great commercial enterprise' but qualified this, in these more enlightened times, by stressing that for Asia this meant the beginning of European domination and eventually Empire.[3] Sponsorship by Standard Chartered, (in association with the newspaper the *Daily Telegraph*) a bank formerly targeted by the anti-apartheid movement for its trade links with pre-democratic South Africa, revealed the first anomaly. In the press release the chair of Standard Chartered refers to the objectivity of the exhibition as he celebrates his bank's achievement in developing international free trade via words like 'progress' and 'advancement' (www.bl.uk). But what does it mean when an international bank sponsors an event which draws attention to unfair trading practices of the past? One reading is that it situates exploitation, economic and otherwise, as a thing of the past and discourages the public from making connections between the brutality of colonisation and its modern equivalents in global trading practices. This leads us to a place whereby the modern world appears far too conscious to ever condone the exploitation of foreigners for the economic gain of the West. Another reading is that *Trading Places* makes us think critically about how exploration and capital informed museum collections and practices in the *past*, but again appears to locate this as now being over. However, capital has, and continues, to play a defining role in exhibitionary practices, through, for example, sponsorship, the privatisation of the public sector, and donations from the wealthy. How radically different is bank sponsorship of an exhibition on The East India Company from the British Museum being sponsored by nineteenth-century colonialism? Strategic corporate sponsorship is so much part of our landscape that, as a public, we rarely question the ironies of oil companies sponsoring ecological exhibits or of billionaire royalty speaking for the poor and dispossessed.

Lynda Dyson, in her chapter in this book, notes the pressure on museums to be commercially viable and populist and to present revised versions of the meaning of nation, noting that they have to present 'a version of nation fit for the neo-liberal global economy'. In her consideration of the Te Papa Tongarewa museum in New Zealand she discusses a section of the exhibition which appears to give voice to different views of the Treaty of Waitangi (1840) which effectively handed New Zealand over to the colonists. She notes, '[t]his device, apparently giving "voice" to a range of ordinary opinions, is used to signify the nation's capacity for "democracy", "egalitarianism" and "openness", thus silencing any contentious claims to different forms of sovereignty'. This has a resonance with the versions of Britain being presented in *Lie of the Land* and *Trading Places*. The contemporary sense of a 'knowingness' suggests that current exhibitions are more authentic because they are 'truthful' about past wrongs, misrepresentations and forms of brutality. There is a sense of a Britain ready to confront its colonial past but this confrontation is not necessarily desirable.

First, it is entirely possible to have a neo-liberal multiculturalism which demonstrates a willingness to confront the thornier issues of imperialism in order to perpetuate continued celebration of the 'achievements' of Empire. There has been a resurgence of histories which, while noting the 'downside' of colonisation, maintain the defence of Britain's global civilising mission (Ferguson 2003). Can the Empire and colonisation exhibitions in one sense provide a means of revisiting 'Great Britain', albeit with some 'guilt'? Is this a way of reminding people of Britain's glorious past and a means of adding credence and historical context to, for example, Tony Blair's desire to carve up Iraq just as his predecessors did? Second, it seems heritage projects which revisit colonisation and the high point of Empire rarely draw attention to what a historical blip a unified (mythic or otherwise) 'Great Britain' was. Even a liberal reformed story of empire can perpetuate the idea of a long, unbroken, glorious past and so establish a dangerous duality between the past as unified, safe and knowable (albeit a bit brutal) and the present as post-modern, fragmented, multicultural and 'politically correct'. To really tackle British history in a radical way it would be clear that debates about 'blackness' and Britishness are part of larger contested ideas about what 'British' means and would expose the foundational myths of England, Englishness and Britishness. As Raphael Samuel noted:

> The break-up of Britain in the present, and the uncertainties attaching to its future, necessarily make us more aware of its contingent character in the past. The unity of the British Isles, so far from being the norm, can appear rather as an exceptional condition, with a lifespan of less than two hundred years, from the Battle of Culloden, say, in 1746, to the Irish Treaty of 1921.
>
> (Samuel 1998: 22)

Third, another sleight-of-hand which can occur, and which Dyson also notes, is the sense of being in a phase of 'post-constructedness' in so far as national identity is concerned. If our attention is being drawn to the instability and representational nature of national identity and belonging in the past, such as around the notion of 'Great Britain', but not drawn to its current manifestations, it appears as though we have reached the end of history in relation to national identity. The project of modernity appears alive and well and functioning for the gradual embetterment of all. In *Trading Places* in particular there is a sense of coming to terms with the past and an acceptance of a 'new' multicultural Britain.

Trading Places highlighted some crucial issues by asking: 'What has been the human cost of cheap Asian goods?', as well as by noting that the onset of colonial rule meant Asian economies were manipulated to turn them into producers of raw materials for Europe as well as consumers for European (mostly British) manufactured goods. But after making these important points, we learn that since 1945 and the demise of the British Empire, powerful Asian economies have emerged and are exporting goods to the rest of the world. This tale of 'successful' Asian economies is only part of the story; and we hear nothing about ongoing poverty in Asia and the historical legacies of colonialism. The following quote from the exhibition continues to reinforce the idea of the problems of colonialism as being resolved. 'The successors to the

Company's trade are perhaps the great industrial-financial complexes to which it gave birth – Bombay, Calcutta, Singapore and Hong Kong and the now familiar Asian presence and contribution to Britain's rich cultural diversity'. This one sentence encapsulates two narratives – one of progress and the linear development towards racial and international equality, and the other the language of inclusion and 'celebration' of Britain's cultural diversity. Until exhibition narratives in major public institutions find a way of clarifying the link between history and ongoing forms of economic exploitation, they will always remain unsatisfying accounts of the nature of global power relations, historical and contemporary. *Trading Places* links the age of exploration to the era of high imperialism to the modern tiger economies. It could just as seamlessly have linked them to continuing forms of economic exploitation, which have their roots in the organisation of the world economy under British rule.

Shifts in how Britain appears to be representing itself must be considered in relation to global economics and politics. If there is a sense of a Britain willing to confront its colonial past and embrace its 'new' multiculturalism it seems pertinent to ask – why now? Perhaps as we as a nation are currently reviled around the world for re-engaging our old imperial desires (albeit on the back of US neo-imperialism) it is especially important to project an image of a 'modern' liberal country whose agenda for invading others comes from a moral rather than economic position. After all, a war-mongering Britain is totally at odds with the New Labour version of a 'young' Britain marketed so assiduously at the beginning of its tenure in government. 'Young Britain' was heavily dependent on the image of a vibrant and creative multiculturalism. But how can a Britain of 'multicultural drift', as Stuart Hall has called the process whereby images of black and Asian people are slowly pulled into the mainstream of representation (see Hall's chapter in this book), be squared with a Britain with its old imperial desires and ambitions seemingly intact and updated?

It is often Britain's racial 'others' who can be useful in plugging gaps between 'old' and 'new' Britain. Like the inclusion of Notting Hill Carnival costumes at the Queen's Golden Jubilee celebrations, a non-white presence conveys an accommodation between two Britains – one 'old', traditional, transcendent and intact and signified by royalty and stately homes – the other 'new', young, energetic and multicultural, magnanimously accommodated by a benign monarchy and 'tolerant' white majority. The 'white past/multicultural present' binary in the historical understanding of Britain is a fallacy that wipes from public consciousness the fact of a long-standing non-white presence on these islands dating from Roman times, the view of a Britain fundamentally and irrevocably shaped by its relations with other countries, as well as obscuring an understanding of Britishness itself as a historically unstable and contested national identity (Littler and Naidoo 2004). The fact that Britons of Asian, Caribbean and African descent are perpetually figured as a new phenomenon and continually and consistently expected to account for our presence here is underpinned by this national reluctance to appreciate that Britain was multicultural long before the *Windrush* arrived (Hall 2000b: 230).

This 'old/new' binary is not accidental or a consequence of naïvety. Neither should it be seen as simply a process on the road to enlightenment on 'race' and national identity. We must ask why, after so many decades of quality scholarship on the black and Asian presence in Britain (Visram 1986; Edwards and Dabydeen 1991; Walvin 1992; Gerzina 1999; Dabydeen 1987; Fryer 1984; Ramdin 1987 to name a few), very little beyond the existence of a few isolated individuals such as Crimea nurse Mary Seacole has penetrated public consciousness or the national curriculum. Surely if it had there would be a much greater willingness to accept that people with black or brown faces may also be English, Scottish, Welsh or Irish. This is not simply a question of having got the analysis wrong – there is a deep economic, political and psychological investment in this 'white past/multicultural present' view. For example, a country which appears able to engage in a limited celebration of its 'new' multiculturalism can also legitimately pathologise and abuse asylum-seekers under the guise of preserving its older more primary identity as a white, 'British' nation. A government who are tough on foreigners but keen to improve the lot of 'legitimate' immigrants can appear liberal and inclusive as they simultaneously deprive people of their human rights. If there was more public consciousness of Britain's role in creating the conditions that give rise to the need for asylum, or of the country itself being created by waves of immigration, it would be much harder for right-wing newspapers to complain when lottery money is spent on asylum-seekers. There must, for example, be some correlation between the widespread unease and objection to the invasion of Iraq and the fact that popular consciousness was raised, not only over US oil interests, but also over Britain's long-term role in manipulating the Iraqi regime.

A section of *Trading Places* was dedicated to the early presence of Asians in Britain, with a focus on cultural influences such as language and early Indian eating houses. These fascinating exhibits with thoughtful illuminating text did disrupt the view that Asian faces in Britain were a post-war phenomenon. Just like the sections of the exhibition which drew attention to Britain's corrupt role in the opium trade (though not sufficiently – see www.bl.uk) *Trading Places* undermined many popular myths about Britain's historical relationship with Asia and why there are Asian people in Britain today. At the beginning of this piece I expressed the view that it was harder in certain ways to express disquiet with these sorts of exhibitionary practices than those which celebrate a more 'gung-ho' reactionary version of Britain's past. The point above would seem to negate the arguments and criticisms I and others in this collection have levelled at established heritage practices. So why is it that one's spirits drop when, after being taken on a fairly ambitious look at colonisation, one is once again left with food and language as the means through which Asians are able to feel acknowledged as being part of Britain?

I, and many like me, have sat in heritage meetings and listened to proposed joint ventures between established heritage institutions and projects which promote black and/or Asian history, with mixed feelings. While they increasingly propose stimulating takes on this history one is still often left with a deep dissatisfaction and no framework in which to discuss it. It may be that after many years of fighting against liberal erasure of difference, we are once again back in a situation where we have to ask what differences are being foregrounded, and why? To include, for example, British Asians, into a narrative of national belonging requires a move beyond the signalling of accepted signifiers of difference. Being 'marked' as Asian seems to have more currency in the heritage sector's attention to 'ethnicity'. Perhaps now a recognition of our 'sameness' as well as our differences is required. To complain about being overly 'marked' runs the risk of slipping into a liberal pluralism of 'we are all the same under the skin', but to ask for an acceptance of sameness as well as difference is more complex. One needs to ask whether there is a preference for invoking easily visible manifestations of ethnic communities.

For example, although it is important to produce language-sensitive leaflets, is this sometimes perceived as the only necessary challenge to our heritage landscape? As I have said there are numerous radical individuals and projects working to undermine such trenchant views and representations, but while there are so many that continue to approach ethnicity and community as though they were finite categories, we must air these concerns. Often there is a belief that 'white' institutions are naïve but are having a go at tackling their former prejudices and therefore should be supported, engaged with and steered in the right direction. But is this assumption of naïvety dangerous? Does the preference for projects which address easily visible, apparently bounded and unified communities play on a particular binary, with the state representing all that is best about the liberal tradition and the 'ethnic community' representing a manifestation of a 'traditional' culture? Hall notes that the 'multicultural question' has a 'transruptive' effect on our understanding of culture (Hall 2000b: 225).

> The binary opposition derived from the Enlightenment – Particularism *vs* Universalism, or Tradition *vs* Modernity – produces a certain way of understanding culture. There are the distinctive, homogenous, self-contained, strongly bounded cultures of so-called traditional societies. In this anthropological definition, cultural tradition saturates whole communities, subordinating individuals to a communally-sanctioned form of life. This is counter-posed to the 'culture of modernity' – open, rational, universalist and individualistic.
>
> (Hall 2000b: 225)

Cultural differences, such as food and language, can be noted and affirmed in the public sphere but through the process of institutionalising them 'ethnic' communities can be assimilated into a liberal pluralist version of the nation and help stem the tide of decline of public faith in the legitimacy of state institutions.

'Ethnicity', like 'race', is a term which falls apart quickly if one tries to link it to any biological essentialised difference or to a set of unified cultural or communal characteristics (Morley 2000). However, it is still approached with too little attention paid to its shifting, negotiated and partial character. As Hall notes: 'We should remember that "ethnicity", with its naturalized relationship to "community", is another term operating "under erasure"' (Hall 2000b: 233). As well as 'race' and 'ethnicity' there is the problem of the notion of 'community' as it is understood and figured. The question of who or what is a community has preoccupied academics, policy-makers, practitioners, artists and writers, but is often skipped over, again, as an annoying theoretical hurdle. However, without proper debate about this, attempts to reach out to marginalised communities can be self-defeating. The liberal face of a heritage project can meet the reactionary face of a community and little progress is made. If communities are homogenised by institutions they never assume that the bulk of a community might object to a particular set of representations or activities which are ostensibly 'for' them.

Liberalism, as Hall continues, is the political tradition which has won – its appearance of universalism marks the triumph of a particularism rather than it being the 'culture beyond cultures' (Hall 2000b: 228). Liberalism as a political ideology has historically had little to say about 'race' (on migration for example, see Cole 2000) and what is apparent is how much 'race' disrupts its foundations. In attempts to convince us that 'the liberal state has sloughed off its ethnic-particularistic skin and emerged in its culturally cleansed, universalistic, civic form' (Hall 2000b: 228) there must be a preference for particular ways of addressing cultural communities and particular discourses of 'race', nation and belonging. This may account for why there is rarely any focus on the 'ethnicity' of the state or on the English hegemony over Britishness. However, the visible 'ethnicity' of communities secures the power of the state to be 'neutral'. It would be more radical to imagine us all as 'multicultural' rather than bringing 'others' into the public sphere as an act of benevolence.

In assessing the success of both *Lie of The Land* and *Trading Places* we have to ask if there is a sufficient sense of radically rethinking how British heritage is approached, represented and circulated or whether there is a sense of simply 'fixing' exhibition practices to make them more in tune with current sensibilities around 'race' and colonisation. Those who criticise how the heritage sector approaches 'race' are often accused of having unrealistic expectations. Surely it is better to make some progress, have some visibility of a black and Asian Britain? After all it is very hard to get every project to stand up to such intense political scrutiny. The next section suggests how we can move forward on issues of 'race' and national identity without recourse to easy essentialisms and in a way which can write new narratives of what it means to 'belong' in Britain.

New nation

A few years ago, I took a group of undergraduates on S. I. Martin's excellent *Black London Walk*. Those who have been on this illuminating excursion are struck by how the history of black London is simply the story of London – of riots, of political confrontations, of boozy night-spots, of intellectuals, traders and abolitionists, all shaping the city – a history of London without it is partial and meaningless. At the end of the walk Martin explains to the company that eighteenth-century London had a significant black population which had dwindled by the early twentieth century. Where did they go? The point when the party of 'black' and 'white' realise that their descendants are all around is very moving. The power of this should not be underestimated in a country where every day non-white people are still asked where they come from. The walk did not only bring into view a 'hidden' history, but directly challenged the foundation of current historical understandings of Britain. The depth and simplicity of such a moment proves that 'doing' black history is about bringing British history in general into view with a more astute eye.

Martin's approach is typical of a vein of historical research into black and Asian Britain which, more than just foregrounding individuals, uncovers the 'blackness' of British heritage causing us to rethink what we perceive of as national history. The research around Robert Wedderburn similarly brings into view ways of being British which are neither racially exclusive nor politically conservative (McCalman 1991). Wedderburn, of Caribbean and Scottish parentage, was a radical intellectual and activist in the early nineteenth century whose abolitionist writings made links between the treatment of West Indian slaves and the working classes in Britain. Wedderburn's political activism locates him as very much part of a British radical tradition – one which should have as much currency as being at the locus of our national culture as the monarchical tradition. He is also part of a rich black Scottish history which has been written out of the national story at the Museum of Scotland.[4] National culture is borne out of conflict, not out of consensus, and at every stage of the last few hundred years Britain's racialized 'others' have been present. Being British is as much about being a black radical firebrand as it is about being a white Admiral of the fleet. As Jagdish Gundara and Ian Duffield say in the introduction to *Essays on the History of Blacks in Britain*:

> What point is there in our children being taught that Waterloo Station is named after a famous British victory over Napoleon, if they do not understand that this was the *dénouement* of a struggle in which Black people played a part too; not merely as cannon fodder for the Royal Navy, West India Regiment and so on, but also as revolutionary activists in their own cause?
>
> (Gundara and Duffield 1992: 3)

46

One could quite easily make a connection between figures such as Wedderburn and political activists of all kinds who have shaped labour history. For example, the Asian women who stood on the picket lines in Grunwick in the 1970s provide an interesting take on how one can approach a British Asian history without recourse to Asian dress, food or language, and one which could make connections between, for example, Asian women in the suffrage movement, serving in the Second World War, and participating in anti-colonial struggles in Asia and Africa (Wilson 1988). To hear that an institution or organisation wants to explore British Asian culture via Bollywood, for example, must arouse our suspicions. This is not to denigrate this aspect of Asian culture, but too often the multitude of ways of being Asian in Britain are condensed around particular oversimplified and retrograde signifiers. Institutions which suggest that there is a current vogue for all things Asian often prefer to channel this via a 'celebration' of predictable cultural practices. The story of all sorts of minorities in Britain is simply the story of Britain and not something that can be hermetically sealed off from 'mainstream' heritage representations. The presence of non-white people disrupts the view that the nation is a legitimate site for a unified 'ethnic' cultural identification and therefore it may be easier to persistently locate them as 'outsiders'. Diasporic people also demonstrate that cultural identifications have always been selected from world-wide resources, long before the planet was imagined as globalised and post-national.

To acknowledge traditions as invented (Hobsbawm and Ranger 1983) doesn't make them necessarily null and void, and – as Jim McGuigan notes in this book – the more readily we accept the idea of the nation as a fiction, the easier it is to write new ones. Perhaps we should take our cue from the royal family which, primarily through the House of Windsor, has, in a relatively short historical period, turned the British royal family from a signifier of a European, internationalised upper class to one of a domesticated, semi-bourgeois British entity with long and established traditions (see Wilson 1989). It has done this through the invention of ceremonies for the investiture of the Prince of Wales and through a shrewd understanding of the importance of television during the Coronation in 1953. Raphael Samuel, commenting on the portraits of 111 Scottish kings in Holyrood Palace in Edinburgh painted by Jacob de Wet, makes a similar point: 'the portraits purport to cover some two millennia of Scottish history, giving fleshly embodiment to those royal genealogies and origin myths in which the idea of Scottish nationality seems first to have taken shape.' The fact that most are made up and the pictures make no pretence at historical accuracy demonstrates that myth and history coexist (Samuel 1998: 11). This shows how easy it is, in one sense, to write new national myths.

As museums look around desperately for where they can find black and Asian history it is usually under their noses. Moira Simpson says:

National Trust properties often epitomise the British upper classes and show little indication of their multicultural heritage. Like the Geffrye Museum, collections which seem to be the epitome of white British upper-class culture, taste and history, can be utilised to draw out a wealth of cross-cultural connections relating to matters such as design, social trends, trading activities, and so forth. Guides to the properties rarely give any indication of the heritage of black people yet the histories of many of them are frequently incontrovertibly entangled with that of the black British population. Wealth derived directly or indirectly from the slave trade funded the building of numerous stately homes while many of them had black servants, yet such histories remain hidden.

(Simpson 2001: 17)

There are a myriad of ways of 'putting your own house in order' which the heritage sector could manage quite quickly to address a more diverse history. If focus was shifted away from doing something *for* a community to one which approaches these marginalised histories as something *for* the museum and all its audiences, many of the pitfalls discussed here could be avoided.

We all need to make a profound ideological shift in our understanding of national history. Only then can heritage be a useful tool against the exclusive xenophobia which has traditionally been associated with the concept of Britishness. Perhaps we have been lulled into a false sense of security – if we are not apoplectic with rage as we walk around museums and heritage sites, but rather mildly disturbed, perhaps liberal inclusion has 'worked'. It should be possible to write a new story of Britain anchored in a different set of facts and of myths. A Britain always multicultural and a place of shifting 'ethnicities' – a Britain always globalised and always shaped by waves of migration – a country always hanging together different nations and kingdoms which have never really hung together as a coherent whole – a Britain where to be black and English, Scottish, Irish or Welsh are not anomalies – a Britain always shaped by difference – a Britain which can admit the myths and fictions upon which it is built. A very different national culture is ready and available.

Notes

1 Panels from *Lie of the Land – The Secret Life of Maps* July 2001 to April 2002 transcribed February 2002.
2 For a discussion which does, see Jordan and Weedon 1995: 284–9.
3 Panels from *Trading Places – The East India Company and Asia 1600–1835* May to September 2002, transcribed August 2002.
4 The interesting People's Story Museum is left to explore a Scotland shaped by waves of migration.

3

COMMEMORATING THE HOLOCAUST

Reconfiguring national identity in the twenty-first century

Sharon Macdonald

Introduction

Holocaust Memorial Day was first held in Britain on 27 January 2001, the 56th anniversary of the liberation of Auschwitz. This chapter addresses the question of why, at the beginning of the twenty-first century, a state-sponsored commemoration should be initiated of an event which took place over half a century ago and outside Britain's shores. The creation of a new, national, ritual – even one ostensibly about a past event – is not just an outcome of a mounting impetus to remember: it also speaks of, and to, the time and place of which it is part. Among other things, I argue, Holocaust Memorial Day articulates a reconfigured vision of national identity, legitimated through reference to the past and the iconic evil of modern times.

My interest in Holocaust commemoration in Britain, and Holocaust Memorial Day in particular, stemmed from having spent the academic year 1999–2000 researching representations of the Nazi past in Germany, where I was surprised by the considerable number of acts of commemoration and museumisation in relation to the Second World War and the Holocaust. These were not only the major projects, such as the new Jewish Museum in Berlin and the planned 'national' Holocaust Memorial, or the redisplay of Nazi sites such as the Nuremberg rally grounds, but also many smaller exhibitions and acts of remembrance, such as the erection of plaques on buildings which had previously been inhabited by noted Jewish citizens.[1] This was accompanied by numerous publications and almost daily television programmes.[2] There were also other signs of what Elisabeth Beck-Gernsheim (Beck-Gernsheim 1999) has described as a shift in the 'memory landscape' (Erinnerungslandschaft), such as the opening of Jewish restaurants and courses in Jewish studies, the latter being, she notes, now more popular – overwhelmingly with non-Jewish Germans – at the University of Munich than is gender studies. Some

49

Jewish-German commentators have described this as a growing 'Jewish pseu-doculture' (Rosenberg 1997, in Beck-Gernsheim 1999: 263) which, they sug-gest, has more to tell us about majority non-Jewish German identity than it does about Jewishness.

Increased levels of public commemoration of the Holocaust are also evident in other countries: Sweden and Italy have begun Holocaust memorial days in recent years; Rachel Whiteread was commissioned to create a Holocaust memorial for Vienna; and across Europe synagogues have been restored and Holocaust exhibitions opened. The United States has witnessed particularly extensive Holocaust commemoration, with a flurry of Holocaust museums and memorials opened in the 1980s and 1990s (e.g. in Los Angeles, Detroit, New York and Florida), including, in 1981, the federally supported US Holocaust Museum in Washington. This activity has provocatively been dubbed a 'Holo-caust cult' (Goldberg 1995, quoted in Flanzbaum 1999: 12) and 'the Holocaust industry' (Finkelstein 2000), and, as in Germany, questions have been raised about what this might indicate about wider American culture (e.g. Flanzbaum 1999; Novick 2000).

Returning from Germany to Britain, I was struck by a new level of public activity in relation to the Holocaust. The new Holocaust Memorial Day included a major ceremony, attended by numerous dignitaries, televised on prime-time television, and thousands of smaller commemorations and events across the country. The Imperial War Museum opened its Holocaust exhib-ition in 2001, and in 2002 the Imperial War Museum of the North, designed by Daniel Libeskind, architect of the Jewish Museum in Berlin, opened in Salford.[3] The Holocaust Centre, Beth Shalom (meaning House of Peace), opened in Nottinghamshire in 1995, and has played an important role in raising Holocaust awareness, for example by creating mobile exhibitions to tour the country (e.g. in Sheffield's Millennium Galleries in January 2002). In Britain, as in Germany, the early years of the new millennium have also seen fairly relentless screening of television programmes and production of publications about the Holocaust and World War II.

Looking at the German case, I had already come to the conclusion that this new level of public Holocaust commemoration could not be explained in entirely the same way as the US – at least as in the arguments advanced by Peter Novick (Novick 2000) and (less convincingly) Norman Finkelstein (Finkel-stein 2000). Britain – a country in which 'having won the war' has been argued to be a significant aspect of self-identity (e.g. Kushner 1997: 8) – seemed to require another strand to the argument again. At the same time, the very fact that the Holocaust had become such a focus of public memorialisation and museumisation internationally called for explanation which would cut across the national differences.

Holocaust heritage

To some extent, the new level of public marking of the Holocaust could be seen as part of a more general public preoccupation – often dubbed an obsession – with the past that seems to have grown up especially since the 1970s (Huyssen 1995; Lowenthal 1998). Yet many of the arguments typically used to try to explain this do not seem to work for the case of Holocaust remembrance. This is clearly no nostalgic looking back to a time of tradition, community or greater stability. More than anything the Holocaust clearly highlights precariousness, even – and indeed especially – in the midst of modernity and rationalisation (Bauman 1989). While there surely is an element of recuperating the voices of those whose experiences have been left out of many historical accounts – in this case the victims/survivors[4] – this is not all there is to it, and it does not explain the state-sponsorship and the form of much Holocaust commemoration. Nevertheless, cutting across all of the many debates about the late twentieth-century heritage and history preoccupation – and indeed situating those debates themselves – is a casting of the past as a subject through which to debate moral and political concerns. In other words, it has become a moral forum, perhaps even the pre-eminent moral forum of our times. While the past may to some extent have long played something of this role, a more widespread public acknowledgement of differences among historians, historical revisionism, debates about school curricula, identity politics, public controversies over matters such as commemoration, and the spreading of a conception of history as potentially regressive rather than progressive (Wright 1985), have all contributed to history being publicly debatable, and to its centring as a site for political and ethical contemplation today.[5]

Within this, the Holocaust has emerged as one of – or perhaps even the – pre-eminent foci of such political and moral activity: not perhaps entirely the 'moral and ideological Rorschach test' that Novick dubs it (Novick 2000: 12) but a moral and ideological touchstone none the less (Thomas 1999). The reasons why it has become so are partly shared across those nations in which the Holocaust is commemorated and to some extent are nation-specific, as I explore for the case of Britain below.

British identity and World War II

In order to understand the course of Holocaust commemoration in Britain, it is worth looking at why the Holocaust was not the subject of such memorialising and interest earlier. After the war, the language of Holocaust was not yet part of the vocabulary and in Britain, as Tony Kushner has written, 'Dunkirk, the Blitz, D-Day, the flying-bomb raids and, to a lesser extent, the prisoners of war in Japan were the British reference points for war suffering' (Kushner 1997: 10). He further explains:

Britain's war memory was essential to its post-1945 national identity. It was too precious, it must be argued, to have been brought into question by the experiences of another people whose suffering and losses made British sacrifices pale into insignificance. Moreover, the history of the Jews in the war was particularly problematic; it was a story with no redemptive ending, which contrasted markedly with the British case. VE Day, in a European Jewish context, fitted very uneasily with the reality of the war.

(Kushner 1997: 8)

Remembrance Day, on 11 November, Armistice Day of World War I, was extended to commemorate also those fallen in World War II. While this day could be said to serve to remember all those who lost their lives in these wars (as some who opposed establishing a Holocaust Memorial Day have argued), it was, from its initiation and in terms of how it has come to be seen and performed, primarily focused upon the heroism and loss of soldiers, and specifically on providing a funeral substitute for the military dead who were not repatriated (Moriarty 1997). While Remembrance Day observations had a clear tone of sadness, they also carried a military symbolism (the presence of uniformed veterans and the playing of the Last Post) and, even though there were surely countervailing private memories, they nevertheless helped sustain the post-war identity story of a heroic nation which had suffered in order to bring greater peace and stability to the world – the 'Britain alone' myth (Kushner 1997: 10). They were accompanied too by the more directly celebratory Battle of Britain and VE Day events, which also helped to shape British war memory. As journalist Martin Wollacott (in Cesarani 1997: 27) suggests: 'Second World War celebrations have a meaning in Britain that they do not have in any other former allied country. The war, for some Britons at least, is a kind of icon of our inner superiority'.

Public acknowledgement of the enormous and particular sufferings of Jews in the war does not seem to have become at all widespread until the 1970s (Kushner 1994, Kushner 1999: 228; Hartman 1994), though there was plenty of evidence available, not least from the war trials (e.g. Cesarani 1997; Frei 1999). Kushner notes that there seems to have been greater awareness of 'the destruction of European Jewry during the war' (Kushner 1998: 228) than was the case afterwards, when – with the exception of the Nuremberg trials – it was rarely deemed newsworthy. He argues that there were even attempts to suppress Holocaust testimonies which resulted 'not simply [from] benign, naive ignorance, but was part of the informal workings of a liberal ideology under the added restraints of an exclusive Englishness' (Kushner 1998: 228).[6] Public discourse on 'the Holocaust', specifically using this language, seems even more recent, with the first sustained uses having only been in the 1980s and 1990s. Historian Peter Novick, looking at the US, notes how different this is from many other cases. In relation to Vietnam, for instance, he writes that '[t]he most viewed films and best-selling books about the Vietnam War almost all appeared within five or ten years of the end of the conflict, as did the Vietnam Veterans memorial in Washington. With the Holocaust the rhythm has been very different: hardly talked about for the first 20 years or so after World War II then, from the 1970s on, becoming ever more central in American public discourse' (Novick 2000: 1–2). Why should this be so?

Novick rejects the psychoanalytic answer so often given, that the trauma has been so great that it is only later that this 'repressed' subject could be contemplated at all. Instead, he gives a historically situated account of the formation of, and change within, public memory, leading to what he refers to – in a mocking twist of the psychoanalytical position – as a 'Holocaust-fixation' (Novick 2000: 10). Immediately after the war, he writes,

> the Holocaust was *historicized* – thought about and talked about as a terrible feature of the period that had ended with the defeat of Nazi Germany. The Holocaust had not, in the post-war years, attained transcendent status as the bearer of eternal truths or lessons that could be derived from contemplating it.
>
> (Novick 2000: 100).

In Britain this was also the case, feeding in to the redemptive allegory of Britain having overcome this evil. Moreover, there was also a significant discourse of 'moving on' – Macmillan's 'you've never had it so good' – that was allied with a christianised discourse of forgiveness, and which regarded looking back at the horrors as essentially psychological unhealthy as well as politically unhelpful in a world in which one needed to 'do business with' the Germans.

The rise of Holocaust remembrance in the US

Novick's account of the growing public discourse of Holocaust shows a detailed interweaving of activity by American Jews – including growing fears of losing their identity in the face of *reduced* evident anti-Semitism in the States – and wider events which changed the frameworks within which the events of the 1930s and 1940s were talked about. The latter included the founding of the state of Israel, which was often publicly legitimated through reference to the Holocaust and a discourse of 'the world's silence' and 'the abandonment of the Jews' (Novick 2000: 158). It also included the rise of identity politics – of groups which self-identified as having suffered discrimination making political claims on the basis of, and on behalf of, their shared ethnic, gendered, sexual or other identities. The idea of 'exclusion' – of having been denied full social participation in some way – was central to this identity politics. It was also bound up with what Novick describes as 'a change in the attitude towards victimhood' (Novick 2000: 8; see also Furedi 2001). As he puts it, 'victimhood' has moved from a status all but universally despised to one often eagerly embraced. On the individual level, the cultural icon of the strong, silent hero is replaced by the vulnerable and verbose antihero. Stoicism is replaced as a prime value by sensitivity. Instead of enduring in silence, one lets it all hang out. The voicing of pain and outrage is alleged to be 'empowering' as well as therapeutic.

(Novick 2000: 8)

Leaving aside the question of whether articulating pain does or does not in fact alleviate it, this alleged shift is worth considering further, not least because in the British context it would jar with the celebratory heroism of much British war commemoration.

If the rise of Holocaust remembrance in the US was bound up with identity politics and the motif of individual survival, it was so in a particular way. One dimension of this was what in crude terms was almost a competition over suffering in which the black experience of slavery was the main contender (Thomas 1999); with the Holocaust in Europe sometimes even seeming to be being turned into an icon of past horror shared by all white Americans, to vie with the historical experience of slavery shared by blacks. While it would take considerable liberties with historical fact to maintain this explicitly, the fact that federal funding was provided for the Holocaust Memorial Museum on Washington's famous Museum Mall, where so much US identity-proclamation goes on, whereas proposals to fund a museum of slavery were thrown out at an early stage (Novick 2000: 194), suggests at least a positioning of the Holocaust as more central to American identity than slavery.

National identity formation and dilemmas

Before moving on to look at the rise of Holocaust remembrance in the UK, I want to consider briefly the question of the formation and maintenance of 'identity', especially national identity. Identity theorists have long argued that collective identities are produced relationally, typically through processes of opposition – of defining 'Us' in relation to 'Them' (Barth 1969; Cohen 1985; Jenkins 1997). This is then consolidated by identifying content which is taken as marking 'Us-ness' – the construction of differentiating symbols and what in German are called 'Gegenbilder' (counterimages) (Beck-Gernsheim 1999). Thus, black and white identities might, for example, be relationally constructed in opposition to one another, and experiences such as slavery be made symbolic of difference.

With regard to national identities, two oppositional processes in particular seem to go on. One is externally oriented: self-definition in relation to other nations, e.g. British versus French. War has always been one of the most fertile arenas for this kind of definitional activity, though it also goes on in more 'banal' ways, such as sport or media discussions of food (Billig 1995). The other means is internally oriented: the identification of the 'really Us/British', through contrast with the 'not-Us/not-British', within (e.g. Gilroy 1987). In the histories of all modern nation-states we can see the identification of 'out-groups' within, which serves to foster and maintain a majority identity in relation to the minority, and also processes such as the scape-goating of these minorities as sources of blame for the fact that the nation-state does not achieve the perfection to which it aspires. Nazi Germany is, of course, the most striking example of this, Jews being the principal 'Other' in this process. But the very overt and state-perpetrated way in which this process occurred in Germany should not obscure the fact that the same basic process has been at work in identity formation in other nation-states too. Even in the 1950s, for example, Jews were not allowed to be members of various sporting organisations in Britain such as the English Golf Union (Kushner 1998: 229).

Another feature of the construction of nineteenth-century national identities was the relating of positive, heroic narratives which depicted the nation as an active and successful entity. National rituals and memorials played an important role in providing occasions on which to remember heroism and triumph even in the face of loss, and in symbolically performing the nation as a united entity (Hobsbawm and Ranger 1983). Continuity over time – and preferably over a considerable time-period – was one of the properties through which the newly imagined communities were legitimated (Anderson 1998); and strength, manifested especially in military success, seems to have been regarded as the proper correlate of the right to political power. It was through such means that this new form of statehood, and the nation-states created according to this model, were imbued with moral legitimacy.

Today, however, many aspects of these identity processes have become problematic and the moral legitimacy of existing nation-states has been brought into question. Self-definition in contrast to national others – though it still goes on – has become less advisable in an era of increased global communication, trade and supra-national organisations. Self-definition by majorities through opposition to minorities has also become less advisable, not least because minorities may be crucial in electoral terms. Moreover, the rise of identity politics, and the growing awareness of the Holocaust itself, have contributed to a widespread recognition of and distaste for such processes. They still continue, of course, as in relation to asylum-seekers for instance, but they run alongside what has become a preferred language of liberal inclusiveness and multiculturalism. The use of heroic narratives – though it too still continues – has also become less confident and widespread; as witnessed, for example, in challenge to the canon and curriculum (see, for example, Samuel 1998; Phillips 1998).

As a consequence, the identity processes that nation-states have formerly employed are today more problematic. Moreover, globalisation has called the status of nation-states into question (e.g. Hall 1999a; Held et al. 1999). Even if the predicted demise of the nation state has been exaggerated, it has surely become more difficult to 'do nationness' in quite the ways in which it was formerly done. At the very least, gestures to alternative narratives and to other kinds of moral legitimacy need to be made – and perhaps harnessed to a reconfigured way of being national. This, I suggest, is something which Holocaust commemoration helps achieve.

The rise of Holocaust remembrance in the UK: Holocaust Memorial Day

The most recent forms of public Holocaust commemoration – most notably Holocaust Memorial Day – have been realised largely in the context of international developments and actions by government. This is not to say that they have lacked involvement by non-governmental organisations or interest groups but that it is change at the political centre that seems to have allowed – and also has provided a good deal of the funding for – them. In the process, they have also become broadened out from specific interest groups and cast as matters that should inform the identities of all citizens.

This state support contrasts markedly with earlier. For example, in 1965 a group of Holocaust survivors was refused permission to take part in events at the Cenotaph to mark the 20th anniversary of the end of the war – a refusal which was endorsed by a leading Jewish and Christian organisation (Kushner 1998: 230); and in 1980 the erection of a Holocaust memorial next to the Cenotaph was also refused, though the placing of a small – and largely forgotten – memorial stone in Hyde Park was allowed (Kushner 1998: 230).

It was not until 1999 that a proposal for a Holocaust Memorial Day was put before parliament, by MP Andrew Dismore who had recently visited Auschwitz-Birkenau on a tour organised by the Holocaust Educational Trust. The consultation paper produced in 1999 achieved widespread support. Then, in January 2000, an international forum of high-level government delegates from many countries, including Britain, was held in Sweden, which led to a signing of the Declaration of the Stockholm International Forum on the Holocaust. This declaration consists of eight statements serving to recognise the magnitude and horror of the Holocaust and a set of commitments to certain actions in the present (www.holocaustmemorialday.gov.uk).[7] This includes declaration number six: 'We share a commitment to commemorate the victims of the Holocaust and to honour those who stood against it. We will encourage appropriate forms of Holocaust remembrance, including an annual Day of Holocaust Remembrance in our countries.' The first Holocaust Memorial Day in Britain, organised by the Home Office one year later, was a direct honouring of this commitment.

An important backdrop to the holding of the Stockholm forum was a growing fear, and growing evidence, of rising neo-Nazism in Europe. Even Sweden, which like other Nordic countries had tended to pride itself on low levels of far-right activity, had witnessed examples of neo-Nazi and explicitly racist incidents; and this spurred its prime minister to hold the forum. Other countries which participated, especially Germany in which racist attacks and support for Nazism had grown since unification, had also experienced apparently growing far-right activity; and there was too the continuing presence of Holocaust deniers. Although far-right parties generally did not do well in elections, there were enough examples of them showing increasing support – including, later, in the British General Election of 2001 – to cause concern. What was going on, it was suggested, was that as memory of the Holocaust was receding – a new generation which did not know of the horrors was growing up – this was allowing the rise of dangerous reactionary currents which might even threaten to destabilise democracy. The call for remembrance was also a call for education, civic ritual being explicitly framed in these terms. This was needed in order to guard against the risks of forgetting – the risk that the same, perhaps in different form or with different targets, might happen again.

This 'risk' was no mere speculative projection. In addition to the continued existence of racism and anti-Semitism in the countries which signed up to the declaration, was also the war and 'ethnic cleansing' going on in the former Yugoslavia. The reporting of these terrible events, and debates about it, frequently made direct and indirect allusions to the Holocaust against European Jewry. Some of this, such as the rather pointless quibbling over whether the word 'genocide' was fully applicable in this case, seems to have been employed to try to play down the extent of the horror (it was, for example, used to justify not intervening by the US); though horribly reminiscent images of 'concentration camps' (and those words themselves) seemed to finally galvanise military intervention. The fact that, as was often said at the time, this atrocity was occurring in the 'heart of Europe' was, like the Holocaust, regarded as particularly shocking. In stating his support for a Holocaust Memorial Day in 1999, the Prime Minister had stated: 'The ethnic cleansing and killing that has taken place in Europe in recent weeks are a stark example of the need for vigilance' (www.het.org.uk/MemorialDay.html).

Together, these formed part of the broader European context in which Britain began a Holocaust Memorial Day; and we can see signing up to, and putting into action part of, the declaration was also a means in which the New Labour government could participate in a collective European project. But, because of the particular place of war memory in British national identity, the context for Holocaust commemoration in Britain was not quite like that in other European countries, especially not in Germany. As Will Hutton, writing in the *Observer* shortly before Britain's first Holocaust Memorial Day put it: 'the same memorial day plays rather differently in Britain. The extreme British Right has the insuperable problem when it flirts with neo-fascism and Nazism that Britain fought and won the Second World War' (21 January 2001). And because of that 'inner moral superiority' (Wollacott in Cesarani 1997: 27) that Britain's war role was supposed to confer, this meant, feared Hutton, that instead of genuinely confronting racism and anti-Semitism, Holocaust

Memorial Day just played lip-service to these and allowed that sense of British superiority to go unchallenged.

Criticisms of Holocaust Memorial Day

Hutton was particularly critical of what he saw as the shortcomings of the education pack to accompany Holocaust Memorial Day which had been issued by the Department of Education. It concentrated, he claimed, far too much on the crimes of the German Nazis rather than more long-standing and continuing anti-Semitism and racism. This created:

> the scarcely subliminal message [that the Holocaust] was perpetrated by Germans . . . the crazed mix of eugenics, anti-Semitism and barbarism were and are unique to Germans and Germany, rather than something which we all must face. Euro-scepticism receives another boost. And, of course, the Israeli lobby will be quietly happy – remembrance cast like this is a powerful relegitimisation of the case for a Jewish state, notwithstanding its own endemic racism.
>
> (*Observer*, 21 January 2001)

If it really were the case that Holocaust Memorial Day were to provide the opportunity to look at the nation's own past – as is one of the stated aims of the day – then, he argued, there would at least be mention of the pogroms against the Jews in England in the twelfth century, the requirement that the few who remained during the thirteenth century had to wear yellow stars, and the fact that all Jews were expelled at the end of that century (*Observer* 21 January 2001). This long-standing anti-Semitism has been argued by Simon Schama, in his popular *A History of Britain* (Schama 2000), to be a fundamental, though often overlooked, constituent of the historical definition of Britishness. The very choice of the date for commemoration – the liberation of Auschwitz – is argued by Nira Yuval-Davis and Max Silverman to 'reinforce the canonical status of Auschwitz' and, because it does not evoke any obvious 'British' connection, contributes to a conception of the Holocaust which 'completely removes Britain from any direct contact with the event' (Yuval-Davis and Silverman 2002: 115), thus avoiding any critical reflection on Britain and its continuing racism.[8]

Questions were also raised about the Labour government's motives in establishing Holocaust Memorial Day. Howard Jacobson, 'Jewish novelist and TV presenter', was particularly blunt in his assertion that the new event was 'all so Blairite' and basically about New Labour trying to present itself as 'caring':

> Ready-made victims give you an appearance of being caring. That's what this government does – it cares about things. And of course, it doesn't have to spend very much money by caring, or expend a great

deal of thought on what things it cares about, or generally inconveni-
ence itself in any way whatsoever. Especially when there's something
like the Holocaust to remember, which gives the government victims
and the ability to 'care' on a plate.
(www.spiked-online.com/Articles/0000000545C.htm)

Whether a memorial day would foster 'real' remembering was also raised,
Ann Karpf, *Jewish Chronicle* columnist, alerting readers in the *Guardian* (26
January 2001) to the argument by James Young (Young 1993) that
memorials are often as much about forgetting – letting us now move on and
ignore them – as about remembering. She also expressed distaste that atrocities, such as those perpetrated in Cambodia, Rwanda and Bosnia, could all be
brought together and 'boiled down to a set of neat, progressive maxims'.
One problem with the idea that the Holocaust could provide lessons, she
said, echoing Novick (and indeed other commentators such as Lang 1999;
see also Clendinnen 1999), was that such an extreme event perhaps provided
very few lessons for everyday life and led us to overlook more 'ordinary'
instances of discrimination. Instead of sensitising us, it could have the reverse
effect.

There were too those who questioned whether it was right to be looking
back at this past – or indeed any past – today. On a web-site set up by the
BBC (http://news.bbc.co.uk/hi/english/talking point/newsid 177400/
1774160.stm) to allow members of the public to voice their views on whether
there should be a Holocaust memorial day there were several responses to this
effect, such as that from Sue of London: 'Better to get on with life now than sit
around bemoaning what happened to your ancestors . . . Ditch all these commemorative days for the navel-gazing nonsense that they are'; or that of Greg,
UK: 'If someone wants to honour the victims of holocaust, war etc., then they
should do so in there [sic] own private way. National "memorial" days just
drag up the past. Look to the future!'.

These, however, were in the minority and the great majority who chose to
post views were supportive, though there was a good deal of questioning of
whether a day such as this should be *Holocaust* memorial day or a day dedicated
to genocide and other atrocities more generally, some suggesting that the name
should be changed, perhaps to 'Genocide Day'. In fact, such a day already
existed – European Union Genocide Day – also on 27 January, though it has
passed largely unmarked in Britain. In contrast, it is 'Holocaust' – now so
thoroughly part of public discourse and iconography – that has succeeded in
mobilising political and popular action to establish and participate in public
commemoration. Having an almost totally agreed-upon atrocity as the core of
the commemoration also lessens to some extent the difficult business of what
to include, exclude and prioritise; though it does not remove such concerns
entirely, as seen in objections by the Turkish government to the inclusion of
reference to the Armenian genocide in the first national Holocaust Memorial

Day ceremony. By contrast with the Turkish case, and perhaps uniquely, the German government, far from objecting to the world being reminded of atrocity perpetrated in its name, is itself engaged in efforts to ensure that this is remembered.

One of the most public objections to Holocaust Memorial Day was the decision in 2002 by the Muslim Council of Britain not to take part in the main commemoration event in Manchester. As the Secretary General of the Council, Yousef Bhailok, explained:

> In its present form the ceremony excludes and ignores ongoing genocide and human rights abuses around the world and in the occupied territories of Palestine. Genocide is the most abhorrent and outrageous crime against humanity and we are not going to prevent it by selectively remembering only some of its victims. Inhumanity, brutality, hatred and such evils keep on recurring.
> (www.totallyjewish.com/news/stories/?disp
> type+0&dispstory+1QaWuh)

In its reference to the omission of Israeli activity in Palestine as a human rights abuse, and in its call for the day to be renamed and reorganised, the Muslim Council shows its concern that Holocaust Memorial Day is at heart – and as some representatives of the Jewish community, such as the Board of Deputies of British Jews, have also asserted – a Jewish commemoration.

Creating a national occasion

One notable feature of Holocaust Memorial Day, however, has been the considerable participation of non-Jews, including a wide range of religious groups. From the government's point of view, as evident from the various official statements and the nature of Holocaust Memorial Day events themselves, commemorating the Holocaust was as much about articulating a particular vision of Britishness, as about responding to long-standing requests from Jewish organisations for national commemoration. Indeed, the government proposal for a Holocaust Remembrance Day, published in October 1999, only mentions Jews in order to emphasise that the Holocaust should not be regarded as concerning them alone: 'Although it was a tragedy whose primary focus was the Jewish people, many other groups were persecuted and it has implications for us all' (Home Office 1999: 2). These implications concern the nature of society, and different groups within it:

> The Government has a clear vision of a multi-cultural Britain – one which values the contribution made by each of our many ethnic, cultural and faith communities. We are determined to see a truly dynamic society, in which people from different backgrounds can live and work

together, whilst retaining their distinctive identities, in an atmosphere of mutual respect and understanding.

(Home Office 1999: 1)

A Holocaust Remembrance Day (as it was at that time called) was seen as providing the opportunity to articulate this vision by reminding of 'the evils of prejudice and racism' (Home Office 1999: 2) and of 'the period of Nazism and the Second World War [which] remains of fundamental importance to both our national values and our shared aspirations with our European partners' (Home Office 1999: 2).

In order to put this into effect, the Home Office set up a steering group of 16 members: three Home Office staff and a member of the Communication Team working on the event, historian Professor David Cesarani, and representatives from five Jewish organisations as well as from the Commission for Racial Equality, the London borough of Barnet, the Pink Triangle Coalition, the Refugee Council, the Inner Cities Religious Council and the National Youth Agency. While there were more representatives of Jewish than any other grouping on the committee, these were not in an overall majority, reflecting the government's intention, stated even more directly by Gaby Koppel, responsible for producing the inaugural national ceremony: 'we were very clear about one thing. Holocaust Memorial Day wasn't to be an event just for Jews. It was a national occasion, relevant to all British citizens' (Koppel 2001: 7).

In its realisation this national occasion included a high-profile televised ceremony and numerous locally organised events. Considerable guidance was made available for the latter through the government website, educational and other materials. These included suggestions of activities to be organised by local councils or community groups, such as tree-plantings, possible sermon topics, suggested texts and programme outlines for memorial services and educational events. The website archive of the 2001 day lists some of the numerous local forms of commemoration that took place: ranging from Ashford Borough Council where a new bench was put in the Memorial Gardens to Wyre Forest District Council which unveiled a memorial plaque (www.holocaustmemorialday.gov.uk/2002). Local events, such as the moving commemorative service that I attended in 2002 in Sheffield's Peace Gardens, were surely important in making the event seem less state-orchestrated and more part of local communities. Moreover, such events could allow local inflections in the interpretation of the newly inaugurated event – though the extent to which 'vernacular' interpretations would differ from the 'official', as John Bodnar argues is typical of national rituals (Bodnar 1992), is difficult to say. Overall, this was a commemoration with a strong guiding impetus, manifested especially in the televised national ceremony, which the Home Office specifically intended to 'set the tone' for the new event (Home Office 1999: 4). For this reason – and because a nationally orchestrated ritual is inherently a performance of a particular, though not necessarily coherent, rendition of the nation – the inaugural ceremony can be explored as a kind of semantic template of this new Holocaust commemoration.

The inaugural national ceremony

The national significance of the inaugural ritual was signalled by its location – Westminster, in the political centre of the nation's capital – as well as by the presence of 'senior public figures' (Home Office 1999). As part of the government's more devolved approach to politics, the main ceremony would in future years move to other locations: in 2002 to Manchester and in 2003 to Edinburgh. The London event was held in the Methodist Central Hall, a nominally religious – though not Jewish – space.

Unlike commemorations such as Remembrance Day, the national ceremony was not a single ritual but a show – a sequential set of pieces, some performed live on stage and others relayed on screen – culminating in a ritualised participation from the audience. This format, while more explicitly pedagogical than many memorials, nevertheless retained ritual's capacity to bring together individuals and groups with different interests within a common frame and to an ostensible common purpose (Turner 1967). It was also highly amenable for televising live, being divided into fairly short and varied pieces, each ready-framed on stage. My own impression was of a curious cross between a state funeral – beginning with David Dimbleby's commentary on who was arriving – and a royal variety performance.

The 'show' itself entailed a careful choreographing of pieces commemorating the Holocaust perpetrated by Nazi Germany, primarily, though not exclusively, against Jews (other victims were also mentioned, homosexuals being the focus of a piece called 'The Forgotten Holocaust') and more recent atrocities. As such, it performed a movement between the Holocaust and other atrocities but, because of the form, without ever needing to address the awkward question of comparison and relative evil. As evident from the brief description below, although the atrocities commemorated were all perpetrated outside Britain, the ceremony nevertheless provided an implicit commentary on, and performed certain conceptions of, British national identity. It is useful, I suggest, to see the ceremony as divided into four stages, moving from past, into present and towards a preferred future.

Anchoring: the Holocaust in Europe

The first part of the ceremony anchored the event in the Holocaust through a set of pieces which incorporated iconic Holocaust referents – chimneys (in the opening poem, 'O the Chimneys'), 'the Final Solution' (a short film), Anne Frank (a choral work), Auschwitz (survivor accounts from), and Bergen Belsen (contemporary film footage). This constructed an already familiar Gegenbild, a vision of a horrific society against which to define our own. That this is not just of Jewish concern was signalled right at the beginning of the ceremony by having actress Emma Thompson reading German Jewish Nelly Sach's poem; and that this past is not so distant was emphasised by the presence of survivors, living today in Britain. The revisiting of 'national values' of 'the period of Nazism and the Second World War', as the Home Office envisaged above, was fairly subtly, but nevertheless surely, achieved: through the fact that the Auschwitz survivors found haven in Britain, through the film about Belsen being liberated by British troops, and in a piece about the Czech Kindertransport, which depicted endangered children being brought to Britain by Nicholas Winton. In all of these, Britain is depicted *contra* Nazi Germany as a nation opposed to racist terror and open to the persecuted.

Extension: continuing atrocities

That atrocities have continued since the Holocaust, and that, by extension, we need to keep 'heeding the lessons' from it, was made clear in the next set of pieces, collectively billed under the ironic title 'Post 1945 – "Never Again"'. Cambodia, Rwanda and Bosnia were the examples presented. The emphasis in all of these was not on political analysis but on the terrible suffering endured and of individuals struggling to cope with the aftermath and memory – accounts by survivors (as they are billed in the programme) featuring here too. There were no references to Britain here, except in the fact that the final survivor to speak, Kemal Pervanic from Bosnia, was currently residing in Britain; thus again depicting Britain as a haven and continuing the contrast of Britain with other, terrible, regimes.

Making explicit: spelling out the messages

In case the point of the two previous stages had not been absolutely clear to any viewers, the next employed direct speeches to make it so. Chief Rabbi Jonathan Sacks gave a speech entitled 'Why the Holocaust is important for everyone in Britain today', in which he argued that globalisation is bringing 'a new and aggressive tribalism', and that Holocaust commemoration provides 'a universal story' which reminds us 'and our children what happens when we forget that the people unlike us are still people, like us' (www.churchnet.org.uk/newsfiles5/holocaust-day.html). The fact that the speech was made by the chief rabbi also helped to effect a return to the Holocaust focus of the event (as too did a Jewish Memorial Prayer 'for the Six Million who perished in the Holocaust (Shoah)'), while simultaneously emphasising its continuing and universal relevance.

The Prime Minister, Tony Blair, continued this making explicit, and in doing so invoked the notion of sacrifice: 'Let not one life sacrificed in the Holocaust be in vain' (www.pm.gov.uk/news.asp?NewsId=1754). As Michael

Rowlands has suggested in his examination of the workings of war memorials, the idea of sacrifice is generally crucial to these and allows what might otherwise be experienced as 'negativity and impotence' (Rowlands 1999: 142) to be resolved, and suffering to be seen as a move towards a higher end. This is a notion steeped in Christian metaphor, though also partly shared by Judaism (Thomas 1999: 201). However, the trope of sacrifice is seen generally as utterly inappropriate to the case of the Holocaust, in relation to which, as Rowlands points out, 'nobody can claim that the deaths served any purpose whatsoever' (Rowlands 1999: 142). Nevertheless, the misguided employment of this trope reflects both a wider cultural drive towards 'making good' from experiences of suffering, and the Government's more specific use of the Holocaust as 'a powerful way of writing its lessons onto our national conscience' (Blair 2001: 5).

This third stage ended with a screening of the 'Statements of Commitment' – the explicit commitments to avoiding racism and so forth, derived from the Stockholm forum. These were introduced by Sir Trevor McDonald. Sometimes referred to as 'a national institution', the presence of this well-known black newsreader was also part of the symbolic enactment of the culminating stage of the ceremony.

Symbolic enactment: ritual performance of the multicultural nation

The final stage, which involved a ritual lighting of candles, might be seen as the 'real' ceremony, and certainly as the crescendo to which all of the earlier parts of the event led. It was initiated by another national figurehead, this time 'HRH The Prince of Wales . . . on behalf of the Nation', as the programme stated. However, the prince played a fairly inconspicuous role, uttering no words and merely lighting a candle, to be quickly followed by a stream of other people also lighting candles. It is notable that it was the prince, rather than the queen, who participated. When the programme was first announced, the fact that the queen would not be attending occasioned some headlines, Buckingham Palace providing no explanation. Yet, the absence of the monarch is, I suggest, in many ways necessary in order for this not to be symbolically a national event in the same way as other national days, particularly Remembrance Day in which the queen plays a central role.

Instead of having a single focus, at Holocaust Memorial Day the nation is presented as made up of numerous different communities. This contrasts with, say, Israel's Remembrance Day ceremony, in which, as Don Handelman points out in his insightful analysis (Handelman 1998), national unity is symbolised by the fact that only the president plays an active role and political leaders do not, and also in the single flame that is lit. In the Holocaust Memorial Day ceremony numerous candles are lit by representatives of different groups, thus representing the idea of Britain as a nation of many faiths and cultures. This is not a symbolism of disorganised communities of self-interest, however, for all participate in the ritual, making the same journey to each perform the same act. Collectively the candles blaze impressively. Enacted here is a form of unity, based not on allegiance to a monarch or the idea of a nation that should be fought for, but against a generalised enemy of racial purity-seeking evil.

Conclusion

If nations can no longer so easily define themselves against contemporary others, as I have suggested here, self-definition in relation to the past remains a possibility. This has two possible elements: (1) *contra* others (or potentially, as in contemporary Germany, *contra* a past self), and (2) through drawing self-continuities over time. Holocaust commemoration in Britain entails both of these. It evokes a direct contrast between Britain and Nazi Germany, and, by extension, those other countries that have continued to perpetrate atrocities. It also reminds national subjects of a time which is popularly seen as one when Britain was strong, people 'pulled together', shared common values, and exhibited 'moral backbone'. Thus, while on the one hand entailing a contrast with an 'extreme' form of nationalism, Holocaust Memorial Day simultaneously allows for a revisiting of some positive imagery of British heroism and of Britain as a moral stronghold and world leader in the fight against evil.

In the Holocaust Memorial Day ritual, Britain during the World War II period is cast as open to outsiders and opposed to intolerance and racism. Were this to be stated outright, its veracity might be questioned but the more oblique form of 'saying' this through the techniques of the ceremony allows it to emerge unchallenged. A historically- rooted narrative of 'British national identity' as open and tolerant is related and performed, thus challenging right-wing efforts to define 'Britishness' as exclusive. Because the Holocaust is such an iconic example of the horrific outcome of ideologies of racial purity, it provides a clear counterimage against which to define a different kind of identity – an identity open to, and accommodating of, difference. This is not a 'post-national' identity, however, but a reconfigured – multicultural – way of being national. The World War II period was one by which, for the most part, nation-states in Western Europe had come to feel relatively inevitable and Nazi Germany's lack of respect for the national sovereignty of others was one of its crimes. Revisiting this period affirms, rather than questions, the legitimacy of nationhood.

In the post-war years, it has been argued (see above), public recognition of the Holocaust would have threatened senses of national identity by relativising the collective mourning of 'British' suffering (soldiers and victims of the Blitz) in the face of a massively greater loss, and by undermining the redemptive focus on sacrifice for the sake of victory. Since the 1970s, not only has an international traffic in Holocaust (through film, images, facts and figures) made it impossible to ignore, the war itself has receded in time, and those who fought through it have become fewer and perhaps less likely to feel affronted at a commemoration which might be perceived as 'competing' with theirs. Moreover, the idea that World War II might have signalled the end of tyrannical regimes has become less sustainable and, informed too by a questioning of militaristic imagery that is itself bound up with the growing critique of the nation-state, there has been a shift towards emphasising victims rather than victory.

This shift is also seen in a change in forms of commemoration themselves, which have become the subject of considerable debate and some interesting experimentation over the past 25 years or so. Some memorials, such as Maya Lin's Vietnam memorial in Washington, challenge the ritual resolution that has been generally characteristic of war memorials (Rowlands 1999). Instead, through their form, they question the notion of sacrifice and 'higher gain'. The Holocaust Memorial Day ceremony, it seems to me, does seek partial resolution in Rowlands' sense in that it attempts to draw some gain from suffering and loss, and in its 'deification' of the dead 'in the sense that they become embodied in the idea of the collective' (Rowlands 1999: 144). At the same time, however, in its focus on victims and its extension to the present, it serves to act as a constant reminder of the horrors of atrocity rather than of their overcoming.

Holocaust memorialising in the US has been discussed in terms of 'the Americanization of the Holocaust' (Flanzbaum 1999), to highlight the way in which Holocaust representation has been put to work to express American values and ideologies, in ways which have inevitably entailed, sometimes rather crass, historical selectivity and sometimes distortion. Holocaust Memorial Day in Britain could be seen as part of a 'Britishisation': an account of the Holocaust that helps define a particular vision of Britishness, and that is embedded in a narrative of British national identity. As Flanzbaum writes in relation to 'Americanization', we should not see such processes as necessarily negative (Flanzbaum 1999: 8). Sometimes, they may well entail a crude papering over of uncomfortable details – such as Britain's less than wholly open policy towards Jewish immigration during the war – but at the same time, they can contribute to more discussion, debate and keeping in mind of the Holocaust and, as in the British case, to an assertion of positive values.

Although I have suggested that this new form and level of Holocaust commemoration in Britain helps articulate a particular vision of British national identity, this does not exhaust its meanings. The shift from a focus on 'the war' to an emphasis on 'the Holocaust' also allows for a less nation- and more European-based form of commemoration. The fact that Holocaust Memorial Day has been achieved as part of a European initiative, to coincide with commemoration in other European countries, is expressive of European cooperation. And although, as Armin Heinen observes, 'the Holocaust . . . belong[s] to the negative legacy of Europe that discredits every attempt to foster European myths in the form of national myths' (Heinen 2000: 109), it does provide a shared, collective counterimage from the past against which a more positive European identity for the future can be defined. In just the same way that Holocaust Memorial Day has allowed for the articulation of a reconfigured national identity, the commemorative form likewise can allow – simultaneously – the articulation of a reconfigured European, and even wider, identity.

Acknowledgements

Thanks are due to Rob Phillips for inviting me to contribute to the *British Island Stories* conference, for which I initially wrote on this subject, and for his many helpful suggestions; to David Brown at Beth Shalom for providing me with invaluable materials; to Andrew Hoskins, Hilary Smith, Jo Britton and to audiences at a Durham University *Tradition and Change* workshop and a Lancaster University Sociology seminar, and especially their respective organisers, David Chaney and John Urry, for numerous provocative suggestions; and to Jo and Roshi for their extremely constructive editing. I apologise for not having been able to include all of the useful points and for remaining infelicities.

Notes

1 Accounts of the Jewish museum include Lackmann 2000 and Young 2000 ch. 6; and of the planned Holocaust memorial: Jeismann 1999, Niven 2002 ch. 9 and Young 2000 ch. 7. For more general accounts of the German case see Beck-Gernsheim 1999, Fulbrook 1999, Michman 2002, Niven 2002 and Reichel 2001. I am currently writing an account of German treatments of the Nazi past focused on the former Nazi party rally grounds in Nuremberg. A preliminary account is Macdonald 2003.
2 For example, the televising of Victor Klemperer's diaries, German-made series such as those by Guido Knopp, and the showing of British-made series, such as the BBC's *World at War*, though not the US-made *Nuremberg Trials*, which was not shown in Germany as it was regarded as trivialising the subject.
3 The IWM North is not a Holocaust museum, though it was often talked of as such before it opened. It also employs some of the same Jewish and Holocaust iconography in its architecture as does the Berlin museum. On the IWM Holocaust exhibition, see Hoskins 2003.
4 The term 'victims' seems to have begun to be superseded by 'survivors' in the 1980s. While this could be seen as a positive move to try to accord more agency to those involved, instead of linguistically denying them this agency, some 'victims/survivors' have expressed discomfort with their 'reclassification' partly because it seems to accord agency where they felt they had none. See Greenspan 1999 and Novick 2000 for discussion.
5 The rise of 'public history' as a focus of academic interest in the US and more recently in Britain is itself indicative of this. See Jordanova 2000.
6 Henry Greenspan describes how in the immediate post-war years survivors – or 'victims' as they were then generally called – generally seemed to have a great urge to recount their experiences, contrary to the myth that later grew up that they were initially too traumatised to talk. The shift in the 1970s and 1980s towards survivor

testimonies 'finding voice' was less a change in their own sensibility than that of wider society, and it was itself bound up with the shift from talking of 'victims' to 'survivors' (Greenspan 1999).

7 All web references are as at April 2003.

8 Perhaps in response to such criticisms, Holocaust Memorial Day 2002 was given the theme 'Britain, the Holocaust and its Legacy'.

4

MUSEUMS, COMMUNITIES AND THE POLITICS OF HERITAGE IN NORTHERN IRELAND

Elizabeth Crooke

Introduction

The public representation of the past in Northern Ireland has never been the single domain of the 'official' museum and heritage sector. The traditions of marching, murals and street painting has ensured that a sense of history is omnipresent in particular urban and, sometimes, rural spaces. A form of political stability has begun to emerge since the 1998 Belfast Agreement and now military fortifications, ephemera of legal and illegal organisations, as well as oral histories of the Troubles are emerging as 'political heritage' in the landscape of reconciliation. Alongside this, Northern Ireland has three national museums, which together form part of the National Museums and Galleries of Northern Ireland, a number of county museums, and several museums specialising in aspects of local heritage, such as the linen industry or the Battle of the Somme. In addition to this, new museums are currently in planning. As we review heritage provision in Northern Ireland, it can be considered in two ways. The most predominant includes the official representations offered by local and national museums; that preserved by the sites and monuments record; and that provided by other heritage organisations such as the National Trust. An alternative form of heritage in Northern Ireland, which is beginning to come to the fore, is the unofficial, unsafe, contested history of the conflict, which is seeking recognition.

This chapter is a consideration of the presentation of heritage in Northern Ireland, with particular reference to the work of museums and the creation of community exhibitions. Its main interest is two-fold: how museums in Northern Ireland are attempting to engage more successfully with a broader audience by embracing new histories; and how communities are undertaking 'museum-like' activities to communicate their own histories. In order to investigate these themes, this chapter will first consider the redevelopment of the museum idea as a community space. This has encouraged museums to be more aware of the diversity of their local communities. This is followed by a discussion of the development of a community focus in Northern Ireland's museums and how this has been linked to the ideas of inclusion and fostering good community relations. The community sector is considered in the following section, through a discussion of two oral history projects and local exhibition initiatives. This chapter will conclude with a discussion of how this activity relates to the themes central to this book: heritage, identity and nationality.

Museums as a community space

Museums are a contested terrain where the public representation of place, the past and identity is always the subject of debate and sometimes dispute. Once the place of privilege, where state leaders would display the booty of war, travel and exploitation, by the nineteenth century museums were also being established to forge national identities and open to a wider public. In the national museums of Europe, museums were often places where the idea of an ancient and superior national community was presented unchallenged (Bennett 1995). In Ireland, the museum founded in Dublin in 1877 was established as a branch of the Museum of Science and Art in South Kensington and reflected its London counterpart. Although the Irish character of the Dublin institution was still strongly felt, the museum was reinvented in the early twentieth century to reflect more closely the desires of an independent Ireland (Crooke 2000). The history of the National Museum of Ireland in Dublin reveals that museums continually reinvent themselves to reflect the context of changing times. The space of the museum is continually revisited and represented to meet new needs and desires. Increasingly, too, the idea of the museum is being rethought consciously to introduce new hierarchies of power, responsibility and accountability. Today, the move to democratise museums is associated with the issues of community representation and inclusion. One of the most powerful examples of this is the 'People's Movement' in Australia, which aims to recognise past injustices and foster reconciliation among indigenous groups and descendents of European settlers in order to lessen racism and marginalisation suffered by indigenous peoples. The impact of this on the Australian museum sector is illustrated by the ways in which established museums are finding new methods of engaging with indigenous groups. In addition, indigenous groups have established new community museums, expressed as 'Keeping Places' and 'Cultural Centres'. In both cases, the new forms of engagement with museums have developed understanding between indigenous and European communities and raised esteem among indigenous groups (Kelly and Gordon 2002).

The example of Australia is a good demonstration of the two-fold method by which 'the museum' is moving from being a state space, where the winners told their story, to the community space, in which history is told from alternative positions. On the one hand, established museums are beginning to reach out to groups previously excluded from museums, both because of an internal desire to do so and because of pressure from external bodies. On the other, the groups themselves are representing their own histories and identities in self-appointed community spaces. Many of the perspectives presented in *Including Museums* discuss the slow introduction of such changes in UK museums (Dodd and Sandell 2001). The South East Asian Arts Officer at the Victoria and Albert Museum (V&A), for instance, illustrates how the V&A is attempting to represent a multi-ethnic Britain better through improved collecting and appropriate interpretation of existing collections (Shaikh 2001). Within South Africa the political changes brought in with the end of apartheid have been expressed in the rise of community-based museums. In the District Six Museum in Cape Town, for instance, former residents who were forced out of the District during land clearances are using the museum as part of the political campaign to bolster support for reclaiming that land. In this example the idea of being a museum is paramount as public display of personal stories develops self-esteem and community confidence (Rassool and Prosalendis 2001).

Museums are now establishing themselves as community spaces, as places where the personal and the local are of equal importance as the state or national story. Lost or hidden histories are now coming to the fore – histories of slavery associated with a painting in the National Gallery in London (Hooper-Greenhill 2000: 147) or with silver candlesticks in Nottingham Museum and Art Gallery (Wallace 2001: 84) have now been brought out in the open. Women's history, as well as the experiences of ethnic groups, disabled and children are gaining prominence in museum spaces. In a bid to increase their relevance, museums are improving links with local groups – be it through the health, social and educational sectors, or by working with leaders of neighbourhood groups. There are diverse stories to be told, more ways of telling those stories, and a wider range of people prepared to share their experiences in public spaces. Memory work in history museums, through oral history and reminiscence, has revealed the value of telling and sharing stories (Kavanagh 2000). Reminiscence work, responsibly handled, has been shown to have numerous positive benefits. It becomes a means to preserve and transmit cultural and community history; promote effective communication between groups of people; enhance self-esteem; aid the preservation of unique individual identity; enable life-review; promote self-development; and is an activity that many find enjoyable (Gibson 2000: 26). It is the recognition of these new stories and the mutual benefits of learning about them that is encouraging museums to diversify.

The concern for museums attempting to become relevant to more diverse audiences is to understand the communities outside the museum. Together we need to realise there is no single national group; rather, collectively we form a myriad of sometimes shifting communities. Communities can be identified by activity, gender, interest, ability and economics; we move between these communities and sometimes feel uncomfortable in the categories we are placed. Nevertheless, we need communities in order to build our experiences and forge our identities. Together these experiences produce 'communities of practice' in which knowledge and relationships are socially constructed (Falk and Dierking 2000: 46).

In Northern Ireland the identification of communities of practice is intertwined with the political environment. The politics of the region has not only ruined lives, it has also formed our understanding of identity, history and culture – both our own and that of others. When the Community Relations Council was founded in 1990, its aim was to promote better relations between the two communities in Northern Ireland; in other words, among Republican and Loyalist groups; or, Nationalists and Unionists; or, Protestants and Catholics. The 'two traditions' model never really worked in Northern Ireland; the conflict may often be reduced to this binary but the reality is more complex. In order to investigate the creation of identities, the Community Relations Council embraced cultural traditions work that encouraged the affirmation of personal histories, reflection on beliefs, the sharing of information between groups and the legitimisation and sharing of different cultural traditions (Fitzduff 1993). The practice of inclusion policies in Northern Ireland's museums reflects this political context. While the region's museums attempt to embrace the ideology of inclusion, as they aim to incorporate diverse histories and new audiences, they are continually brought back to the question of how to represent the Troubles in museum spaces (Crooke 2001). Questions being asked include: how do you tell the history of the conflict in museums; what is the material heritage of the Troubles that could be displayed in exhibitions; should we preserve the built remains of the Troubles; whose story should we tell, and what if that story causes offence? Of course, there are 'communities of practice' that need not reflect on the Troubles but, for now, one of the most significant issues facing the heritage sector in Northern Ireland is the method and purpose of the public representation of the history of the past 30 years.

The official community heritage sector

There are numerous reasons why Northern Ireland's museums are being nudged into asking both how and why they should represent the Troubles. In the first place, national and international debate on museum definition and purpose is encouraging the sector at large to make exhibitions and collections more representative of different people's histories, rather than one grand narrative. Second, and as a consequence of the previous point, museums are exploring local stories, identities, and the means to express these in collections representative of the way most people live. In Northern Ireland, this interest links to the activity of community groups that increasingly are engaged with the public expression of their histories. The region's museums are recognising that they must involve themselves with local groups and their histories in order to maintain relevance and not to lose core, or potential, audiences to these alternative initiatives. A third reason for the museum sector taking part in the representation of the Troubles might also be the potential positive impact of working together on interpreting the conflict. Community-relations work in Northern Ireland has long used history and heritage as the basis for exploring identities and division. Finally, underpinning all of these considerations is the more subtle point that representing the Troubles in museums and as part of our 'heritage' is a confident move for Northern Ireland. Through display, this process can present a changed place and suggests for us and to our visitors that the Troubles have ended.

In Northern Ireland, museums are linking with new communities principally through outreach and the development of new more challenging exhibitions. The county museum services have small numbers of staff and often a low budget. Frequently, the key concerns of dealing with documentation backlog, collections care, funding applications and staff training can dominate everyday work, and for some it is difficult to see where the museum fits into the wider community agenda. There is still innovative work in the local museums – an exhibition entitled *Local Identities* that toured in 2000 is an example. This exhibition explored the construction of identity in Northern Ireland and the diversity of faith, leisure and politics (Pollock 2000). Such work is often achieved in collaboration with other local museums or through the support of the Community Relations Council or the Northern Ireland Museums Council. The contact between museum work and community relations varies from place to place. In some museums it is minimal or low-key while in others it is very apparent. Community-relations work at a local level is supported by the district councils, of which there are 26 in Northern Ireland. Although each council has a community relations officer, Down District Council is unusual in placing its officer within the Department of Museum Services. In the Down County Museum Plan the rationale for this was expressed thus:

> The community-relations section of the department is an expression of Down District Council's commitment to improving and supporting good community relations in its area. Its work is concerned with bringing about equality, promoting reconciliation and mutual respect for the various traditions which exist within Northern Ireland, and creating a community which accommodates people's differing beliefs, aspirations and traditions. This brings it very close to the cultural concerns of the museum and arts functions.
>
> (Down District Council 1997)

The 'Community Education Officer' in Down County Museum has developed a programme focused on developing a sense of community identity, civic pride, the appreciation of the diversity of cultural traditions and museum staff believe they have created a shared and safe museum space (McKenna 2003 personal communication). The museum has attempted to broaden its audience through a diverse range of activities: events in association with the bicentenary of the 1803 Rebellion, for instance, include lectures, living history, mock trails and a play hosted by the drama department of a local school (Down County Museum 2003).

In the Ulster Museum, part of the National Museums and Galleries of Northern Ireland group, the European Union's Special Support Programme for Peace and Reconciliation has funded an outreach officer working in the history department. The post is closely associated with the Community Relations Council – the council administers its funding and monitors activity through regular reports. The outreach activity has taken the form of working on new exhibitions linked to exploring identity in Northern Ireland (some of these are referred to below), identity workshops based around a CD-Rom on the Troubles, and community history projects based in areas that have had high rates of violence or polarisation as a result of the Troubles. Through this post, the museum has made a number of new links with cross-community and single interest groups in Northern Ireland (Leonard 2001 personal communication).

The Ulster Museum has often been criticised for giving scant consideration to the events of the past three decades in its permanent history displays (O'Toole 2000). A more holistic view of the museum gives a better picture – often the events of the recent past can be linked to temporary exhibitions and less high-profile outreach work. In 1998 the exhibition *Up in Arms! The 1798 Rebellion in Ireland* got considerable press attention for providing the opportunity for a cross-community contact. In search for a venue in which both sides would feel at ease, a cross-community group from a village outside Belfast visited the 1798 exhibition in the Ulster Museum. Led by a member of the Orange Order and a Catholic priest the visit was considered as something they could do together that would not compromise each other's principles (Sheridan 1998). The exhibition was well attended by community groups: of the 22,500 visits the museum recorded approximately 1,500 from members of community groups; in addition, 7,000 members participated in linked activities and resources developed specifically for such groups (Parkhill 2003).

Opportunities for further cross-community impact were provided in 2000 with the *Icons of Identity* exhibition, also at the Ulster Museum. In Northern Ireland, symbols are widely used to bind communities, represent allegiances and mark territory. In this exhibition nine symbols of life in Northern Ireland were selected: the mythical warrior Cu Chulainn; the Virgin Mary; Christ crucified; Saint Patrick; Erin, the female embodiment of Ireland; King William III; Sir Edward Carson (1854–1935), leader of the Ulster Unionists and one of the creators of Northern Ireland; the Somme and the contribution to of the 36th (Ulster) Division to this battle on 1 July 1916; and the republican revolutionary leader Michael Collins (1890–1922). Some symbols are predominantly Protestant (King William, Carson and the Somme); others are used mainly by the Catholic community (such as Collins and Erin); and, the remaining icons are used by both, but often in very different ways. Interpretation of the icons acknowledged associated myths, contradictory interpretations and the various ways the icons were understood in different communities, and how some have been used to fuel sectarianism. The introductory essay in the exhibition catalogue provides a record of some of the questions the exhibition team faced and the approach they took to their subject. To begin, they quoted from Carlo Gebler to convey the purpose of interpreting a troubled history: 'you cannot change the past, but with understanding you can sometimes draw the poison out of it' (Gebler cited in Warner 2000). The purpose of a museum in such a context was defined as: 'to preserve and present for discussion and information the cultural heritage of its community . . . [It should include] objects that illustrate the history, warts and all, of *all* the members of that community'. Finally, the essay concludes on the most significant question for Northern Ireland: 'why do we want to learn about the past, when it seems to be responsible for the Troubles of today?' The answer provided is: 'a community without a sense of past is a community in denial' (Warner 2000: 2). People in Northern Ireland have a very keen sense of the past; it is how the past is used to inform the present that is the issue.

Although the introductory booklet gives a sense of the aims of the exhibition team it is almost impossible to tell if such an impact was achieved. One of the methods employed to collect visitor reactions was the provision of blank postcards and the invitation to provide feedback. The exhibition ran for 6 months and got feedback from about 1,400 visitors, approximately half of which were from children. The exhibition seems to have received a generally positive response – it brought many requests for peace to be brought to the region and a fairly equal number saying that it was either too nationalistic or unionist. For some it emphasised a void in their own understanding, one visitor wrote: 'Excellent exhibition. Very evocative for me of good feeling for my own identity and growing appreciation of other folk'. Another visitor wrote: 'as a 37 year old brought up in the north of Ireland, I never once seen a photo of Michael Collins – so I think this exhibition is long overdue'. A number of visitors commented on evidence of bias; one visitor wrote: 'I thought it was a very good exhibition, but slightly biased. I found the amount of information noted to the Orange Order and Carson quite intimidating'; however, on the other hand, another wrote: 'as a prod, I notice a few attempts to debunk Protestant myths, the commentators should resist the urge to write judgments'. One visitor questioned the very approach of the exhibition: 'Surely Northern Ireland gets enough exposure by media etc what about real art we're very disappointed that the more orthodox viewing has been closed due to Icons which should remain in the past' (Ulster Museum, Icons visitor cards).

The outreach work undertaken in the history department at the Ulster Museum has a deliberate community-relations agenda; much of it has been achieved through funding administered by the Community Relations Council.

The actual impact of museum outreach on community-relations is almost impossible to quantify; as noted by one commentator 'if reports, conferences, exhibitions, think-tanks and books were enough, the Northern Ireland question would have been solved long ago' (Longley 2001: 41). However, some indication of the success of the outreach work must be taken from the fact that the Ulster Museum has continued to secure support for outreach from the EU Special Support Programme for Peace and Reconciliation. When considered together, the museum exhibitions and outreach described above do have resonance. Histories that were previously taboo and symbols that were misunderstood are now beginning to be discussed in public and secure spaces. However, the true impact of these museum initiatives can only be measured through forms of evaluation. The creation of an appropriate methodology for measuring the real impact of museum initiatives on behaviour and attitudes is a growing area of concern in museum studies (Hooper-Greenhill 2002). The Northern Ireland example helps to complicate such investigations: are museums being visited by those most closely involved in sustaining division; if they do visit, what do they gain from their experience; and, can a museum visit have a long-term impact on deeply held views? Research has shown that it is often the visitor who has the most influence over what is learnt from an exhibition, rather than the curator or designer. Instead visitors bring their own personal experiences, histories and beliefs to the exhibition and it is through these that he or she will interpret the exhibitions.

The unofficial community-heritage sector

Away from museum debate and government policy, rural and urban groups are coming together to explore their history and heritage and forming their own exhibitions and collections. These community groups are not interested in the concerns of the museum profession, yet they are engaging with the past in ways to which museums aspire. As regards representing the recent past in Northern Ireland, a gap seems to be growing between the official museum sector, which is trying to find its direction, and the unofficial heritage sector, which is more confident about how to engage with notions of political heritage. In Northern Ireland numerous groups of people are engaging in local history work, in the way that museums are being encouraged to in various recent 'inclusion' publications published in Britain. Over the past decade, with the increasing availability of peace, community-relations, and sometimes National Lottery funding, there has been an increase in people coming together in groups to engage in heritage-based activity.

One of the trends likely to have the greatest impact on creating an archive of the Troubles is the growing interest in collecting oral histories of the conflict. In both Belfast and Londonderry, local groups have gained government and European funding to support such initiatives. In Derry a proposal has been put forward to establish 'The Bogside History Centre', located in an intensely republican part of the city. Acknowledgement seems to be key – the centre seeks 'recognition' of the history of the area of the city known as 'the Bogside'. The stated aim of the group is to contribute to 'the process of community regeneration through increased community confidence and esteem'; and, to aid 'the process of reconciliation and healing between our divided communities, by increasing knowledge of our troubled past'. They acknowledge their use of cultural identity as a tool with which to 'tackle social and economic marginalisation'. The proposed centre will have an exhibition area, research room, collect experiences of the Bogside community and provide tours for school groups and tourists. The main subjects to be investigated are civil rights and the events of Bloody Sunday, 30 January 1972 (Bloody Sunday Trust: 2003). The Derry initiative seems to follow the format of that developed by the Falls Community Council in Belfast, which is well underway. The Falls Community Council was established in the 1970s to represent people in the mostly nationalist Falls Road area. In the mid-1990s the group developed the idea of a community oral history archive and a living history centre. The project, known as Duchas, which means 'heritage' in Irish, was made possible through the availability of funds associated with the peace process. At the moment the Duchas project takes the form of a drop-in centre where people can access the archives of interviews, and where they can go to gather advice and support for groups interested in gathering oral histories. Again, the long-term objective is the creation of what has been described as a 'living history centre' with open access to a listening archive and, possibly, exhibition panels and objects to support the oral history (Hackett 2002 personal communication).

These two examples of urban oral history projects are closely associated with experiences linked with the Troubles, and the characteristics of the projects have important implications for our understanding of the role of public history-making in societies emerging from conflict. The themes chosen by the Duchas project to shape the oral archive are intensely political. Oral testimonies of internment and hunger strikes have been collected – selected because they are of greatest relevance to the local community (Hackett personal communication 2002). Internment, in this case, refers to the Special Powers Act of 1922, an emergency law in Northern Ireland, which was, in 1971, used to legalise detention without trial. Between 1971 and 1975, over 2,000 republicans and about 100 loyalists were detained until the power was withdrawn in 1975 (Arthur 1980: 107–14). The hunger strikes were a protest tactic used by IRA prisoners for 6 months in 1981, leading eventually to the death of ten of the strikers. Both of these themes, internment and the hunger strikes, are intensely emotive. These are histories that do not want to be forgotten; in the case of both the Duchas and Bogside initiatives the most contested aspects of the history of Northern Ireland in the past 30 years have been selected for representation. These histories are ideal for creating a sense of community because they are histories that still have a lot at stake. The events shaped lives, are highly emotive and already in the public domain. When captured in a living history centre the stories will take on a new dimension; this new representation defines them as central to understanding the place in which they are exhibited. The local accounts, once handed down through story-telling, can now be made tangible in exhibition displays. Recognition of these local experiences, and how they are part of the national or state history is central for community empowerment. The authority brought by self-representation binds the community. An essential characteristic of this work also seems to be that it is independent of the 'official' heritage sector. Duchas is not interested, for instance, in liaising with the local or national museums in the creation and preservation of its oral archive; it does not want a state institution to be put in charge of its story (Hackett 2002 personal communication).

Both the Duchas and the Bogside initiatives claim a community-relations agenda, and the nature of this invites consideration. In Northern Ireland community-relations work has taken various forms. In some cases it has been learning about the 'other' tradition, in the hope that myths can be expelled and common experiences valued. Other forms are based around learning about one's own history, on the premise that only when we are secure in our own identity can we be expected to understand difference. Certainly, the oral history projects described above are centred on the experiences and interpretations of one community. However, irresponsibly managed, the risk with such an approach is that the work will fall into the old stereotypes and prejudices and only serve to isolate and divide the communities further. Such local stories have the potential for both a positive and negative impact. In a divided society, this experience can be used to bind one community against the other. It is important to allow people to be in control of their own history and therefore 'outside' interference in the collection of those stories would be anathema. However, when those individual stories become a collective heritage and when they move from the realm of the personal to the public, their purpose changes. There is a difference between stories shared privately between groups of people and the public display of those stories in history, community or heritage centres. The public dimension adds a new significance, is a form of recognition, and provides endorsement. We must, therefore, consider the impact of displaying oral testimonies that are largely partial in public spaces.

The Derry and Belfast initiatives are just two examples of projects that hope to become a permanent contribution to the Northern Ireland heritage landscape. In addition to these there are numerous other heritage initiatives that complete their life cycle more quickly. If it is possible to keep up to date with the numerous community exhibitions reported in local papers and developed in local community centres or parish halls, one would get a sense of the high level of local heritage activity and awareness. Many of these initiatives have modest, but nevertheless highly significant, aims. One example is the exhibitionary enthusiasm generated by the recent Royal Jubilee. Numerous local history societies and groups used the jubilee as an opportunity to create exhibitions on their local area – the *Diary of Events for the Jubilee Year* provides a list of these (Golden Jubilee Unit 2002). One such exhibition held in a village church hall in County Fermanagh was an opportunity for the local community to develop an exhibition on life in the area. During the jubilee weekend, visitors in a packed hall were treated to 50 years of local news, awards and achievements. The contribution to local cohesiveness and community memory-making was undoubted. This rural example can be compared with the work of the People's History Initiative, a course hosted by the Ulster People's College in Belfast. The college was formed in 1982 with the aim to 'support people tackling social and economic problems as well as overcoming cultural, educational and political divisions' (Ulster People's College 2002). The People's History Initiative, funded by the Community Relations Council, takes the form of an adult education class with the main aim to explore how 'local people have shaped the story of our common past'. Participants are both student and teacher: they learn about the history of Belfast and share their own expertise of their area of the city. By researching and eventually creating an exhibition or CD-Rom of an aspect of their history, the process aims to allow participants to take control of the interpretation and presentation of their own community. Belfast community groups have produced exhibitions that have covered subjects such as shopping; life, work and entertainment; boxing; history of women; housing, dock life; the Troubles; and, the Second World War.

   In the examples of community exhibitions discussed above both the processes and the product are important. In the example from County Fermanagh and those of Belfast, the exhibitions were part of a process of celebration and remembrance. Not only were the exhibitions ends in themselves, they were also a means to an end. The exhibitions were the by-product of processes based on needs of the local community. In the People's History Initiative, for example, the process was a regular meeting of groups, within which they discussed the history of their community and area. Meeting, discussing, sharing experiences, and developing a historical record aided the development of friendships, community pride and good self-esteem. The final product is also significant – public display and acceptance brings with it a sense of value and importance. In both the smaller initiatives and those developed for a national and international audience, such as the Duchas project, recognition is key. The most significant benefits of this recognition are the likely political outcomes: community confidence, empowerment and cohesion.

Conclusion: heritages, identities and nationality

This chapter has considered two forms of heritage production in Northern Ireland: that undertaken by the county and national museum services; and the local initiatives generated from within the communities themselves. Each of these initiatives contributes to our understanding of the interlinked notions of heritage, identity and nationality in Northern Ireland.

   The initiatives discussed in this chapter illustrate a key characteristic of heritage: its fluidity. In Northern Ireland the interpretation of the past is changing, who is doing that interpretation is broadening, and the past remembered in public spaces is more wide-ranging. The creation of history, and its presentation as heritage, is an ongoing and live process. History is continually being written and rewritten, and the definition of heritage shifts according to current need. Public display, in books, exhibitions and monuments is not limited to the official academic, museum or heritage sectors. As well as the revision of well-known events, who is included in the process of creating history is becoming more diverse: wider ranges of people are both telling their histories and are being listened to. Some histories are being told for the first time, such as that emerging from the People's History Initiative, and other histories are being retold, such as that of the Bogside and Duchas projects. There is little permanence in Northern Ireland history, and the established museum sector is approaching these histories with caution. This point is demonstrated by the Ulster Museum, which in 2001 removed its permanent history gallery; instead, they will use the space for a series of temporary exhibitions, before attempting another permanent exhibition. The presentation of history in the museum is being tested, sampled and evaluated. The museum realises they have to tread carefully on the Northern Ireland story. One of the reasons for this sensitivity stems from the interest local and national museums have in establishing themselves as neutral venues for the presentation and negotiation of history. Museums often hope to achieve 'neutrality' through the creation of safe and open spaces where all personal experiences are valued. The notion of neutrality is, of course, highly problematic, as is the view that all versions of history command equal respect. Similarly, diversity of involvement does not always bring with it the benefits associated with a policy of inclusion. Just because more diverse histories are being made known, it does not mean they are being told in a less exclusive or partial manner.

Together, the heritage initiatives discussed in this chapter are an important contribution to the creation of identity in Northern Ireland. Analysis of the move to record the events of the Troubles in public spaces reveals the complexity of identity in Northern Ireland. For many, the experiences of the Troubles are personal and only shared with a limited group within well-defined boundaries. The impact of the Troubles may have been very public, but individual experiences were often kept private. Now, with the collection of oral experiences of the Troubles, the creation of history centres and other proposed memorials to the Troubles people are choosing to place their private story in the public domain. A high-profile example is the proposal to preserve part of the Maze Prison site as a museum, which is being forwarded by a Republican ex-prisoner group. With these new initiatives accounts of the Troubles that were previously concealed are now being disclosed. People and events that may have only been commemorated in private are now entering the public domain in the form of archives and exhibitions. It is important to evaluate the consequences of the shift from the private to the public domain. We must ask what is being recorded, why is it being shared, and for whom are these initiatives being created? Such moves to create a heritage out of the Troubles also challenge us to reassess the contribution of the Troubles to identity formation and re-formation in Northern Ireland. Rather than wishing to believe that the Troubles only impacted on certain people or places, with public display we are invited to consider the broader influence of the Troubles in shaping the identity of everyone in Northern Ireland. Furthermore, these initiatives will have an impact on the perceived national identity of Northern Ireland, whether that is Irish or British. It is likely that as the heritage sector becomes more confident in telling the history of the past 30 years, the identity of the six counties as a unique place will gain prominence. Within both the United Kingdom and Ireland, the history of the Troubles is essentially a local story – together many of these heritage initiatives tell the 'Troubles experience'. No one in Northern Ireland is outside the Troubles; to a greater or lesser extent it has impacted on everyone. This is an aspect of the past in Northern Ireland that everyone shares, even if they experienced it, and remember it, in different ways.

5

GHOSTS

Heritage and the shape of things to come

Jonathan Rutherford

The past has to 'wear out' before we can go on. And that applies
not only to our personal lives, but to countries as well.
All Souls' Day (Nooteboom 2002: 167)

Now and then

Howarth in Yorkshire was home to the Brontë sisters. It is now a heritage site
dominated by the narrow lane which passes through the village, rising up the
hill, lined with gift shops and tea houses. It is a caricature of Olde England
whose claim to authenticity lies in the displays of ersatz Victoriana, New Age
products and Third World handicraft which have become the ubiquitous
emblems of the English idyll. The reason for the existence of this commerce
and the visitors crowding the narrow lane window-shopping is hidden away
behind the church. A surprisingly small and modest parsonage which, when I
entered, had only a handful of visitors musing around its rooms. I had expected
to be subjected to an overweening Brontë myth, but it was the pathos of their
home and the story of their hard, closed and short-lived lives that made the
impression. A graveyard dominates the immediate surroundings. Its heavy,
oppressive stones and slabs lend the place a dark foreboding of death. Returning to the small main street and the crowds enjoying the sunshine, it was as if
this was the true heritage experience, a welcome distraction from the past
hidden away in its deathly surroundings. Howarth represents heritage as a dislocation from history. An opportunity to side-step the reverberations of the
past and enjoy the simulacrum.

The day out had been part of a journey up north with my partner to visit
relatives. Such occasions bring the past into sharp relief. Memories of childhood are evoked by the changed urbanscape of what had once been home. The
journey itself becomes a liminal experience as a familiar, ordered, temporal
living is disrupted. We began in Daubhill in Bolton, historically the immigrant
area of the town, once inhabited by the Polish and Irish and now by the Asian
community. The terraced housing was interspersed with the detritus of old

mills and workshops. We had been looking for an early childhood home but all that survived of the street was a short length of cobbled stone which led into a rubbish-strewn strip of ground trapped between the brick wall of what had once been the de Havilland factory and a new building which looked as if it housed an electricity generator. Across the road was the iron skeleton of a new mosque under construction, the emblem of a community establishing a per-manent cultural landmark. It would displace the Catholic church down the hill, which had secured the presence of an earlier marginalised ethnic minority. The traces of a multitude of pasts and histories lay scattered everywhere; an aunty's old house, the ruin of a mill, the Co-op and library; like footprints they led back into previous ways of life now ended. Howarth is an example of how heritage can commodify the past and create a culture which denies decay and transience. But this wandering on foot through the narrow terraced streets of Daubhill made their traces both visible and real. The effect of their reverber-ation in the present is paradoxical. The past can be related to and in the process let go of and allowed to give way to emergent life. The signs of racial difference, English Islam, the gaudy structures of the modern service economy grow through the ruins of an industrial society. And with them, what history can bring to people which the heritage industry can tend to obscure: difference, displacement, and a questioning of our ordinary, mortal lives. What will become of us in the future?

England is full of ghosts. They constitute an absence which defines us. In the three decades after the Second World War the English imagined themselves a natural given like the rolling green of the south or the bleak moors of the north, sustaining themselves with visions of a warrior nation of virtue, endur-ance and physical courage. And yet for all this national myth-making there was a dissonance in its telling. We were living through the final years of the long, stubborn demise of the late Victorian imperial age, a Teutonic nation of class deference shuddering to an ignominious end with the birth of youth culture, modern consumerism and New Commonwealth immigration. Even today this martial, status-obsessed world erupts into public view with a royal funeral, the anniversary of a military event or a skirmish overseas, its archaic symbols of royalty and tradition reinvigorating a glorious myth of England. Gripped in this dreamlike version of the past, the English are very close to the ghosts we have inherited; the dead which our heritage frequently evades confronting.

We have appeased these ghosts with legends about Alfred burning the cakes, the courage of Richard the Lionheart, the compassion of Florence Nightingale. The past has been depicted as a magical place and history a reverie in which the English can affirm our conservative soul. Its mythology has shaped how we think about ourselves and who we think we are, the horizon and background for our everyday experience. The promotion of a national heritage connects our consciousness of our individual pasts to a social past in which 'I' becomes the 'we' of a singular, ethnic national community. Its narratives, ideologies, metaphors and fantasies fuse together the present and past into an undifferentiated union. Heritage becomes the attempt to make sense of the social past without disturbing the social and symbolic order of the present. In *The Birth to Presence* Jean-Luc Nancy describes the task of making sense as 'death work'; the work of mourning as an act of fending off the dead. It is he argues 'the very work of representation. In the end, the dead will be represented, thus held at bay' (Nancy 1993: 3). Heritage, in its attempts to bring the past back to life, epitomises this paradox. Symptomatic of a state of unresolved mourning, it represents a loss that cannot be accepted and must be continually returned to, even as it is denied.

John Everett Millais' painting *The Boyhood of Raleigh* (1870) hangs in Tate Britain, the museum dedicated to the history of British art. The painting is a precursor to the heritage industry of the late twentieth century; a masculine, romanticised story of an empire built on virtue and idealism. In Millais' homage to the progenitor of Victorian imperialism, two small Elizabethan boys listen intently as a Genoese sailor, his finger pointing to the open sea, regales them with his stories of seafaring adventure. The young Walter Raleigh, his hands clasping his knees which are drawn up to his chest, does not look at the sailor, nor follow the man's pointing finger. Even as he listens, he is lost in his own thoughts, day-dreaming of his own destiny. What holds the attention are Raleigh's eyes. Roland Barthes describes how images have 'punctums', the element of a picture which arrests our gaze, and which makes it meaningful and memorable. It is what the viewer adds to the image but which is none the less already there; a form of aesthetic communication which draws us into an emotional engagement with the image (Barthes 1982: 27). Raleigh's eyes are an invitation to identify with his earnest self-reflection and recall our own memories of childhood day-dreaming. What is the boy's destiny, Millais tells us, is also our destiny: England's destiny.

In a nearby room is John Singleton Copley's painting *The Death of Major Peirson* (1781), the chronicle of an event of tragic, youthful heroism which gained iconic status in Georgian England. Its raw depiction of the chaos and violence of battle contrasts sharply with Millais' pre-Raphaelite wistfulness. The French have invaded Jersey and its capital St Helier has fallen. The young Major Peirson rejects the surrender and leads a successful counter-attack. In the mêlée of soldiers fighting in the small square he is killed, and as he swoons back into the arms of his brother officers, the centre of the canvas is dominated by a lone, black soldier firing his musket at the assailant. Where is the punctum in this picture? Two figures stand out. Who is the black protagonist, where has he come from and what is his history? And in the bottom right-hand corner of the square is a frightened boy, the young Singleton Copley, witness to the event, being hurried away by his fraught mother and nurse. Unlike Millais' romantic imperialism, Singleton Copley's picture is an act of remembrance which prompts us to ask questions about race, difference and history. It is a memory which allows an event in the past to become an object of thought.

Walter Benjamin, in his essay on his childhood, 'A Berlin Chronicle', wrote that 'memory is not an instrument for exploring the past but its theatre. It is the medium of past experience, as the ground is the medium in which dead cities lie interred' (Benjamin 1985: 314). He describes a discovery of the socially significant past which comes about not in an excavation of archives and texts, but through the archeology of one's own self, in the relationship between actual events and cultural texts and the daydreams and fantasies evoked by them. Benjamin advises us to approach our buried pasts 'like a man digging' and not to be afraid to return again and again to the same matter. It is a past which is like an absence in the present. As André Green describes it, absence is an intermediary situation between presence and loss; it is something which is felt but its exact nature remains unknown (Green 1986: 50). It awaits meaning, and in this sense it represents the future. This essay poses the past as a question. Dominant discourses and practices of heritage, in their attempt to bring the past into present life, can end up achieving the opposite effect. Past and present are fused together and neither can be separated out nor understood. What might come into being in the process of undoing this union? What would it reveal about who the English are, the nature of our individual selves?

Then

A good place to begin this investigation of subjectivity, and to trace its relationship to ideas about the past and heritage, is the late seventeenth century. It is the historical period which began to give form to the contours of our contemporary world: the 'possessive individualism' of commerce and trade capitalism; the cultural differences of femininity and masculinity; the emergence of colonialism and empires; the conflict between reason and feelings, commerce and sensibility; the divide between the public and private spheres of life; the making of the modern self. With the emergence of science and a metropolitan public culture over the following century, there occurred the secular development of the individual's inner life. The idea of reason began to challenge the parameters of ecclesiastical tradition. The religious ethic of righteousness was gradually surpassed by a pragmatism and psychology of the self. The Puritan's anxiety 'how can I be good?' became the secular 'how can I be happy?' At the same time, seventeenth-century maritime exploration and the colonial settlements which followed established a new understanding of the world which was central to the imagining of empire and empire-making. The birth of modernity is characterised by this new spatial, geographical conception, and by the beginning of a language of the inner, psychological processes of the individual. Both are central to the modern articulation of identity and difference.

Daniel Defoe's *Robinson Crusoe*, published in 1719, arguably the first novel of modern England, offers a representation of this development. Historically located between the era of exploration and the birth of British colonialism, Crusoe is part missionary, part conquistador, part trader, part colonial administrator.

September 30, 1659. I, poor miserable Robinson Crusoe, being shipwrecked, during a dreadful storm, in the offing, came on shore on this
dismal unfortunate island, which I called the Island of Despair, all the
rest of the ship's company being drowned, and myself almost dead.

(Defoe 1994: 89)

Shipwrecked on a slaving expedition to Africa, Robinson Crusoe begins his
recollections in the diary he keeps on his castaway island. His despair is overcome by an extraordinary economic activity which transforms the uninhabited
island into his 'little kingdom'. Crusoe's work orders time and space; 'Nov, 4th.
This morning I began to order my times of work, of going out with my gun,
time of sleep, and time of diversion' (Defoe 1994: 88). He produces an astonish-
ing array of products: his fortress home, his domesticated animals, candles, clay
pots and plates, and after three years his field of barley and rice and earthern
vessels for baking bread. Crusoe is a figure of an ascendant middle-class culture,
preoccupied by commerce, whose principle of freedom lies in unfettered economic individualism. For such a middle-class culture, the ideal free man is the
man unconstrained by social relations.

The story of Robinson Crusoe lies on the threshold of modernity and marks
a break with what Michel Foucault, in *The Order of Things*, calls the classical age
(Foucault 1986). Crusoe tells us early on in the story that he leaves his family
for the adventures of seafaring because he wants to evade the calling of provi-
dence. His adventure is an allegory for the birth of 'the West' and the social
category of man. The idea of the individual becomes the subject of language
and representation.

No doubt modernity begins when the human being begins to exist
within his organism, inside the shell of his head, inside the armature of
his limbs, and in the whole structure of his physiology; when he begins
to exist at the centre of a labour by whose principles he is governed
and whose product eludes him . . . modern man – that man assignable
in his corporeal, labouring and speaking existence – is only possible as a
figuration of finitude.

(Foucault 1986: 318)

While the classical age was able to allot human beings a privileged position
in the order of the world, Man could not appear as a subject of knowledge. In
representation and language he is without boundaries or finitude. Crusoe tears
himself free of this undifferentiated state in order to possess himself and secure
an identity. He experiences his aloneness, and in his abandonment of providen-
tial fate, he is confronted with his finitude. This coming into being as an individual sets up a temporal and spatial polarity between now and then, presence
and absence, self and other. Foucault writes that, 'The profound vocation of
Classical language has always been to create a table – a "picture" '(Foucault

1986: 311). This is the space of representation that the category of Man destroys with his newly acquired form of knowledge or *episteme*. He brings himself into being through narrative, the advance of time, the recognition of his finitude, the knowledge of his death and the destruction of the old order.

On the island, Crusoe reflects on his lack of company, but dismisses the value of other men. His aloneness leads him to reflect on the benefits of his isolation. He has nothing to covet, nobody to lust after. Crusoe's island is one of intense privacy, a masculine idyll in which women are entirely absent. Emotion is subordinated to rational discourse. Scientific observations and the classification of experience distances him from compromising feelings. Everything Crusoe was capable of enjoying he has made himself, for himself alone; 'I was lord of the whole manor . . . I might call myself king or emperor over the whole country which I had possession of' (Defoe 1994: 139). There are no rivals, no competition, nobody to dispute his omnipotence. But the movement which has created this isolated, utopian self-sufficiency, promises its destruction: 'Time – the time that he himself is – cuts him off not only from the dawn from which he sprang but also from that other dawn promised him as still to come' (Foucault 1986: 335). In his liminality and finitude, uprooted and adrift, man is confronted with difference and what is other to himself. Time, and with it experience, passes, and neither can be recovered.

The category of man is founded on his capacity to think and the knowledge he establishes of and about himself. But this *episteme* does not affirm his being, rather it suggests a further binary of thought and the unthought: 'What must I be, I who think and who am my thought, in order to be what I do not think, in order for my thoughts to be what I am' (Foucault 1986: 325). Descartes seminal 'I think therefore I am' is split. It can no longer guarantee the individual self, but plagues man with self-doubt. Between the 'I think' and the 'I am', between the cogito and being, lies man's unthought. It is this unknown which perpetually summons the individual toward self-knowledge, but thought alone cannot any longer think itself. It is not possible for man to describe himself, without thought at the same time 'discovering, both in itself and outside itself, at its borders yet also in its very warp and woof, an element of darkness . . . an unthought which it contains entirely, yet in which it is also caught' (Foucault 1986: 326). The category of man is established in a confrontation with difference, in time passing and in the loss of experience.

Robinson Crusoe is an allegory of a European colonialism whose history has been man's attempt to overcome difference. Everything which has established Crusoe's sovereignty, what he imagines to be his ontology, hewed from one foundation, is divided. 'It happened one day about noon going towards my boat, I was exceedingly suprized with the print of a man's naked foot on the shore, which was very plain to be seen in the sand.' After 15 years, Crusoe's kingdom is shattered by the discovery of what does not belong to and of him. He hurriedly builds extra fortifications, all the while fearful of the threat from the 'out-side of my outer Wall'. So begins the years of primordial fear, of living in dread of being captured by savages and eaten. Crusoe's confrontation with the Other marks the end of his innocence. Its foreignness confirms, in his own mind, his identity and legitimate authority, but at the same time it signifies the unthought which divides him from himself. For Foucault, 'Man and the unthought are, at the archeological level, contemporaries' (Foucault 1986: 326). The other is born beside man in an 'unavoidable duality', 'both exterior to him and indispensable to him . . . the shadow cast by man as he emerged in the field of knowledge . . . the blind stain by which it is possible to know him' (Foucault 1986: 326). In recognising both the interior and exterior of the unthought, what he imagines himself to be is no longer possible without the erasure of this threatening other. For weeks afterwards, Crusoe's mind is filled with a desire for revenge. He sleeps fitfully, dreams of the pleasures of murder and suffers lurid nightmares. War must be declared, both within himself for mastery of his fear and against others for the threat they pose to his existence; either he devours or he will be devoured.

The purpose of such a war is to modify the spaces of the other and incorporate them into the self. Its purpose is to collapse difference into sameness, to banish the unthought and once more fuse together 'I think' and 'I am' and recover the illusion of an homogeneous, internally undifferentiated individual. Man must become master of himself and of all that he sees. But this defensive strategy is impossible to fulfil because it undermines the preconditions of his existence. It is fuelled by a primordial desire to recapture the past and return to a state of non-differentiation with the world. The birth of 'the West' and its colonialism was not simply the assertion of economic and racial supremacy. The confrontation with difference precipitated a war of conquest to sustain man's viability against the other.

After 24 years alone on his island and 9 years under the threatening shadow of the other, Crusoe rescues Friday from ritualistic death and summons the era of the monologic, colonial imaginary:

> I smiled at him, and looked pleasantly, and beckoned to him to come still nearer; at length he came close to me, and then he kneeled down again, kissed the ground, and laid his head upon the ground, and taking me by the foot, set my foot upon his head; this it seems was in token of swearing to be my slave for ever; I took him up, and made much of him, and encouraged him all I could.
>
> (Defoe 1994: 207)

Not only does Crusoe rescue Friday from his own culture, he saves him from his own debased desire to be enslaved. In Friday's gratitude and Crusoe's benevolence the transgressive nature of otherness is wiped away and the dominion of man is confirmed. It is the relationship of the colonist to the native, the missionary to the convert and man to his Other. Friday is incorporated into the colonial imaginary as the shadow of Crusoe's being, not a threatening unknown but a mimicry. Crusoe teaches Friday English – 'I . . . taught him to say Master' – and like his parrot, Friday's language is a debased simulacrum of Crusoe's own imperial identity: 'Yes, master' to Crusoe's 'No, Friday'. After all the threat and the terror, there is nothing to fear. The colonialist may now rule his territories as if they are uninhabited. On having to take notice of anyone, he will see only himself. Anything else is simply timeless and ghost-like.

For Foucault the project of the *episteme* of man is bound to fail. The other, what is unthought, is larger than man or his history and will expose the 'hollowness of our existence' (Foucault 1986: 375). Confronted with his own apocalyptic vision, Foucault can only ask himself a series of rhetorical questions about the nature of the modern *episteme* and the form of thought which might come after it. He replies, that while he has no answers as to the future of European subjectivity, the significant fact is that he is able to ask these questions about its contemporary nature. 'I now know why I am able, like everyone else, to ask them – and I am unable not to ask them today' (Foucault 1986: 307). Foucault makes us question ourselves and our relationship to the other, to time past and time present, but what do we do when we have asked the questions? There is an absolutism in his work that undermines the possibilities of ordinary human agency. For Foucault the unthought has the characteristic of being an inevitable and overwhelming force of negation which flattens temporality into space, turns history into geography and disintegrates the meaning and integrity of the individual self.

A more pragmatic response to the idea of the unthought is that it constitutes an absence which is filled with potential meaning. Just as it is the place in which the subjectivity of man is threatened, so it is also where new subjectivities might emerge. The problems associated with the *episteme* of Western individualism can be recognised and challenged without surrendering its positive achievements. Jean-Luc Nancy writes that 'whoever comes after the subject, whoever succeeds to the West' will be a coming into presence. 'Presence is what is born, and does not cease being born' (Nancy 1993: 2). Subjectivities are always 'in the midst of taking place' (Nancy 1993: 2). The Manichaean world of Robinson Crusoe originates in his fear of this indeterminacy, projected out on to foreign lands and peoples different from himself. In Defoe's fiction Crusoe's supremacy over Friday is conclusive. It is a desire to fix identity and make it incommensurable to others. Its modern subjectivity attempts to 'master' the past, a relationship borne out of colonialism and capitalist modernity. However, even the most emphatic, monologic commentaries on race and cultural identity contain their ambiguities. The most conservative forms of heritage reveal the fault lines of their instabilities. An example is the work of Rudyard Kipling. Two hundred years after the fictional trials of Crusoe's early colonialism, Kipling's clarion call of imperialism is not the seamless voice it appears to be. In his writing we can recognise the contradictions and doubts of our own modern English identities.

Here and then

In 1902, Rudyard Kipling moved to his house 'Batemans' in Sussex and wrote to an American friend, C. E. Norton.

> Then we discovered England which we had never done before . . . and went to live in it. England is a wonderful land. It is the most marvellous of all foreign countries that I have ever been in. It is made up of trees and green fields and mud and the gentry, and at last I'm one of the gentry.

Kipling personifies the culmination of Defoe's nascent imperial man. He is remembered for his bellicose, barrack-room jingoism, and his promotion of the empire and its pageantry. But the truth is more complex. He was an Indian-born Englishman who became an immigrant in his native land and a foreigner in his own home. He belonged in neither one place nor another. Kipling lived at Batemans until his death in 1936, but he remained an odd man out and never quite made it into the ranks of the gentry. Unlike the fictional Crusoe he never succeeded in defeating the difference which haunted him.

In 1906 he published *Puck of Pook's Hill*, a book of stories which was an attempt to make himself feel at home in the Sussex landscape of Batemans (Kipling 1975). The stories intertwine a heritage of the English with the lives and the future of his own two children:

> Land of our Birth, we pledge to thee
> Our love and toil in the years to be;
> When we are grown and take our place
> As men and women with our race

The central figure of the book is Puck, the Gate Keeper of Old England. Kipling uses him to introduce the children to men and women from England's past. He writes about heroism, moral courage, warriors, journeys, frontiers, explorations and the establishment of overseas territories. But rather than symbolising adventure and escape to foreign parts, the narratives are interred in the locality the children belong to, and seek to establish their relationship to the land. The book is a romanticised, sometimes sentimental version of history, but despite this, Kipling does not offer his children a celebration of a familiar heritage.

The final tale of the book 'The Treasure and the Law' is about Kadmiel, a Jewish wanderer living in the early Middle Ages, and so Kipling's mythical vision of England is confronted by European modernity's symbolic figure of difference. The Jew is the stranger who is everywhere out of place. The story reveals Kipling's ambivalence about his own belonging. A frisson of uncertainty and doubt starts to unravel the fabric of the heritage he has taught his children.

'The Treasure and the Law' begins with Kadmiel's birth and the foretelling that he would be 'a Lawgiver to a People of a strange speech and hard language' (Kipling 1975: 228). Kadmiel sails to England to work for his uncle. The country is in a state of turmoil. The barons are fighting King John, borrowing money from Kadmiel's uncle to finance their war. When the barons attempt to secure another loan, Kadmiel demands that the barons amend the fortieth law of the Magna Carta which declares that 'to no *free man* will we sell, refuse or deny right of justice'. Kadmiel insists the words 'no *free man*' are replaced by the word 'none'. His demand is agreed, but then Kadmiel discovers that his uncle is planning to loan King John a secret hoard of gold which will enable him to raise an army and defeat the barons. The treasure has been hidden at the bottom of a tide-well in Pevensey Castle. In order to recover it, Kadmiel dives repeatedly into the tide-well, loads it into a boat, sails out into the English Channel and drops the treasure overboard. Kadmiel saves England from further war and ensures that 'there is but one Law in Old England for Jew or Christian' (Kipling 1975: 228).

Kipling gives no hint in the story that such tide-wells were used as privies and that Kadmiel would have been forced to dive into 'Christian smelling' sewage. In a further twist to the plot, the gold originally belonged to two knights, Sir Richard and Sir Hugh who, in a previous story in the book, had sailed to Africa where they had acquired it in exchange for worthless trinkets. 'Well', said Puck calmly, concluding the story of Kadmiel 'the Treasure gave the Law. It's as natural as an oak growing' (Kipling 1975: 239). But the story is not 'natural'. Nothing is clear. *Puck of Pook's Hill* had appeared to be an unambiguous and seamless history of old England. But by its end it is riven with ambiguities. Puck's statement is full of unconscious irony. African gold, discovered hidden beneath English shit, contributes to the development of an egalitarian English law. A Jew is the creator of free-born Englishmen. The treasure does not give the law, but must be given up in order for there to be the law. Loss establishes meaning. What is considered to be the same, is created out of difference. What is foreign is the source of what is familiar.

What paternal lesson was Kipling imparting to his children in this final story? Perhaps he was unclear himself about his intentions. Tolerance of difference? A reflection of his own indeterminate status? Or a belief that the antithesis of ourselves is not to be feared but can be a source of renewal. These are radical and democratic sentiments one would not expect from a conservative imperialist. They might have taken root in his boyhood when he endured the misery of childhood exile from his home and family in an English prep school (Kipling 1991: 5). His holidays were spent in a foster home he called 'the House of Desolation' where his 'terrors' precipitated a nervous breakdown (Kipling 1991: 12). He could not endure the loss of his home and mother. It was a trauma that would not wear away into the past, but instead seized him in present time and evaded his understanding. He was a man who could never quite put the past behind him. Kipling was a patriot, but he was also a product of colonialism. He shared with Kadmiel the experience of being a man between places who was never sure of his identity. His story teaches us that what appears to be familiar always contains the seed of its own strangeness. We are never altogether what we imagine ourselves to be.

Now

Like the Styx which must be crossed to reach the underworld, the past is viewed as a boundary between the living and the dead, presence and absence. Heritage becomes an effort to mitigate its disruptive power, not so much by expelling it, but by attempting to incorporate it into the present. In the eighteenth century, prints of ruined castles and abbeys had a popular market. They provided the opportunity to reflect on transience and loss. Ruins were depicted as places of solitude and contemplation which could bring about a change in being. As Geoff Dyer remarks, '[r]uins don't make you think of the past, they direct you towards the future. The effect is almost prophetic. This is what the future will end up like. This is what the future has always ended up looking like' (Dyer 2003: 204). Ruins are only ruins if history passes them by and they are given up to the vagaries of time. Today, representations, artefacts and edifices of the past are integrated into the media, heritage and leisure industries in the form of reconstructions, tourism and pageantry. What matters is their recovery and preservation. To allow them to rot and fade back into the earth would be considered a transgression against a national culture. But their commodification encourages the idea of a perpetual present in which the past becomes a simulacrum. As a culture it becomes difficult to experience the loss of the past. Modern consumerism collapses the past into the present, death into life. Post-war Englishness has been informed by a mixture of nostalgia and bereavement. We have ended up wanting something that never goes away.

The heritage industry is shaped by this relationship to the past. It manufactures ghosts; the dead who cannot settle and remain caught in limbo neither fully present nor absent, prowling in the hope of release. As Freud noted we unconsciously invent ghosts because of our sense of guilt in relation to the dead. They are the 'evil demons that have to be dreaded' (Freud 1985: 82). Our dread comes from our fear of their retribution. It is only in the process of mourning that this fear of ghosts will diminish. When mourning has 'renounced everything that has been lost, then it has consumed itself, and our libido is once more free' (Freud 1975: 307). In other words we have to remember before forgetting. Such a release transforms our relationship to the past. 'The same spirits who to begin with were feared as demons [are now] revered as ancestors and appeals are made to them for help' (Freud 1990: 122).

Released from the grip of the past, how might we think historically in a way which helps us to face the future? I don't have an answer, but I have the idea that Freud's 'dreaming in broad daylight' might help me think about it. Imagine if Kipling, the estranged son who wrote the 'Treasure and the Law', sat down in the same room as the anti-colonial revolutionary Frantz Fanon. He would have been meeting his nemesis, the personification of everything his imperialism feared and hated. We could imagine him stepping into H. G. Wells' fictional time machine and taking a short trip into the future to see what had become of the imperialist world after the Second World War. The machine would have landed him in its heart, in Washington, USA in December 1961. Here he would have found Fanon bedridden with leukemia. Fanon was 36 years old and in the last days of his life. He had come to America for medical treatment and found himself marooned and isolated in a strange country. His fame, which would sweep through the national liberation movements of the Third World, was still to come.

Picture the short, dapper Kipling with his Edwardian reserve sitting rather formally by the bedside of this infamous, once elegant black man. Fanon, who fought in the Algerian war of independence against France in the 1950s, was committed to destroying everything that Kipling had once championed. European humanism, he declared, had eulogised on the rights of man and yet 'murders men everywhere' (Fanon 1990: 200). Colonialism was the systematic negation of the other person, a furious determination to deny them all attributes of humanity. The people it subjugated were robbed of their identities and must, even now, constantly ask themselves: 'In reality, who am I?' (Fanon 1990: 200). Fanon had spent his life seeking an answer to this question. He was a man who embodied Nancy's successor to the West and the philosophy of the other coming into presence. The bloody and terrible affair of the successor the 'West always demands, and always forecloses' (Nancy 1993: 2).

Despite Kipling's antipathy, Fanon's sad plight might have reminded him of his own beloved son John who was killed on the Somme, and whose death brought his trumpeting regard for English imperial bravado to an abrupt end. In this loss, Kipling might have recognised the common traits both men shared, not just the loneliness of dying, but a history of European colonialism which had united them in their difference. And with this in mind he would have found the opening gambit of a conversation: 'In our difference what might we hold in common . . .?'

6

MAKING PLACE, RESISTING DISPLACEMENT

Conflicting national and local identities in Scotland

Siân Jones

> The so-called homogeneity of 'Britishness' as a national culture
> has been considerably exaggerated. It was always contested by the
> Scots, Welsh and Irish; challenged by rival local and regional
> alliances; and cross-cut by class, gender and generation.
>
> (Hall 2000b: 217)

Introduction

In recent years, many commentators have stressed that cultural diversity and
immigration are integral features of British history (e.g. see Hall 2000b; Kushner 1992; Merriman 1997; Ramdin 1999; Walker 1997). Furthermore, 'four
nations' histories of 'the Isles' have highlighted the fault lines of an internally
divided series of cultures, which are emphatically hybrid and riddled with conflict (Samuel 1998). Nevertheless, the cultural fault lines that lie *within and across*
the imagined national cultures making up the British Isles tend to be ignored
or smoothed over in the context of museums and the presentation of archaeological and architectural heritage. Discourses of national heritage routinely
focus on normative cultures which are presented as contained, coherent and
homogeneous in essence (Handler 1988; McCrone 2002), and Britain is no
exception (Kushner 1992, Hooper-Greenhill 1997). Admittedly, the 'Celtic
margins' have been portrayed as a locus of cultural and racial difference in
opposition to an English core lying at the heart of Britishness (Norquay and
Smyth 2002; Harvey *et al.* 2002). But this tension has in turn often been associated with an emphasis on smaller-scale, normative, Scottish, Welsh, English and
Irish national cultures (e.g. for Scotland see Cooke and McLean 2001;
McCrone *et al.* 1995); a tendency that devolution threatens to enhance. *Within*
these imagined national entities, cultural difference is almost always situated
in relation to 'minority-"non-white"-immigrant' communities, with the

'majority-white-indigenous' population regarded as culturally homogeneous and unproblematic in this respect (Hesse 2000: 10; see also Hall 2000b). Not surprisingly, strategies of social inclusion, which play a key role in the contemporary political discourse and social policy of New Labour, tend to mirror this dichotomy in the sphere of heritage and museums. Cultural difference is seen as a basis for exclusion and alienation among ethnic minorities, but among the majority 'white' population exclusion and marginality is attributed to economic depravation or physical factors, such as ill-health and disability (Sandell 2002: 3). The result of these combined strategies is that a core underlying homogeneous national heritage is maintained, with the 'problem' of cultural difference located either at national boundaries, or in terms of 'non-white', post-1945 immigrant multicultural heritage.[1] Thus, Britishness (and increasingly, in the context of devolution, Englishness, Scottishness and so forth) is 'the empty signifier, the norm, against which "difference" (ethnicity) is measured' (Hall 2000b: 221).

This distinction between 'majority-white-indigenous' heritage and 'minority-"non-white"-immigrant' heritages is problematic in a number of respects. It allows multiculturalism and cultural difference to be situated outside of the constructed core of these normative national cultures. Thus, in the sphere of heritage and museums, cultural difference is largely addressed through 'social inclusion' strategies focusing on how to incorporate 'non-white' cultures into existing national spaces without fundamental disruption of existing heritage narratives.[2] At the same time, the denial of cultural difference at the heart of the imagined national cultures of the British Isles, and the explanation of tensions or fault lines in terms of economic (and sometimes social) disadvantage, enables the authority and stewardship of national heritage organisations to remain unchallenged at heart. Above all, the distinction prevents connections being made between the historical conditions of production of these spheres of heritage, which are artificially divorced from one another.[3] Historical processes, such as colonialism, agrarian reform and industrial revolution, population displacement, and the fragmentation of communities, as well as discourses of 'race', 'improvement' and 'civilisation', are central to both 'majority-white' and 'minority-non-white' heritage. However, such politically and ideologically laden issues tend to be written out of mainstream heritage management and presentation. Furthermore, whilst they are sometimes addressed in the sphere of multicultural heritage, there is a tendency to simply celebrate cultural difference rather than risk disrupting mainstream national narratives through the introduction of subject matter which demands recognition of relationships of power (see Kushner 1992: 5–6; Hooper-Greenhill 1997: 9).

In this chapter I intend to question the notion of a contained and homogenous 'majority-white-indigenous' cultural heritage, and probe the limits of the nation as an imaginary site for the production of identity. In doing so, I will focus on the twentieth-century biography of a specific nationally acclaimed monument derived from the maritime margins of northeast Scotland – the ninth century AD Pictish symbol-bearing cross-slab known as the Hilton of Cadboll stone (see Figure 6.1). Often described as a 'masterpiece' and regarded as one of the most important pieces of early medieval sculpture in Scotland, if not north-west Europe, the Hilton of Cadboll cross-slab is famous for its 'exquisite' carving and for its depiction of a hunting scene with a woman riding side-saddle (see Carver 1999: 51; Ritchie 1989: 9).[4] This kind of early medieval sculpture, produced throughout much of Britain and Ireland under the influence of early Christianity, has figured prominently in the production of national heritage, particularly in Scotland and Ireland. However, as we shall see in the case of the Hilton of Cadboll, the authority of national heritage organisations is often challenged when it comes to conserving, managing and (re)presenting these monuments (see Foster 2001 for further examples). Based on ethnographic research, involving in-depth qualitative interviewing and participant observation,[5] I will suggest that official representations of national heritage are frequently recast, reformulated and contested in the production of other kinds of meaning and identity (cf. Herzfeld 1997: 1–2). These processes, I will argue, form part of the way in which those 'pushed to the edges' (in this case geographically, as well as culturally, politically and economically) seek to resist their marginalisation and reclaim a space for themselves. Issues of cultural difference are equally relevant in the context of the predominantly white, rural community concerned, rather than merely economic disadvantage. Moreover, I will suggest that that the histories of displacement and fragmentation with which they are grappling, open up unexplored paths 'across the margins' that could contribute to a more radical remaking of heritage in the 'Atlantic archipelago'.[6]

Hilton of Cadboll and the making of national narratives.

On descending to the 'Early People' galleries (c. 8000 BC to c. AD 1100) in the basement of the new Museum of Scotland, one is encouraged to move along a broad 'walkway' surrounded by representations of people (see Figure 6.1). On either side, two groups of futuristic figures by the modernist sculptor Eduardo Paolozzi represent the four themes of the archaeology galleries ('A Generous Land', 'Wider Horizons', 'Them and Us', and 'In Touch With the Gods'), with cases for the display of prehistoric artefacts set within the modern sculptures. At the end of this almost 'processional' route, standing discrete on a raised and wired-off platform, is the Hilton of Cadboll cross-slab.[7] The elaborately carved images of the cross-slab, specifically the hunting scene in the central panel, are intended to provide visitors with their first encounter with the anonymous people who inhabited the prehistory and early history of Scotland.

The Keeper of Archaeology and curator of the new 'Early People' exhibition, David Clarke, explicitly tried to evade a nationalist agenda when designing the exhibition (Clarke 1996). Nevertheless, the very nature of the institution and

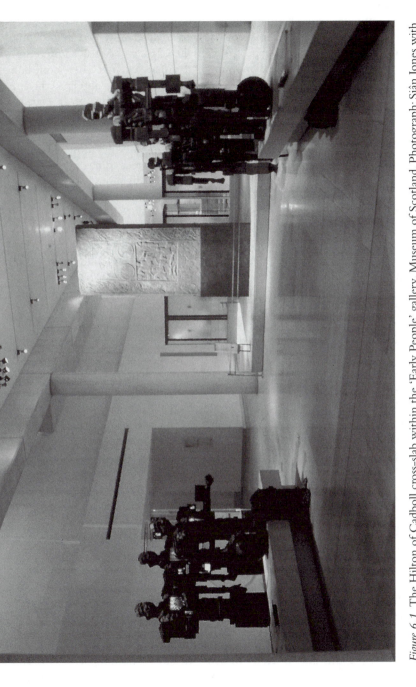

Figure 6.1 The Hilton of Cadboll cross-slab within the 'Early People' gallery, Museum of Scotland. Photograph: Siân Jones with permission from the National Museums of Scotland.

the increasing pace of devolutionary politics have meant that national narratives seem to entwine themselves around the exhibits (Cooke and McLean 2002: 119–20). The Hilton of Cadboll cross-slab was deliberately used in an iconic fashion within the 'Early People' galleries (D. Clarke, personal communication). It is meant to provide a monumental visual statement that confronts visitors as they enter the galleries, and whilst some resist the anticipated route its placement at the end of the walkway is intended to encourage an engagement with this nationally and internationally acclaimed piece of Scottish sculpture. It can be argued that the juxtaposition of the Hilton of Cadboll cross-slab alongside the sculptures of Eduardo Paolozzi, one of the most acclaimed Scottish artists of the twentieth century, serves to create a connection between the distant past and the present, thus alluding to an indigenous national artistic tradition. Furthermore, the deployment of Christian-influenced early medieval sculpture from the eighth to tenth centuries AD in the 'Early People' gallery is arguably essential to the creation of a national artistic canon for the early (pre)-history of Scotland with a strong 'indigenous' tradition of figurative art. Without it, the 'indigenous' artistic tradition in the 'Early People' galleries would be confined to the Pictish symbol stones and abstract prehistoric art, both of which are widely regarded as more 'primitive' forms of art, and the only figurative 'high art' would be represented by the classical tradition brought to Scotland by the Romans.[8] On the next floor up, in 'The Kingdom of the Scots' galleries (c. 900 to 1707), early medieval sculpture is employed again alongside earlier Pictish symbol stones, providing a material linkage between the early history of the nation and its prehistoric forebears.[9] Here such sculpture is situated within more explicit national narratives through the text panels that deal with the origins of the Scottish nation, its ethnic make-up and political formation.

The place of early medieval sculpture within such modern national narratives is prefigured in Scotland, as well as in other parts of the Atlantic archipelago, by longstanding traditions of enquiry into national origins; traditions that have often focused on early medieval peoples and which became increasingly racialised during the late eighteenth and nineteenth centuries (see Ferguson 1998; Kidd 2002). In Scotland, early medieval sculpture was the focus of antiquarian research from the eighteenth century onwards, and by the nineteenth century it was firmly embedded within Scotland's national heritage as the 'high art' associated with a formative period in the history of the Scottish nation (see McEnchroe Williams 2001 for an Irish comparison). The arguments of Joseph Anderson, Keeper of Archaeology at the National Museum of Antiquities (the forerunner of the Museum of Scotland) between 1869 and 1913, are instructive about the national symbolic value of monuments like the Hilton of Cadboll cross-slab. Anderson argued that centralised collection in museums is in the best interests of sculpted stone monuments themselves, preserving them from dispersion and weathering. But also that centralised collection is in the 'public interest' because:

The formation of such a gallery of art materials in the country to which they are indigenous would [. . .] restore to the native genius of the Scots the original elements of that system of design which are its special inheritance.

(Anderson 1881: 134)

The relationship between such monuments and Scottish national heritage was further articulated by Anderson as follows:

if our monuments be all destroyed, it will be nothing to us that those of England or Ireland or France or Scandinavia are still preserved, for Scotland's antiquities are not the same as those of Scandinavia or England . . . They belong to Scotland because they are inseparable features of her individuality, and they belong to Scotchmen in general in a sense which they can never belong to the holders of the lands on which they are placed [i.e. private landowners]

(Anderson 1881: 9)

When the Hilton of Cadboll cross-slab entered the collections of the National Museum of Antiquities late in 1921, the furore surrounding its initial donation to the British Museum earlier the same year added further weight to its place in the production of Scottish national heritage. Although many of the articles and letters of protest in regional and national newspapers focused on the detailed history of the cross-slab or issues of conservation, most were also couched in discourses of patriotism and nationalism. For instance, one article in the *Scotsman* compared Scotland's attitude to its national 'treasures' unfavourably with that of Ireland:

Ireland, a poorer nation than Scotland, has never dreamed of parting with the Book of Kells, the Cross of Cong, and the other priceless treasures that make Dublin one of the most interesting cities in Europe. Why should Scotland be in such indecent haste to write herself down a mere tributary province, and part with the tangible expressions of the national soul?

(*The Scotsman*, 14 February 1921)

The authors of much of the commentary were primarily concerned with its return to Scotland and not its subsequent locality of display. However, many felt that the National Museum of Antiquities in Edinburgh was the most appropriate location, serving to represent Scotland's national patrimony as a whole. The 1921 debate dealt with Scotland as a homogeneous entity and asserted a generic model of patriotic feeling and behaviour in relation to national heritage, which all 'Scotsmen' should conform to. Furthermore, the successful return of the cross-slab to Edinburgh later in the same year has conferred upon it a further element of national symbolism in terms of the nation's rights to its own heritage.[10]

Fragments from the margins

In the Museum of Scotland the small, discrete text panel next to the Hilton of Cadboll cross-slab provides an approximate date (c. 800 AD) and a location map showing its find spot. The text reads:

> *A Female Aristocrat*
> Before the Romans invaded Scotland, images of people are very rare indeed. From then onward, there are more of them, almost always seen on monumental sculpture.
>   Here a female aristocrat, riding side-saddle, is the central figure in an elaborate panel depicting a hunting scene. Hunting was a favourite aristocratic pursuit; and this scene is more concerned with honouring the aristocracy than with picturing a real hunt. The sculptor's placing of the woman in the scene is a tribute to the person who commissioned the cross – a woman of some importance.

The approach is typical of that adopted throughout the 'Early People' galleries and in museums more generally: one aspect of the multidimensional nature of the object is pulled out and used as a component in the exhibition narrative (D. Clarke personal communication). It would of course be naïve to suggest that there are no limits to the number of dimensions of any particular object that can be drawn out in a given exhibition. But in this case the museum exhibit not only represents just one dimension of the narratives surrounding the monument, it also physically constitutes only one fragment of the monument (the largest), among numerous smaller fragments. The text panel concentrates on the original context in which the cross-slab was commissioned and carved, omitting any discussion of its later biography. Hence, it does not refer to the burial inscription to 'Alexander Duff and his three wives' carved on to the cross face of the sculpture in 1676. Nor does it mention the absent lower third of the monument. Instead, there is an attempt to effect 'wholeness' by writing these elements in the biography of the monument out of the display even though the traces are inscribed on its material form. The side with the seventeenth-century burial inscription is placed at the back of the museum display and visitors are discouraged by the architecture and the signage from viewing it from that angle. The missing base is physically replaced by a copper plinth, to suggest the original height of the monument, and provide a reconstruction of the missing carving which is etched on to the copper surface, thus 'completing' the lower panel.[11]

    However, over the last 5 years a large section of the missing base containing elaborate carving, and thousands of the fragments making up the cross-face prior to its removal in 1676, have been discovered and retrieved from the Hilton of Cadboll chapel in Easter Ross where the cross-slab derived from (see Figure 6.2). The excavations leading to these discoveries took place in 1998 and 2001 (see James 2002; Kirkdale 1998, 2001) and were stimulated in part by an intensification of local interest in, and grievance about, the absent cross-slab during the 1990s. During the mid-1990s, a full-scale carved reconstruction had been commissioned from sculptor Barry Grove and was erected at the site of the medieval chapel at Hilton of Cadboll in 2000. The reconstruction can be seen as a means to 'presence' the monument in the village in the absence of the original, but the subsequent discovery and excavation of the missing fragments provided the locus for conflict between heritage organisations and local inhabitants.[12] This conflict concerned the ownership of the new remains – essentially whether they should be placed in the Museum of Scotland with the rest of the monument, or whether they should remain locally within the village of Hilton of Cadboll. The Hilton of Cadboll Chapel where the excavations took place is a scheduled monument and an Historic Scotland *Property in Care*. The organisation's normal policy regarding early medieval sculpture under its jurisdiction is to maintain it *in situ* within the landscape or in the immediate vicinity. However, where a museum has already acquired part of an object, as in this case, the integrity of the object is prioritised and new discoveries are usually allocated to the same museum.[13] Nevertheless, local residents contested this position, claiming that ownership of the newly excavated material rightfully belongs to the village, and that they would not allow the carved 'base' (effectively a lower portion of the cross-slab) to be removed.

A public meeting at the site of the excavation in August 2001 provisionally resolved the stand-off when the chief inspector of ancient monuments for Historic Scotland agreed that, once lifted, the large decorated lower portion would not be removed from the village until ownership had been formally established through legal channels. Ownership has now been attributed to the National Museums of Scotland.[14] To date (August 2004), however, the lower portion of the monument remains in the village of Hilton of Cadboll in a secure location, and its long-term location and mode of display is still subject to negotiation and debate between the National Museums of Scotland and the Historic Hilton Trust (formed in December 2001), who have subsequently acquired ownership of the chapel site (in March 2002). For the rest of this chapter, however, I wish to move beyond the actual developments concerning ownership of the cross-slab, to examine the meanings, values and interests embedded in, and negotiated through, the cross-slab during 2001 and subsequently.

Hilton of Cadboll and the symbolic construction of community

The Hilton of Cadboll cross-slab is associated with an array of meanings (For a full discussion see Jones 2004). It is regarded as: a sculpture of national and

Figure 6.2 Fragments: the large lower fragment *in situ* during excavation. Photograph: Siân Jones.

international significance in the context of early medieval European art; one of the symbols of the nation's rights to its own treasures in the context of its 1921 sojourn in London and 'repatriation' to Edinburgh; a major 'document' in the early history of Christianity in Scotland; a monument intimately connected with the Picts and thus laden with the popular associations of a heroic, painted people who successfully resisted the Romans; a memorial to one of three drowned Norse princes in the context of local folklore; and a stone which is bound up in family stories and genealogical accounts in the context of local oral history on the Easter Ross seaboard. But it is also associated with a range of metaphorical and symbolic meanings in local contexts, which are not immediately evident in terms of the meanings sketched here.

One of the most striking aspects of the cross-slab, and indeed the reconstruction, in local contexts, is the way in which they are conceived of as 'living things'. Sometimes such meaning is produced through the metaphorical attribution of organs, or processes, that are fundamental to life, to the monument. For instance, the cross-slab and the reconstruction are both referred to as having been 'born', 'growing', 'breathing', having a 'soul', 'living' and 'dying', having 'charisma' and 'feelings'.

A few informants and interviewees were more explicit about this symbolic dimension of the monument drawing direct similes rather than relying on metaphor. For instance, one local resident, Christine, noted that the cross-slab (specifically discussing the large carved section of the base after it had been excavated): 'was like something that was born there and it should go back [. . .]. It's, it's like people who emigrate or go away, they should always come back where they were born and I feel that that stone should go back.' Another, Duncan, remarked that if the main part of the cross-slab returned from Edinburgh

> there'll be a party maybe and there'll be things going on here that'll be absolutely unbelievable like a, like a how would I put it now, an ancient member of the village coming back, if that came through here on a, on a trailer and everybody would be here. [. . .] Coming home where it's always been. [. . .] If the stone had a soul it would be saying oh there's the Port Culac you know, there's so and so's house you know I'm going over to the park and there's, there's the other bit of the stone and it broke off a hundred and fifty year ago or whatever.

Here the monument is not merely conceived of as a living thing, but as *a living member of the community*. Not only is a direct analogy drawn between the cross-slab and an 'ancient member of the village', but it is also attributed the kind of social knowledge which is essential to establishing a person's membership within the community; knowing who lives in which house, recognising local landmarks and beauty spots, and so forth.

The use of discourses of kinship and 'belonging' in relation to the cross-slab

103

also reinforces its place as a living member of the community. 'Belonging' is one of the key concepts in the identification of kinship and other relations of identity, particularly among the older generation who were born in Hilton and/or have spent most of their lives there (and see Macdonald 1997 for a discussion of the concept in a Western Isles context). Thus the term regularly crops up in daily conversation, for instance, in an interview with Maggie: 'she *belongs*, they're both Sutherland in their name', or 'it was the first of the Sutherlands that *belong* to my granny'. Such statements do not simply relate to actual kin relations, but are also extended to others who are considered part of the community. Indeed rather than a reflection of static relationships they provide a means of articulating and negotiating 'who is and who is not "part of the place", and who is and is not authentically "local"' (Macdonald 1997: 131). Given such usage the widespread extension of the concept of belonging to the cross-slab by local residents carries a connotation of kinship. Thus, for instance, when Mary, a local resident, argues that 'I still think that the stone *belongs* to the people here', this is not a straightforward ownership claim of the kind that might be associated with property, but rather the assertion of an inalienable relationship of belonging in the sense of kin relations.

One rite of passage that is of particular importance in terms of 'placing people' within a network of social relationships, and in particular negotiating degrees of 'belonging' is that of birth. Being born in Hilton, or related to someone who was born there, is central to being accepted as an insider or a 'local'. Again, this process of social identification is applied to the cross-slab; like people, the cross-slab belongs in Hilton because as Christine puts it, it is 'like something that was born there', and 'that's where it was created'. The close association between the monument and the soil, which local residents bore witness to during the excavation of the fragments, is also important metaphorically in terms of the life-force attributed to the cross-slab and its ability to 'breathe' and 'grow'.

There is thus a whole body of metaphorical and symbolic meaning which surrounds the monument in local discourse, concerning its place within the community. In this way it facilitates the negotiation of identities and the expression of boundaries. However, it should not be assumed that it simply allows fixed, pre-existing categories to be mapped on to it. On the contrary, the categories of 'local' and 'incomer', and through them the boundaries of community as a whole, are fluid and continuously subject to negotiation.[15] As well as being conceived of as a living member of the community, and therefore acting as a mechanism for the negotiation of personal identities and relationships, the monument is also simultaneously an icon for the village as a whole. This iconicity is expressed metaphorically in the following statement by one of the local activists that: 'that stone is the heart of Hilton'. Here, it is portrayed in its entirety as one of the bodily organs of the community, the heart. Thus, the cross-slab is both a member of the village community and a microcosm of it in its entirety; symbolism which is central to its role in producing a sense of place.

Making place, resisting displacement

Anthropologists have recently turned their attention to a reconsideration of the relationship between community and territory, and in particular to the ways in which, in a world of deterritorialisation, people often deliberately and laboriously construct their places in particular locations. Gray (2002: 40) has argued that 'place-making and the resultant sense of place are an essential part of how people experience community' and that a sense of being in a community and a sense of its place emerge simultaneously and mutually constitute one another. Furthermore, it has also been observed by Gray (2002) and others (Gupta and Ferguson 1997; Kempny 2002; Nadel-Klein 1991) that processes of displacement, decline of community institutions and blurring of community boundaries, often lead to a more explicit and urgent emphasis on the production of a sense of *community as place*.

Given the way it mediates the symbolic construction of community, it is perhaps not surprising that the Hilton of Cadboll cross-slab also plays an integral role in the production of a sense of place. Conceived of as a living member of the community, the monument provides a mechanism for expressing the relationship between people and place. Place, and indeed placing people, is very important to people living in Hilton and the other seaboard villages. There are constant references to who is related to whom, particularly among the elderly who were born and brought up there. People are said to 'belong' to places as well as to each other, for instance, someone might comment, ' she belonged over to the Nigg area', or ask 'did he belong to here, or did he belong to Portmahomack' (a village about 5 miles from Hilton). Thus, discourses of belonging incorporate a strong spatial dimension, and on this basis it can be argued that statements of belonging in relation to the cross-slab serve to conflate community and place. This conflation is captured, for instance, in the statement: 'it belongs to the village, it *is* Hilton'.

Furthermore, the monument not only 'belongs' to the place, it is simultaneously constitutive of place and therefore part of the fabric of people's existence in that particular place. Associations between the monument and other aspects of the landscape, such as rocks and sea, serve to place it as an integral component of the landscape. For instance, one interviewee, Màiri, commented:

> the Hilton stone, you almost feel attached to it, it's almost like being attached to rocks or the sea or it's always been here, it's part of the place and for generations, I don't know, it was a close community you know

Such a conceptualisation of the monument, as one of the physical constituents making up the 'world', enables it to act as a metaphor for the relationship between people and place, referencing the closeness between people and the landscape, as well as the closeness of the community as a whole.

However, there is a tension underlying the process of place-making in Hilton and the other seaboard villages; they are not locales of timeless, stable relationships to place that are often attributed to such rural communities, particularly in the oppositions that are frequently made between urban and rural heritage (see Agyeman and Kinsman 1997). Although archaeological evidence indicates prehistoric, early medieval and medieval habitation along the seaboard, the origins of the contemporary seaboard villages are largely tied to the history of population movements during the late eighteenth and early nineteenth centuries, and to the development of the modern fishing industry. Between 1750 and 1850 the Highlands underwent fundamental change in the name of 'improvement'. The Improving Movement focused on reorganisation of the rural landscape and agricultural practices, as well as the reform of rural peasantry who were regarded by the Improvers in racialised terms as primitive, indolent, unhygienic and uncivilised (Nadel-Klein 2003: 32–3; also Smout 1969). One of the most overriding transformations wrought by the Improvers was the massive depopulation of the Highlands of Scotland to make way for sheep farming, a process which involved the 'clearance' of people from what were densely populated valleys and glens. In the process it was assumed that the landless poor would be converted into an industrious and efficient working class, fully integrated into the capitalist economy (Smout 1969). In practice, the 'small and large evictions, voluntary and forced removals, . . . outright expulsion of tenants and resettlement plans' (Richards 2000: 6) carried out by lairds (landlords) and their factors (estate managers) were often forced upon an unwilling population, resulting in the pain of dislocation and the destruction of a way of life. Encompassed by the phrase 'Highland Clearances', these traumatic events in the history of the region became a prominent aspect of oral history and social memory, associated with a sense of anger and loss within the Highlands and beyond (elsewhere in Scotland and among Scottish diaspora communities) (Ascherson 2003; Basu 2002; Richards 2000; Withers 1996).

The population displacement associated with these processes resulted in migration to urban industrial centres and mass emigration to the New World. One further aspect, however, was the resettlement of the remnants of Highland communities on the most marginal land, often coastal margins where it was assumed they would take up fishing or kelp working. The seaboard villages of Hilton of Cadboll, Balintore and Shandwick provided a refuge for displaced people during the late eighteenth and early nineteenth centuries, and grew rapidly as a result (Ash 1991: 156–7; Macdonald and Gordon 1971). A plan of Hilton in 1813, for instance, shows two streets with 24 houses, but by 1832 there were 58 families (Macdonald and Gordon 1971: 18). Furthermore, many people who were born in the villages recount personal genealogical connections with Clearance histories. The subsequent history of the seaboard villages was tied to the fishing industry, and following its decline in the Moray Firth during the earlier twentieth century, the North Sea oil industry took its place as one of the main sources of employment for the local population during the

1970s, also attracting new residents from the central belt and elsewhere in Scotland. However, since the recession of the 1980s, employment opportunities have significantly declined, as has the socio-economic infrastructure of the villages.[16]

The particular social and historical contexts that have just been summarised make processes of 'place-making' in Hilton, and the seaboard generally, distinctly fraught and problematic. There is an ambivalence associated with local residents' consciousness of place, for Hilton is both a place of deep significance and value, and a marginal place associated with deprivation, particularly as refracted through the eyes of those involved in social and economic development. Furthermore, social discourse surrounding this tension is replete with processes of historical emplotment, whereby current concerns about decline and marginality, as well as the need to fight against them, are framed by past events and injustices, such as the Clearances.[17] The history of the cross-slab means that it is eminently suited to the task of metaphorically dealing with dislocation between people and place, the resulting fragmentation of communities, and the pervasive sense of loss surrounding such processes. In the perception of many of the inhabitants the displacement of the upper part of the cross-slab in the mid-nineteenth century, and the recent excavation and possible further displacement of the new fragments, represent the power of certain individuals and organisations, notably landowners and national institutions, forcibly to move people/things against their will and without their consent. Furthermore, the fragmented nature of the monument can serve to provide an iconic image of the fragmentation of communities wrought by processes of displacement. The Highland Clearances provide the main focus for the historic emplotment of these processes of displacement and fragmentation, and the frequent uninitiated references to them in conversations about the Hilton of Cadboll monument highlight its symbolic role in this respect. Such references take the form of a slippage between those with power and authority today and their perceived counterparts in the past, namely landlords and church ministers. Or sometimes they even seem to involve a direct relationship between people's longing to reconstitute or reconstruct the Hilton of Cadboll cross-slab, and their desire to destroy other monuments associated with the Clearances and their landlords. For instance, one man noted in passing, 'Aye, we'll sort our stone and then we'll sort that stone' referring to the controversial statue of the 1st Duke of Sutherland, on top of Ben Bhraggie hill overlooking the small town of Golspie in east Sutherland. The Duke of Sutherland is one of the most notorious and despised of the Clearance landlords, and his statue, which was erected in 1834, has been the focus of a campaign to knock it down, taking the form of formal requests through the Planning Office of the Highland Council from 1994 onwards.[18]

Thus, it can be argued that opposition to the recent excavation of the base of the cross-slab, and to its potential removal to Edinburgh, provides a means symbolically to resist the historic processes of displacement encompassed by the

Clearances; processes which ironically contributed to the development of the villages in their modern forms. There is also a redemptive or restorative dimension to the role of the monument in place-making. The historical association of the monument with a wealthy and aristocratic group of people in archaeological and art historical accounts, as well as the national significance attached to the sculpture in heritage discourses, are actively appropriated in making Hilton a 'place of significance'; a place worthy of such a 'fine stone'. But of equal, if not more importance, is the way in which, when conceived as a living member of the community, it provides a means metaphorically to make the community 'whole' once again, against a historic background of fragmentation. For instance, reflecting on the impact of the carved reconstruction on Hilton when it was erected in 2000, one local resident, Christine (my emphasis), suggested that:

> I think people in Hilton were proud although they hadn't got the original stone they had something at last that they could associate with the Hilton stone. Because they had nothing and all they could say was oh, it's in Edinburgh. *But now they've got something, they can go and look at it and it is part of them.* [. . .] *I think Hilton became whole. Something was missing. So erm, at long last something came back to what was taken away.*

Furthermore, the metaphorical association between the fate of the stone and the fate of the community is also extended to the 'life' of the community in social discourse. Thus, another local resident, Alan, comments that:

> I look at [the] Hilton stone when it's in the Edinburgh museum it's just a dead headstone among other headstones, just a dead you know whereas in Hilton it could be a living stone, hopefully as a focus of a living community again and also indirectly basically the catalyst for more development in the place.

Conclusions

As pointed out at the beginning of this chapter, there is a danger that an artificial dichotomy is created between a 'majority-white-indigenous' national culture (perceived as settled and homogenous) on the one hand, and 'minority-"non-white"-immigrant' cultures (perceived as displaced and marginal) on the other. The conflict surrounding the Hilton of Cadboll monument exposes some of the limits of the nation as an imaginary site for the production of identity and brings into question the notion of a 'core', homogeneous and settled national culture and heritage. It reveals that the conservation, management and (re)presentation of heritage is actively involved in the negotiation of power and identity, and that issues of displacement, fragmentation and marginality extend beyond post–1945 immigrant minorities.

Attempts to conserve, manage, and (re)present early medieval sculpture in Scotland have been characterised by local protest and resistance. This resistance suggests that the official discourses surrounding these monuments and their designation as national patrimony are not shared by everyone. Hilton of Cadboll's fragmented history provides a unique window on these processes and illustrates how the meanings attached to objects change as they pass through different systems of classification (cf. Clifford 1988: 189–251). In terms of its display in the Museum of Scotland, the biography of the monument is largely silenced and strategies are employed to effect wholeness through physical reconstruction. Furthermore, in relation to the collection of early medieval sculpture in the National Museums of Scotland, the Hilton of Cadboll cross-slab is seen as a key piece in representing a particular type of sculpture, without which the collection would be less 'complete', and thus less authentic (see Clifford 1988: 215, 232). Here too then there is an emphasis on unity and wholeness, on the production of a 'complete' representation of a particular type of national heritage in one place; a place which constitutes an abstract national space. In this way, through the production of coherent, integrated collections in museums, or through the preservation of representative types of monuments distributed across the national landscape, representations of the nation as a coherent, homogeneous community are produced, creating a façade of national unanimity. However, in the case of the Hilton of Cadboll cross-slab, the discovery and excavation of the missing lower section and thousands of smaller fragments has thrown these processes into relief and contestation. At the outset of the excavation it was assumed by the national heritage agencies involved that the new discoveries would be allocated to the National Museums of Scotland in order to maintain the integrity of the monument. Although it is not the intention physically to reconstitute the cross-slab by attempting to put the original fragments back together (indeed NMS has recently proposed local display in Hilton of Cadboll), such an allocation symbolically reinforces the completeness of the object through the incorporation of the material within the same collection. The anger and protest expressed by many in Hilton of Cadboll and the other seaboard villages over the excavation of the new discoveries and the question of ownership revealed other processes at work.

In local contexts, the various fragments of the cross-slab act as a mechanism, mediator and metaphor for the production of embodied relationships between people and place; between Hilton the community and Hilton the place. The national significance of the monument, and obvious excitement over the recent discoveries, are of course central to people's engagement of the monument in making Hilton a 'place of significance'. In this respect, whilst apparently contesting state authority in relation to the monument, local residents are also complicit in the reproduction of the cross-slab's national significance. However, at the same time the role of the cross-slab as a means of making place and identity serves to contest and recast official national discourses. As discussed above, these local discourses surrounding the cross-slab in its various forms – the largest fragment in the Museum of Scotland, the recently recovered fragments, and the Reconstruction – are embedded in culturally specific and localised meanings surrounding the monument. Conceived as a living member of the community, the cross-slab mediates the production and negotiation of identities both within and out with the village – of 'locals', 'incomers' and complete 'outsiders' or 'strangers' – and, through them, the expression of the boundaries of community. Furthermore, through the application of discourses of belonging to the cross-slab, reinforced by reference to its 'birth' and 'growth' in the village, it also serves to articulate the relationship between people and place. Here then the national significance of the monument is directly contested, as people use it to express and negotiate culturally specific discourses of identity and belonging. These culturally specific discourses create what are perceived to be inalienable ties between the cross-slab and community; ties that are incommensurable with its significance as an important item of national patrimony.

However, perhaps the most far-reaching challenge to the imagination of a core national community posed by the conflict surrounding the Hilton of Cadboll cross-slab lies in its significance as an icon of displacement. The fragmented biography of the monument is integral in respect to this iconic role. Although dating to a much earlier period, the cross-slab is something (a 'living thing') that has been fragmented and displaced, and which is therefore eminently suited to the metaphorical task of engaging with, and contesting, the traumatic history of the Highlands between the mid-eighteenth and late nineteenth centuries. This history involved the displacement of communities in the name of agricultural and social 'improvement' supported by racial discourses about the primitive and backward nature of the Highlanders (see Ascherson 2003: 209–12). I have argued here that recent resistance to further displacement of the fragmented remains of the cross-slab provides a means of symbolically resisting these historical processes of fragmentation and displacement. Such forms of resistance and negotiation surrounding heritage bring into focus the dislocation and uneven relations of power underlying the formation of modern nation-states, which were embedded in processes such as agrarian reform, industrialisation and colonialism. They also expose cracks in the façade of national unanimity which all too often underpins the conservation, management and (re)presentation of the past. The historical contexts and discourses underpinning this particular conflict, agrarian reform, industrialisation and so forth, as well as the discourses of race and 'improvement' which accompanied them, are related to those, which, at different times and places, underwrote the creation of 'multicultural Britain'. Local residents in Hilton and the other seaboard villages are seeking to resist their historical and contemporary marginalisation, and reclaim a space for themselves, just as Asian, African and Caribbean communities, for instance, are doing elsewhere in the 'Atlantic Archipelago'. I do not wish to imply that their conditions and experiences are the same, but merely to suggest that the histories of displacement and fragmentation with which they are grappling open up unexamined paths 'across the margins'. These paths should be explored in the context of heritage conservation, management and (re)presentation, rather than closed down by a false dichotomy between core 'white' homogeneous national cultures on the one hand, and immigrant 'non-white' minority cultures on the other.

Conventions

All names used in relation to interview citations are pseudonyms, with the exception of individuals speaking or acting in an official capacity either in (or in relation to) public forums, whose identity is intimately tied to that official position.

Acknowledgements

I owe thanks to a great many individuals and organisations who have contributed to this chapter in one form or another. Historic Scotland and the University of Manchester contributed towards the costs of fieldwork, and this chapter has been written during a period of research leave funded by the Arts and Humanities Research Board. Thanks to Sally Foster at Historic Scotland for unflagging support and insight, and David Clarke of the National Museums of Scotland for his candid reflections on the 'Early People' exhibition design, and for supporting my research within the Museum of Scotland. Thanks to everyone who helped me at Groam House Museum, GUARD, The Highland Council, Historic Scotland, National Museums of Scotland, Ross and Cromarty Enterprise, Seaboard 2000, Tain Museum and the Tarbat Discovery Centre. Colin Richards, Helen Rees Leahy and Thomas Dowson at the University of Manchester have provided much support, enthusiasm and constructive criticism, as did the editors of this volume. Above all, thanks to Dolly Macdonald, and the other residents of the seaboard villages of Easter Ross, in particular Hilton, who provided a wealth of information and insight, and without whom this research would not have been possible.

Notes

1 Such an approach is starkly exhibited, for instance, by English Heritage's (2000) MORI-based survey, *Power of Place: The Future of the Historic Environment*. Here statements concerning social exclusion and inclusion, broadening audiences and widening understanding, are almost entirely supported by reference to the 'MORI Ethnic Minority Focus Group' and not the main MORI survey with the implication that difference and marginalisation are absent from the latter constituency. Problematically, however, the dichotomy between core national normative culture and minority 'non-white' cultures is also perpetuated by the gulf between scholarly

111

studies of 'four-nations' and 'multicultural' history. Indeed this gulf was also evident at the *British Island Stories* conference which fed into this volume. The conference deliberately incorporated both 'four-nations' and 'multicultural' agendas, but it was notable that much of the discussion, engagement and debate took place within rather than between them.

2 In the sphere of heritage and museums such policies and strategies have started to make headway (see contributions to Sandell 2002 and Hooper-Greenhill 1997). However, as Hooper-Greenhill points out, the number of museums addressing cultural diversity are still disappointingly small. Tellingly, much of the commentary focuses on repeated references to a few temporary or travelling exhibitions which have achieved almost iconic status, such as the *Peopling of London* exhibition at the Museum of London, and *Warm and Rich and Fearless* displayed at Bradford Museum and Walsall Museum and Art Gallery. There has been little progress in terms of large-scale exhibition projects and permanent displays. Furthermore, strategies of social inclusion focusing on cultural difference in the sphere of heritage are almost always restricted to heritage institutions situated in the heart of Britain's urban metropolises. In rural areas the emphasis is almost entirely on economically disadvantaged communities, and the social problems attributed to them.

3 See Kushner for a similar point regarding the dangers of leaving the history of minorities as an isolated specialism; 'By studying responses to minorities the identity and nature of majority society comes into focus.' (Kushner 1992: 10).

4 The design incorporates a number of Pictish symbols (including a crescent and V-rod, a double disc, and double disc and Z-rod), and is framed by vine scroll border inhabited by winged beasts or griffins (the vine scroll has stylistic parallels with contemporary Northumbrian art and is one of the parallels used for dating the sculpture to c. AD800). It is referred to as a 'cross-slab' as it would originally have depicted a cross on the other face, the arms of which would not have projected significantly beyond the dimensions of the slab of sandstone.

5 The field research on which this article is based was carried out over a period of 3 months between August and November 2001 with follow-up research trips in 2002 and 2003 amounting to a further 3 months. For a full discussion see Jones (2004 and in preparation).

6 Here I have been influenced by the agenda set by Norquay and Smyth (2002), who adopted the term 'Atlantic Archipelago' (after Pocock 1975) in place of the more nation-centred, politically engendered terms that can be used to refer to Great Britain and Ireland, to use two of the prime examples.

7 The special treatment afforded to Hilton of Cadboll is further reinforced through comparison with other examples of early medieval, and indeed Roman, sculpture in the exhibition. These are mainly grouped together for comparative purposes, located in more discrete areas of the gallery, and not fenced off from visitors: all factors indirectly implying a lesser value.

8 Interviews with the Keeper of Archaeology, David Clarke, suggested that this had been an implicit aspect of the exhibition design, even if it had not been a fundamental guiding principle. For instance, with respect to the location of the Hilton of Cadboll cross-slab, he acknowledged that it had been important politically to have something 'indigenous' in such a prominent position, rather than, for instance, an item of Roman monumental sculpture (e.g. the Hawkshaw Head). Furthermore, he acknowledged that visitors were likely to 'read' the sculpture in terms of the history of Western figurative art. However, the concentration on figurative art at the beginning of the 'Early People' galleries is a by-product of the broader exhibition narrative, which opens by introducing the inhabitants of Scotland's ancient past.

9 The Pictish symbol stones (unshaped stones bearing symbols) are regarded as precursors of the Pictish symbol-bearing cross-slabs, and are conventionally dated to

c.400–700, a period pre-dating the stated chronological framework for the 'Kingdom of the Scots' galleries.

10 The relationship between cultural property and the construction and negotiation of identity, particularly in the context of repatriation, has been addressed in a number of publications (e.g. Barkan and Bush 2002; Simpson 2001).

11 Early in the exhibition design there had been plans to produce a multimedia database called Mosaic, which would have enabled visitors to explore multiple dimensions of the objects on display, including their later biographies (D. Clarke personal communication). However, this was abandoned due to financial constraints, and therefore the overriding emphasis in the display of objects is on their original meaning and function, rather than their biographies.

12 Four organisations funded the excavations: Historic Scotland, National Museums of Scotland, Ross and Cromarty Enterprise, and the Highland Council. Local protest in Easter Ross largely focused on the former two organisations, which are based in Edinburgh in the central belt of Scotland rather than the Highlands. These two regions have been enmeshed in a core–periphery relationship associated with oppositions in many aspects of social and political life; a relationship which is also central to the historiography of Scottish identity (Withers 1996: 328).

13 This latter response follows the principle enshrined in guidelines for the allocation of finds from excavations, where the integrity of the object or assemblage is privileged and therefore in cases where material from the same site (or object) is already part of a museum collection subsequent finds would normally be allocated to the same museum (see, for example, Scottish Executive 1999: 6).

14 Initially, it had been anticipated by heritage managers that future ownership would be legally determined through the treasure trove system. However, in the early half of 2002 the Queen's and Lord Treasurer's Remembrancer (the Crown's representative regarding treasure trove) declared it to be outside the remit of treasure trove as he did not regard the new finds as 'ownerless'. The identity of the 'owner' was not initially specified in communications from the Crown Office, but subsequently in 2003 the Q&LTR stated that as the NMS already owns the upper portion of the monument, the lower portion, by default, belongs to the same organisation.

15 Once symbolically conceived as a living member of the community, the cross-slab becomes a medium for the reproduction and negotiation of relationships. 'Locals' could negotiate relative positions of authority and status through their association (and their forebears' associations) with the biography of the monument. 'Incomers' on the other hand could negotiate greater degrees of 'insiderness' through adopting, or respecting, the socially constructed authentic position of 'the village' demanding that the new discoveries remain there. In contrast, the few local residents who asserted that the base should go to Edinburgh were cast as 'incomers', thus questioning the authority of their opinion.

16 On the basis of the 1991 census, the Highland Council and Ross and Cromarty District Council identified the seaboard villages of Easter Ross as the second most deprived area in the Region and the District, respectively (Barr 1996). The affect of this 'social disadvantage' and the associated concentration of development activity on people's consciousness is palpable, captured by one local resident in the statement that 'Hilton is a backwater on a backwater on a backwater'.

17 See Nadel-Klein (2003 ch. 5) for an analysis of the ways in which fisherfolk's experience of crises in the fishing industry is conditioned by specific historical processes, particularly the social memory of injustice and stigma.

18 As Withers (1996) points out in his analysis of place and memory in Highland Scotland, for those supporting the campaign the proposed destruction of the monument, which provides a symbolic representation of power within the landscape, was a means of erasing a dominant memory. However, others felt that it

should be maintained as an icon of past iniquities and as an embodiment of memory and identity. Whichever stance is adopted, it is clear that the Duke of Sutherland monument provides a focus for the negotiation of power and identity in respect to memory. The connections that some local residents in Hilton made between this monument and the Hilton of Cadboll stone serve to highlight similar processes at work surrounding this latter monument even if they are manifested in different ways.

7

REINVENTING THE NATION

British heritage and the bicultural settlement
in New Zealand

Lynda Dyson

Cultural identities are not obvious or 'natural' propensities of populations living in territories delineated as 'national'. In the white settler colony of New Zealand, two dominant ethnicities – Maori and Pakeha – were produced as distinct collectivities through the colonising processes of modernity. Before the arrival of Europeans, Maori people had no single term for themselves. There was no pan-tribal form of identification, not least, because the three islands, which came to be known as New Zealand, were not conceived of as a unified geographical entity. In other words, the First Peoples of the territory did not imagine themselves as a unified grouping. Tribes were distinguished from one another by *whakapapa* (genealogies), narrated in terms of links with specific geographical locales and pre-dated by ancestral links with the canoes which brought the Polynesian settlers across the South Pacific to Aotearoa around AD 950 (Durie 1998: 53). The word '*maori*' meant 'normal', 'usual' or 'ordinary' but after the Treaty of Waitangi was signed in 1840 between the British and tribal chiefs, the term was capitalised to refer to a newly racialised collectivity.

> Defining the Maori as a unified ethnic grouping was an important part of the Treaty of Waitangi's constitutive role in the formation of nation but, more crucially, the Treaty's designation of the indigenous peoples as a collectivity ensured that all inhabitants of the territory were drawn within the jurisdiction of the Anglo-settler state and defined in terms of their 'race'[1].

Confronted by Europeans for the first time, the indigenous people referred to these white folk as '*Pakeha*' which had meant 'imaginary beings resembling men with fair skins'. Over time this term changed from designating those perceived as 'strangers' to referring specifically to European settlers (Salmond 1992).

During the nineteenth century settler communities were founded by groups who were recruited by the New Zealand Company from economically deprived rural areas in Britain with the promise of cheap land. Scots, Danes, Germans and Norwegians also formed settlements in the colony. In the early days communication networks were almost non-existent between settlements and it was many decades before the white settlers ('*pakeha*' to the Maori) identified as a collectivity, not least because of their regional and religious disaffiliations. Their eventual collective identification with the emerging nation was based on their 'whiteness' which set them apart, in national discourses, from the colony's others – the Maori.

In recent times New Zealand's dominant ethnicities have been recast in a new version of nation, 'biculturalism', which repositions Maori and Pakeha as 'partners'. This 'bicultural settlement', as it has come to be known in New Zealand, is an important element in the reparations made to Maori after long years of struggle to have the terms of the Treaty of Waitangi recognised. However, despite the significance of the 'partnership' between Maori and Pakeha, the new version of nation continues to be contested, not least because it delegitimates the claims of a whole range of other ethnic groupings such as Chinese and Pacific Islanders who have a long, albeit largely invisible, history in the territory.

'Biculturalism' has transformed New Zealand's founding assimilationist myth of 'one nation, one people' into the binary 'two peoples, one nation'. This shift, which has come about after many decades of political struggle by Maori to have their sovereignty and rights to land recognised, has challenged the historic formation which centred the white majority within narratives of nation.

The development of a new national museum – Te Papa Tongarewa – has played an important role in reconfiguring the nation's heritage within the context of biculturalism.[2] The museum, which opened in 1998 on a prime waterfront location in the nation's capital, Wellington, represents a substantial state investment in the new version of nation. In order to construct a monument to the nation's 'settlement' with Maori the museum indigenises both Maori and Pakeha. This article will argue that Te Papa Tongarewa addresses 'the people' and 'the nation' through a complex matrix of racialised, gendered and class-based distinctions which continue to privilege hegemonic versions of 'whiteness' whilst incorporating the new commitment to 'biculturalism'. It shows how the complex distinctions made in relation to British heritage have been reworked in a post-colonial context.

Building the nation

Constructions of 'whiteness' in New Zealand are in a sense 'janus-faced'; looking outwards from the nation's peripheral position (in terms of global circuits of cultural goods) for legitimation through cross-border flows of images and narratives, and inwards for 'indigenising' symbols which can be appropriated for local forms of ethnic self-fashioning. Benedict Anderson has described national identity as a particular way of 'imagining' in which the mass consumption of forms (such as the novel and the newspaper) provide the collective means to experience the nation as a 'deep horizontal comradeship' existing in 'homogenous empty time' (Anderson 1998: 6). Anderson's formulation is useful in detailing the complex ways in which modernity (defined by secular rationalism, a calendrical perception of time, mass literacy and mass communications) has given rise to forms of cultural production and circulation through which the nation can be imagined as a bounded, unified space.

In New Zealand the predominantly one-way flow of cultural products from other places, together with local struggles over ethnicity, have meant that the 'imagined community' of nation has always been fragmented and discontinuous. The 'constructedness' of nation is all too apparent as the place has a short and uncomfortable colonial history, and local versions of 'whiteness' have been historically based on the maintenance of racialised boundaries and myths of common descent extending beyond the territory of nation back to the imperial heartland of Britain.

During the nineteenth century, civilising missions in the colony valorised 'whiteness' as a repertoire of behaviour, rules and ideas organised around the notion of autonomous individuals regulated by codes operating in both public and private spheres of national life. Notions of 'whiteness' underpinned the organisation of everyday colonial life, administered through independent spheres of social and cultural activity designed to 'safeguard' the moral and spiritual fibre of the nation with the Maori positioned as inferior. As Edward Said suggests, national culture operates as a system of exclusions which define the limits of the national 'imaginary'. He describes it as a process legislated from above but enacted through the polity in order that: 'such things as anarchy, disorder, irrationality, inferiority, bad taste and immorality are identified and then deposited outside the culture . . . kept there by the power of the state and its institutions' (Said, 1983: 94).

Nation-building in New Zealand involved the centring of white settlers within narratives which interpellated them as both 'citizens' and imperial subjects through the production of 'creolised' forms of Britishness/Europeanness. Historically narratives of '(white) nation' have been reproduced within the educational system (for example through standardised curricula in English and History) while local cultural production (particularly in the spheres of literature, art and cinema) has always been bound up with 'imported' canons of taste and value. Although, in the colonial context, cultural forms have addressed distinctive national preoccupations, most notably a concern with the specificities of 'place', the forms themselves are institutionalised by repertoires of taste and value measured against norms defined elsewhere, at the 'centre'. (Ashcroft *et al.* 1989).

While national imaginings are always geographically delimited, or as Anderson puts it, 'no nation imagines itself coterminous with mankind' (Anderson 1998: 7), in New Zealand, the creolised culture of the white settler majority has historically been based on a shared language (English) and a shared myth of descent (British). Thus when applied to a marginalised locality such as New Zealand, the notion of an 'imagined community' needs to be considered in relation to the peripheral context within which cultural production and consumption takes place not least because local cultural production competes unevenly with a flow of artefacts from elsewhere.

At a symbolic level, the 'invented traditions' of nationhood, exemplified by forms of pageantry and 'pseudo-tradition' – including a familiar repertoire of symbols and rituals (the national anthem, public holidays, and the rituals surrounding sporting events) – provide a focus for collective identifications. New Zealand's colonial legacy has meant that the even the most fundamental signifiers of nation (such as the currency, the flag and postage stamps) have been inscribed with imperial iconography. New Zealand's currency, symbol of the 'national economy', bore the British Queen's head on one side until 1990 while the national flag connotes 'New Zealand of the South' with a Union Jack nuzzling the top left corner in a sea of blue overlaid with a five-star Southern Cross.

The process of nation-building in the colony required a means to delineate the 'uniqueness' of the national collectivity within the context of strong imperial links with Britain. In order to achieve this distinctiveness, Maori cultural forms have been appropriated in various ways. Maori *kowhaiwhai* (scrolls) have been used on banknotes and stamps as the border design framing representations of enduring colonial icons such as the British monarch and the explorer, Captain James Cook (Thomas 1995: 91). 'Indigenous' songs and dances furnish the symbolic regalia of nation with the tourist industry reproducing an internationally recognised repertoire of 'miniaturised' Maori artefacts – greenstone and bone pendants, flax bags, and wooden carvings – as souvenirs of the nation. And importantly for the purposes of this chapter, the national 'archive' of Maori artefacts has been appropriated as an important part of the nation's 'heritage' (Butts 2002: 227).

Despite attempts to define a 'common culture' in New Zealand, any sense of 'nation' based on collective memories and an idea of common destiny, has been fractured and discontinuous not least because Maoris have long contested the colonial land-grab and transfer of sovereignty to the British. How do such constructions feed into, and reflect, what Bhabha has described as 'the complex strategies of cultural identification and discursive address that function in the name of "the people" or "the nation"'? (Bhabha 1991: 291)

The role of museums

Museums have been described as 'secular temples to the nation' providing the means by which a nation represents its relationship to its own history and to that of 'other' cultures (Hutcheon 1994: 209). As authoritative public spaces (institutionalised as apolitical, objective and empirical), museums function as monuments to the nation and as such they have played a pivotal role in the formation of the modern state. Their imposing architecture and prime metropolitan siting, together with the arrangement of an interior space designed to regulate forms of behaviour for visitors, variously positioned as 'citizens' or 'tourists', endow them with an authority and historic role unlike any other public institution (Karp and Levine 1991).

Historically, national museums have played a central role in defining hegemonic versions of nation and have therefore been sites of struggle over competing definitions of national culture. Within these institutions the collections of artefacts have been constructed within the rule-governed systems of anthropology and art which have reproduced hierarchies of difference. Historically, national collections (organised within the disciplinary distinctions of art, ethnology and natural history) represent power/knowledge relations through the delineation of familiar hierarchies and exclusions: men over women, European over non-European, modern over pre-modern, high art over traditional crafts. Thus the collections themselves, in terms of both content and presentation, invest artefacts with particular meanings which are, more often than not, legacies of a colonial history, while the history of the acquisition of artefacts themselves tends to be erased in public displays. In New Zealand collections, these hierarchies have marked out the shifting parameters of 'Maori' and British/'European' culture.

For example, in ethnological collections Maori artefacts have been used metonymically to fix 'tribal' forms as specimens of an authentic, pre-modern culture existing outside the time of the nation, while examples of European/ Western art and artefacts have been classified differently within a canon defined predominantly by the teleological narrative of art historical discourses (Clifford 1988: 192). In ethnological terms the 'modern' culture of the white settler majority has been unrepresentable, but with the nation's recent 'bicultural turn', museums have become sites where the contemporary struggle over definitions of national culture have been played out.

Long-standing Maori tribal grievances have included claims for the return of artefacts confiscated by the colonisers, often as trophies of war during the nineteenth century. Many of these – including a meeting house displayed in London's Victoria and Albert Museum – have been returned to the tribes as museological practice has been forced to consider the politics and ethics of collecting (Allen 1998: 144).[3]

National museums in New Zealand have been established at key historical moments. For example, during the decade prior to the centenary of the signing of the Treaty of Waitangi (1840) there was an intense period of cultural nationalism in New Zealand. In 1936 the Centennial Branch of the Department of Internal Affairs was established in order to develop a sense of nationhood. The setting up of the Centennial branch which, within a decade, had founded the

119

national archives, produced the 11-volume series *Making New Zealand*, a centennial atlas and a *Dictionary of New Zealand Biography*, coincided with the development of a national museum and gallery in Wellington (Oliver 1984; Phillips 1996). The National Art Gallery and Museum opened in the capital in 1936. The building's architecture and the collections housed within were shaped by the way in which the colonial state imagined its dominion at that time (as part of the British Empire). The architecture drew on neo-classical motifs – the front colonnade was modelled on the portico of a Greek temple – signifying the nation-state's 'civilisation' and power. On the front facade of the building, an inscription dedicating the building 'to the services of Art and Science' was embellished with icons relating to the various fields represented within the museum and gallery; painting was depicted by a palette; sculpture by a roman bust (toga-clad and bearded); architecture by a building; and ethnology with a tattooed Maori head. This depiction of a Maori head highlights the way in which New Zealand's museum collections have represented Maori culture. The heterogeneity of European culture (exemplified in this case, by the references to painting, sculpture, architecture) stands in contrast to ethnology's construction of 'the Maori', essentialised as a homogenous object of study with the tattooed head displayed as an icon of a knowable entity – the nation's 'others'.

In the past, the selection and presentation of Maori objects displayed in New Zealand's museums of ethnology have been based on the perceived 'cultural purity' of the artefacts. In ethnographic collections dissimilar groups of objects have been invested with meanings relating to notions of 'tradition' and 'authenticity' and displayed within interpretative contexts emphasising a pristine culture untarnished by European contact. Examples of Maori sculpture have been exhibited alongside utilitarian objects – such as spoons, bowls or spears – as representative of an atemporal, pre-modern culture. Defined within such a taxonomy, carving has been collected and displayed as an instrumental tribal practice, its status within collections signalled by the absence of the sculptor's name. Conversely, in art museums, 'works of art' are displayed for their aesthetic qualities; selected on the basis of 'beauty' or 'originality' or because they represent a defining moment in the teleology of the Western art historical discourses (Clifford 1988: 226). Such works are identified as the creations of named individuals; their place in everyday cultural practices (including the art market) is irrelevant in a context where categorisation is based on 'transcendant' aesthetic attributes defined by a canon. Therefore in the case of New Zealand, distinctions employed in the selection and display of collections in ethnological museums have developed taxonomies which by omission, furnish dominant constructions of 'whiteness'. To parody Eric Wolf, whites have been represented in New Zealand national collections as 'the people with History' (Wolf 1982).

In 1984 New York's Metropolitan Museum's staged an exhibition of Maori artefacts which transformed the way in which Maori culture was perceived in New Zealand and has informed the development of the Maori section at Te

Papa Tongarewa (Butts 2002: 228). While curatorial direction of the *Te Maori* exhibition in New York remained in the hands of white ethnologists and museum professionals, the exhibition marked a shift in the way Maori people were involved in various aspects of the exhibition. This shift inaugurated a wider debate about the management and exhibition of material culture in New Zealand and has been crucial to the development of the Maori section of Te Papa which is curated and managed by ethnologists, archaeologists and technicians appointed by a Maori advisory group (Tamarapa 1996: 160).

Described by publicity material as 'a place to stand for all New Zealanders', Te Papa Tongarewa is officially designated as 'a museum of art, history, Maori art and history and the natural environment'.[4] The need to specify the inclusion of 'Maori art and history' signals the difficulties of representing the duality demanded by the discourses of biculturalism in a place where white dominance is structured into the cultural formation and lexicon. The generic categories 'art and history' continue to naturalise 'whiteness' while the emphasis on 'Maori art and history' makes visible categories submerged within discursive practices of ethnology. The display of artefacts in the new museum makes a powerful statement about the place of the *tangata whenua* (people of the land/ Maori)) within the reconfigured nation and also demonstrates the museum's commitment to museological practice informed by a new approach to collecting and exhibition.

The museum can be read both as a public space representing a collective imaginary based around a new legitimating myth – 'biculturalism' – and also as a national institution geared to consumerist culture. In line with the market-driven approach of New Zealand's public sector, the museum's mission statement included, from the outset, a commitment to be 'customer-focused and commercially positive' in its 'celebration of the *mana* of the two mainstream heritages – Maori and Pakeha'.[5]

Representing Biculturalism

In a private interview, a historian involved in the design of the Pakeha exhibits expressed disquiet at the way the 'politics had been sucked out of the exhibits'.[6] His inability to speak publically about behind-the-scenes disputes which dogged the development of Te Papa, demonstrates the difficulties and limits involved in reading-off museum exhibits as 'text'. While the minutes of committee meetings and related policy documents reveal, to a certain extent, the institutional tensions steering the development of the museum, the gradual 'neutralising' of the museum's approach to 'biculturalism' is only evident in the absences and shifts which can be gleaned by examining changes evident in development plans for the museum.

Revealed in these documents are the contradictions involved in working to an explicit state-funded brief to showcase the commitment to 'biculturalism' whilst attempting to reflect current museological debates in relation to the

121

politics of collecting and exhibition. This tension has resulted in a disjuncture between the way in which the two 'mainstream' cultures are exhibited. The requirement to be commercially viable in terms of attracting corporate sponsorship, maintaining a balance between populist entertainment forms geared to income generation (such as themed rides, cafés and souvenir shops) and the role of preserving and presenting national collections in a new context, have heightened the institutional tensions underlying the museum's development.

In order to accommodate these conflicting interests, the nation's history has been sanitised by exhibits which downplay the inequalities and injustices underpinning it in order to construct, yet again, a unified version of national identity. Instead of acknowledging the significant political and social changes which have come about as a result of the contemporary renegotiations, particularly in relation to tribal claims for reparations under the Treaty of Waitangi, the museum indigenises the 'treaty partners'. In a space publicised as 'Our Place' the museum performs a 'bicultural' balancing act – presenting an empowering and unified 'Maoriness' alongside a hybrid and potentially decentred version of whiteness. Te Papa Tongarewa invites visitors to participate in and celebrate the shared cultures of New Zealand's 'treaty partners'.

The discourses of 'biculturalism' sever the time-space co-ordinates of the nation from connections with Europe. In the architectural space of the museum, Maori and Pakeha are joined together in the deep ahistorical space of land and nature. This dehistoricising of the colonial phase is evident in conceptual plans used in the development of the museum. The design of the space was based on a tripartite axis with the *tangata whenua* (those belonging to the land by right of first discovery), and the *tangata tiritiri* (those belonging to land by right of treaty) entwined with *papatuanuku* (the common land).

In planning documents the connections between these areas were depicted figuratively in the form of a venn diagram; intersecting circles showing each of the three elements conjoined. The museum's architects have explicitly stated that the building was designed to represent the anchoring of the nation in 'deep time' through the connections of both Maori and Pakeha to 'nature'.[7]

Architect Peter Bossley draws on the discourses of biculturalism to naturalise 'shared' connections to the land, describing the relationships between 'sub-cultures' as expressed in the museum's architecture: 'Common to both sub-cultures were attitudes to openness relationships with sea and sky, the transitional nature of the occupied space between land and ocean.'[8]

At Te Papa, the positioning of the Treaty of Waitangi display and the natural history section, play an important part in making explicit these connections for visitors as they move through the space of the museum.[9] The Maori and Pakeha exhibits sit alongside one another on level 4, connected by a central atrium area dedicated to the Treaty of Waitangi. This 'treaty space' is designed to resemble a chapel (Figure 7.1). A facsimile of the original treaty document, meshed between blue glass and embellished with gold leaf, hangs high in the ceiling like an enormous stained glass window. Visitors walking beneath this structure are dwarfed by the scale of the object and need to look up in order see it. The movement of visitors passing through the space triggers recordings housed in pipes embedded in the floor (resembling the pipes of a church organ), which comprise loop-tapes of positive and negative opinions about the role of the Treaty in contemporary New Zealand. This device, apparently giving 'voice' to a range of ordinary opinions, is used to signify the nation's capacity for 'democracy', 'egalitarianism' and 'openness', thus silencing any contentious claims to different forms of sovereignty. Significantly, it does not provide any context for the treaty's turbulent history. Instead, the religious iconography of the space elevates the treaty to spiritual status thus avoiding materialist issues connecting the treaty to a political and legal struggle over land rights.

The Pakeha exhibits at Te Papa, which represent white identities as contingent, heterogeneous and unstable, occupy the museum space alongside a version of 'Maoridom', which appears timeless and pure. Yet, however powerful the 'Maori' space in the museum is – artefacts presented in a beautifully lit space; with the meeting house, works of sculpture, painting, clothing and the use of photographs and video to anchor the collection in relation to specific tribal connections – the exhibit appears to have been designed primarily to connect the history of European settlement to the 'deep' history of the land.

The Pakeha exhibits were developed by a government department; it appears the 'centre' continues to speak for the 'dominant'. In New Zealand's deregulated environment the contract for 'conceptual input' into the section was awarded to the Department of Internal Affairs. Jock Phillips, head of the department's historical branch, has described the department's function as 'a business with a public mandate to strengthen national identity'.[10] According to Phillips, the department's task in designing exhibits for the museum was to tell 'the story of the *tangata tiriti* – the Pakeha who were there by virtue of the Treaty of Waitangi' (Phillips 1996: 115).

Defining Pakeha history continues to be a major conceptual issue for New Zealand historians but as Phillips puts it, 'we solved the matter quickly and argued there was no Pakeha identity as such' (Phillips, 1996: 115). As a result the three exhibits representing the majority group have been designed within a contingent, non-linear interpretative framework. It remains to be seen the extent to which such a context enables visitors to 'read in' the nation's troubled colonial history, particularly given the museum's showcase status as a tourist-oriented 'gateway to New Zealand'.[11] Phillip's account states that the colonial encounter will be subsumed by what he calls a 'universal truth' of Pakeha 'non-identity'; that the core of 'Pakehaness' is based on 'a founding trauma':

Figure 7.1 'Giving voice' to opinions about the Treaty of Waitangi in Te Papa Tongarewa, Wellington, New Zealand. Photograph: Lynda Dyson. Signs of the Nation exhibition area copyright Museum of New Zealand, Te Papa Tongarewa.

'the fact that we are migrant people, attempting to make a new home . . . is the central truth to our identity' (Phillips 1996: 119).

In a reversal of the way settler differences (regional, religious and so on) were collapsed in the nineteenth century in order to construct white settlers as a collectivity of New Zealand 'citizens', the museum's interpretation of 'biculturalism' recuperates diversity and pluralism, presenting migration stories based on the travelling experiences of 'ordinary folk', in an attempt to deconstruct the now-discredited settler narratives of dominant white identity which have been mythologised in local culture. Development documents stress the way each component of the 'Pakeha' section avoids an overarching 'master narrative'.[12] This 'post-modern' approach draws instead on anecdotal material to present an account which is intended to signify a decentred whiteness in keeping with the museum's 'biculturalism' (Phillips 1996: 117).

In the exhibit called *Passports*, visitors are able to open drawers containing details of individual settler stories and miscellaneous artefacts, most of which are related to the journey from Europe to New Zealand: 'visitors will be able to play off generalisations about New Zealand identity against particular lives' (Phillips 1996: 119). This exhibition is sponsored by Air New Zealand and the trope of 'travel', used to describe settler migrations, represents colonial settlement as mere 'event'. This is reinforced by the use of Air New Zealand's corporate logo (the koru scroll) on exhibition signs suggesting a teleology of travel in which ships have simply been replaced by planes. More broadly, the presentation of these 'stories' exemplifies the tensions which exist in a public institution burdened with the task of redefining national identity for a society 'hungry for a vision of itself' (Phillips 1996: 108).

Heroising whiteness

Historians designing the exhibits were battling against public pressure to establish a Pakeha 'gallery of heroes', despite the fact that, as Phillips puts it, 'the clamour for such a solution came from Pakeha who sensed the Maori exhibitions would be affirming of identity and therefore hagiographic in tone' (Phillips 1996: 115). One of the sections – *Exhibiting Ourselves* – is described as 'potentially the most subversive' because of its interpretation of the way in which versions of national identity have changed historically (Phillips 1996: 116). The interpretative device for the exhibit is a re-creation of New Zealand's displays at four international exhibitions spaced 50 years apart: the 1851 Great Exhibition in London, the 1906 Christchurch International Exhibition, the 1940 Centennial Exhibition in Wellington and the 1992 Seville Exposition in Spain. At each of these events, it is suggested, a different version of a mythologised 'New Zealand' was exhibited: the 1940 exhibition in Wellington represented the nation as an economically progressive welfare state while the 1992 version, at Seville's Expo, projected New Zealand as a 'go-getting nation of entrepreneurs' (Phillips 1996: 116). Phillips suggests Te Papa's visitors may be able to read these constructions as 'puffery and propaganda designed to sell goods and to attract immigrants and foreign investment' (Phillips 1996: 116).

For the curators, *Exhibiting Ourselves* may well demonstrate how different versions of national identity have been 'self-serving projections' linked to specific temporal conjunctures, but it is questionable whether the interpretative capabilities of museum visitors will lead to similar readings in the present. To what extent will visitors share the values and assumptions that have informed the representation of these exhibitions in the new museum? And, if these versions of identity are interpreted by visitors as 'constructions', will this, lead in turn, to a deconstruction of Te Papa's 'bicultural' projection of national identity?[13]

In the latter phase of the museum's development, a media campaign was fought over plans to use a collection of eighteenth-century antiques of British origin to produce an exhibition about class relations in the early days of settlement. Donated to the nation by a descendant of a wealthy hill-farming family, the Elgars, the collection was to be integrated into an exhibit about wool production in the colony, in order to make connections between class, labour and the generation of wealth in the early days of settlement. According to Phillips:

> We decided to look at the wool barons by focusing on Mrs Elgar. We planned to reconstruct her drawing room using the furniture and around the walls tell how her family had acquired the wealth which purchased the collection. Well of course, this was not quite what the Elgar lobby wanted.[14]

After a public campaign the artefacts were housed instead in a glass compartment and anchored by a large sign entitled *Grassy Empires*. In two short sentences, the text of a caption trumpets the achievements of nineteenth-century capitalists exercising their freedoms in the colonial zone: 'It was thanks to sheep farming that Ella and Charles Elgar owned Fernside. In the 1840s a few canny entrepreneurs got in quick, leasing and then buying cheap acres.'

Interestingly, it is through a collection of artefacts belonging to 'common' people that connections are made in relation to colonial appropriations. John Guard was sent from Britain to Australia as a convict and subsequently settled in New Zealand in the 1820s, marrying Betty, the first white woman to live in New Zealand's South Island. The national museum in Wellington inherited a collection of the couple's possessions including John Guard's pistol, sword and whaling implements, Betty Guard's wedding ring, and perhaps most importantly for the mythology which surrounds the couple, a tortoiseshell comb which is supposed to have saved Betty's life when she was struck by a mere (Maori club) during a tribal attack which took place when their boat was shipwrecked off the New Zealand coast. As a result of the collection, which

126

provides material evidence of their existence, the Guards have appeared at regular intervals in New Zealand historiography, usually narrated as courageous pioneers (with John Guard portrayed as the archetypal 'kiwi bloke'), despite the evidence which shows he and his wife were involved in corrupt dealings, most notably involving unscrupulous land deals and the exchange of sexual favours in which John Guard traded his wife. Phillips reports:

> To present them as noble pioneers was not acceptable . . . instead it seemed necessary to confront visitors with the reality of power implied by Pakeha settlement. We hoped to show that John Guard's settlement in New Zealand emerged from a personal history of oppression and a struggle to survive . . . we used him not to condemn him but to make the point that Pakeha settlement inevitably involved conflict with Maori.[15]

While it may be the very fact of this collection's existence which explains the prominence of the Guards in local historiography; the collection has produced the narrative with the artefacts providing material evidence which has guaranteed the couple's place in New Zealand history albeit because it continues to be less controversial to critique the actions of those occupying a less privileged place in the social order.

Commodified heritage

Discourses of commerce and consumption have permeated the museum's design and development with an emphasis on creating a populist space geared to attracting a demographically wide audience. The conceptual plan, around which the museum was developed, proposed to organise the museum in order to give the visitor an experience described as 'malling'. According to the plan, a tour of the museum was designed to function as a circulation loop which constantly returned the visitor to the atrium which forms the spine of the building. It was envisaged in the plan that those on a quick tour could window-shop; café facilities and souvenir shops were placed in strategic positions 'similar to the way anchor shops are placed at opposite ends from each other in a mall'.[16]

At the risk of overinterpretation, it is significant, in terms of links between the imposition of capitalist relations and the white settlement of New Zealand, that the shopping theme has been extended to one of the most popular exhibits in the Pakeha section – *Golden Days*. Visitors queue to enter an old-fashioned shop where they face an array of merchandise displayed in front of a window which depicts an 'olden days' Wellington street scene beyond. With lights dimmed, a 20-minute audio visual show unfolds. The window becomes a screen for the projection of a series of 'magic moments'. Clips from films, television news and advertising are edited into themed sequences (from sporting triumphs to protests – anti-nuclear, land rights – and royal visits) condensing a familiar visual repertoire projected over a sound track of aural nostalgia (ranging from the bird call of the native 'tui' to the national anthem). Visitors are offered the opportunity to consume the unchallenging banalities of 'Kiwiana' (described in the programme as 'the spirit of New Zealand') in a space created by the omission of a social history section called 'Life in New Zealand'.[17]

Te Papa Tongarewa is described as New Zealand's most significant piece of contemporary architecture. As a result the building's material infrastructure has provided the means for a cross-section of commercial companies to enhance their corporate identities through their connection to the museum. In the months following the opening of the building, images of the museum were used to promote a range of products and services – acoustics, electrical, engineering, lighting, graphics, interactive technologies, interior fittings, landscaping, steel, cladding, precast concrete – that had been involved in its building. Thus the museum has become a site for transnational companies keen to be associated with and demonstrate their commitment to the 'new' nation through their involvement with the museum.

Conclusion

The development of Te Papa Tongarewa has involved a complex process of resistance and accommodation in the production of a 'bicultural' identity during a period of economic, social and cultural transformation which has seen the historic ties of empire severed. By collapsing the hierarchical boundaries traditionally organising museum collections, Te Papa can be read as attempting to construct a 'heterotopia' in which, for the museum's management at least, 'taste and caste have been dismantled' in a celebration of the post-modern nation.[18]

It remains questionable whether the museum's new version of nation provides an interpretative space where the tensions of New Zealand's bicultural settlement can be interrogated by visitors. Rather, the development of Te Papa Tongarewa can be seen as a public investment in a site committed to representing a reworked version of nation in order to reconcile a range of conflicting pressures stretching beyond the institution. As such, the museum functions primarily as a monument to a state which appears to have settled accounts with the 'indigenous' people. More pragmatically, in the context of New Zealand's refocused economic interest in the Asia–Pacific region, together with the growing importance of tourism as the primary service industry, the museum's version of nation demonstrates how the settlement between Maori and Pakeha produces a 'strategic biculturalism' which strengthens the national 'brand' in the international marketplace. 'Whiteness' has been indigenised as cultural hierarchies, which historically produced British heritage as 'superior', have been displaced in a museological celebration of 'ordinariness'. 'Kiwiness' is partnered with a homogenised, neo-primitive 'Maoriness' to produce a back-projection of the nation's history which skips the colonial phase in order to produce a version of nation fit for the neo-liberal global economy.

Notes

1 The Treaty of Waitangi (which has only retrospectively been written into the narrative of the colony's past as a historic turning point) was at the time simply a means to facilitate the appropriation of Maori land. Acquisition of cheap land paved the way for the transition from the 'scavenger' economy based on whaling, sealing and forestry to pastoralism, as permanent white settlements were established on territory acquired through the massive transfer of land from tribal 'ownership' which followed treaty-signing. From this point onwards the privileging of settler interests (largely coterminous with capitalist interests) over those of Maori was enshrined in a panoply of laws and statutes. Initially legislation which directly involved the Maori people was based on an assumption that they could be assimilated into white society. The Treaty of Waitangi acknowledged the presence and rights of the tribes but at the same time the colonial authorities sought the voluntary acceptance by Maori of British institutions, believing the Maori could be evangelised, educated and made subject to European law (Belich 1997).
2 Te Papa Tongarewa translates as 'repository of things precious'. The museum's website can be found at http://www.tepapa.gov.nz.
3 Mataatua was installed in the courtyard of the Victoria and Albert Museum in London in 1882. Following the recommendations of a tribunal investigating reparations in relation to the Treaty of Waitangi, the house was returned to its tribal owners in New Zealand in 1992 – it is now exhibited at Te Papa (Allen 1998: 152).
4 Annual Report of Museum of New Zealand Te Papa Tongarewa, 1995–6.
5 Museum of New Zealand Te Papa Tongarewa, statement of intent for the financial year ending 30 June 1997.
6 Interview with New Zealand government historian, Jock Phillips, Wellington, May 1998.
7 'The Designing of Te Papa', *Architecture New Zealand*, special edition, February, 1998.
8 'The Designing of Te Papa', *Architecture New Zealand*, special edition, February, 1998.
9 The museum's website uses hypertext links to connect these sections.
10 Comment made in a private interview, Wellington, March 1998.
11 Museum of New Zealand, Te Papa Tongarewa statement of intent for the financial year ending 30 June 1997.
12 *The Peopling of New Zealand: Concept Development Report*, history exhibition team, February, 1994.
13 This interpretation of the representation of New Zealand in the context of Empire also glosses broader issues about the way the settler colonies were hierarchised in relation to other territories. Annie Coombes argues that empire exhibitions represented the white dominions at the 'top of a racially hierarchised ladder' (Coombes 1994: 192).
14 Interview, Wellington, March 1998.
15 Interview, Wellington, March 1998.
16 'The Designing of Te Papa', *Architecture New Zealand*, special edition, February, 1998.
17 Plans to exhibit a collection of contraceptives dating from the 1930s in an exhibit

about 'love in New Zealand' were shelved when, as historian Jock Phillips put it, the Chair of the Museum Board decided 'it would appeal to young people who did not know the difference between love and sex'.

18 Ian Wedde, museum curator quoted in the *Australian*, 6 June, 1998.

Part II

PROCESS, POLICY, PRACTICE

8

TAKING ROOT IN BRITAIN
The process of shaping heritage

Naseem Khan

A not particularly distinguished church, on the south side of the River Thames and within sight of Parliament, holds an interesting take on the development of 'Britishness'. The church was rescued from obscurity in 1977 and turned imaginatively into a Museum of Garden History. But the telling element in this case lies not so much in the body of the church itself, but in the little garden to the rear. Here, among the old tombstones, you can find a planted bed of what might seem incontrovertibly British native plants – those well-known and much loved denizens of the English country garden: hollyhocks, roses, peonies, irises, evening primroses, marigolds and geraniums.

Except that they are not English. They are immigrants, as careful notices by each – detailing when the species was first officially recorded – show. Hollyhocks were first noted in 1573, and the others officially entered the English garden in 995, 1370, 1200, 1621, 995 and 1629, respectively. Reading the notices, it is hard not to conclude that virtually all the colour – all the plants that feature so prominently in literature inviting people to an isle of tradition and longevity – has been provided by tourists, interlopers and sometimes illegal immigrants.

The eighteenth century saw a great upsurge of activity among plant collectors, with Joseph Banks – founder of Kew Gardens – travelling with Captain Cook and sending back 316 hitherto unknown plants from Brazil alone (Hoyles 1991). A thousand new strains of orchids were brought to Chatsworth House from India, by a collector who had been sent out to India by Joseph Paxton, in the train of the new governor-general of Bengal. But the English landscape had been affected by immigration long before that. It was the Romans, for instance, who had imported roses, while the New World was responsible for the arrival of potatoes, tomatoes, chocolate and tobacco.

Without the immigrants, it is a sad scene. The 'traditional' garden lacks the elements that not only bring scent and colour but also are believed so fondly to be the very essence of Englishness.

133

This simple act of subtraction prompts the question – how does a nation evolve an idea of its national character? Is the process always as open to accident and self-deception as the garden test suggests? And what implications does this act of exclusion have for the body of immigrants – horticultural and human – written out of narratives of heritage?

Of course the fact of constructed identity need not surprise us too much. Human beings define themselves not only by which groups they belong to but also which groups they consider anathema. Racial stereotypes can affirm (the British are 'tolerant', 'fair minded', 'love an underdog') as well as demean (Leonard 1997). Racial myths are part of a daily stock-in-trade. Governments themselves trade on a recognisable brand: 'archaic and ageing diplomats and missions filled with Chippendale furniture; pompous heraldry in official publications; titled diplomatic envoys; tourism advertising displays of thatched pubs and classic cars; and cardboard cut-out Beefeaters at trade fairs,' notes Mark Leonard scathingly in his Demos report. Indeed, remarks Wally Ollins, the current trend is for governments and businesses seemingly to change their traditional places. While governments are embracing branding – developed by business as their marketing tool – businesses are attempting to take on 'socially engaged' roles in the communities in which they are based (Ollins 1999).

Leonard argues for diversity as being one of *Britain TM*'s unique selling points. There is certainly some way to go. Diversity may be part of overseas marketing, but it is not part of the internal heritage myth. The countryside is represented in tourism as inalienably white, pointed out photographer and critic, Ingrid Pollard. Her witty series of pictures that put black people into the frame of Wordsworth's Lake District make her point. Artist Yinka Shonibare has also mischievously inserted his black dandy, like an elegant fifth columnist, in his scenes of eighteenth-century polite society.

While Pollard deals with the present, Shonibare infiltrates history and challenges ideas of heritage. Rebranding, in other words, is not just a matter of re-envisioning the present, but of revisiting the canons of history and heritage too. Consider, for instance, the custom of London's Geffrye Museum in labelling the furniture that forms the *raison d'être* of its historical collection, with the original source of the material of which various pieces were made – malacca, teak, mahogany, and so on. This simple act discreetly shifts the viewer's understanding. Instead of seeing the objects as simply isolated examples of British craftsmanship, in a frozen time-warp, they are able to sense the web of trade and empire connections which lies behind and which produced the artefact.

This tension between illusion (the all-English cottage garden) and diverse reality might have been a creative one for artists, but it has confused the quality of Britain's cultural policy over the years. Caught between ideas of the ideal society and the immediate facts, it has shifted its stance and objectives around a series of accommodations – assimilation, integration, coexistence in a tolerant parallel existence. Each has carried with it different ideas about rights and duties. But the most central question is, who shapes policy? What is the relationship between – in this case – the artist and the policymaker? Who leads? Can policy ever shape public opinion – or does it always follow after, like a submissive handmaid? And can the people for whom policy is intended effectively intervene? Signs today suggest that the voice of the artist has become more heard, a shift that could introduce a different sense of reality. Policy that had historically been relatively single-stranded is having to shift its ground, to challenge its own basic assumptions. But in order to test that progression, we need to retrace the journey.

The territory in which 'race' is located has evolved over time. Its ambiguities have been well laid out by, for instance, Kenan Malik in his book *The Meaning of Race* (Malik 1996). The British experience is distinct, some argue with Bhikhu Parekh who has differentiated interestingly between German and British takes on policy (Parekh 2000c). Incomers to this country, he argues, find it easier to gain citizenship, compared with the case in Germany. Hence the focus in this country has been on racial and cultural difference, while in Germany it has been on the struggle for political rights.

In fact, the struggle for rights preceded the argument over culture. This effectively began in the mid-1970s, as a result of a wider enquiry into the role of the arts on society that had previously encompassed community arts. This extended into questioning the existence and nature of what, in 1974, were called 'the arts of ethnic minorities in Britain'. They formed the basis of a research report that I was asked to write. The arts in question were largely unknown to the report's commissioning bodies – the Arts Council of Great Britain, Communities Relations Commission (CRC) and Calouste Gulbenkian Foundation. The focus on ethnicity to date had been primarily around rights – issues of discrimination and racism in employment, housing and policing. These formed the central thrust for the activities of major groups such as CARD (Campaign Against Racial Discrimination). Meanwhile, there was considerable counter-agitation against immigration and immigrants, voiced most prominently by the MP Enoch Powell with his apocalyptic warnings about the country becoming like the River Tiber, 'foaming with blood'.

Ethnically based culture, in the public arena, was part of political ammunition of activists. The race relations industry with its networks of very active local community relations councils (CRCs) acted as conduit and cultural promoter. CRCs organised regular 'multicultural evenings' – variety nights that brought in ambassadorial examples of other cultures, presented as kindly, colourful, non-threatening, interesting and exotic. Some communities appreciated the platform and did not feel it was irrelevant. Polish and Ukrainian communities for instance already had an established practice of taking their many and very skilled folk dance groups out on goodwill visits to hospitals or fundraising evenings for charitable causes. But other artists who were aspiring to professional status felt some unease at being crammed, in a sense, into a jar of All Sorts, where there was little understanding of their art form and more than a whiff, at times, of being patronised. The classical dancer, Pushkala Gopal, who is a proponent of the rigorous Indian style, Bharat Natyam, recalls being introduced, 'And now we are really lucky to have Bharat Natyam with us, and she is going to show you her dance, Pushkala Gopal.'

In the private arena, things were very different. Behind the public displays a complex network of impressive and elaborate organisations and ambitions was slowly growing. It lay below the official waterline, little documented in official records and little funded by official bodies. Research for the report — that was published in 1976 as *The Arts Britain Ignores* — was virtually all primary research. Guided by an excellent advisory group,[1] I travelled the country, knocking on doors, walking the streets, following up leads.

The picture that emerged was impressive in its reach and vigour — scores of community associations, artists in every discipline, centres and schools. They were inspired by two main and largely separate desires — first to maintain the culture of their homelands (many at that time had come to Britain as young adults), and, second, to present culture as part of a wider political struggle. Fixed events like the annual African Liberation Day, evenings of the nascent Black Power movement and the foundation of publishing houses such as Bogle L'Ouverture and New Beacon Books were such rallying points.

They were overwhelmingly self-funded, existing on community support or the support of the like-minded. Few surfaced in records of local authorities to whom I referred for information for *The Arts Britain Ignores*. Indeed, a number of local authorities took issue with the very terms of the enquiry, stating that they 'treated everybody in the same way', and did not create categories. Although this was a fine principle, the facts showed that it did not apply in practice. 'No discrimination' paradoxically meant discrimination. There was little communication between arts funding bodies and the arts in question, and very little knowledge of the other on either side. The artists themselves were, I found, often surprised that they might be eligible for funding at all, because 'we're not English'.

The Arts Britain Ignores argued that the canon of funded arts should change: that artists (and audiences) paid their taxes and should be accommodated equally. Furthermore, the presence of new arts and artists should impact on major British institutions and arts training courses. These needed to expand their agendas and widen their perspectives in order to take advantage of what was seen as a potentially richer cultural life for all. It also recommended the development of a network of black infrastructure in order to provide the breeding ground for new artists and showcases for existing ones. Funding, promotion, training and infrastructure — these were its broad areas of attack.

The principle of equal treatment was accepted readily by the Arts Council of the time, and the regional arts associations. However, although the door was now open, it became apparent that very few artists were making their way inside. Why should this be?

Very simply, it was because the product did not fit the vehicle. The arts funding system had been constructed with certain assumptions in mind about the way the arts functioned, who they were for and in what sort of contexts. By and large, the newcomers confounded the system. They tended to cross boundaries between art forms, combining music and dance, for instance, in one event. This created difficulties for a system that (despite the existence of opera) divided them up for funding purposes into Music, Drama, Dance and so on. The context in which the new arts existed also crossed boundaries too, blurring the lines between cultural, social and religious occasions. This tended to be seen as producing 'impure' art by the funders, and a bar to support. Lastly, they were largely created by people who did not (indeed, could not) depend on their art for a living. This meant, in the eyes of the time, that they were 'amateur' and hence suspect in terms of quality.

These factors and others meant that artists from these areas were inevitably debarred, regardless of the standard of their work. This resulted in confusing messages: a welcome mat by the closed door. Nor did it did help that the arts funding system lacked in-house expertise to deal with these arts. While it is true that appreciation and understanding is not ethnically limited, it is also true the sense of gut familiarity that comes from daily immersion is hard to reproduce. One music officer at a regional arts association of the time put it very well and honestly: 'When it comes to the twenty-first application to put on The Messiah', she said, 'I know exactly where it's coming from, but I just haven't got that feeling with this work'. How could dance officers who don't know the style assess the claims of a Bharat Natyam application? Or the rival claims of carnival applications? The system attempted to address this vacuum of expertise by co-opting ethnic spokespeople on to its voluntary panels, but more often than not this resulted in tokenism, with the people themselves feeling marginalised in an opaque culture with its private language.

This impasse was tackled in 1986 by the 4 per cent rule. This was a strong recommendation from the Arts Council that all its funded bodies and regional arts associations should make sure they spent 4 per cent of their budget on what had now come to be called 'black arts' over the next 2 years. (The figure was selected because it corresponded to the percentage of ethnic minorities in the overall population at the time). On the plus side, this did address the block whose existence was now beginning to be accepted. It was an appropriate challenge.

However, three factors played against it. First, it encouraged tokenism. Bodies clearly felt this was yet another Arts Council diktat that they needed to take into account, without addressing the reasons for the diktat. The classic example is of Glyndebourne Opera House that records show to have reached the 4 per cent target in the following year. However, this was because they had staged a production of 'Porgy and Bess' with its all-black cast. No one who has been to Glyndebourne recently would be able to see the continuing effects of that brush with diversity.

Second, it failed to address the central problem of how change should be 'mainstreamed'. A theatre might, for instance, employ a black writer or choreographer in residence for a time, but how should their impact be built into the system? How would the writers' groups, youth dance groups and networks that could have resulted be sustained? How would that be covered in the budget? Diversifying an organisation needs structured planning, long-term commitment, insight and vision.

Third, it inspired resistance on the part of both white and some black artists and arts organisations. White organisations intrinsically in favour of diversity rejected what they felt was instrumentalisation of the arts. They claimed the right to reserve their artistic freedom and not to paint, as it were, by numbers. A number of black artists felt that it ghettoised them, painted them as victims, and also would give the impression – where they got jobs – that they had got them not for their talent but for their race.

However, although it is easy to excoriate the 4 per cent rule (and the Arts Council's heart seems not to have been in it since it was not systematically monitored and pursued), the attempt does bring us back to the important questions. How is change achieved in the arts? Does an Arts Council – or policy-making body in general – lead public opinion or follow it, and what is the role of the artist? The moral of the 4 per cent history needs to be interrogated. Was it a failure of nerve or a failure of timing?

Although it is frequently claimed that 'you can't change human nature', it is clear that policy can change ideas of what is acceptable. Smoking, seat belts and alcohol consumption are all cases in point. Old films show cigarettes as an accoutrement of sophistication, their heroes and heroines lighting up with not a hint of anxiety. Clicking one's seat belt into place in a car is now almost second nature. And who would now approve of the person who cheerily calls, 'One for the road!' before downing another pint and driving off unsteadily into the night? Smoking, drinking and road safety have all been the object of sustained government education programmes. They have all worked against ideas of physical attraction and personal freedom that were embedded in the culture. And they all appear to have succeeded in changing people's views and values. It would not seem out of the question for cultural policy to assist in a change whereby an all-white (or all-male) board room, audience or arts programme comes to feel instinctively wrong.

Although it always seems as if 'nothing has changed', there have been quite significant changes in attitudes and policy since 1976. Initially, the policy aim was benign acceptance. The arts were seen as belonging to previously excluded minorities, and moreover people whose exclusion in the social sphere was well documented. A decent society, it was felt, would appreciate difference and support peoples' right to self-expression, albeit of a different type. In the 1970s, immigration was still new, and ties to mother countries for many were strong and vibrant. Cultural policy endorsed the right to be different, and for society to support self-chosen difference. But although there was lip-service paid to the principle of equality, the tools and structures were not put in place to make that aspiration a practical reality.

By the 1980s, protests from the artists themselves had had an effect, encouraging a recognition that the mainstream itself needed to shift. Funding was finite, so redistribution of funds had to be considered. A return to 'zero funding', one activist demanded – in other words, every arts body, whether the Royal Opera House or Adzido, would start at the same point with no points given for longevity or status. The 4 per cent rule was the funding body's attempt to respond to this very real claim of disadvantage. However, it is notable that the terms of the debate were still based on a form of essentialism: black arts and white spaces. But it was even then becoming harder to define exactly what 'black arts' were. The increase of public voices by the artists themselves meant that easy solutions or formulas would be challenged and would not always hold water.

In response to the recognition of complexity, theories have shifted. Where the category was once 'black arts', now 'cultural diversity' reigns: a term that is both frustratingly and usefully vague. What is 'diverse', ask critics: surely every society is diverse? Surely it means everything and nothing? Interpretations of the term compound the difficulty. For some arts funding bodies, 'cultural diversity' includes disability issues. The Arts Council's new Diversity Directorate now has three strands – disability, social inclusion and ethnic (or cultural) diversity.

Meanwhile, moves through UNESCO and the Council of Europe press for a view of cultural diversity that will acknowledge the intrinsic distinctiveness of each country, in the face of homogenising America-led globalisation. This would support a form of protectionism that would, for instance, defend threatened languages or art forms like film that haven't (unlike Hollywood) the sheer base of audience numbers to provide a livelihood. The main danger of this is that the heritage views of national cultures so frequently promoted under its banner tend to be conservative and traditional, and not to take in the diverse mix that now makes up all Western nations. It also tends to isolate and to ignore the dynamic relationships being forged across cultures internationally, sometimes from the basis of diasporic thinking.

While the UK's own formulation of 'cultural diversity' can be criticised as meaningless and negative, it can also be seen as visionary and positive. What it still lacks is the kind of methodology to make it a realistic instrument of policy rather than a catch-all. 'Cultural diversity', said the earlier Museums and Galleries Commission (precursor of Re:Source),

> refers to the complex composition of society. It acknowledges that it is made up of interest groups that are often very distinct, while holding to a general commonality. These interest groups may be regionally-based, ability-based and so on. Each can have its own sense of history, its values and a specific "language" or form of self-expression. Put together they are responsible for the rich layering that constitutes society.
>
> (Khan 2000)

What this useful definition does not touch on is the fluidity of boundaries. By the 1990s, the difficulty of identifying 'black arts' had become more acute. Some artists rejected the term, stressing their right to be regarded as an artist first and foremost. And art forms that had emerged from an ethnically distinct base, like Bhangra or Bharat Natyam, acquired a different patina by association with different art forms. How to place the work of Akram Khan, say, who uses his training in Western contemporary dance as well as his strict training in the South Asian classical style of Kathak? If white people participate in playing carnival, are they *de facto* 'culturally diverse'? If Talawa chose to stage *Antony and Cleopatra*, is this 'black theatre'?

Borrowing, sharing, exchanging became more and more common across racial lines, with the road being opened significantly by music, so often in the vanguard. This sense of ease is new, quite different from the impulse that once upon a time inspired 'fusion arts', that often concentrated on the destination and the outcome rather than the journey. Talvin Singh, Nitin Sawhney, Shobana Jayasingh, Keith Khan and many others pick and choose elements that relate to their own aesthetic imperative. The result is filtered through British society and Britishness, because this is where they live and this is the air and the influences they breathe. Even calling the work 'hybrid' assumes a state of affairs in which the arts were ever 'pure' and uninfluenced by outside forces.

This ambiguity is why the term 'multiculturalism' has been quietly dropped in arts funding circles. They have long been aware of the traps it contains, such as those listed by Yasmin Alibhai-Brown in *After Multiculturalism* (Alibhai-Brown 2000a). Ambiguity is in many ways at the core of new developments. It can be found in the work of the artists cited above. It can be found in the inspired mixing of hip-hop and performance art in the work of Benji Reid, in the fascination that so many artists of 'ethnic' backgrounds find in life at the crossroads or on the sharp cutting edge of identity. It is embedded in the personae of Homi Bhabha's 'vernacular cosmopolitans' (Bhabha 1994) and the writers of *Voices of the Crossing* who talk about the impact of relocating themselves from the Caribbean, Africa and the Indian sub-continent on their creative processes (Dennis and Khan 2000).

The growing acceptance of multiple identities as a reasonable concept recognises ambivalence as a simple fact of life, part of the diversification of society as a whole. The characters in Zadie Smith's *White Teeth* live happily enough in a world where the races mingle. Monica Ali's streetwise young Bengalis in her novel, *Brick Lane*, have constructed their own idea of Bengali roots and the nature of Islam. The agony of choice and of a 'culture clash', so meticulously documented in earlier novels, has diminished. This is no longer – the message appears to be – where it is at. The message now is negotiation rather than choice.

This is a very different lesson from the one posed in the 1970s where ethnicity was a matter of separation, and of the right to be separate. The new perception is complex and still has to be satisfactorily decoded by arts funding bodies. What is clear is that it carries profound implications for the way that arts and heritage are seen as a whole.

In 1999, the Arts Council was joined by the Heritage Lottery Fund, Museums and Galleries Commission, North West Museums Service and North West Arts Board in a major national conference that directly addressed the issues of heritage. Called 'Whose Heritage?' it had a keynote from Stuart Hall that proved to be seminal, ably backed by a second keynote from Maya Jaggi. The series of workshop groups tackled different aspects of heritage – the redefinition of landscape and natural heritage sites by the Black Environment Network (BEN), the documentation of heritage from Black Cultural Archives, Talawa Theatre and Pigeon Films, the impact of new technology on the work of artists like Simon Tegala, and the power of networks by the African and Asian Visual Artists Archive (AAVAA). The central theme however involved a paradigm shift, requiring an acknowledgement of the way in which concepts of heritage are formed. The arguments and examples all pointed to the need to deconstruct the idea of heritage as an absolute version of truth, and for groups that had been cast as marginal bit-players to find their place in the main drama.

The excitement of the event sprang overwhelmingly from Hall's keynote – when walls come down, fresh air bursts in – but it was compounded by the presence in equal measure of three constituencies that rarely met in one room. These were representatives of the museums and heritage sectors (including major funders), black, Asian and Chinese artists, and arts administrators, funders and policy-makers. The mix made for a number of powerful exchanges and an escape from that bane of conferences: rows and rows of safely unchallenged faces, the familiar 'usual suspects'.

The conference reconfigured ideas of culture and identity. It turned its back on old ideas of 'in' and 'out', the core and the 'other', and sought a new interpretation of relationships. For those of us who had been at the packed meetings of ethnic minority artists in 1976, to consider the findings and recommendations of *The Arts Britain Ignores*, the distance covered was staggering. The first meeting had carried a powerful charge – it was the very first time that representatives of different ethnic groups had come together across the country *en masse* to state their case and to make common cause. The power of association was palpable. This conference had a similar feeling of energy arising because people had been released from constricting frameworks. In 1976, it was escape from invisibility; in 1999, it was escape from marginality.

The status of the debate confirmed that. This was a conference constructed with the artists and their experience very much in the driving seat. The strength of the arguments directly affected Arts Council and museums' thinking, demonstrating a subtle change in the relationship between the funders and the funded.

This was noticeable in the following Arts Council conference (with the British Council and London Arts). This one examined the way in which diaspora perspectives on the part of artists affected ideas of nationality. Called *Connecting Flights: New Cultures of the Diaspora*, it brought together concrete examples of thinking and working across boundaries.[2] Sample partnerships between London, Johannesburg, New Delhi and New York provided fodder for debating the nature of cross-frontier partnerships. This was an exercise diaspora communities have long mastered, since they have an ability to think double: to be based in one country and to think globally. But this is not just a diaspora skill now. Increasingly, artists of all backgrounds are using the internet to locate partners of choice rather than of shared ethnicity. The connections made often exist outside official and conventional channels, and in their own way subvert both nationalism and global homogeneity. 'Globalisation from below', it was called approvingly by Stuart Hall, when he responded to Shekhar Kapoor's keynote speech.

The panorama presented by both these conferences was so dazzling as to make an observer feel all is right in the world. The thinking was profound, the vision was startling and its humanity was central. What more can be wanted?

Unfortunately, the view from the high ground is not the whole story. While some artists can climb the heights and feel it is their natural element, the view from the ground is far less glittering. Here statistics show ongoing inequality in the matter of jobs, opportunities, training and grants. Almost all the 65 black, Asian and Chinese arts administrators interviewed for the Independent Theatre Council's *Glass Ceiling* report had directly experienced racism. Hardly any non-white person heads a major arts venue, and very few make it on to the boards of national flagship institutions. Reports that probed the causes of the disturbances in northern mill towns in 2001 deplored the gulf that existed between Asian and white communities – different schools, different jobs, different geographical areas, different lifestyles. The Arts Council's *Arts: What's in a Word?* (Jermyn and Desai 2000) recorded the views of black, Asian and Chinese people who would not visit mainstream arts events because they thought they would feel 'out of place'.

At the same time, arts policy-makers are faced with other agendas – the desires of people who desperately want to maintain their own culture in its apparent original purity and feel the funders fail to understand it, the under-recognised needs of refugees and asylum-seekers, the anxiety of mainstream Britain at its own loss of identity with devolution, the voice of a number of black artists who themselves are now rejecting the term 'cultural diversity'. The time for a single black arts policy has long passed. The implications of diversity now infiltrate a wide range of areas – urban planning, international cultural policy, social policy, employment, equal opportunities. Diversity has moved, imperceptibly, from a marginal matter concerning immigrants, to a theme that runs through the whole of society.

More than that, it has consistently proved to be a dynamic agent for change. In the 1980s, it was a catalyst for the rethinking of arts funding structures. In the 1990s, it stimulated rethinking over heritage. In the 2000s, it suggested that borders and boundaries are porous, and the world is actually connected. It has generated controversy, it has challenged convention, it has signalled the need to find alternative ways of thinking. The modest phenomenon of 1974 has turned into a major factor.

Ironically, though, its very energy could work against it. High-profile practitioners put out the message that all is well with the world, and that quality will naturally rise. The Ofilis, Kureishis, Kapoors are all there: *ergo*, no action is needed. The new myth of multicultural Britain allows uncomfortable facts to be ignored. The success of the Ofilis does not mean that the world from which they have emerged has become miraculously transformed. Inequality still reigns – it would be surprising if it had slunk away so easily. The voices – honest though they may be – that proclaim all is well are siren voices. They attract those for whom change is troubling, and in the process they run the danger of shipwrecking a genuine push for social change and cultural regeneration. To be holed by failure is regrettable; to be holed by success is tragic.

Notes

1 A. G. Hines (Chair), Taiwo Ajai, Norman Beaton, Peter Blackman, Stuart Hall, Ravi Jain, Shantu Meher and Ossie Murray.
2 *Connecting Flights: New Cultures of the Diaspora*, conference organised by the Arts Council of England, the British Council and London Arts, held at the British Library, 7–8 November 2002.

9

WHAT A DIFFERENCE A BAY MAKES

Cinema and Welsh heritage

Gill Branston

Introduction

Cardiff, where I live and work, is still sometimes conceived of as part of a 'non-authentic' or 'English' Wales. It gets represented as cosmopolitan, English speaking and urban, in a perceived opposition to an indigenous, 'language-d' (by which is always meant only the Welsh language), and rurally rooted Wales. Such a city's presence within an overall nostalgic national image has its advantages, especially when attempting to re-brand that country as both quaintly archaic and multiculturally modernised.[1] But it has tended to marginalise the complex experiences of those Cardiff dwellers who, historically, lived an earlier, often painful but also zestful 'cosmopolitanism'. Their memories, with a now familiar irony, have been recollected partly through a history project subsisting in the space left by demolition of their part of the city in the drive to waterfront modernisation. The precariousness of this memorialising process seems related to difficulties representing, as part of Welshness, other contemporary global flows and their consequences, especially the range of asylum-seekers and new languages which now inhabit the city and elsewhere in Wales (see Speers 2001; Welsh Language Unit 2003).

The research took the form of oral history work and archive/cultural studies exploration of memories and histories from the 1940s and 1950s (with a few reaching to the 1930s) of that part of the one-mile long docks area of Cardiff where 'mixed race' people tended to be concentrated until around the 1960s. It was named Butetown after the Marquis of Bute, a key figure in Cardiff's heritage, celebrated as one of a local family which later indulged in some wonderfully baroque castle building, but also describable as part of Scottish aristocracy, who made economic migrations from time to time to their South Wales estates. He was one of the biggest landowners in nineteenth-century Britain (see Davies 1982), whose enormous land and coal revenues financed the development of Cardiff docks, which further added to his fortune. His family name was given to the building where I work, and to many other landmarks in Cardiff. Butetown seems to have been divided into the northern part, 'Tiger Bay' or 'the Bay', and the southern 'docks' area. However, the whole was often called 'the Bay' or 'Tiger Bay'. Its image now resonates 'Shirley Bassey', literally wrapped in the Welsh flag at the millennium celebrations, but with only vestigial ties to the Bay, which she left aged two. Since the history project uses the term 'Butetown', so will I, mostly, though with a sense of its trickiness.[2]

Researching past cinema-going in such a racially and ethnically complex[3] area of Cardiff inevitably involved me in powerful popular discourses around 'heritage' and 'Welshness', still played out in dominantly masculinist histories and heritage displays. At the same time they highlight a long established, fluid multi-ethnic community within a South Wales which is often perceived as white and emphasised as indigenous. Both the emphasis on a dominantly rural nation, a 'long-rooted' Welshness (the image is striking in this port context), and also the emphasis on heavy industrial production are perceived as masculine and primary, and are emphatically separated from consumption, gendered as female, and secondary. Both, of course, are implied to be 'white'.

This piece is part of recent efforts to render visible non-white experiences of Welsh residence, including anti-'black' racisms across Wales, which are by no means limited to the activities of the British National Party (BNP). Such practices are rather different to political positions which locate racism and migration solely in Welsh–English conflicts, including blaming 'inward migration' of the English for the demise of the Welsh language and especially of that oddly designated group, imagined as both genetic and cultural: 'native born Welsh speakers'.[4]

In focusing on cultures of leisure rather than of work, and mostly on Hollywood movies, such research also cuts against other grains in histories of Wales. Where these attend to cinema-going at all, they have tended to construct Hollywood films as leisure activities associated with a suspicion of consumption, and therefore as trivial and illegitimate (and by implication female?) compared with more virtuous, male-dominated leisure worlds – the respectable activities of choirs, rugby, boxing and Working Men's Clubs, 'chapel' and miners' institutes. Mainstream cinema audiences' pleasures are often simply not included in the mass of nostalgic and communitarian celebrations of such 'typically Welsh' shared activities. This 'virtuous leisure' of course is rarely perceived as having functioned to reprime ordinary people for their working existences, as cinema regularly has been. And audience engagements have often been excluded from writings on Wales and cinema, which proceed mostly via textual analysis, presuming certain effects on audiences.[5] Ironically, within such powerful contrasts, *male* enjoyment of Hollywood cinema forms is also often written out, or simply not recollected, perhaps as part of an attempt to deny the pleasures of 'Mam' and her world. As a result, the history of mainstream cinema exhibition and reception in Wales has also been constructed in opposition either to documentary, or to the revolutionary cinema of the 1930s (see Ridgewell 1995 for the complexities of this contrast), sometimes crystallised around the black political activist and star, Paul Robeson, with his many and inspiring links to South Wales.

The research and its issues

I began the research along two routes. First, I got to know the work of the Butetown History and Arts Project (BHAP), founded in 1987 and emerging from interview work by African-American anthropologist Glenn Jordan who had set about creating an archive of local people's memories, documents and photos, initially via a weekly oral history class (see Benjamin: 2002). This work crystallised, most recently via the hard work of getting Home Office and lottery grants, into the BHAP. However to Jordan's and others' disappointment, rather than having its own building, where this part of the Cardiff story could be represented and even intervene in the ongoing redevelopment, it is still only a small gallery space which houses its 450 hours of oral histories and 3,000 photographs, plus videos. It is an unjustifiably marginalised part of the Cardiff Bay Development Corporation's (CBDC) £1.66 billion 'redevelopment' of the docks begun in the 1960s, which redesignated the whole area 'Cardiff Bay'. At the time of writing Jordan and other project workers have never been consulted by the CBDC as to how the multicultural history of the area might play into 'heritage' developments.

Maybe now, in 2004 there are only a few people without 'a friend, relative, or co-worker who is not on the road to somewhere or already coming back home, bearing stories and possibilities' (Appadurai 1998: 4). But I was struck by the *early* historical-cultural richness of Butetown. It grew from 'black' settlements, beginning in the nineteenth century, of resident and transient seamen. Some of them jumped ship, seeking a kind of asylum, keen to conceal/change their identity, and then married into families which were already ethnically complex, notably from Ireland and England, economic migrants drawn to South Wales by heavy industrialisation and unemployment elsewhere. All this offers a vivid contest to 'sealed' versions of Britain as a sceptred isle, and of the edges of Wales as landlocked, rooted in Celtic mists, the 'border country' of Raymond Williams' writings on South Wales. For 'black' does not begin to describe the set of richly mixed ethnicities and imaginative affiliations in the history of 'the Bay'. I was proudly told there had been 57 different nationalities there, a statement which the BHAP verifies, and is more than a play with the old 'Heinz 57 varieties' advertising slogan (sometimes used negatively to signify 'mixed race' communities): 'We even had a Red Indian. Do you remember his tent? But we never had an Eskimo, did we?' (Olwen Watkins). All this was well before the 1948 *Windrush* and those other immigrations usually given as dating the beginning of 'multicultural Britain' and seen as part of 'post-modern hybridity'.

Second, I was excited by Joanne Lacey's work (Lacey 1999) with white working-class women cinema-goers in Liverpool and their 'utopian' enjoyments of 1950s Hollywood musicals. She focused on the ways that a port location and its immigrant communities (white Irish in this case) constructed ways of locating 1950s 'American-ness' within often hostile British discourses around the US and consumerism in general. I wanted to see how this applied to 'Tiger Bay' but, as it turned out, I had delusions about how precisely focused the work could be. It had to subsist in the spaces left by other parts of my life and job, and, unlike Lacey, I did not come from the neighbourhood being researched. Her all-women interviews were able to centre tightly on the 1950s, and shared viewings and discussion of *Calamity Jane* (US 1953). I made 13 interviews – six women and two men plus one man who emailed answers about his early life in nearby Grangetown. I used open, fairly non-directive questioning, at people's homes, in coffee mornings or small group discussion at the BHAP. Since they are now mostly in their sixties and seventies their memories range from cinema-going in the 1930s to the 1950s. This made a fine grained focus on one film impossible and, indeed, less interesting than the speculations and archival research prompted by such memories. To my surprise, discussions also opened into the topic of film production, since 'the Bay' was used as a source for the casting of at least two major British films: *Tiger Bay* (UK 1959) and *Sanders of the River* (UK 1935).

I'm aware such work raises familiar theoretical and methodological issues, and the relation of power between interviewer and interviewees such that I could take this whole chapter discussing them. A delicate balance is needed between an academic authorial voice displaying its self-reflexivity, and a certain sidelining of other collaborators, voices, within such an article. The prime author's self-reflexing can further make the retrieved voices themselves seem less self-reflexive than they give evidence of being. Yet precisely these power imbalances means it seems wrong not to briefly mark the narratorial problems in some way. So this research does not escape discursivity, and especially the ways that memory is never simply about the past but about the relationship between past and present, including the interview, the 'material conditions of remembering' (Lacey: 56). In this case the Butetowners' remembering was made with a white, female, middle-class academic, *audibly* from outside the area (though I have now lived in South Wales for the largest part of my life) who had herself to be hospitably 'translated into' some discussions. The sheer demands of sociability needed for such interview work (far from unpleasant) meant that I could not easily impose my imagined priorities on the flow of the conversations. I experienced the 'important methodological possibility . . . of being surprised, of reaching knowledge not prefigured in one's starting paradigm' (Willis 1980: 90).

A special kind of 'double discourse' (Stacey 1994: 318) operates in discussions with those who are part of a well-established history project. Personal memories, the first discourse, seemed to be put in play with and take on the lustre of a more elaborated historical self-awareness. (This is over and above the issues raised for oral history of older people's memories, discussed so well by Thompson: 2000.) Some anecdotes seem to have sedimented down, told already, and then solicited again and again in funded oral history work operating over 15 years. Partly, too, the stories themselves often seem to have been shaped by an awareness of the 'inside/outside' structure of remembering painful experiences of racial identity (see Jordan and Weedon 2002: 175; and Dicks 1999), people using several names (from 'community' to 'ghetto') for the place where they happened. For me all this played with my structures of expectation, which were partly the usual academic fantasies of power in organising an object of research. But also, coming from a university sector structured in competitiveness, I enjoyed the Butetowners' hospitality, and the nostalgic 'inside' tales of past 'community'- the houses unlocked all day, money left on the table for the milkman to collect, the sharing of both hardship and entertainments, and so on. This pleasurable exoticism exercised a power both for me and, it seemed, for those relishing the memories, *despite* an awareness of the always double-edged nature of 'community', and the golden tinge to the memories, inflected by the Butetowners' need to try to reverse racist accounts of their area. These other accounts, featuring images of knives, drug dens, prostitution and criminal darkness, were drawn on as late as 1997 by the Crown Prosecutor during the now notorious wrongful arrest and conviction of the 'Cardiff Three' for murder of a prostitute in Butetown (Jordan and Weedon 2002: 171; also *www.innocent.org.uk*) in a trial held forty miles away in Swansea where jurors were less likely to have first-hand knowledge of 'Tiger Bay'.[6]

What difference(s), what 'escape'?

Within general histories of Wales, Hollywood cinema has been mostly ignored, or if mentioned, is implied to be outside properly political concerns (apart from its assumed reproductive function for oppressive ideologies). This is despite its popularity: Miskell cites admissions at over a million a week in 1951, easily outstripping those for rugby or football matches (Miskell 1997: 53). In some work (Richards 1997; Smith 1984; Stead 1986) such figures are often written off as simple cultural colonisation, and further, the output of 'the Dream factory' seems dismissed because it was enjoyed mostly by women, in 'escapist picture palaces'. Explicitly or not, a gendered contrast is presumed not only with work but also with the validated leisure activities of rugby or choral singing. Cinema-going is constructed as almost the defining opposite of the Welsh virtues of tough sporting solidarity and a communitarianism embodied in song, all imaged, until very recently, as exclusively masculine. Even within a valuable recent account of film and Wales (Berry 1994) cinema-going practices and audience accounts of their experiences remain relatively unexamined.

However, other recent cinema-cultural work (see Geraghty 2000; Hansen 2000) suggests two helpful moves. First, Hollywood's highly successful idiom, developed in the early US domestic market to appeal to diverse ethnic constituencies, has been a major factor in its hegemony all over the world, a success

148

achieved 'not monolithically, but by translating differently into a variety of . . . contexts' (Askari and Yumibe 2002: 432). This translation of course is not simply a textual matter but also involves audiences' take-up of the stylings and 'product placements' of a Hollywood closely meshed with other US export drives from almost its earliest years (Branston 2000: ch. 1). Second, the activity of going to see the most 'frivolous' film is a more complex matter than 'mere escapism' would suggest. Terms such as 'coping' and 'negotiating' are used now, though are still perhaps inadequate in suggesting its imaginative relation to the lives of audiences and their inventiveness around the screen.

The key differences 'the Bay' made for my interviewees involved their experiences of a both mundane and ritual cinema-going in the 1940s/50s – mundane because, as children, the low prices allowed them to cinema-go several times a week; ritual in its role as focus of fantasies, and the way 'cinema was a social place: we made sandwiches and passed them along the row' (Marcia Barry) as whole families went to the movies together and shouted at the screen. Rita Delpeche spoke of how she and her brother loved the chance to go to the Central twice a week, especially for *Three Stooges* films, when they were sent down to the front row by their mother to 'screech and hug each other with delight'. Equally, being one of seven children, she loved going to the cinema with her mother because 'then I had her to myself '.

Yet even among these memories there was evidence of coping, and of a skidding improvisation rather than simple escape. This went along with early experiences of the hybrid identities involved in viewing. Girls like Olwen Watkins, eager to get into the boys only serials on Saturday mornings, used to borrow sailors' pea jackets to wear, 'passing' as boys. Tales of under-age cin-ema-going and successful strategies for getting someone to act as accompany-ing adult for A-rated movies were told to me with an awareness that these functioned as a kind of baby-sitting device for parents. Yet, further than this, some of the girls learned to deal with 'dirty old men' who tried to touch them in the cinema, though they never told their parents of this.

Within a neighbourhood that was racially discriminated against, cinema-going took these people literally into another space than the home or the often hostile parts of the city outside the Bay (the Central cinema in the Hayes was close to but not part of 'Butetown'). It lit up another set of imaginative possibilities and connections further than the 'given-ness' of things (see Appadurai 1998 for the distinction 'fantasy' and 'imagination' in such con-texts). The Butetowners knew poor housing conditions, a low standard of living and local authority policies which favoured the segregation of the black population (Sherwood 1991). They, or their families, often had memories and stories of the post-war 1919 Cardiff race riots, when white returnees found many jobs filled by non-whites: the canon on the bridge at the top of Bute Street, police lined up there, the white mothers from the Bay going into town to find things out and shop when it was dangerous for others (Rita Delpeche). And they knew the 'banal' racism (Billig 1995) of a range of lived cultural practices.[7] It is hard to tell how explicitly formulated these perceptions were at the time: 'we just knew' was a phrase repeated: about where not to walk, try for work, play, go dancing. In such contexts, it is understandable that terms like 'escape' and 'dream' are reached for to describe the imaginative possibilities of the lives and goods on screen. Yet such cinema seems to have engaged more than a blanket escape, an easy blissing out from racism and poverty. For a start those very conditions were partly embodied in the cinema building itself and in the Butetowners' lived practices of cinema-going (Figure 9.1).

The Central Cinema, to which Butetowners began going in the 1930s (Sinclair 1997: 95), offered a very different cinema-going experience to the city centre's 'dream palaces' (Figure 9.2). Devoid of the Orientalist splendour, the first experience of central heating or fitted carpets which many of Annette Kuhn's working-class interviewees recalled in Manchester cinemas (Kuhn 2002), the Central was 'poor people's cinema'[8]: a fleapit, a bughouse, a 'sit and scratch' as such places are now remembered (Thomas 1997), a small building with a metal roof on which the rain played, showing second- or third-run films, for very low prices – 10 pence in the Central (compared with 28 old pence in Empire on Queen St). Disadvantage was embodied, rather than escaped from, in the racial discrimination of cinema owners: I was told several times that the Central began to be popular with Butetowners as 'blacks' were barred from nearby cinemas such as the Pavilion. It was closed in 1959 after fire damage; a local paper had reported a hoax fire in 1957 when a gun powder tin was 'planted next to some coloured people'.[9]

Within this socially shaped space and time, these people encountered moving images of Americanness. These were experienced within their very early sense of what certain discourses now name as the complex relations between subjectivity, 'the global' and nationhood, itself complicated for 'black' Welsh people by the British context. The way these experiences were imagined was shaped by earlier generational stories involving ethnic complexity and unpredictable connections. Rita Delpeche told me how her Jewish grandmother, aged 16, met her future husband (a seaman from Barbados with a Cuban passport) in Camden, London, around the 1890s, the first time she'd ever seen a black person. She was a little shocked, but as he came close, saw he was handsome and dropped her glove to draw his attention. They met secretly (her family was horrified – non-Jewish and black!) and she gave up all to marry him ('Fool!' said Rita, for he later left her). He was based in London but got a lot of work in Cardiff so she, then with twins, began to board here, and finally decided to move.

In 1940s and 1950s British cultural discourses, American-ness was often set up as the 'glamorous unknown', its dazzling movies and the consumer products they showcased evoking a mixture of cultural sourness and excitement from British commentators and politicians. But for my interviewees the USA was not a wholly unknown fantasy space existing only on screen. A rethink is needed of those histories telling that they and other audiences were sucked

Figure 9.1 Central Cinema, Cardiff. Reproduced with the permission of the Butetown History and Arts Project.

Figure 9.2 ABC Cinema, Cardiff. Reproduced with the permission of the Ronald Grant Archive.

unthinkingly into identification with exotic consuming passions on screen – so different to the passions and politics around industrial production, and indeed other kinds of leisure, related to male forms of work and usually identified as 'Welsh'. Like Lacey's Irish Liverpudlians (who had often seen Liverpool as simply a stopping-off point on the way to the US) the Butetowners viewed the US with the savvy of port-dwellers who were related to sailors over several generations, with relatives in the US and family experience and tales of that fabulous modernity over the Atlantic. Family and neighbourhood memories include those of Olwen Watkins, whose aunt knew and danced with Josephine Baker in the New York Cotton Club and who brought back to Olwen's home a trunk full of clothes, and photos of her and Baker. Olwen found the key to it, got her father, a docks electrician, to set up some lights in their attic and sold tickets for little concerts to her school friends. The trunk, its clothes and photos, were simply thrown out of the attic window when the demolitions of 'redevelopment' began in the 1960s. Little chance that archaeology would recover heritage material from the disposable dwellings of the poor.

Although the 'exotic' Tiger Bay was 'off limits' to GIs and British armed forces during World War Two, they nevertheless found their way there. Cardiff brides later went all over the US – to Louisiana, New York, California. The GIs brought over magazines like *Ebony*, sometimes baseball bats too – as important as movie products for the men of the bay, for whom sport, especially football, cricket and rugby, were more important activities than for the women. 'Cinema going and sport were part of a seamless whole. They felt like my culture, what anybody, growing up in the area, was interested in' (Alan Lovell). For some of the women, however, these interviews evoked a golden age of cinema-going before their lives became dominated by marriage and house-work. None of them had the tales of travel and movie-going overseas which 'call-up' meant for Freddie Manny and others.

These people's global connections and the products they saw unloaded at the dockside meant, for example, that when they saw newsreels at the end of the war, they were amazed, from the voice-overs, to realise that the rest of the audience were assumed to have never seen bananas (Marcia Barry). This was told me with a kind of pride in 'wordliness'. Location of course produced different engagements with cinema. While Kuhn reports that women who'd worked in the textile industry in Manchester loved not just the tactile impression of fabrics in Hollywood films, but the amount, the sense of abundance (Kuhn 2002), the Butetown fans Vera Johnson and her sister Woodie Wilson (grandmother to the footballer Ryan Giggs), growing up near the waterfront, loved the films of the swimming star Esther Williams. (To the horror of one of the men interviewed, children attempted to copy her baroque formation routines in a canal, which regularly claimed young lives.) Rita Delpeche told me that when she was on leave from the army (the ATS) and her sister about to have a baby, the zinc bath and hot water ready, her younger sister was told to go to the chemist for castor oil. But there was an Esther Williams' film showing,

153

and the story goes that she was so entranced by it that she stayed to see it twice to learn the words and only returned after the baby was born. Freddie Manny recalled that when *Sanders of the River* (UK 1935) was shown he and other boys rode the logs moored in the canal and chanted, pretending to be Africans in a scene from the film. He fell in the water three times doing this.

Like many other cinema-goers, these fans watched movies partly with an eye on how to achieve the performance of style. They often spotted and looked for clothes, or hats, or shoes, or simply movements, or pithy phrases, still recalled with their American inflections. The women tried to copy the fashions show-cased in American films as ingeniously as they could, sometimes requesting clothes from contacts or family in the USA. Freddie Manny got hold of a shirt with a particular neckline he had seen in a film. 'It looked so comfortable' he said. Again, the screen seems experienced, even by men, not as narcotic but through a give and take of both wonder and sharp-eyed savvy.

Casting for other connections

One intriguing difference that 'the Bay' made was to the involvement of my interviewees with non-Hollywood films. Unsurprisingly, this does not take the form of a love of Griersonian documentaries, or of British/English films of the 1940s and 1950s. Like many working-class audiences, they seem to have found English/British films 'naff'. Several disliked the accents used, the voices, as key signifiers of class, and region, contrasting unfavourably with the apparently class and region neutral accents in American movies. From another part of Wales comes a vivid account, though with a more exoticised view of America than the Butetown fans had:

America was what I admired . . . because really for Britain . . . you had the damn class system. All you could look up to was Kenneth More, patches on his jacket, like, cap and all that . . . Bloody brogue shoes, give me a break! So it was America that was classless, America that was cool. I remember thinking it would be great to drink Coca-Cola, and . . . going to Cardiff market and . . . drinking it from the bottle and thinking, this is fabulous, this is like being at some drive in or some-where, but oh it wasn't . . . a lot of people, when we were kids, would talk about going to America . . . I think it was more of an impossible dream. There was just no need to go to America. America came to us.
(Thomas 1997: 54)

Tales of discrimination from family members in the States gave some in 'Tiger Bay' a rather different take. Yet these Butetowners' non-Hollywood viewing does not relate in predictable ways to the American left-wing activist, singer and star, Paul Robeson, most famously linked with the heroicised male workers of the Rhondda Valleys via solidarity campaigns around the General

Strike and unemployment, the 1936–9 Spanish Civil War, and struggles for him to recover his passport, impounded by the US government in 1950. Such solidarities are rightly celebrated, and the Central cinema, according to several accounts, rang with cheers and applause whenever his films were shown. But Robeson was specifically connected to Butetown by visits he made there to Aaron Mossell, a black Communist activist who'd fled the USA, and an uncle by marriage. Such links are sometimes integrated into modernising discourses which seek to secure Wales for a tolerant internationalism, emblematised by the scene in *Proud Valley* (UK 1940) where the Robeson character (all too easily) overrides the mildly racist hesitancy of the colliers to admit him into their choir.[10]

Robeson was several times involved in films whose politics turned out to disappoint him (see R. Dyer: 1986). *Sanders of the River* (UK 1935) celebrated, as usual, the 'civilising mission' of an Empire defined partly by whiteness. Robeson, who, along with future African political leader Jomo Kenyatta, was enthusiastic during the production, was said to have been shattered when he saw the final version (Duberman 1989: 78–80). The film was partly marketed for 'authenticity' through documentary footage shot by Zoltan Korda in East and West Africa, and songs based on African chants. But the black baby lullabied by Robeson in the studio footage was Deara Williams, one of several Bay people who became dancers in London (Sinclair 1997: 44). Another imperial film, *Men of Two Worlds* (UK 1947) is discussed by Lola Young:

> films like [this] . . . slide between an aggressive objectification of black African subjects, marking them as an ignorant 'primitive' undifferentiated mass, and an acknowledgement that specific individuals can be redeemed by being properly schooled in the moral and cultural values of western Europe.
>
> (Young 1996: 80–1)

But Neil Sinclair, the local historian of the Bay, observes of this 'imperial project' film that many of the Bay viewers knew that the

> fire dancer was the cousin of Olwen Blackman Watkins. We all knew the witch doctor dancing wildly in the centre of the film's version of an African village was Mr Graham, the "Bengal Tiger" from Sophia Street. And that was Uncle Willy Needham leaping around in the loin cloth which he kept for years after the film was made.
>
> (Sinclair 1997: 43)

Speculatively I'd suggest that such practices produced another potential for these viewers' 'take' on British and US imperialised film practices. Bay people knew the filmic construction of 'the jungle' from the inside, indeed Robeson's films for Pinewood are part of their repeated if occasional involvement with

155

the making of such British films (Sinclair 1997: ch. 3), which of course needed black faces. Freddie Manny heard as a child that extras were transported to Pinewood studios for 2 guineas (£2.10p) a day (at a time when the average weekly wage was 15 shillings) and later that seamen from Liberia and 'the Gold Coast' were preferred for their dark skins. Racist employment practices in Cardiff meant such black seamen were likely to be unemployed and therefore the film company could confidently advertise in employment exchanges.

Such memories flash the relationship of these people's cinema-going to both play and work possibilities. The 'doubleness' of engagement is evidenced in their enthusiasm for those energetic Hollywood forms like musicals, whose numbers and songs they could learn and adapt, often by repeat viewing in such a cheap cinema (Woolworth's 6p song sheets came out about a year after the films, said Vera Johnson). But this seems to have combined with a critical awareness of such Hollywood practices as the racist treatment of black dancers or the obnoxiousness of its imperial assumptions. At least one anecdote suggests that family connections to Africa and other 'jungle' regions represented so predictably in so many films led to a lively awareness *at the time* of the limits of Hollywood imagery. Olwen Watkins as a child often went to the cinema with her Spanish-named part-Irish Filipino grandmother whose fury at the 'Filipinos are savages' parts of one unnamed film was still a vivid memory. (How can I transcribe Olwen's chuckle and tone as she told me that this gran 'also had Irish blood' as one of the Irish fleeing to Liverpool 'from the English tormentors'? She seemed aware of the excess of the description, yet also unapologetic and unironic. I asked what her gran was able to do with her anger: 'Ma used to say Gran was like Mr Micawber, "waiting for something to turn up"). Tales of relatives' experiences in the US must have further complicated simple viewing positions. Rita Delpeche told me of one Tiger Bay émigré to US 'modernity' who was told to go to the back of a queue because she was black and retorted 'I'm English and I'll behave as the English do'. This piece of self-definition struck me as revealingly different to the way that Olwen will now, very deliberately, and with a sense of how the statement resonates with her appearance, say 'I'm Welsh'.

Conclusion

The Butetowners' cinema involvements, like those of many other fans, enabled them to enact dreams of abundance, of joyful and powerful *movement* in musicals, moves which they could take out with them on to the street as they often danced away from the cinema. But these went alongside an awareness of structures of discrimination on screen, and off, and with learning the valuable tricks of a trade, of style, in conditions where jobs were scarce, usually allocated, and experienced in racist ways. These people were often defined, through their skin colour, as 'exotic' and possessed of 'natural rhythm', which in the 1950s was part of a demonised or exoticised 'jiving' and 'jitterbugging' culture (and which had partly defined the sexualised exoticism of Josephine Baker in the 1920s). No wonder some of them watched the cinema screen with an eye both to employment possibilities within a raced world of entertainment, as well as to their pleasures in dance, emphasised to me time and again – 'that was our life, dancing' (Vera Johnson). Radio and its opportunities for keeping up with popular music, in pre-television times, along with their attendance at little dance schools in the neighbourhood, were a huge source of enjoyment.

Their stories give a twist to the limited ways that the pleasures of the 'dream factory' are often understood within many versions of work, leisure and cultural heritage in Wales. Like the cinema of the Liverpool women, it seems to have been part of a conscious and creative kind of 'coping', in their case involving daily negotiations of structures of hardship and racism. These are recollected now with a little sadness and a lot of verve, largely through the activities of a marginalised history project which could and should have been given a strategic role in opening a truly contemporary sense of heritage around Cardiff's waterfront. The occasional image of Shirley Bassey as signifier of a glamorous multi-ethnicity does less than justice to the extraordinary experiences of the ordinary people of the Bay. Similarly, the modernised yet also 'heritage-d' image of the Bute family as local benefactors of Cardiff and the Bay does little to illuminate abiding structures of cross-border privilege and economic exploitation stretching back beyond feudal times – though of course it fits with the deference of many British tourist discourses in one of the few remaining monarchies of the modern world. Interestingly, the present marquis also reinvented himself, out of whatever desires and images, 'passing' for some time as Johnny Dumfries, a racing driver. He inherited £110 million in 1993 and also passes as Earl of Windsor, Viscount Ayr, Lord Crichton of Sanquhar and Cumnock, Viscount Kingarth, Lord Montstuart Cumbrae and Inchmarnock, Baron Cardiff and Viscount Mountjoy (www.grandprix.com/gpe/drv-dumjoh.html).

I hope this small-scale research can strengthen understandings of the ways that Welsh history needs to be rethought as partly constituted in long standing cross-border flows and imaginings, involving both work and leisure activities, a matter of routes rather than roots. Globalised experiences now highlight these, currently in the 'extreme' form of asylum-seeking, but they are far from new. For Wales a particularly useful contrast might be with a supposed indigeneity, often claimed to originate in a 'Celtic' Welshness (see James 1999), but also with the limiting, and white, histories suggested by the over-emphasis on a Welsh-English language binary.

Acknowledgements

Most of the voices quoted here are those of Butetowners I talked with in interviews which have been agreed by them and are transcribed in the BHAP archive: Marcia Brahim Barry, Jim Cowley, Rita Hinds Delpeche, Gerald

Ernest, Mavis Jackson, Vera Roberts Johnson, Molly Maher, Freddie Manny, Olwen Blackman Watkins. Thanks also to Alan Lovell for e-mail interviews on his childhood memories of nearby Grangetown.

Further acknowledgements

Thanks to Alun Burge, Ursula Masson, John Robinson and Charlotte Williams for help and comments; to Glenn Jordan, Tony Lewis, Chris Weedon, Julia Young, and others at the Butetown History and Arts Project (www.bhac.org), and to Dave Berry for help in the early stages of this work.

Notes

1 See recent Wales Tourist Board images (especially those targeting/seeking to construct a US/Welsh link, 'diaspora tourism' and a 'cyber-Cymric community'); the Cardiff Capital of Culture bid on *www.cardiff2008*; the *Guardian* 'Capital Cardiff' supplement 17 May 2003 and Rhodri Morgan's history of Cardiff (Morgan 1994) with its comment: 'being cosmopolitan meant that instead of just having anti-Irish Catholic and anti-black race-riots in Cardiff, we had anti-Chinese riots as well'.

2 'another area which had a similar reputation, though on a lesser scale, to Tiger Bay . . . was upper Grangetown, the area around the railway line as it leaves the Central station and crosses the Taff. Different ethnic groups settled there and apparently similar stories were told about policemen having to go in twos.' (Alan Lovell: 16 February 2001)

3 See Williams (2003) and Sherwood (1991) for useful distinctions between 'race' and 'ethnicity', and Gilroy (2002) for his provocative new term 'planetary humanism'.

4 The latest manifestation of a 'genetic' Welshness position was Jane Aaron's lecture *The Welsh Survival Gene: The 'Despite' Culture in the Two Language Communities of Wales*, Institute for Welsh Affairs Annual National Eisteddfod Lecture, August 2003.

5 See for example Richards 1997 and Christine Geraghty's review in A. Kuhn and S. Street (eds) *Journal of Popular British Cinema* vol. 2, 1999: 140–142.

6 The police reopened the investigation, after protests, in 2000 and in July 2003 Jeffrey Gafoor of Llanharan confessed and was convicted, as a result of elaborate, globally connected DNA work.

7 Olwen Watkins, as a child, was surprised, when she and her mother went into town, to be touched on the head by white people she had never met, hearing them say 'Go on, there's one, go touch it' since to touch a black child's head was believed, superstitiously, to bring good luck.

8 Alan Lovell, film-maker and theorist, who grew up in nearby Grangetown, remembered it thus. He gave me an e-mail interview in 2001 after hearing an early version of this paper.

9 *South Wales Echo*, 12 September 1957.

10 However compromised the film may now seem, Duberman notes that Beaverbrook refused to let his papers review or advertise it (Duberman 1989: 646).

10

HISTORY TEACHING AND HERITAGE EDUCATION

Two sides of the same coin, or different currencies?

John Hamer

Although much of what takes place under the title of 'heritage education' is not new, the use of the specific term appears to be of relatively recent origin. In the earliest mention I know of, Asa Briggs in an article entitled 'Heritage Education in Action' refers to the Heritage Education Group which was established as a by-product of European Architectural Heritage Year in 1975 (Briggs in M. Dyer 1986). He also notes the appearance of *Heritage Education News* first published in the same year and distributed to all schools in the country. Given its origins, heritage education was here closely linked to furthering knowledge, understanding and appreciation of the historic built environment and to using it as a resource to support the teaching of a range of subjects. In this chapter, however, I have considered 'heritage education' both more narrowly – that is I have been concerned only with its relationship to the teaching of history – and more broadly, by which I mean: first, that I have seen heritage education as relating not solely to the use made in teaching of the physical survivals of the past – buildings, historic sites, museum artefacts – but as also encompassing the non-institutionalised and less tangible – customs, folk stories, festivals, symbols and ritual. This I refer to as the *resource model* of heritage education; and, second I have taken heritage education to include the view that there is a body of essential knowledge about the past which should be handed on from one generation to the next, and that it is primarily the role of history teaching to do this. This I call the *transmission model* of heritage education.

In exploring the issues raised by the relationship between history teaching and heritage education, I want to share with you something of a personal journey. For 40 years or so I was a student, teacher, inspector – and occasional writer – of history. History was a stern taskmaster. It demanded knowledge of a wide body of data, rigorous scrutiny and analysis of sources, engagement in debate, considered judgement in the light of conflicting interpretations and strict adherence to the historical record.

Over and against history there was an odd hybrid called heritage. Heritage was frivolous – history with the difficult bits left out. It was about nostalgia. It offered a pre-packaged chocolate-box view of the past: a world where people lived out their lives in country mansions, thatched cottages set in rolling countryside, or cosy terraced houses in cobbled streets free from the grime and pollution of smoke and dubious sanitary arrangements. It was a world of cathedrals, castles and – because Britain had an industrial as well as a rural past – of redundant coal-mines and cotton mills turned into heritage centres. It was about the acting out of customs, ceremonies and Civil War battles. The maintenance, not to say the exploitation, of traditions and national icons – many of which, because I had read Hobsbawm and Ranger on inventing tradition and Roy Porter on English myths – were either spurious or of recent origin – or both (Hobsbawm and Ranger 1983; Porter 1992). Heritage, or, 'history as . . . an exploration of the frilled knickers and tapestries of the past' as David Starkey characterised it in his 2001 Medlicott Lecture, was a bad thing (Starkey 2001). The very word was, according to an editorial in *History Today* some years ago, guaranteed 'to make the crustier sort of historians reach for their revolvers' (*History Today* 1988).

And that was heritage at its best! In more sinister vein, the idea of heritage might also be used to promote notions of exclusiveness. It had overtones of national, cultural and racial superiority. No less disturbingly, appeals to heritage could be used to support repressive actions and to justify the perpetuation of injustices and inequalities. Heritage, as a former staff inspector for history in Her Majesty's Inspectorate (HMI) warned, 'has too often been the ally of despots' (Slater 1995: 8).

Given such a doubtful – even dangerous – concept, therefore, what was I, a responsible historian, doing in 1997 accepting the post of education adviser to the Heritage Lottery Fund? Here was an organisation which was unashamedly about preserving and furthering people's awareness, understanding and enjoyment of the heritage; and did so by awarding grants to the tune of over £300 million a year to heritage related projects. Was this a proper place to be? What was I doing swapping the respectable world of history teaching for the seemingly tainted waters of heritage?

I took some comfort from the words of the same *History Today* editorial that I quoted from earlier, namely that ' "heritage" . . . [is] probably still, despite overuse, the best portmanteau word we have for attempts to present the past to a general audience not already convinced of the "magic of history" ' (*History Today* 1988). And I was reassured by Raphael Samuel's argument in his essay, 'The Return of History' (Samuel 1990). Here he suggests that, despite the reluctance of scholars and purists to admit it, 'the commodification of the past', as he puts it, has been influential in the retention of history in schools. Its popularity as a hobby, a holiday pursuit and a form of mass entertainment is, according to Samuel, one of the great arguments supporting history as a class-room subject. The pioneers here, identified by Samuel as the railway preser-vationists of the early 1950s, have been followed by the vast development of history-based tourism which has disseminated the idea of a more immediate past; history as an experience to be shared rather than a remote object of classroom study. Perhaps, then, there was after all some hope that I had not moved too far in the direction of serving Mammon.

Worries about seeing history in terms of heritage were apparent in the report of the working group set up under the 1988 Education Reform Act to develop for the first time in England a set of statutory requirements for the teaching of history. As Samuel noted, the chairman of the group was not an academic or history teacher, but the owner of a Norman castle, President of the Historic Houses Association and a founder of the Heritage Education Trust. Nevertheless, in its final report the National Curriculum Working Group was coy about referring too overtly to the notion of heritage.

> We have been careful to minimise the use of the word 'heritage' because it has various meanings and is in danger of becoming unhelp-fully vague. For historical purposes the word 'inheritance' may be more precise in its meaning.
> (National Curriculum History Working Group 1990: 10–11)

Even so, whilst eschewing the word, the report's recommendations placed the transmission model of heritage education firmly at the heart of the history curriculum. Indeed, the supplementary guidance to the working group's terms of reference required it to do so – 'the programmes of study should have at the core the history of Britain, the record of its past and, in particular, its political, constitutional and cultural heritage' ((National Curriculum History Working Group 1990: 189).

In a paper published 2 years before the appearance of the working group's report, HMI, whilst noting that the concept was a complex and problematic one, had been less reticent about referring openly to heritage. One of the main reasons, they suggested, for offering a course in history to young people is that

> *the school curriculum provides one of the fundamental ways in which a society transmits its cultural heritage to new generations* (their italics) . . . History should give pupils . . . the knowledge to make sense of the many heritages they inherit and which they will be offered.
> (Her Majesty's Inspectorate 1988: 1)

That this is a primary function of the curriculum and of history's role in it are reflected in the current National Curriculum's statement of aims that, *inter alia*, 'the school curriculum should contribute to the development of pupils' sense of identity through knowledge and understanding of the spiritual, moral, social and cultural heritages of Britain's diverse society' (National Curriculum 1999: 11).

The view that developing young people's knowledge of their heritage is integral to, or indeed, synonymous with, the teaching of history has a long pedigree. And, although we would now perhaps be more hesitant than was the case 50 years ago about entitling a school textbook series 'The Heritage of History' (Davies 1950), it is a view that survives. It surfaces, for example, in the recurring debates about whether or not the curriculum contains sufficient British history. For much of the time that history has been taught in schools such a view went largely unquestioned. Seeing history as heritage was valuable not only because it informed pupils about the environment in which they would have to live and act, but also because it was a necessary part of the moral training that history teaching should provide (Board of Education 1929). An inherited past introduced pupils to their present and future responsibilities.

> If the soldiers and sailors who followed Marlborough and Wellington, Drake and Nelson, had defended the independence of this country from foreign danger, they in their turn might be called upon to do likewise. If the yeomen who supported Pym and Hampden had won parliamentary liberties, they might be called upon to defend and also to exercise these liberties. If Galileo and Newton, Pasteur and Lister and all their less famous collaborators had extended human knowledge, then here was a tradition that might be followed. If the group who supported Wilberforce or Lord Shaftesbury had reformed the conditions of the poor and the oppressed, they might also do so, or lend intelligent support to others who were doing so.
>
> (Ministry of Education 1952: 13)

By the 1950s, if not earlier, however, heritage had become problematic. Fewer history teachers now saw the past as a storehouse of moral and civic virtues which it was their job to enable pupils to enter. In an ever more pluralistic society the idea of heritage appeared redundant, even divisive. The idea that the nation's history could be presented as a series of agreed and unbroken narratives was increasingly challenged. Not, as a Ministry of Education publication in 1952 suggested, that the motive for history teaching as the conveying of tradition had radically changed; but what had changed – as it must in every age – were notions about what that tradition was and what was important to us within it (Ministry of Education 1952: 15).

It was this argument in particular – that the selection of what we teach about the past should be based upon what the present deems to be important – that influential trainers of history teachers such as W. H. Burston writing in the 1960s were unhappy with. Burston conceded that for pupils in newly formed states, where some feeling of having roots could constitute an element of stability in the community, the deliberate fostering of a consciousness of heritage might be justified. But, this caveat apart, he rejected it as a principle for deter-mining the content of the history syllabus. Inevitably, he argued, it leads to our presenting a distorted and propagandist picture of the past. 'Like happiness', he suggested, 'a true view of our heritage is most likely to come if it is not con-sciously pursued' (Burston 1963: 164–7). The teaching of history may in the event promote feelings of heritage – but only as a by-product.

Burston's position is curious in two respects:

1   Whilst rejecting the idea that making young people aware of their heritage is a proper reason for teaching history, at the same time he also appears to regard this as a desirable outcome. This apparent contradiction suggests that his primary concern relates more to teaching strategies than it does to curricular aims – about how we should go about the business of promoting a sense of heritage, rather than whether or not we should embark on the process at all. But, as a strategy, it is not immediately obvious why Burston's preferred tactic of 'heritage by stealth' as it were is any more desirable – or potentially less dangerous – than a more up-front approach.

2   Much of his argument for rejecting introducing young people to their heritage as a principle for selecting the content of the history syllabus hangs upon equating having a consciousness of heritage with the possession of particular virtues, for example patriotism or courage in the face of the enemy. But, over and against this we also have 'a true view of our heritage'. Although he does not elaborate what this might be, Burston is here acknowledging that 'heritage' does not necessarily carry with it the conno-tations that he attributes to it earlier in his argument. What he offers us, therefore, is at least two senses of heritage; and the latter he appears to applaud as a legitimate and worthy aim for history teachers.

More recently, Peter Lee in *History and the National Curriculum in England* (Dickinson *et al.* 1995) echoed something of Burston's argument.

Another agenda for the History Curriculum is offered by those who wish to promote history as heritage, or, more far-reaching, as a means of developing patriotism . . . This is unfortunate, first because history cannot *guarantee* to deliver any of the wider aims, and secondly because it has no prospect whatever of delivering them if it is transformed into something else. This is a kind of Heisenberg principle of history educa-tion: the more one tries to make history meet external priorities, the less likely it will be that they can be met.

(Lee in Dickinson *et al.* 1995: 111)

The substance of Lee's argument is that the selection of content for the history curriculum has to be governed by historical rather than some other kind of criterion – such as inculcating a love of country. To do otherwise would be to turn what is claimed to be history into something else. This is not to say that teaching history is incompatible with developing patriotism; but it is to say that such a wider priority cannot be a proper basis for judging whether or not we are successful. If in the end our pupils turn out not to be patriotic, that is not a reason for changing the kind of history we teach.

If the purposes of history teaching and heritage education – in the transmission sense – thus threaten to part company, does the resource model fare any better? In recommending that field trips, museum and site visits should form an integral part of the school history curriculum, the original National Curriculum Working Group for all its worries about heritage appeared to be on long familiar and non-contentious ground.

> The use of all the senses can help convey an image of living in the past in a way that a narrative account may fail to do. The rough feel of woven cloth, the smell of the stable or of primitive sanitation, the taste of food smoked over an open fire, the sound of horses' hooves on cobble stones, can evoke images as strong as the written or spoken word. Children can quickly become acquainted with differences between living in the past and living in the present through the use of, for example, artefacts from and visits to historic sites. They may learn, for example, of the physical efforts involved in former times when motorways, canals and railways were not available for the transport of daily essentials and of people themselves.
>
> (National Curriculum Working Group 1990: 117)

But, even here, we may have to tread warily. Not all have been as sanguine as Samuel about the growth of history-based tourism. Hewison, for example, in a book published shortly before the working group's report, saw the proliferation of museums, heritage centres, conservation and restoration projects and the like – summed up as the 'heritage industry' – as a morbid obsession with the past signifying a society in cultural, economic and social decline.

> . . . we have begun to construct a past that . . . is a set of imprisoning walls upon which we project a superficial image of a false past, simultaneously turning our backs on the reality of history, and incapable of moving forward because of the absorbing fantasy before us. This is the meaning of the heritage industry.
>
> (Hewison 1987:139)

Recently (August 2003), the BBC has screened *Restoration*, a series of programmes which focus on a number of dilapidated buildings and invite viewers to vote for the one they feel should get £4 million towards its renovation. At least one critic has attacked the programme on the grounds that 'an educated interest in architecture is one thing, but an unreflective sentimental reverence for a structure merely because it is old is sick'. He sees it as further evidence that 'In Britain today we are living not so much a restoration tragedy as a restoration farce' (Bayley 2003).

There is, then, a clutch of arguments that history and heritage, and by extension history teaching and heritage education (however it is construed), make uncomfortable bedfellows. Namely that heritage:

- focuses on the superficial and the frivolous – 'the frilled knickers and tapestries of the past';
- makes no attempt to assess the significance of things or to give them meaning;
- embodies a nostalgia for the past which stifles creativity;
- manipulates the historical record in order to serve current priorities;
- promotes values that are antithetical to history and the teaching of history;
- deals, despite appearances, not with the past at all but with a made-up commodity masquerading as the past.

What are history teachers to make of such arguments? Even where they might have felt themselves to be on safer ground, does heritage education invite history teachers and their pupils to participate in at best the trivial, and at worst a sham and a conspiracy?

Some of these dilemmas seem to be more readily resolved than others. That there is an unambiguous dividing line distinguishing those aspects of the past which merit serious examination from those which are trivial, for example, is a difficult argument to sustain.[1] Any charge of superficiality points more to matters of treatment and interpretation of the past rather than to issues of content. Hewison, whilst damning the pernicious impact of the heritage industry, suggests that the way forward is not to empty the museums and sell up the National Trust, 'but to develop a critical culture which engages in a dialogue between past and present' (Hewinson 1987: 144). And Donald Horne's proposed escape route from heritage tourism is to develop the ability 'to contemplate a monument not just according to the present stereotype, but to give it one's own meanings – and to know something about the other meanings it has had', but this 'is something that needs its own training' (Horne 1984: 251).

What is required, therefore, is that history teaching should approach those things that are presented as part of a heritage as it would other activities – film, drama, literature – that purport to offer portraits of the past. That is as a potential means of firing the imagination and of providing a gateway into the complexities of the past. But it is a gateway to be approached cautiously and critically with the awareness that what is on offer is an interpretation to be scrutinised, not a story to be assimilated. To turn to Raphael Samuel again:

> [History] teachers, enjoined by ministers to regard themselves as custodians of 'heritage', might consider the past as a means of symbolic

reassurance, as a source of borrowed prestige . . . On school trips, negotiating a world of appearances, they might like to speculate on the
deceptions of immediacy . . . And, if [they] saw their task as training
children in the use of sources, they might find costume drama or
romantic fiction more appropriate for critical viewing or reading than
pre-selected documents or graphics.

(Samuel 1998: 222)

Teaching should address not only the record of the past but also 'the hidden
forces shaping contemporary understandings of it' (Samuel 1998: 222). And
heritage is one of the shapes that understanding assumes. Approached in this
way, the resource model of heritage education is no less intellectually rigorous
and disciplined than the best of history teaching – and is integral to it.

It is not here, however, that the nub of the problem lies. Many history
teachers, as Robert Phillips and others have pointed out, become especially
uneasy when heritage, overtly or otherwise, becomes 'national heritage' and is
linked to the promotion of a national identity (Phillips 1997). Fears that behind
talk of heritage lies the presumption that there are things rooted in the past that
all who form part of the nation should be taught to value and that should be
handed on intact. To which the proper response is to maintain that heritage
education in the transmission sense forms no proper part of history teaching's
domain. Let those who will – in government, the media, advertising, the tourist
industry – take it on: history has other concerns.

Appealing though this argument is, it is not wholly persuasive. Partly this is
because of the difficulty with which, for example, Burston and the National
Curriculum Working Group wrestled – with only limited success. However
hard history teaching attempts to avoid admitting notions of heritage as part of
its purpose, or to by-pass them with alternatives such as 'inheritance', they insist
on slipping back in. And further, on the more pragmatic grounds that those we
teach will inevitably be assailed at one time or another by exhortations justified
by appeals to a national heritage – save the pound, preserve fox-hunting, retain
the House of Lords, show the Dunkirk spirit – and so on. If heritage is the ally
of the despot, then our pupils will need to know their enemy. I want to argue,
then, for seeing the transmission model of heritage education – or a refined
version of it – as integral, rather than inimical, to the teaching of history.

As we are often reminded, 'the bulk of those who listen to us, and read our
writings, and work with us, come to us not as potential historians, but as potential citizens' (Barraclough 1955: 28). This is not easily reconciled with assertions that purely historical criteria should determine the content and manner
of teaching history. Rather, the nature of the audience suggests that answers to
the question – 'why should history have a place in the school curriculum?'-
have to be more instrumentalist than such assertions would allow. Although
Peter Lee congratulated them for not doing so, the original National Curriculum Working Group recognised this in their statement of the purposes of

school history. In *History in a Changing World*, Geoffrey Barraclough went even further. He suggested that we must seek not merely for history teaching but for history 'an end outside itself . . . its study should have a constructive purpose and a criterion of judgement, outside and beyond the historical process' if it is to be taken seriously as other than an abstruse and irrelevant activity meaningful only to historians (Barraclough 1955: 29). The notion of heritage provides the sense of relevance that Barraclough was concerned history should offer.

To describe something as part of a heritage is to pick out those features of the past that people – as a country, as a community, as a family or as individuals – perceive to be valuable and wish to preserve because they believe them to be a significant part of their story. Significant either as a cause for celebration or as a means of affirming identity; or, and equally importantly, because they point to evils and injustices to be avoided in the future. Heritage points to both the collective and personal relevance of history. It is a powerful and enabling concept that history teaching should not ignore.

In the book *Lost Communities, Living Memories* Sean Field writes about what he describes as the 'living heritage inside people'. 'Living heritage is also about the social connections and cultural relationships between people. People express themselves through gossip, folklore, urban legends, traditions and other forms of storytelling. These are the colourful threads that weave the fabric of communities' (Field 2001: 120). Sean Field is the director of the Centre for Popular Memory at the University of Cape Town and the book which he edited is built around the recorded memories of some of those caught up in the forced removals in Cape Town in the 1960s. The work of the centre is closely linked with the District Six Museum that has been created to capture what life there was like before District Six was designated a whites–only area in 1969 under the Group Areas Act. Field quotes one former resident visiting the museum:

> The day I left our house in District Six, never to return, I knew my life had changed forever . . . I thought my happiness had received a blow from which it would never recover. Who would have thought that, with the establishment of the District Six Museum, there would be a return of meaning into my life.
>
> (Field 2001: 121)

Admittedly, the example of District Six is an extreme case. But what I think this example shows is that presenting history in terms of people's heritage can be very powerful. It is powerful in helping individuals to build (or in the case of District Six to rebuild) a sense of self and community both by sharing what they have in common and by the realisation that what they have in common is capable of capturing the imagination and excitement of those who have not had the same experiences. It is a public acknowledgement that individuals' experiences matter.

Translating this into the school setting, I am reminded of the pupil interviewed by Denis Shemilt as part of his evaluation of the Schools Council 13–16 History Project. This boy was convinced that the events and occurrences that he would witness and in which he might be involved could never be recorded in future history books. History was about political leaders, famous people, rich people – and possibly people who lived in the home counties. History, he was sure, was not about the experiences of people who lived in Castleford (Shemilt 1980: 21).

In slightly different ways both Burston and Peter Lee equated what I have called the transmission model of heritage education with certain substantive values – notably those related to love of country. Viewed in this way, they were right to be concerned that heritage education should be seen as something apart from history teaching. Put succinctly, their argument is that heritage education here seems to be about the transmission of values which are (1) shared; and (2) validated by being inherited from the past; whereas history teaching should be concerned with the examination of the differing values which society or societies have espoused at different times.

Their arguments rest in part, however, upon something of a sleight of hand. This is apparent in Burston's indiscriminate moving between the two meanings that he accords to heritage; and in Peter Lee's distinction between 'history as heritage' and history 'as a means of developing patriotism'. In both cases, condemnation of the one – history as promoting patriotism – is offered as condemnation of the other – history seen as heritage. But, as they at least implicitly acknowledge, the promotion of patriotism and history as heritage are not necessarily the same thing. Heritage can accommodate the undesirable as well as the desirable; the unworthy as well as the worthy.

A less-confined and more multi-faceted concept of heritage – and national heritage – raises fewer anxieties that the transmission model of heritage education involves the mere handing on of a monolithic version of the past which precludes a critical approach. It retains the powerful and motivating hold that looking at the record of the past in terms of heritage can have on young people; whilst avoiding the dangers that 'teaching about' becomes 'teaching acceptance of' and 'my heritage' is presented as being superior to 'your heritage'. Pupils, as the 1988 HMI Curriculum Paper argued, should be given 'the knowledge to make sense of the many heritages they inherit and which they will be offered'. History teaching and heritage education – in the fullest sense – are then complementary activities.

Note

1 For instance, in his introduction to *The English Court: From the Wars of the Roses to the Civil War*, Starkey compares the approach adopted by the authors with that taken earlier by GR Elton. 'Professor Elton regarded "reveries on accession tilts and symbolism" as mere diversions from the job in hand' whereas 'we have found that tournaments say much about the origins of Henry VIII's Privy Chamber, and the symbolism of masques still more about Charles I's management of his court' (Starkey *et al.* 1987).

11

PICTURE THIS
The 'black' curator

Carol Tulloch

Any project concerned with reconstructing a sense of place must
be prepared to consider the definitions of the temporal and spatial contexts which are important to the development of different
phenomena within places.

(Walsh 1992: 153)

This essay has developed out of the paper *SW7 to SW9: A Case Study of
Exhibitions on Black Culture* given at the conference *Connection and Disconnections: Museums, Cultural Heritage and Diverse Communities* held at the Victoria
and Albert Museum (V&A) in 2002.[1] The impetus for the conference was an
opportunity to bring together a range of institutions and individuals from
across the country to:

examine how those involved in cultural heritage are responding to the
challenge to draw on, reflect and engage with the cultural diversity and
complexity of today's society. It will explore the nature of existing and
potential relationships between museums, material culture and communities at a local, national and international level . . . Set within the
context of broader political and social realities the conference is
designed to bring together key stakeholders, museum professionals,
educators, diverse communities and members of the general public
with a view to fostering networks, promoting debate and informing
future practice. One of the central aims of this programme is to
disseminate findings and share experience with others.

(V&A 2002)

Hence *SW7 to SW9* was one of some 19 presentations of various projects
which reflected this conference framework. It acted as a mapping exercise of
the curatorial projects I undertook during 2001, all of which raised a number of questions associated with the agency of the 'black curator' of a 'black'

organisation, and the notion of the 'black' or 'white' organisation. The presentation of an extended version of that paper here is to try to answer those questions. By choosing to do so through personal experience is an exercise in understanding an individual's sense of place in the burgeoning black heritage project in Britain. I feel this applies to all those involved, regardless of 'race' and ethnicity, and has an impact on the work conducted. In my example this takes place within the context of being black, British and a curator.

Who am I and what use am I to you?

In January 2001 I was appointed 'curator and exhibition organiser' of the Archives and Museum of Black Heritage (AMBH). This was a short-term project funded by the Heritage Lottery Fund for 18 months. AMBH was established through a partnership between Middlesex University and the Black Cultural Archives (BCA) and was based at the BCA premises in Coldharbour Lane, Brixton, London.[2] The primary aim of the project was to create a major repository of black heritage:

> AMBH aims to make its resources available and accessible to as wide an audience as possible by disseminating information on the history and culture of black people in Britain nationally and internationally . . . This pioneering heritage development will make explicit the links between the descendants of the Windrush settlers and their predecessors who came to Britain 2000 years before them . . . It is now more crucial than ever to acknowledge the historical dimension of the complex diversity which is an integral part of this country's heritage. This project will clearly be of benefit to Britain's black communities whose historical presence here has been under-represented for so long but access to the information and resources at the BCA is crucial for all communities.
>
> (AMBH: 2001)

This objective was to be achieved by disseminating information about the history of black people across the country through a programme of research and exhibitions, education and outreach. AMBH wanted to conduct some of this work in partnership with other 'black' and 'white' organisations. By working in this way AMBH, itself a product of a union between one 'black' and one 'white' organisation, actively pursued the potential to work with difference in Britain whilst simultaneously communicating the roots and connections of that difference.

My post at AMBH required me to translate this stance through exhibitions and events, rather than the establishment and care of a collection. This was my first post as a curator and came at a time when the issue of 'cultural diversity' and 'social inclusion' were urgent missives within British museum culture, the push for which is now taking successful root. I decided that of the various definitions of what a curator can be, I wanted to be an 'agent of change' who would use primarily material culture to consider the ways in which objects and forms are used to shape and define lives whether culturally, socially or politically. My vision was to employ this tenet alongside visual culture to counteract stereotyped representations and unwarranted beliefs about black Britons and the African diaspora, and a whole host of meanings and emotions that both terms resonate: migration, emigration, the control and abuse of power, the creation of new relationships and identities, the act of renewal and reconstruction of the self, the concept of 'home', the co-optation and blending of shared and/or different experiences, travel, exploration, the concept of borders and boundaries, the centre and the periphery, to be in a place but not of it. These issues forged the philosophy of AMBH's exhibition policy I constructed and was partially incorporated into the AMBH website, the organisation's global marketing tool, as a statement of intent:

AMBH wants to create a space within museum culture to question, articulate and celebrate the history and culture of the African diaspora in England, Scotland, Wales and Ireland, and thereby redeem black Britons from the sense of being 'heritage-less'. The project's exhibition policy is constructed to reflect this aspect of AMBH's identity and to gain the confidence of the public in our commitment to represent black British history and culture . . . The exhibitions will draw on the collections held by BCA and other organisations to:

- demonstrate the need for a national organisation devoted to the telling and interpretation of black history and culture, which is key to the development of a black British heritage, that will act as a major repository where exhibitions expounding information and debate on black heritage can be communicated.
- be a showcase for the rich source of material on black British history held in archives throughout Britain and to reflect the national outreach of the project, and its collaborative intent with other organisations and professionals.
- a primary aim of the exhibition policy will be to develop a collection belonging to the BCA/AMBH, therefore the exhibitions will be a ready source to acquire material.
- the exhibitions will be a means to assess the future categories of AMBH.

The exhibitions will take the form of historical surveys on particular aspects of black British culture, and will draw on other resources in addition to the collections held by the BCA.

(Tulloch 2001)

How were these goals to be realised? What value did they give to the building of black heritage in this country, and AMBH's identity during its lifetime? On reflection, as a new organisation that was burdened with being a prime mediator of how to confront difference and champion black heritage in museum culture, a series of questions arise in terms of my place within the project: what does it mean to be the new curator, who happened to be black British, of a new black project based in the so-called black area of Brixton, where all the staff were black (and predominantly female), which intended to present exhibitions that focused on black history and culture? How does one consider the binary categorisation implied by being a black heritage organisation? And what is the agency of the 'black curator' in this context? My original desire to work within the framework of a new black heritage institution, and consequently the exhibitions I hoped to undertake within its agenda, confronted issues that have already been considered by Mari Carmen Ramirez, and which provide a basis from which to help address the questions raised above. Her essay 'Brokering Identities: Art Curators and the Politics of Cultural Representation' considers curators who engage with art, identity and the periphery in the presentation of Latin American art in the United States, asking '[H]ow, then, can exhibitions or collections attempt to *represent* the social, ethnic, or political complexities of groups without reducing their subjects to essentialist stereotypes?' (Ramirez 1996: 23).

In addition to the objectives of AMBH one had to respect the differing curatorial responsibilities to Britain's black inhabitants: to consider the needs of black Britons – their hunger for their history – in a way that did not patronise them, but which matched creatively their historical relevance. Also, there was the agenda of Britain's museums and their attempts to represent this audience and draw them into their spaces. I soon realised that this was not a gentle world I had entered into, but a high-profiled programme driven by a social responsibility to ease the differences between 'black' and 'white'. I now wonder how I positioned myself *vis-à-vis* the identities of the African diaspora in Britain I wanted to represent (Ramirez 1996: 24). This aspect of the evaluation of my curatorial role at AMBH has intensified my reflective deliberation. I worked with a number of black and white organisations and individuals during the 17 months I was with AMBH, but the collaboration with the V&A was the most profound exercise in the working possibilities between two vastly different organisations – one 'black' the other 'white', one with a long established international reputation as a museological force, the other a new heritage institution with a focused agenda to champion all aspects of black history – to discuss black history and culture within a museum context to advance a more plural perspective of British history.

Worlds apart?

These very different organisations occupy vastly opposing geographical spaces – the V&A in South Kensington, generally viewed as white, safe and privileged, and AMBH's home at the BCA premises in Brixton, often stereotyped as black, crime-ridden and underprivileged. Yet the collaboration between the V&A and AMBH culminated in a dynamic force. The representatives from the respective institutions shared a 'structure of feeling' with regard to 'living with difference' (Hall 1999a: 34) which further fired their mutual desire to encourage a new audience of black people, as well as non-black visitors, to view and discuss black history and culture within their respective spaces. Thereby, together the collaboration assisted different groups to cross boundaries into spaces generally regarded as out of bounds or of no interest to them: in this case encouraging people of the African diaspora that they have a valued place in the 'white' space of the V&A. I use the term 'white' here as it was the word black visitors applied to the museum in their comments on evaluation sheets and their description of the V&A as somewhere alien, and as a space to enter with caution.

This nomenclature derives from the V&A's historical profile: 'a formidable colonial institution, situated only yards from the sites of such imperial spectacles as the Great Exhibition of 1851, the 1886 Indian and Colonial Exhibition, and the former Imperial Institute . . . indicating the web of continuities between colonial past and post-colonial present' (Barringer and Flynn 1998: 1). As the museum developed from the mid-1800s it became part of the British imperial machinery. In the expansion of the diversity of objects it collected, the museum became what Tim Barringer calls 'a three-dimensional imperial archive. The procession of objects from the peripheries to centre symbolically enacted the idea of London as the heart of empire' (Barringer 1998: 11).

Times have changed the V&A. Since 2000 the museum has made a concerted effort to embrace cultural diversity and its social inclusion initiatives have been supported by such institutions as the Heritage Lottery Fund and the Arts Council of England.[3] Effectively, this push has helped turn on its head the meaning of the V&A's engagement with the peripheries: from wanting to possess the objects of 'others', to help 'others' tell the history of those from the margins, and to encourage black people, specifically those of the African diaspora to come into the 'centre' and enter and interact with the galleries of the museum. One such example was the *Day of Record* event of 2001.

Nails, Weaves and Naturals: A Day of Record

In the summer of 2000 I was invited by Shaun Cole and Susan McCormack of the V&A's new curatorial department, 'The Contemporary Team', to work with them on their next annual one-day event, *A Day of Record*. The department introduced this innovative curatorial exercise of museum documentation to catalogue applied and decorative arts in relation to the body under a single themed day. The system forms part of the department's curatorial objective to devise a means of recording a contemporary art form. The first was held in 2000 on the subject of tattoos, and the second was on black hair and nail art entitled *Nails, Weaves and Naturals: Hairstyles and Nail Art of Black Britain – A Day of Record*, held on Bank Holiday Monday, 7 May 2001 (Figure 11.1). The decision to host this particular event had the extenuated function of contributing to the renewal of the museum's profile and desire to connect with new audiences. The organisation of *Nails, Weaves and Naturals* was supported by another V&A department, Access, Social Inclusion and Community Development. Both sections envisaged *Nails, Weaves and Naturals* as the test case for the long-term objectives of finding new ways of presenting the V&A to the outside world, addressing new constituencies and sustaining and building on work already undertaken to reach diverse audiences.[4] I was approached due to my research on dress and the presentation of self among women and men of the African diaspora, and because of my long-standing working relationship with the V&A since 1992. When I joined AMBH in January 2001 I was able to bring the event with me. The project was perfect for the initiatives that drove the establishment of AMBH.[5]

The collaboration between AMBH and the V&A was built on the basis that the former would provide specialist knowledge on the subject of black hair, nail design and black heritage; whilst the latter would supply the expertise in the organisation of such events and the cultural capital of hosting a 'black event' in a high-profile venue like the V&A. Further support came in the form of responses to my reports on the progress of the event at the weekly staff meetings at AMBH, and working closely with the education and press department of the V&A. The *Nails, Weaves and Hair* team pooled all their decisions about the development and marketing of the event, which were discussed with the key representatives of the two institutions, Cole and myself. Within this team there developed a strong working relationship where institutional sensibilities challenged assumptions about what could be provided and gained from hosting an event on black cultural practices, and consequently black heritage, at the V&A.

The remit for the event was to photograph the hundreds of hairstyles and nail art worn by black women, men and children from various backgrounds of the African diaspora and thereby place a spotlight on the wearer and the cultural impact of their grooming. The event also wanted to include the hairstyles worn by non-black men and women inspired by black culture. Primarily, we wanted to communicate the relevance and need for a discussion of the transient feature of black expression, black hair, nails and beauty that have been created out of fashion trends and cultural heritage, thus providing an invaluable resource of an often misunderstood and mythologised area of black dress. The *Nails, Weaves and Naturals* team developed a programme which extended the central piece to the day. Visitors were also provided with a historical and

174

Figure 11.1 Front view of the promotional postcard for *Nails, Weaves and Naturals: Black British Hairstyles and Nail Art*, a collaborative project between the Victoria and Albert Museum and the Archives and Museum of Black Heritage held at the V&A on 7 May 2001. Poster: photographer: Michelle Jorsling, copyright V&A Images. Reproduced with the permission of the V&A.

social-cultural context to the history and meaning of these cultural practices in order to understand the relevance of such potent black aesthetics to black identity and history. In addition, they provided a broader international perspective as many of the style motifs witnessed during the day had connections across the diaspora. This was conveyed through a series of lectures presented by practitioners and academics in the lecture theatre. Tina Daley of Ritchina Nail Art gave demonstrations and produced examples on visitors. As part of my contribution to the event I curated the photographic exhibition *Grooming an Identity: Hairstyles of the African Diaspora*, which consisted of 36 images featuring black people in Britain, North America and Africa dating from the late 1890s to the late 1990s. It was displayed in the Link Gallery of the museum from 23 April to 20 May.

The result was an incredible day. There was an unprecedented presence of black people within the museum. Of 1,236 people who attended the event, 95 per cent were black. A main concern for some of the black visitors was that the V&A was attempting to appropriate black culture, whilst others decried the use of white speakers on black issues. None the less, the majority saw the day as a positive first step in the right direction, and wanted to see more events like this within the V&A, with the possibility of them lasting more than one day and even being televised. *Nails, Weaves and Naturals* had a life beyond the walls of the museum in the form of a website curated by Cole, and a tour of *Grooming an Identity* which included the Afro Hair and Beauty Show London 2001.[6] This event provided an additional dimension and successful collaboration to *Nails, Weaves and Naturals*. Grace Kelly, organiser of the event, wanted to provide an historical context for the contemporary exposition of black hair and beauty featured in the show. The acts of documentation and practice from three very different British organisations reaffirmed the cultural importance of a phenomenon generally misunderstood as frivolous, thereby further underlining the relevance of black aesthetics on the black body to black and British heritage.

What these series of events achieved for the identity of the V&A and AMBH was immeasurable. Essentially, it was confirmation that both organisations understood the delicate balance needed to present black culture and heritage. Evidence of this was the marketing material associated with the event. The decision as to what was the appropriate image for the poster and postcards was given lengthy deliberation. Cole and I chose the image photographed by Michelle Jorsling which was used on all promotional material as well as the key press image. The poster and postcard (see Figure 11.1) were designed in-house at the V&A and the design proofs were presented at the weekly AMBH staff meeting, the *Nails, Weaves and Naturals* team and to black V&A wardens. There was a unanimous agreement on the material's potential for public appeal. This was also supported by the positive response to this material from black visitors attending and contributing to the event.

In addition to the wealth of support from black people in attending the day, the media was like-minded in their documentation and promotion, which included a 30-minute interview on *BBC London Live*, coverage by *Pride Magazine*, *Time Out Kids*, the *Independent*, the *Daily Telegraph*, *New Nation*, the *Voice*, *Metro*, *South London Press*, *Hampstead & Highgate Express* and websites such as www.wondernails.com and www.absolutarts.com. A lasting impression of the day was to see the target audience of black visitors engage with and enjoy the different spaces of the V&A – from the lecture theatre to the Indian galleries, to taking tea and cakes in Milburns restaurant. They changed the internal landscape of the V&A. *Nails, Weaves and Naturals* went beyond the limitations of a single site-specific exhibition space to a multi-spatial dynamic within the museum itself. Holding this 'black event' in a 'white' space placed all involved not only as 'agents of change', but as what Mari Carmen Ramirez calls the curator as 'cultural-broker', who has the role

> to uncover and explicate how the practices of traditionally subordinate and peripheral groups or emerging communities convey notions of identity . . . By selecting, framing, and interpreting peripheral art in exhibitions and exhibition catalogues, for instance, art curators can claim to be shaping a more democratic space where specific cultural groups can recognise themselves.
>
> (Ramirez 1996: 22–3)

In terms of the collaboration between AMBH and the V&A, this was described in the evaluation meeting by the latter as being one of the best collaborative experiences they had ever had. Thus the working partnership between a new black heritage organisation and an established 'white' museum does not have to be about co-operating traitorously with the enemy, but can achieve 'a new critical environment . . . a *mis en scéne* or setting-in-place of a sphere of interaction where the work and the curatorial strategy are intimately bound together, triggering off new technologies about making and thinking about art' (Deliss 1996: 286), and equally black heritage.

Bringing it back home

The AMBH management felt the success of *Nails, Weaves and Naturals* should be extended to other local authorities far removed from Kensington and Chelsea and so it became the focus of their Black History Month 2001 programme. For this programme I did not want the continued discussion of black hair to replicate the issues aired at the V&A event, which had concentrated on the wearer of black hairstyles and nail art and the cultural impact of their grooming. In my first solo exhibition on behalf of AMBH, which would be shown at the BCA gallery in Brixton, I decided to bring to the fore the black hairstylist in the exhibition *Tools of the Trade: Memories of Black British Hairdressing*. Here the art of hairdressing among black people in Britain could be celebrated. I wanted to alert visitors to the exhibition that black history is not only about pain and power struggles, it can also be about pleasure and constructive dialogue among and between different cultural groups. *Tools of the Trade* was supported by a simultaneous display of eight images from *Nails, Weaves and Naturals*. This display, entitled *Hair Pieces: Black British Hairstyles*, was co-curated with Joelle Ferly. It was shown simultaneously in three London establishments related to hairdressing.[7]

Tools of the Trade was built on the oral histories of six male and female practitioners who had practised hairdressing in London, Birmingham, Jamaica and Guyana and the objects associated with their craft and business profile. The first contributor was Mrs Beryl Gittens who began her hairdressing training in Guyana in 1947. She came to England in 1952 and opened the first black hairdressing salon on Streatham High Street in 1962. The second was Winston Isaacs, the co-founder of the West London-based hair salon *Splinters;* the third, Cynthia MacDonald, who opened the haircare establishment for dreadlocks *Back to Eden* in New Cross in 1986; and the fourth, Errol Douglas, based in Knightsbridge, who has been the winner of 'Afro Hairdresser of the Year'. The fifth, Sharon Miller, was originally trained by her mother in Birmingham, went on to establish her own salon, *Expressions in Hair*, in Lewisham and was personal stylist to Nina Simone up until her death in 2003; the sixth, Faisal Abdu'Allah, an artist and barber who has used the head as part of the narrative of his work.

The exhibition provided visitors with a chronology of development from the late 1940s to 2001 through the voices of the contributors. In addition, they were asked to select the hairdressing tool they viewed to be *the* essential element of their art. I wanted to give this aspect of the exhibition a special treatment, when shown alongside the owner's testimony, to enunciate the importance of the tools to their creativity. By guiding the visitor around the exhibition through personal testimonies I hoped to convey the value of black hairdressing and their practitioners. With its focus on 'things' and memories associated with an individual black hairdresser, *Tools of the Trade* illustrated what Judy Attfield has defined as being 'part of the mediation process between people and the physical world at different stages of their biographies' (Attfield 2000: 3). Here then, like the one-day event *Nails, Weaves and Naturals*, was a living exhibition with the supporting premise of how this aspect of material culture can add to the expansion of black British heritage and consequently allude to the development of another aspect of British hairdressing and its history. Essentially, it was saying that the people and their objects matter – the tools, the hairdressing certificates, the photographs, business cards, the oral histories. They matter because together they provide a history of black creativity, business and careers that is hairstyling, and the lives devoted to that practice. They matter because together they tell another story of the journey from migration to confident, vibrant communities in post-war Britain.

The experience of co-organising *Nails, Weaves and Naturals* and the consequent evaluation of the event instilled in me that to be part of the mediation of black history to a more general audience requires sensitivity. There is a particular responsibility when the process is brokered by a 'black' organisation, intimately and historically connected with the target group. This is especially acute when black people in Britain hunger for more of its history and are vigilant against acts of trivialisation of that history. I decided that for this inaugural solo exhibition for AMBH I did not want to frustrate the black public with exhibition concepts that left them gasping for explanation – this could come later. I first wanted to draw them into the gallery, win their confidence, feed their intelligence and ultimately build relationships. The architecture of the gallery heightened this desired bond. The full length of the walls which face on to the streets of Brixton are glass, which furnished the space with tremendous natural light to provide a jewelled quality to any exhibition (see Figure 11.2). Similarly, this feature allowed the passer-by to stop and view the exhibition, and so one effectively took the exhibition on to the streets of Brixton. Within consumer culture it is believed that a retailer has only 6 seconds to capture the attention of the passer-by with a window display. AMBH had on offer edification on black heritage. Bearing all this in mind I wanted AMBH's first exhibition to be straight talking.

I invited the curator and exhibition designer Judith Clark to design the exhibition space. A specialist in dress history and theory, and owner of the Judith Clark Costume Gallery, Clark was the ideal person to interpret the tangential elements that constituted the exhibition and empathised with the extenuating issues mentioned above.[8] The BCA gallery consists of two rooms divided by a beamed opening. The first and larger room housed traditional museum cases which featured the archival material of the contributors such as photographs and journals, corporate identity material, hairdressing tools and manuals. It was into this space that the visitor first entered. The second room, clearly visible from the first, featured the 'precious objects' selected by five of the exhibition contributors.[9] Clark developed this feature of their essential hairdressing tools to display them on plinths. She contextualised and connected the individualised choices with the origins of black hairdressing in Britain by using a backdrop of an interior photograph of the hairdressing salon established by the Trinidadian pianist Winifred Atwell in Brixton in the 1950s. This was reproduced into six two-and-a-half metre long vertical panels. The desired effect was achieved – not only did visitors enter the gallery and view the exhibition, but as expected, passers-by were intrigued by what was on display in the gallery and pressed their noses against the windows to study the exhibition.[10]

The promotion of the exhibition was not as extensive as that of *Nails, Weaves and Naturals*.[11] However a press release was made available, and interest was secured from BBC Radio 4's *Woman's Hour* which consisted of an interview with Mrs Gittens and her daughter Sandra Gittens, although the interview was never aired during the life of the exhibition. The exhibition was listed on the Judith Clark Costume Gallery Website, and as a result of the private view of the exhibition, I gave an interview for BBC World Service which was aired in

Figure 11.2 View of the 'precious objects' section of the exhibition *Tools of the Trade: Memories of Black British Hairdressing* in the gallery of the Black Cultural Archives. Reproduced with the permission of the photographer Alan J. Robertson.

Croatia. The exhibition leaflet acted as a substantial introduction to the exhibition's agenda, as it was the main text available to the public. Again, the image was paramount. By choosing a classic hairdressing pose of Mrs Gittens attending to a client at the Roy Lando School of Hairdressing in 1961, I hoped to convey the 'normal' quality of hairdressing among black people, which equally has its history of unique techniques and processes of styling.

As a curatorial package within the context of AMBH's aims, the event *Nails, Weaves and Naturals* and the exhibition *Tools of the Trade* and its complimentary tour of photographs, force one to evaluate the agency of the curator:

> From this point of view, curators must be able to recognise that what holds an individual or group together cannot be reduced to a particular set of traits or to a specific essence embodied in . . . [black heritage]. Neither can it be apprehended in a single exhibition or collection . . . Therefore, it is to the diversity of each group's experience, in its contradictory stances and multiplicity of approaches towards . . . [black history], that curators must turn their attention. This approach should ultimately pave the way for new exhibition models and a more authentic renewal of curatorial practice.
>
> (Ramirez 1996: 34)

The meaning of that agency has broader significance when applied to the 'black curator' of a 'black organisation'. It is not helpful to have labels such as 'black curator' as this only leads to generalisation of an individual's range of knowledge or interest. Yet within the context of the AMBH project, to be considered a 'black curator' was an inevitable label. In this light 'black curator' automatically imbues the individual with the power of a 'natural' understanding of heritage intervention and with the notion that she/he arrives readily equipped for all aspects of the post. This is a heavy burden to bear, as the curator (black or white) pursuing the progression of black heritage in Britain needs the space to develop curatorial techniques.[12] I say this because the establishment of black heritage in Britain is a relatively new process, and therefore those engaged with the building of it are learning about new audiences and new sensibilities, whilst grappling with England's colonial and imperial past in order to move toward a new dynamic museological experience. Whilst curator of AMBH the words 'marginalised', 'boundaries' and 'periphery' were not the driving force of my thinking, and with hindsight what feels more appropriate is the idea of the crossing of thresholds into new spaces – be they 'black' or 'white' – to stimulate responses and develop relationships. The agency for me was in that.

Notes

1 The conference was organised by Eithne Nightingale and Rhondda Garraway of the Access, Social Inclusion and Community Development Department of the Victoria and Albert Museum. This was part of their Heritage Lottery Funded programme *Cultural Diversity and the V&A*.

2 AMBH consisted of: Yejide Akinade, administrator; Sheila Gopaulen, researcher; Roshi Naidoo, education and outreach manager; Alice Robotham, archivist; Sam Walker, co-ordinator, and from January 2002, director; and Lola Young, director (January–December 2001). In 2002 Angela Brevitt, marketing manager, and Devinia Kelly, assistant administrator joined the project.

3 Since 2000 there has been a number of events organised by the V&A, particularly by the Contemporary Team and the Access, Social Inclusion and Community Development Department: these include 'Carnival', an extensive Black History Month programme, and 'Cultural Revolution in Harlem and Paris'. The two departments are currently collaborating to develop a black history programme which will run throughout the year to counteract the criticism that black history is generally relegated to one month – October – of every year.

4 The Contemporary Team has had the initiative to be interventionist and challenge the traditional perception of the V&A as 'élitist' through the introduction of challenging display methods and content. To host a high-profile event on an aspect of black style also fitted with the V&A's Access, Social Inclusion and Community Development Department's cultural diversity drive.

5 The collaborative team that worked on the event comprised of: Shaun Cole and Susan McCormack (Contemporary Team); Eithne Nightingale and Rhondda Garraway (Access, Social Inclusion and Community Development), Helen Beeckmans (V&A press officer); marketing person; and myself from AMBH. Shaun Cole and I were the co-ordinators of the event.

6 This was part of the October 2001 Black History Month events held at the Tate Library, Brixton and the Black British Heritage Group, Notting Hill. The photographs were also exhibited at the Design History Society Conference *Situated Knowledges: Consumption, Production and Identity in a Global Context*, at the University of Wales, Aberystwyth, 3–5 September 2002.

7 From 22 October–2 November 2001 *Hair Pieces* was shown at *Expressions in Hair*, Leyton, *Rick's Place*, Camden and the College of North West London. AMBH's Black History Month 2001 programme was supported by funding from the London Arts Board.

8 The Judith Clark Costume gallery was based in Notting Hill and had the same architectural aspect as the BCA gallery, of a large expanse of glass facing on to the street.

9 Cynthia MacDonald was not represented here as her hands were her essential tool.

10 A memorable example of this was watching three black labourers pointing and talking about the barber clippers once owned by Faisal Abdu'Allah's father, which he used to cut the hair of Faisal and his brothers as children.

11 AMBH did not have the same publicity resources as the V&A but Middlesex University were very supportive by allowing Karyn Michael from the press department to work on the promotion of the event.

12 As I had not undergone any formal curatorial training, it had been suggested by a member of the interview panel for my post at AMBH that I undertake a period of mentoring with perhaps an African–American institution such as the Schomberg research institution, or the National Portrait Gallery, London. The time-frame and funding of the project could not allow for this.

12

A COMMUNITY OF COMMUNITIES

Jim McGuigan

For the British-born generations, seeking to assert their claim to belong, the concept of Englishness often seems inappropriate, since to be English, as the term in practice is used, is to be white. Britishness is not ideal, but at least it appears acceptable, particularly when suitably qualified – black British, Indian British, British Muslim, and so on.

However, there is one major and so far insuperable barrier. Britishness, as much as Englishness, has systematic, largely unspoken, racial connotations. Whiteness nowhere features as an explicit condition of being British, but it is widely understood that Englishness, and therefore by extension Britishness, is racially coded. 'There ain't no black in the Union Jack', it has been said. . . . Race is deeply entwined with political culture and with the idea of nation, and underpinned by a distinctive kind of British reticence – to take race or racism seriously, or even to talk about them at all, is bad form, something not done in polite company. This disavowal, combined with 'an iron-jawed disinclination to recognise equal human worth and dignity of people who are not white', . . . has proved a lethal combination. Unless these deep-rooted antagonisms to racial and cultural difference can be defeated in practice, as well as symbolically written out of the national story, the idea of a multicultural post-nation remains an empty promise.

(Runnymede Trust 2000: 38–9).

Introduction

The Parekh Report, *The Future of Multi-Ethnic Britain* (Runnymede Trust 2000) was not well received on publication in October 2000. It was read as an attack on Britishness and as an expression of the New Labour government's political correctness, although the then Home Secretary, Jack Straw, managed simultaneously to launch the report publicly and distance himself from what he mistakenly construed to be its key argument. In this chapter I shall consider the reception of the Parekh Report as mediated by the national press in Britain and provide my own exegesis of it. Then, I will compare Labour peer Bhikhu

Parekh's thinking on multiculturalism with that of Samuel Huntington, the American policy expert and erstwhile advisor to the Democrats on international relations. It is important to appreciate that the Parekh Report is not only of national but also of global significance, especially so in such a period of martial tension across the world. When considering the politics of heritage in Britain it is necessary to situate particular issues – to do with, for instance, museum policies, public symbols and broader negotiations of identity within the nation-state formation – in relation to these extended theoretical arguments and cross-national debates concerning past and present-day cultural configurations.

How the Parekh Report was (mis)represented in the Press

The Parekh Report was published on 11 October 2000. Its negative reception had already been framed the previous day. A couple of *Daily Telegraph* articles by Philip Johnston, Home Affairs Editor, established the frame. On the front page, Johnston (Johnston 2000a) quoted two Conservative politicians, Margaret Thatcher's old war horse, Norman Tebbit, and Gerald Howarth, who had in his youth been associated with the radical Right. The report was immediately defined as a New Labour document, for which there was some justification. The Runnymede Trust, an independent charity, organised a commission on race relations to inform government policy. Howarth complained about the wish to rewrite British history as multicultural. He said, 'It is an extraordinary affront to the 94 per cent which is not from ethnic minorities. The native British must stand up for ourselves' (quoted by Johnston 2000a: 1). Thus, the distinction was drawn between an overwhelming majority of native Britons being asked to comply with the demands of various minorities that in total only make up 6 per cent of the population. Inside the *Daily Telegraph* of 10 October, Johnston (Johnston 2000b) praised Simon Schama's television history of Britain and the episode on the Magna Carta for recording accurately the history of an island race. He acknowledged that King John and the barons at Runnymede in 1215 spoke French. They, however, were white like 53 million of the current British population of 57 million.

Johnston (Johnston 2000c) felt justified in taking the credit for alerting Straw to the report's key argument that Britishness was inherently racist, an insult to the great majority of Britons. At the launch of the report and in a subsequent *Observer* article, Straw turned on 'the Left' for having let the Right capture 'patriotism' for itself. He went on to say,

> I do not accept the argument that Britain or Britishness is dead. On the contrary, both are now receiving a new lease of life. Enduring British values of fairness, tolerance and decency are at the heart of

the government's reforms to build a more inclusive, stronger society.

(Straw 2000: 27)

It was not far from this to infer that in attacking Britishness the Parekh Report was, in effect, attacking New Labour Britain. Was the Labour Home Secretary, then, lining up with the right-wing critics of *The Future of Multi-Ethnic Britain*? Not in so many words: yet, it was unsurprising that the New Labour government heeded the traditionally Conservative broadsheet, the *Daily Telegraph*, not to mention the populist *Sun* and conservative Middle England's favourite tabloid, the *Daily Mail*. True to form, a *Sun* leader on 12 October castigated Straw for not distancing himself enough from 'the ludicrous "British is racist" report'.

On 11 October the *Daily Mail* had a field day. Its banner headline on the front page made all the necessary connections: 'The flashy vacuity of the Dome, the trashy icons of Cool Britannia . . . and now the idea that to be British is racist. This is a government that knows nothing of our history and cares about it even less'. Inside that issue of the paper, under the heading 'Racism Slur on the Word "British"', Edward Heathcoat Amory and Gordon Rayner (Heathcoat Amory and Rayner 2000: 6) listed and described the Runnymede Trust's 'panel' members. Included, for instance, were Professor Stuart Hall – 'One of the best known class warriors of the Sixties and Seventies' – and commission vice-chair Kate Gavron – 'Third wife of millionaire publisher and Labour benefactor Lord "Bob" Gavron'. There was also a piece by a member of the Commisson for Racial Equality, Dr Raj Chandran, a Sri Lankan Tamil in origin. He defended Britishness from the slur of racism and extolled Britain's history of tolerance towards others: 'So why rewrite British history in order to junk this proud heritage?' (Chandran 2000: 7).

The point about history was picked up in Paul Johnson's (Johnson 2000: 12) article, 'In Praise of Being British': 'Britain, unlike many European nations, has a long tradition of unbiased, objective and truthful historical writing, avoiding propaganda and hagiography, and not fearing to criticise the ruling élite where necessary'. The *Mail's* leader on the same page also emphasised the issue of history and in its headline accused the Parekh Report of insulting Britain's past and the intelligence of its people.

Insults were a common feature of the Parekh Report's reception in the press, perhaps the worst of which appeared in the 'satirical' *Private Eye* on 20 October. The first of three boxed items here was headed 'Who Are They? The Great and Good Who Make Up the Runnynose Commission, Authors of *Britain Don't You Hate It? The Future of Multiculture*'. It renamed and described the members of the commission, such as:

CHAIR Lord Hoohi, lecturer in anti-British studies at the University of Humberside (formerly Grimsby Polytechnic); Mrs Pashmina

Ali–Baba Brown, Columnist on racial discrimination for the Racial Discrimination Section of The Indescribably Boring [*The Independent*]; and, Professor Adolf Wong, Lecturer in Positive State Censorship at the Chow Mein Kampf Institute, Sunningdale.

(*Private Eye* 2000: 19)

Another box on the same page, entitled 'That Runnymede Trust History of the Country Formerly Known as Britain', began '1948 AD BRITAIN first discovered by Afro-Caribbean explorers on their ship the Empire Windrush'. Ho, ho, very satirical.

You might have expected right-wing newspapers like the *Mail* and the *Telegraph* in daily and Sunday editions to be hostile towards the Parekh Report. Less predictable was the critical response it elicited from the left-liberal broadsheets, *Guardian* and *Observer*. In its front-page headline on 11 October, the *Guardian* followed the *Daily Telegraph*'s lead: 'British tag is "coded racism"'. It quoted from the offending passage in the Parekh Report that is quoted at greater length as the epigraph to the present chapter. This was picked up in the leader column on page 21 where it was said that the report's 'prescription for harmony . . . is spoilt by a bad idea'. On the following Sunday, in the *Observer*, Will Hutton (Hutton 2000) reiterated this objection at some length. He accused Lord Parekh of being 'silly', which was not the nastiest epithet applied to the Runnymede Commission's chair and principal author of the report on multi-ethnic Britain. To be fair, however, Hutton also complained of the sensational misrepresentation of the Parekh Report in the press. He argued that 'the racial connotations' of Britishness are probably true but do not actually constitute the inflamatory claim that Britishness is necessarily 'racist'. In the same issue of the *Observer*, Stuart Hall (Hall 2000a) made exactly the same point. Bhikhu Parekh was also permitted to defend the report in both the *Guardian* (Parekh 2000d) and the *Telegraph* (Parekh 2000b), for which latter he received considerable support in letters to the paper. Parekh made it quite clear that rethinking Britain as 'a community of communities' did not mean abolishing the state or outlawing the word 'British'. Nevertheless, the damage had been done swiftly and – yet again – public debate was distorted by perverse misrepresentation in the news media.

The report itself

A striking feature of the Parekh Report, *The Future of Multi-Ethnic Britain*, is its elegant combination of advanced thinking in the social sciences – including cultural studies, political theory and sociology – with a slate of practical policy proposals. The report is divided into three parts. The first part is the most abstractly theoretical, elaborating upon a number of linked themes, in formulating 'A Vision for Britain'. The second part, 'Issues and Institutions' surveys concrete matters in the areas of policing, criminal justice, education, arts, media and sport, health and welfare, employment, immigration and asylum, politics and representation, and religion and belief. The third part, 'Strategies of Change', makes a series of specific recommendations.

The report addresses terminological problems in what is undoubtedly a minefield of potentially explosive words, particularly rejecting the use of 'minorities' because it implies marginality and the existence of a homogeneous majority at the centre, which is not historically so. The British Isles had a long history of conquest, migration and the mixing of peoples and cultures well before the post-Second World War immigration from the former Empire and Commonwealth. This emphasis on heterogeneity in the very make-up of Britain over many centuries is no doubt offensive to those who would like to uphold an essential Britishness. For them the unity of Britain is not only threatened today by devolution on the Celtic fringe but is undermined by the comparatively recent arrival of alien cultures brought by economic migrants and, yet more worryingly at present, asylum-seekers. There has also been a disturbing growth of Islamophobia in response to recent events that are of global but also national significance.

According to Parekh and the Runnymede Trust's Commission on the Future of Multi-Ethnic Britain, the country has reached a 'turning point' in its history. Britain is at a 'crossroads' where choices as to direction have to be made. These alternatives are stated as a set of binary oppositions: 'static/dynamic; intolerant/cosmopolitan; fearful/generous; insular/internationalist; authoritarian/democratic; introspective/outward-looking; punitive/inclusive; myopic/far-sighted' (Runnymede Trust 2000: 4). The second terms in these binaries represent the fresh vision for Britain that is proposed by the Parekh Report: dynamism, cosmopolitanism, generosity, internationalism, democracy, looking outwards, inclusive and far-sighted.

The dominant terms still need to be deconstructed. Britain was, in effect, invented in the eighteenth century with the construction of the United Kingdom. Its values were contrasted with the traditional foe, Catholic and then Republican France. That this 'imagined community' was an historical invention makes its reinvention at a later moment in history a serious proposition. Now, it should be possible to reinvent Britain as 'a community of communities' that does not have to depend on older national and imperial myths. These are increasingly irrelevant in any case. Britain is a multicultural society but this does not mean, as Parekh has argued consistently in his many writings (see Parekh 1999, for instance), that its policies are multiculturalist. It is desirable, then, to go beyond 'multicultural drift' and develop 'conscious policies' of multiculturalism.

In chapter 2, 'Rethinking the National Story', the components of 'the dominant version' of the traditionally 'imagined community' are itemised. The widespread belief that Britain has been unified for a very long time is simply wrong, it states. The idea that Britishness is evenly diffused throughout the United Kingdom is also untrue. English experience has largely stood for

Britishness in a way that is unacceptable and no longer credible. Moreover, the British are not best thought of as an island race set apart from the rest of Europe and the world. Anti-Catholic and anti-Irish sentiment and imperial power may have been unifying, though always seriously questionable, forces in the past but they do not refer to a present reality. Furthermore, 'The roll-call of traditional British virtues – tolerance, moderation, readiness to compromise, fair play, individualism, love of freedom, eccentricity, ironic detachment, emotional reticence [etc.]' (Runnymede Trust 2000: 23) is far too complacent.

The legacy of empire carries with it the trace of white supremacy. The British Empire has gone and Britain is situated at a much more complicated intersection of global processes. Britain was never so internally unified as the dominant version of the country assumes. And, in one way or another, it has become more open to the rest of the world. There are enormous implications for identity in 'a complex, shifting multicultural reality' (Runnymede Trust 2000: 27). The cultures of host and migrant communities are in reciprocal relation to one another. A great many people feel they do not have a single and fixed identity. Multiple identities are commonplace. This has implications for how community relations are conceptualised. It is mistaken to regard ethnic communities as entirely separated from one another, as utterly distinct entities. Instead, they interact quite routinely in various ways, setting up channels of mutuality as well as hostility. There is a constant play of similarity and difference.

The key problem is how to achieve satisfactory cohesion, genuine equality and respect for difference. The Parekh Report identifies five models: pro-cedural, nationalist, liberal, plural and separatist. Neither the first nor the fifth of these models are realistic to follow, which does not mean they cannot exist. Proceduralism assumes that the state is a neutral arbiter without cultural prefer-ence. No state is actually indifferent to the customs and practices of its society. At the further extreme, complete separation between cultural communities is the end of the state and any sense of shared national belonging. The solution must be somewhere in between. Only nationalism, liberalism and pluralism can be seriously considered for the sake of cohesion, equality and difference.

The nationalist model promotes a single, unified national culture. This has already been deconstructed with regard to the multinational structure of the United Kingdom – encompassing England, Scotland, Wales and Northern Ire-land – and the sheer diversity of communities within it. The liberal model partly overcomes this problem by insisting on a single political culture in the public sphere while acknowledging the diversity of cultures in the private sphere. The liberal model is also unsatisfactory because, as the Parekh report argues, the diversity of cultures should be represented with greater symbolic force in the public sphere. This is the 'community of communities' model of Britishness advocated by the Parekh Report: 'Britain needs to be, certainly, "One Nation" – but understood as a community of communities and a community of citizens, not a place of oppressive uniformity based on a single substantive culture' (Runnymede Trust 2000: 56).

For the Parekh Report, it is vital to be clear about the principles underpinning an actively multiculturalist society in order to combat the various racisms that persist in Britain. The report makes what has become a conventional distinction between biological racism and cultural racism. There still are traces of nineteenth-century biological racism across the range of present-day racisms yet cultural racism is by far the most insidious problem now. Respectable racism is enunciated typically today by cultural arguments that may be relativistic, as we shall see in the discussion of Samuel Huntington's (Huntington 1996) 'clash of civilisations' thesis later in this chapter.

The Parekh Report distinguishes between 'overt racism' and 'street racism', on the one hand, and 'institutional racism' on the other hand. Overt forms of racism certainly persist and are stressful and, indeed, dangerous for the victims, especially in conditions of deprivation. Poverty and resentment are often closely associated with racial violence. They occasionally lead to fierce confrontation even in a relatively harmonious country such as Britain. Yet more complex, however, and harder to deal with are forms of racism that may be unintentional but are manifestly evident in institutional processes throughout British society. The notion of institutional racism, long known to sociologists, was revived and given much greater public attention by *The Stephen Lawrence Inquiry* (MacPherson 1999). The Metropolitan Police were found to have been negligent both on the night when the young black man Stephen Lawrence was attacked and in the subsequent investigation into his murder. The police officers involved had mistakenly assumed that Lawrence was involved in a fight rather than having been set upon out of the blue by a group of racists. The police also failed to put a successful case together against the suspects. Behind the police's action was a set of taken-for-granted assumptions about young black men that amounted to an institutionalised form of racism in policing which is not necessarily intended but is deeply embedded in routine practices. According to the Parekh Report, 'unwittingness' is not an adequate justification and solutions to the problem of institutional racism must go beyond 'race awareness' training for police officers and other professionals. Moreover, 'colour blindness' in public policy and practice is not good enough. Different groups are treated in different ways, the specificity of which always needs to be understood and acted upon. Britain should observe international standards of human rights as a minimum requirement for achieving a more just society and which must be supported by specific policies for eradicating racism.

The theoretical part of the Parekh Report concludes with the identification of five urgent tasks:

1 'reimagining Britain's past story and present identity';
2 'balancing equality and difference, liberty and cohesion';
3 'confronting and eliminating racisms';
4 'reducing material inequalities';
5 'building a human rights culture' (Runnymede Trust 2000: 105, 107).

The second part of the Parekh Report addresses practical matters from criminal justice to religion and belief. Here, I shall just concentrate on what it has to say about the arts, media and sport since its views on cultural policy might otherwise be neglected for the more urgent issues of, say, policing and asylum. Evidence is given of what might amount to institutional racism in terms of exclusion in the fields of art, media and sport. For instance, only 0.2 per cent of the first 2 billion pounds of National Lottery funding for the arts was spent on black and Asian artists (Runnymede Trust 2000: 161). There is still plenty of evidence of misrepresentation or non-representation of African, Asian, Caribbean and Irish communities in the media. Sports participation is also very uneven with many evident forms of exclusion, such as exclusion of Asian footballers. Policy statements from New Labour's Department of Culture, Media and Sport place very little emphasis on cultural diversity and social inclusion. Furthermore, the higher echelons of public cultural administration and privately owned media and cultural organisations remain almost exclusively white, with a few notable exceptions. No doubt, there have been positive responses to these claims and attempts at melioration since the Parekh Report was published that are testament to its impact. Nevertheless, such change even where it is actively sought tends to be painfully slow.

Clearly, the arts, media and sport are key to reworking the national story in terms of representation and participation, raising a great many issues concerning the canon, funding and employment. The success of black footballers should not distract from the many forms of exclusion that still exist. The Parekh Report is replete with practical proposals and recommendations for addressing these and other issues.

The practical recommendations are framed by seven general principles:

1 'Three central concepts: cohesion, equality and difference';
2 'Demonstrable change at all levels';
3 'Addressing racisms';
4 'Tackling disadvantage';
5 'Colour-blind approaches do not work';
6 'Empowering and franchising';
7 'A pluralistic culture of human rights' (Runnymede Trust 2000: 296–7).

Clash of civilisations or community of communities?

The Parekh Report is not just a policy-oriented expression of Bhikhu Parekh's ideas on multiculturalism. Other members of the Runnymede Commission on the Future of Multi-Ethnic Britain made important contributions individually and collectively. Any student of cultural studies and sociology, for instance, will no doubt recognise the contribution of Stuart Hall on questions of identity. Nevertheless, the report is very much consistent with Parekh's own thinking, which has been given its fullest theoretical articulation in his great treatise, *Rethinking Multiculturalism* (Parekh 2000a).

It is instructive to compare the Parekh position with that of Samuel Huntington who has also published a major treatise, *The Clash of Civilisations and the Remaking of World Order* (Huntington 1996). Huntington's thesis was first announced in the American journal, *Foreign Affairs*, in 1993. In that article he put a question mark against the title, 'The Clash of Civilisations?'. By the time the book was published 3 years later, the question mark had been removed. The following year, Huntington published an article summarising his thesis in the British magazine, *Prospect*, under the title, 'The West and the Rest'. This article provides a rather more benign version of the thesis than the book. To find out what Huntington is really saying it is essential to address the book-length version, especially its concluding chapter, 'The West, Civilisations and Civilisation'. The clash of civilisations thesis is the successor to Francis Fukuyama's (Fukuyama 1989, 1992) end of history thesis. It was cited widely after 9/11 (or, as comedian Ali G puts it, '7 Eleven'). Huntington's thesis makes a similar argument to Benjamin Barber's *Jihad vs. McWorld* (Barber 1996) but rather more comprehensively and, ultimately, yet more scarily.

According to Huntington (Huntington 1996: 20), 'culture and cultural identities, which at the broadest level are civilisational identities, are shaping the patterns of cohesion, disintegration and conflict in the post–Cold War world'. We now live in a 'multipolar and multicivilisational world'. The main source of international tension after the collapse of communism, in his scheme of things, is cultural – that is, civilisational differences – and not economic interest or political ideology.

Huntington argues for the greater explanatory power of his 'civilisational paradigm' over the four extant paradigms of international relations: 'one world', 'us and them', '184 states, more or less' and 'sheer chaos'. Civilisations are made up of a number of elements: religion, 'race', comprehensiveness, longevity and cultural rather than political identity. The most important, Huntington maintains, is religion and this is uppermost, yet not always congruently so, in his identification of seven or eight civilisations in the world. The first is *Sinic* in which Confucianism is prominent. Although many scholars would include *Japanese* civilisation in the Sinic category, Huntington does not. In his opinion, it is a distinctive offshoot of Chinese civilisation, so distinctive historically that it must be seen as separate. No mention here that Japan is capitalist and China still nominally communist. The third civilisation identified by Huntington is *Hindu*; the fourth, *Islamic*; the fifth, *Western*; the sixth, *Latin American*; the seventh, *Orthodox*. Finally and eighth, somewhat reluctantly, Huntington sees *African* as possibly a separate civilisation in spite of its northern relation to Islam and southern relation to Western Christendom.

I want now to consider three problems with Huntington's clash of civilisations thesis that reveal the questionable nature of his domain assumptions. They are to do with religion, cultural racism and Western identity. Huntington's emphasis on values and their grounding in religion – whether as strength of belief or trace of belief – underplays the role of material interests. It is material interests, diffusely those of the West and, rather more concretely, those related to the particular interests of the United States that are implicit in his general argument.

For instance, Huntington seeks to resolve the issue of Europeanness by equating it with Christendom, thus demarcating Europe along the fault line with Islam and, more perplexingly, with Eastern Orthodoxy, so that Turkey's claim to European community membership is questioned and even Greece cannot be properly regarded as European. The equation of Europe with historical Christendom, made by Huntington, is consistent with the critique of Europeanness from the point of view of the excluded and marginalised, yet the implication of his argument is to justify exclusion.

Huntington is much concerned with the issue of migration. The influx of Muslims into Europe and – again perplexingly – Hispanics into the USA may give rise to what he calls 'cleft societies encompassing two distinct and largely separate communities from two different civilisations, which in turn depend on the number of immigrants and the extent to which they are assimilated into Western cultures prevailing in Europe and America' (Huntington 1996: 204). That these are already 'cleft societies' which need reconfiguring is not Huntington's view: far from it. The problem, as he sees it, is one of assimilation; and, if not assimilation, then what? Exclusion? This seems to be the deeper implication of Huntington's superficially reasonable argument.

The general position enunciated by Huntington is culturally racist. It is the kind of position that allowed Enoch Powell's apologists to deny that he was a racist. Apparently, Powell did not believe that Asian and Caribbean immigrants to Britain during the 1960s were necessarily inferior beings; he just did not want them diluting Englishness. Similarly, Huntington makes no claims concerning the superiority of Western civilisation and like a good postmodernist he rejects any universalistic pretensions associated with its values, such as democracy and equality, or anything of that sort. In fact, Huntington argues strenuously that the West should not interfere in other civilisations. The Rest should be left to deal with their own problems. The West may have institutionalised modernisation but modernisation and Westernisation are not the same. In the later phases of modernisation amongst the Rest, Huntington observes, it is common for anti-Westernisation to arise.

At home, of course, it is important to protect the integrity of Western culture and civilisation, according to Huntington, by fighting off the multiculturalists that have done so much to undermine the American way of life. He is concerned about 'problems of moral decline, cultural suicide, and political disunity in the West' (Huntington 1996: 304). In fact, Huntington makes his position and concerns abundantly clear in a passage towards the end of *The Clash of Civilisations and the Remaking of World Order:*

> Western culture is challenged by groups within Western societies. One
> such challenge comes from immigrants from other civilisations who

reject assimilation and continue to adhere to and propagate the values, customs, and cultures of their home societies. The phenomenon is most notable among Muslims in Europe, who are, however, a small minority. It is also manifest, in lesser degree, among Hispanics in the United States, who are a large minority. If assimilationism fails in this case the United States will become a cleft country, with all the potential for internal strife and disunion that entails. In Europe, Western civilisation could also be undermined by the weakening of its central component, Christianity.

(Huntington 1996: 305)

Huntington wants to resist what he calls the 'siren calls of multiculturalism', which he sees as particularly characterised by the undermining of a culture of individual rights by the myriad calls for collective rights, not only to do with 'race' and ethnicity but also with sex and sexuality.

Huntington's position, in spite of his arguments concerning non-interference, is not strictly speaking one of splendid isolationism and resistance to multiculturalism in the USA and the defence of apostolic Christianity in Europe. The USA has a much larger geo-political role than that to perform. In alliance with Europe, he argues, there should be more integration between Western states, the Catholic countries of Eastern Europe should be included in the West, and Latin America should be Westernised. China and Japan should be kept apart. Russia should be recognised as 'the core state of Orthodoxy'. And, 'Western technological and military superiority over other civilisations' should be maintained while, somehow, the West should avoid destabilisation by refraining from interference in other civilisations. It is a sobering thought that this position is to the Left of the second Bush regime's theory and practice in American foreign policy.

It is also worth noting how the kind of cultural relativism that tends to characterise postmodernism can be given such a conservative inflection by the likes of Samuel Huntington, whose message seems to be, you can hang on to your cultures so long as we can purify ours. The implications for multiculturalism in Western societies are clear: either to assimilate to Western ways or go away. Such thinking, taken to its logical conclusion, might imagine a gigantic programme of repatriation. Where would it stop? At the New England Puritans, perhaps? To be sure, Huntington is defending the indefensible or even the non-existent, a fixed Western identity when, in fact, identity is in flux – and all the better for it.

It has to be said that Huntington's position on cultural identity has a certain resonance in non-Western cultures where the project, for some, is to maintain tradition and restore indigenous identity against the ravages of globalising modernity, driven by neo-liberalism and fast communications. The defence of cultural purity is an impossible as well as a perilous project whether in the West or in the Rest. And, while globalising modernity is in many ways destructive and on a number of counts needs to be challenged, it may also herald the prospect of greater democratisation of life.

Huntington's canvas is the world; Parekh's is Britain. Yet, when looked at closely, it is evident that Huntington's reasoning is preoccupied by Western concerns from a distinctly North American perspective and, specifically, what he considers to be the interests of the USA. Parekh's work is concerned with making multiculturalism in Britain work. It is finely tuned to the specific features of that location but in an international comparative framework (Parekh 1997). An appreciation of local specificity and complexity is necessary wherever you look in the world. The differences, then, between Huntington and Parekh are not reducible to a global framework in one case and a national framework in the other case. The differences are much deeper than that. The nation-state still matters in spite of accelerated globalisation. Citizenship rights remain secured, for the most part, at the national level, qualified to some extent by internationally recognised human rights.

Parekh's position is not faultless. His attempt to reconcile liberal and individualistic rights with collective and communal rights may be queried; and, he may have too sanguine a view of the Canadian resolution where francophone Quebec has become a virtual state within the largely anglophone state of Canada. It is reasonable, however, to expect the future to become increasingly hybrid in political, cultural and personal composition. If there was ever a site of actually existing and potentially greater hybridity, surely it is the state system and network of reciprocal relations that traverse the British Isles, encompassing a diverse range of territories and cultures.

The Parekh Report was criticised for failing to solve the liberalism/collectivism problem, manifest in the fact that its policy recommendations in the main do not transcend the liberal problematic of discrimination (Barry 2001). It has also been criticised for attending insufficiently to actual communities in Britain and for representing predominantly professional-managerial interests (Seaford 2001). Such criticisms must be taken into account in a continuing dialogue over multiculturalism in Britain. However, in the particular context of debate these criticisms may perhaps be regarded as carping. The Parekh Report elicited enormous hostility from the media, thereby poisoning its prospects for widespread public understanding and action. This was especially disturbing at a time when asylum-seekers were also being demonised and treated badly by the government.

In a less immediate context, the value of the Parekh position is pointed up sharply by comparison with the Huntington position. Is the difference between them just that of woolly-minded idealism versus a grim realism? The truth of the matter is that the thinking behind Huntington's clash of civilisations thesis is deeply unrealistic, though it may provide a spurious 'explanation' for lazy minds of events like 9/11, though not so easily the USA and Britain's 2003 assault on Iraq. The economic and political tensions in the world today are not reducible to cultural differences. In any case, Huntington concocts an extraordinarily schematic and simplistic typology of civilisations. A hundred holes can be picked in it and motives for its blind spots and inconsistencies readily discerned. Where does Judaism fit into this scheme of things? And, what differentiates Catholic and Hispanic Latin America from Western Christendom other than economics and politics?

The trouble is, this stuff is taken seriously. The defence of an essential Britishness is as lacking in historical foundation and plausibility as the wish to win back an uncontaminated Western civilisation from the incursion of others. What do we want, a clash of civilisations or a community of communities? This is not only a national question but a global one. German social theorist Jurgen Habermas sums up what it is at stake rather well:

> Equal respect for *everyone* is not limited to those who are like us; it extends to the person of the other in his or her otherness. And solidarity with the other *as one of us* refers to the flexible 'we' of a community that resists all substantive determination and extends its permeable boundaries even further. This moral community constitutes itself solely by way of the negative idea of abolishing discrimination and harm and of extending relations of mutual recognition to include marginalized men and women. The community thus constructively outlined is not a collective that would force its homogenized members to affirm its distinctiveness. Here inclusion does not mean locking members into a community that closes itself off from others. The 'inclusion of the other' means rather that the boundaries of community are open for all, also and most especially for those who are strangers to one another and want to remain strangers.
>
> (Habermas 1999: xxxv–vi)

Relating these broad principles and generalisations to the present discussion, questions of shared identity and multicultural heritage should not be treated in isolation from recognition and respect for difference throughout the world. Across the globe, there are national, local and transnational forces at work in a complex exchange of cultures. The hostile response to the Parekh Report in the media and among politicians gave vent to an out-dated isolationism and self-regard in the British imaginary. Multiculturalism needs to transcend such narrowly nationalistic terms of debate in favour of open-minded cosmopolitanism.

Acknowledgements

I must thank Dave Deacon, John Downey, Mike Pickering and Nathan Vaughan for helping me retrieve some of the material for this chapter.

13

INHERITING DIVERSITY

Archiving the past

S. I. Martin

Many professional archivists in the UK would concur with the claim trumpeted by the King's Own Scottish Borders Regimental Archives in 1999 that: 'Our archives are open to everybody. Colour, race or creed has no bearing on the way we operate. Anybody from anywhere who wishes to make use of our Regimental Archives may do so by whatever means they so wish' (Public Service Quality Group 1999). But when in the same year 77 per cent of all visitors to British archives were revealed to be over 45 (with 43 per cent of retirement age) it came as no surprise that the average visitor was described as 'male and slightly greying'. The least likely groups of visitors were the under-24s (3 per cent of individual users) and ethnic minorities, who collectively made up 2 per cent of the archive-using public.

These figures (which have, more or less, flatlined over the past 3 years) exposed what had long been suspected: that there were profound differences between the ideas of heritage with which the archive community was concerned and the moods, tastes and interests of the population at large, and in particular among non-white potential users of their services. One month after the above findings were made public, Stuart Hall defined heritage as a representation of the nation's collective memory, adding that 'those who do not see themselves reflected in the mirror cannot feel that they belong' (Hall 1999c). On that basis alone it was clear that people of colour would not only encounter problems when seeking a reflection of their experience in the archive environment, but they would largely feel overlooked, forgotten and, in a very real sense, excluded.

The problem, of course, was deeper and duller than Hall's mirror. It went to the very heart of a heritage sector which was still, in part, an outgrowth of its late-Victorian origins. The South Kensington Museum (forerunner of today's V&A) was originally a vast repository in which the arts and handicrafts of imperial subjects were categorised, ordered and ranked by their British rulers (Richardson 1997). Sitting beside the neighbouring Imperial Institute, the

Albert Memorial and the Royal Albert Hall, its consciously didactic function could not have been clearer. Here, in the heart of the capital, selections of the monarch's imperial prizes were displayed to encourage what Eric Hobsbawm has described as 'giant new rituals of self-congratulation' on an almost planetary scale among indigenous Britons (Hobsbawm and Ranger 1983: 53). On a smaller, more suburban, scale the exhibits on view at the Horniman Museum were less about the folklore and traditions of the peoples from which they were taken and more to do with the 'stoutly-earned results of a wide-spread dominion . . . the fruits of British pluck, endurance and industry' (Schneer 2001: 94). Tea-trader Frederick John Horniman's original intention was to bring the world to Forest Hill via his private collection of artefacts. As was the case with the natural history displays, the ethnographical collection stood as a testament to British expansion into and documentation of the world at large. And let us never forget the degrading and enormously popular and large-scale public displays of people of colour (Singalese, Tamils, 'Bedouin Arabs', Matabeles, Swazis, Hottentots, Malays) in so-called 'native villages' where they could be observed going through the motions of snake-charming or performing a 'superstitious bush dance'. For decades, these expositions provided a multi-purpose ideological cement through which the lowliest Britons could feel themselves wedded to notions of progress, racial superiority and the global mission of Christian civilisation. In presenting not only African arts and crafts but especially African bodies to public scrutiny, exhibitions like the 'Great Exhibition of the Industry of All Nations' at Crystal Palace in 1851 solidified once and for all in the public imagination the idea that peoples of colour were objects, and moreover objects that could be validly understood through European interpretation alone (Lindfors 1999). It is no surprise that given this context public record practices have reflected such interests.

It is instructive to see where the black presence in Britain, when actively noted, has surfaced in archives. It is present in accounts of stage-show 'freaks' like Sara Baartman the original early nineteenth-century 'Hottentot Venus' whose enlarged genitalia and steatopygia drew enthusiastic crowds and opprobrium in equal measure, or George Gratton, the 'Piebald Boy' of the preceding century, whose vitiligo earned him the stage-name 'Harlequin'. Criminal activity also features strongly as records of black involvement in urban disturbances from the Gordon Riots of 1780 onwards attest (Fryer 1984). Otherwise people of colour are mentioned as either grateful recipients of imperial benevolence or agents for the moral advancement of white people. Both these elements are noticeable in the popularity of the Crimean nurse Mary Seacole, and Martha Ricks, a Sierra Leonean of advanced years who made a quilt for Queen Victoria and travelled to London to present it personally.

Given such a background it is inevitable that there is long-standing and genuine cultural resistance and mistrust between most black people in Britain and the heritage sector. It has a uniquely low image and poor profile. The crude view is that museums, galleries and archives are still places which tend to be *about* us rather than *for* us. A trip to the British Museum brings us face to face with imperial plunder from Egypt and the Sudan. A visit to any of the Tate galleries prompts reflection on the human cost of the sugar magnate's princely munificence. At Harewood House, Leeds, the delights of Adams' interiors, Chippendale furniture, Sèvres porcelain and the paintings of Reynolds and Titian are obscured by the knowledge of Henry Lascelles' slaving fortunes. A visit to an archive will often reinforce a sense of 'unbelonging': a sentiment captured over 200 years ago by the black writer and shopkeeper Ignatius Sancho who wrote of feeling like 'only a lodger – and hardly that' (Caretta 1996: 91).

Where and how could an individual novice black user access material relating to the historical black presence in the UK? What were the guidelines for black geneaological research? Where were the staff familiar with black history, the black presence in the armed forces, the patterns of black settlement in these islands and the particular ways in which these records can be accessed? Where were the black archivists? Moreover, where was the active and continuous expression of interest in black culture beyond the odd regional open-day featuring music, food and oral history showcases?

The job of diversifying the archive environment was taken up with gusto by the Department of Culture, Media and Sport (DCMS). Communities of colour would seemingly be bundled together with the other individuals or areas which 'suffer from a combination of linked problems such as unemployment, poor skills, low incomes, poor housing, high crime environments, bad health and family breakdown' (Lang and Wilkinson 2000). The excluded were to be included as a policy objective. The opinion from DCMS was that archives needed to be drafted into action (alongside the already recruited museums, galleries and sports centres) to pull their weight in the campaign against social exclusion. The role of archives was to change from being passive monocultural repositories to 'agents of social change' and engines of neighbourhood renewal. Social inclusion was to be mainstreamed.

The view from the already understaffed and overstretched enquiry desks was that resources for expanding into unfamiliar cultural waters were either unavailable or, where available, would require extraordinarily sensitive implementation. Some were already aware that initiatives to extend access and promote archive use among the socially excluded would 'run the risk of simply increasing use by those who are already socially included' (Norgrove 2001: 19) given that traditionally such programmes have tended to be publicised via specialised pre-existing channels rather than minority community, or even popular, media.

The response from sections of the black community to these manoeuvres was to wait and see how a number of hurdles would be surmounted. Primarily, what was sought was recognition of the fact that a significant amount of work had already been undertaken by the community to address the black absence in these institutions. Independent bodies including the Black Cultural Archives and the Black and Asian Studies Association had made considerable headway in the research and dissemination of black history material. Independent writers and researchers such as Ziggi Alexander and Audrey Dewjee had exhumed the story of Mary Seacole (Alexander and Dewjee 1999), and others were lobbying English Heritage for blue plaques to commemorate the lives of black Londoners such as John Richard Archer (Britain's first black mayor) and Dr George Rice (the Woolwich coroner and holder of a number of influential medical posts in south London from 1877 to 1917). It is symptomatic of the whole problem that the Rice family papers and photographs were discovered accidentally by an unnamed black workman during a house clearance. With a few exceptions, the contributions of these pioneering researchers and activists was overlooked in the rush to shoehorn social inclusion into all aspects of government and county council policy.

Called away from their traditional concerns by these directives, archive managers throughout the land vied to outdo each other with mission statements which at times seemed to emanate from somewhere between Madison Avenue and North Korea (for example, 'Our Mission is: To help people determine their place in the world, and understand their identities, so enhancing their self-respect and their respect for others').Mercifully, such posturing was counter-balanced by Vic Gray, former chair of the National Council on Archives, who conceded: 'No parish register or medieval charter is going to change the life of a drug addict' while adding that 'archives – our shared and common memory – can make their own contribution to that complex jigsaw of services and support which together are needed to encourage and facilitate social inclusivity' (Norgrove 2001: 1). These statements were to provide the bedrock for some useful initiatives in a number of cities. Some of these, for the first time, were conducted in partnership and consultation with community organisations. The example of Bristol is interesting. Non-user surveys had revealed that people of African-Caribbean descent were particularly low in the city's heritage sector visitor numbers. They also highlighted the fact that the sector was seen not only as an irrelevance to that community but as also being an active agent in the ongoing omission of the role played by Bristol in slavery and its allied trades, and how these forms of exploitation contributed to the city's growth. To address this situation the Bristol Slave Trade Action Group was set up. This body (comprised of councillors, members of the black community, and museum officers) launched a number of projects including a 40-site black history trail, a pamphlet on Bristol and its links with slavery and a display within the Georgian House Museum which described the plantation-owning background to the Pinney family's wealth as well as items related to the life of Pero, Pinney-household slave who died in eighteenth-century Bristol. Around 300 people outside the heritage sector were involved in ongoing and successful consultations during the development of these programmes. Teachers' packs and extensive advertising in the black press helped to raise the profile in the targeted populations. In brief, the heritage sector was put on the black

Bristolian map, and confidence in it among a number of local African-Caribbeans was raised.

A similar, though smaller, project which would achieve comparable results was underway in the London borough of Lambeth. Here, the local archives took an active lead and initiated the Lambeth Black History Project. The object of this 2-year project was to research the documentary evidence of Lambeth's earliest communities of colour. This would be done with the understanding that society as a whole has become accustomed to discussing what history is and is 'less prepared to leave these processes to professionals' (Newman 2002: 7). To this end the local community was brought on board. Schools, both pupils and teachers, were introduced to the material and consulted on its relevance and effectiveness. The Black Cultural Archives were involved as partners and local libraries also took part. Again the black press and radio was used to keep the project alive in the community's memory. The project concluded with the launch of the teacher's pack and the book *Lambeth Forbears* at the Tate Library in central Brixton before a very large and appreciative audience. These examples appear to have laid down the template for other community-driven black history projects in Tower Hamlets and Northampton.

On a larger scale, there have been attempts at increasing accessibility to archives and increasing minority involvement by other bodies. In 2002 the London Metropolitan Archive produced a multimedia exhibition entitled *Black and Asian Londoners: Presence and Background 1536–1840*. This major research project involved a survey of over 1,000 Anglican parish baptismal registers for entries of black and Asian people. Over 1,800 individuals were located. The results have been exhibited at the Hackney Museum and are intended to become part of an online resource for schools. Another IT-oriented development is the Public Record Office/National Archive's *Moving Here* project, part of which involves the search-enabled digitisation of passenger lists from the Caribbean to Britain between 1948 and 1961. A publicly accessible online database will allow for the preservation of what will surely become a fundamental part of black genealogy in Britain.

Perversely, however, it may be through white genealogy that black history finally makes its mark on the archive world. During my black history walking tours of various parts of London I have been exposed to a rich variety of responses regarding facts about the city's multi-ethnic past. The most unforgettable question (asked on a couple of occasions) was: '*If there were so many black people around in those days, where did they all go? What happened to them?*' The second most unforgettable exchange was with an elderly white woman by the name of Blackmoor. There had always been rumours of an African forebear whose presence apparently manifested in the current generation in large patches of melanated skin (not to mention the family name). This woman had done the research herself and had tracked down her eighteenth-century black ancestor. She is far from unique. It has long been assumed by a number of genealogists and geneticists that a surprisingly large number of white British people would, statistically speaking, have at least one ancestor of African origin. Extrapolating from estimates of eighteenth-century black populations in the British Isles both the geneticist Dr Steve Jones and the genealogist Anthony Adolph have concluded that 20 per cent of the current white population who can trace their families to that period would have had an ancestor of colour. Whilst this fact should be of no consequence, the growing number of books, leaflets and articles percolating around genealogical circles on the subject of 'Finding black ancestors' proves this is not the case.

Will the discovery of black or Asian ancestry confer a new and productive sense of identity to its possessors, or will it merely be another fashionable trans-ethnic cap feather? We can only guess, but there is one probability that seems all too likely. The history, research and archiving of the black and Asian presence in the British Isles may become, to a significant degree, the 'intellectual property' of white family and cultural historians. In an ideal world none of this would matter, but in this one such a move would represent a huge step in the processes by which 'the dispossessed are dispossessed of their dispossession' (Tal 1998).

It is fair to say that many archivists are still taking their first steps on the journey that moves them from providing specialist facilities for the initiated to promoting accessible archive use to the general public. The monastic and foren-sic aspects of their profession are barriers that can clearly be overcome with community involvement and consultation. Most importantly, the sentiment that: '[a]rchives are the raw material for developing a sense of place both topo-graphically and within a wider historical process' (Norgrove 2001: 7) has at least begun to take root, and is providing a platform that future generations of archivists and archive users of all backgrounds can benefit from. For, ultimately, these issues are not simply about blowing dust off parchment in dusty vaults or deciphering seventeenth-century cursive: they are about providing a develop-ing multi-ethnic society with the tools to handle difficult questions about origins, ethnicity, identity and nationalism. Without them, we shall continue to see each other through a glass darkly.

14

KEEP THE FLAGS FLYING

World Cup 2002, football and the remaking
of Englishness

Mark Perryman

For the musician Billy Bragg, World Cup 2002 provided a moment which could be described as 'taking much of the beligerence out of the England flag and making it accessible to everyone' (Bragg 2002a). Billy Bragg is of course a walking–talking–singing advertisement for the cause of English patriotism without prejudice. 'Take down the union jack, it clashes with the sunset and put it in the attic with the emperor's old clothes' he sang on his single 'Take Down the Union Jack' released to coincide with the Queen's Golden Jubilee. Bragg's flag of preference is the St George Cross of England. He asks us not to stop flying the flags: just to change the meanings of the one which we sport. His goal is simple, if ambitious

> We've got to get to a place where when we see a flag of St George we don't immediately think 'racist'. People don't think that when they see the flag of Scotland or Wales, it's a real problem that we have in Eng-land. It's our problem, the BNP are in England. So keep the flag flying people, just understand what it really means.
>
> (Bragg 2002b)

The varied meanings of the St George Cross became a very live topic as the England team progressed through World Cup 2002 in Japan towards their eventual quarter-final encounter, and defeat, to Brazil in Shizuoka. This pro-gress was marked by the extraordinary achievement of victory over a football-ing foe, Argentina, with whom rivalry on the pitch is accompanied by the unmistakable martial baggage of a not long forgotten war.

Something is surely stirring when the *Guardian* runs as its front page lead photo on the morning of the 15 June second round game with Denmark photos of St George flying from vans, cars, motorbikes and buses with the headline 'Flying the Flag: Discerning Drivers with the latest Must-Have

Accessory'. No irony was intended, though, when the *Guardian* thoughtfully provided readers with their own cut-out and display St George flag the morning before the 21 June game against Brazil. Left-liberal anxieties were suitably assuaged with the corner-flash 'New improved flag of St George: No Ugly Connotations, No White Van Required'. The accompanying article by Jonathan Glancey neatly summed up the shifting emotions of *Guardian* writers and readers as they became hopelessly engaged in the football-fuelled emotions all around them.

> Although many of us were brought up to believe that the English had no need to shout their identity and that patriotism was the last refuge of a scoundrel, and many more of us, whatever we feel about England, or In-ger-land, have never waved a red-cross flag (nor even a union flag) in our lives, the fact that so many people from so many different backgrounds can wrap themselves in this antique emblem shows that there might – might – just be a little chivalry behind the effing, blinding, beery bravado after all.
>
> (Glancey 2002)

The week after England's 1–2 defeat at the hands, or should it be feet, of Brazil, Tony Parsons in the *Daily Mirror* was less circumspect than Glancey.

> Far more important than anything that happened on the field was the sudden liberation of English national identity. It looks as if the English are finally allowed to start loving themselves. The sting has been drawn out of the flag of St George. All the old connotations – that a red cross on a white background meant a mindset that was white, racist, boozy, xenophobic, and exclusive – has gone out of the window. The flag of St George has gone from white van man to everyman.
>
> (Parsons 2002)

Though perhaps not everywoman, not yet anyway. Martin Phillips in the *Sun* writing on the morning after the match before marked the team's, and the nation's, defeat with a welcome, and unfamiliar, touch of tabloidesque sobriety.

> This was the World Cup that saw us grow up as a nation. Where before there has been jingoism and contempt for all opposition, the new mature England only sent its heroes off with hope they would do their best. The flags that have fluttered from homes, offices and cars should not be lowered to half-mast or removed just because the adventure is over. They should be raised even higher – with pride.
>
> (Phillips 2002)

It was only a few months later of course that the *Sun* launched its campaign for a toughening of immigration rules to exclude, and expel, asylum-seekers with the front-page screamer 'Lock 'Em Up, Chuck 'Em Out'. Meanings of Englishness, and their articulation through football, will chop and change from the engaging and inclusive, to the threatening and exclusive dependent on a miscellany of factors, some predictable, others not. Les Back, Tim Crabbe and John Solomos describe this as 'contestation' and prior to the 2002 World Cup offered this explanation of how contestation is practised. 'Whilst the side has become a focus for the display of a variety of forms of English patriotism, for a significant proportion of fans the national team represents a means through which to associate with historically grounded notions of a particular white, working-class English identity' (Back *et al.* 2001: 250). This appears to suggest that the authors believe that the site of contestation is heavily weighted in favour of one particular interpretation of Englishness, though they do go on to qualify this: 'the cultures surrounding the England football team are shifting to become more racially inclusive and less insular' (Back *et al.* 2001: 251).

Contestations of Englishness – what it means to fly the flag, to support, or not to support, the team – are intimately connected to the irresistible rise of a multicultural England. Stuart Hall has described this as a fundamental challenge to what we understand as the meaning of culture.

> We tend to see cultures, anthropologically, as well-bounded entities, where difference is fixed and essentialised, indeed naturalised, and sometimes effectively biologised, tied to places of origin, inclusive of all its members and powerful enough to script fixed differences over time, and in that sense is trans-historical. Instead, we need to imagine them as shifting, loosely constructed repertoires which are positional rather than fixed, multiple rather than unitary, connected less with the singular roots from which we came, and more to the roots we have travelled to get to where we are now – less being and more becoming.
>
> (Hall 1999b)

Hall's exploration of how multiculturalism has impacted on how we must conceive of nationality and its attendant baggage of symbols and rituals is explicitly connected by Jim Pines to the flying of the St George Cross up and down the length and breadth of England during World Cup 1998.

> The St George's Cross had become the symbol of a shared national allegiance among England fans during the tournament, both at home and abroad. The English flag invoked a sense of multicultural inclusiveness which had not been seen before, and certainly not in relation to the Union Jack.
>
> (Pines 2001: 57).

Globalisation was supposed to have put an end to a politics of nation and locality but as the drive towards one neo-liberal international political economy gathers pace localisation and nationalism have acquired an unpredictable persistence. Hall described this in the early 1990s as 'a contradiction at the heart of modernity that has given nationalism and its particularisms a peculiar significance and force at the centre of the so-called transnational global order' (Hall 1992b: 6). Hall is not so easily convinced of the automaticity of political affiliations that many critics ascribe to these localist and nationalist tendencies. 'It is capable of being inflected to very different political positions, at different historical moments and its character depends very much on the other traditions, discourses and forces with which it is articulated' (Hall 1992b: 6).

Raymond Williams went further than most in identifying the potential progressive contribution of a nationalist politics.

The moment when we move from a merely retrospective nationalist politics to a truly prospective politics, we begin that affirmative thinking that some of the most developed and intelligent left politics in certain other centres of Europe has truly lost. For however sophisticated, however militant, that politics may be, it has lost something at its heart that is recognised, again and again, by those who are inside it: the sense of what the struggle would attain, what human life would be like, other than mere utopian rhetoric. That sense has been so truly lost that what is now being contributed, I think still very incompletely, from the new nationalist movements is a re-connection inside the struggles of the sense of an objective that has the possibility of affirmation.

(Williams 1992: 10)

Williams' progressivist nationalism was most closely identified with Wales. He was writing nearly 5 years before the Welsh people secured a Wales Assembly, and the Scots their own Parliament. These institutions were voted for by referendums in September 1997. But the devolution argument was in many senses settled during the 4-week campaign of Euro '96. Contrary to the scenes at Wembley almost 30 years to the day previously when England lifted the World Cup amidst a near-universal sea of British Union Jack flags, when England played Scotland in this championship the only flag any self-respecting England fan would be flying was St George. As for the Scots, the faux-fun nationalists of the 'Tartan Army' would never, ever, fly the Union Jack, a flag of another country, not theirs. Two anthems, too, 'Flower of Scotland' for the Scots, while the congenital constitutional confusion that is England's fate meant that the English were left to sing 'God Save the Queen'. Never mind, 'Three Lions on our Shirt' was effectively the popular anthem of the day for England, and for ever afterwards too. Three years later, when England were drawn once more to play Scotland, in Glasgow's Hampden Park and Wembley in a two-legged Euro 2000 qualifying play-off, the separation of Britain into its constituent parts was even clearer with the game billed predictably as the 'Battle of Britain'.

Of course, the hate-filled rivalry that frames in large part encounters between England and Scotland is not the best possible advertisement for the progressive lexicon that a break-up of Britain might deliver. Anything but. Nevertheless, the flying of St George, not the Union Jack, is a vital indicator of the shifts in national identity that football has helped produce. But there are influential voices which seek to ignore this tendency towards Englishness, Scottishness, Welshness, and Irishness too, in place of Britishness. Mark Leonard wrote the highly regarded Demos report *Britain TM: Renewing our Identity* in 1997. Despite the fact that the then yet-to-be elected New Labour government was committed to devolution, the author ignores this, hanging on to a modernising Britishness as his pet project with a missionary tenacity (see Leonard: 1997). His commitment to a modernised national identity is not in doubt; indeed much of what he writes on the crisis of Britishness is absolutely correct.

> Together the new institutions of Britishness and icons of Britishness melded into an extremely robust identity. They crystallised just as Britain rose to success as an imperial and industrial power and they gave British citizens an extraordinary confidence and pride. Today, however, each of the pillars on which that identity rests has been eroded.
>
> (Leonard 1997: 26)

Leonard lists these pillars of Britishness quite correctly as institutions, empire, industry, language, culture and religion, sport. But nowhere does he account for the rise of a devolutionary and nationalist politics that at least in some limited measure would lead to the constitutional fracturing, accompanied by the cultural fragmentation, of long-cherished notions of Britishness. The absence is quite inexplicable.

Yet 5 years later the same author, now the Director of the Foreign Policy Centre, edited an equally important volume *Reclaiming Britishness*. Once more no account whatsoever is given to the political or cultural impact of devolution on Britishness: instead we are promised that the collection of essays will 'explore how a modern, inclusive, outward-looking notion of Britishness can be used as a guide through difficult issues – and how it can become a reality' (Leonard 2002: x). These are laudable enough aims, but – given the intervening 5 years since his first stab at the subject had been marked by referendums, elections, opening ceremonies and the rising fortunes of nationalist parties, all testament to the fact that a fundamental challenge to Britishness was emerging from within its own once easily drawn borders (not to mention the ongoing eclipse of the Union Jack by St George as the English popular flag of choice) – then a comment or two on this might have been called for. No, not a word; Britishness remains unproblematic if 'modernised', enough according to Leonard and his co-thinkers.

But as World Cup fever gathered force in England and St George was daubed on childrens' faces, pinned on a lapel, stuck in a shop window, turned into a fashion icon in outlets from FCUK to Paul Smith and a range of sartorial points in between, voices of anxiety from opposite ends of the political spectrum made themselves heard. Not necessarily in unison with Leonard's pan-Britishness but nevertheless implacably opposed to all this English flag-flying. The conservative columnist for the *Mail on Sunday* Peter Hitchens wrote

> I hope the English football team is rapidly knocked out of the World Cup. I really do. And please don't call this group of people 'England'. They are not England and do not represent this country, at least I sincerely hope they don't. They are people who are quite good at playing football and who happen to be English.
>
> (Hitchens 2002)

For Hitchens, a mass outpouring of national emotion, wrapped around team and flag, is something to be snootily dismissed. What of England knows those who only football know, he appears to be asking. Hitchens is an inveterate unionist and Europhobe, yet he seems to have little inkling of the roles sport, culture and flag-flying have in reconstructing national identity at precisely the conjuncture of devolution and Europeanisation against which he fulminates his opposition week in, week out, in his *Mail on Sunday* column. Or maybe he just doesn't know how to react to a line-up of players, and to an increasing extent supporters, who project a multiculturalism that undermines fixed notions of nationhood.

Meanwhile in the left newspaper *Socialist Worker* all this flag-waving by a huge bulk of the population, including of course many workers, not to mention socialists, was confounding those whose notion of international socialism is as fixed as Hitchens' notion of nationhood. 'Nationalism, however dressed up, is something which helps obscure the real class divide in society and helps divide us from our fellow workers across the world. That is why socialists should oppose all nationalism, and follow no national flag' wrote Paul McGarr (2002: 9). McGarr's furious rejection of 'fluffy, popular or multicultural nationalism' leaves him with a decidedly one-dimensional understanding of politics and surrenders an extraordinary expanse of popular consciousness to those one might expect somebody of McGarr's politics would want to oppose. Contestation demands a complexity of understanding that McGarr rejects in favour of unadulterated, and unsophisticated class politics.

Assessments of the impact of all the World Cup English flag-waving elsewhere were generally more favourable, and more thoughtful, than either Hitchens or McGarr. In *Tribune* Sarah Schaefer suggested that the national feel-good factor of June 2002 represented 'a national pride which has absolutely nothing to do with the nasty ideology peddled in the past by the far Right and their fellow travellers on the Tory fringe. Beckham and his team did not bring back the World Cup, but they gave us something no less precious' (Schaefer 2002:11). The Monday after England's quarter-final defeat the letters page of the *Guardian* featured heartfelt cries for the moment to continue. Karen Clarke wrote 'I can fly my country's flag and celebrate my own culture without being branded a racist', while John Chilton added 'The longer you and I and the rest of us continue to fly the flag the more difficult it will be for the extreme right to reclaim it for their own purposes'. This is now a familiar, and widely held, point of view. That unless the decent, law-abiding, anti-racist majority fly the flag then all icons of national identity, though in particular the flag, will become the property of the far right, most notably the British National Party (BNP). In actual fact unlike the National Front in the 1970s and 1980s the BNP rarely march with their flagpoles, drum corps and honour guard looking for a punch-up. Nowadays the BNP prefer a community activism that has delivered them a frightening amount of electoral success and a credibility that far outstrips even the greatest achievements of Oswald Mosley and his inter-war British Union of Fascists. It is unlikely that simply by reclaiming the flag significant inroads can be made into the layer of racist attitudes that allow the BNP to get away with offering a legitimate protest vote. Although captioning a photo of a St George Cross flag as 'The BNP flies its flag in Burnley local elections' in the *Guardian* of 29 April 2002 betrays precisely the attitudes that on occasion leave all who festoon themselves, their car or house with the flag feeling unwanted and unloved by polite society.

Many commentators, especially following the crowd trouble at England's away game to Slovakia in October 2002, readily wrote off all this happy-clappy flag-waving as a temporary, if welcome, national aberration. Oliver Holt was one; 'Patterns are re-establishing themselves here. Japan was a wonderful aberration. That much is clear now. Maybe our fans weren't entirely to blame for what happened in Bratislava but trouble follows them round like a faithful mutt' (Holt 2002). Holt writes a powerful damnation of the racism that undoubtedly continues to accompany England, particularly at away matches. But he is too quick to write off what happened in Japan, and the circumstances of opportunity and understanding this offers us for a more favourable national future. None of the positive interpretations of England's World Cup 2002 would have been written if it wasn't for the good behaviour of the England fans who made it out to Japan. In so many different ways their behaviour and reception framed how the vast majority of supporters watched the tournament, back home on the TV. Throughout May 2002 readers had been treated to tales of how 'British [sic] soccer hooligans are secretly plotting to wreck the World Cup' (*Sunday Mirror*, 5 May 2002) while the *Evening Standard* reported 'Here are the riot police who will be facing down any badly behaved England fans in Japan' (10 May 2002). The day before the tournament opened the *Sun* treated thrill-seeking readers to the horror story of 'HMS Hooligan, floating jail for England yobbos' (30 May 2002). Less sensationalist, but contributing to pre-cisely the same picture of upcoming England-inspired mayhem, the *Observer* splashed with 'Football thugs free to attend World Cup' (26 May 2002). The reality turned out very differently. But the very fact that these fears, much more strongly expressed in Japan's own media where it was impossible for many months to read any report that didn't picture all England fans as hooligans, exist, and were projected in the press, on the radio and via TV, surely means we must account for the changed outcome.

First, lets discount the idea that it was a different set of England fans compared with those who had been at the trouble-strewn Euro 2000 and France 1998 World Cup. The ticket distribution system administered by the Football Association (FA), which is based primarily on loyalty points secured by attending games, meant that a high proportion of those receiving their England tickets from the FA had been to one, if not both, of these previous tournaments.

Second, and of far greater importance than the reduced numbers due to distance – after all some 10,000 England fans did travel to Japan at some point during the team's 3-week campaign, more than enough for a critical mass to provoke trouble should the fancy take them – was the mood of the support. The dominant attitude was one of exploration, engagement and excitement at being in a country of such a different complexion to the ones even the most well-travelled fans were used to visiting. An England fan who follows the team is by definition one used to flying off to countries all over Europe for competitive, even friendly fixtures. Many of these fans had spent the preceding 18 months on trips to Holland, Germany, Greece, Albania, Italy and Finland. But with no fixtures outside of Europe and the failure to qualify for USA '94, few fans had followed the team beyond the continent. There has always been an element among England's most committed supporters to think of these trips as a match, plus a city or country to visit. But in Europe most destinations are either overly familiar, or, if in Eastern Europe, with a fan culture that can too often be as fearsome as anything England can offer, not to mention with police forces whose idea of low-key policing includes automatic rifles, baton rounds, vicious truncheons and water cannon. Neither factor can excuse the minority of England's fans who go looking for trouble, usually find it, and are eyed with an easy glee by too many of the supporters who justify the fighting as a natural part of following their team to foreign parts, and never mind the consequences. In Japan, none of this applied. There were widely reported accounts of riot police armed with nets to shoot over groups of fighting fans, officers were apparently adept in the martial arts and expected to strike fear into the English. But at each match the England fans were treated to rank after rank of friendly smiling stewards, volunteers and where the police were seen they were the equivalent of the friendly bobby variety of folkloric memory, with an amazingly high proportion of policewomen. And the host population were England fans too. This was a quite bizarre experience. So used are we to striking fear into those we visit (whether deservedly so or otherwise, it hardly seems to matter) that shut shops, full-up hotels, empty streets and alcohol bans have almost become the order of the away day. Japan was the complete oppos-ite of the fans' worst nightmare. Many experienced for the very first time what it was liked to be loved rather than loathed. Those pictures of Japanese Eng-land fans, complete with Becksmania, became one of the most enduring images of the tournament (see Figure 14.1). The Japanese made this a special

Figure 14.1 Japanese fans of the England team during World Cup 2002. Reproduced with the permission of the photographer Anne Coddington.

tournament, and it could only become so because the England fans responded in kind.

Third, the lack of trouble and the relative success of the team, not to mention the tournament location, meant the media had to seek out stories and pictures for those watching, listening and reading back home of a very different variety to what we'd been used to. A great mix of images of what it could mean to be an England fan began to emerge, and with games televised in the early morning or at lunchtime this became connected to, on the other side of the world, a country, and population that for 3 weeks would fit work, school, travel, breakfast and lunch hours around kick-off times.

An aberration? Each tournament of course plays under its own particular circumstances. But if no lessons are learnt from Japan's set of circumstances for Englishness, home and away, then aberration it will surely become instead of opportunity grasped.

The World Cup performs a key function in that it frames a national moment which contributes to how England is imagined as a community (Anderson 1998). The progressive ambition is to shape this process of football framing the nation in order to help, not hinder, the evolution of a pride free of prejudice, to separate hope in the team's success from the hate too often associated with that aim, and give credit to the commitment of fandom without using this as a subterfuge to excuse violent confrontation. This must mean contesting the flag and what it has been allowed to symbolise. To make excuses and exit from this contestation is simply not good enough. It is no longer sufficient to decry the racist, imperial and martial baggage. Scottish and Welsh devolution, Europeanisation, immigration and globalisation mean the long neglected English question is never far away from emerging as a shadowy presence in the background, and increasingly moving towards the foreground. As Tony Wright has pointed out 'from now on devolution stops being an argument about somewhere else and starts being an argument about England' (Wright 2000: 13). The ways in which the question emerges will be unpredictable but it would be foolish to assume it won't nevertheless be ever present. From the row over Scottish Labour MPs voting on foundation hospitals that will only ever be built in English constituencies, to Scots celebrating an Olympic gold medal in womens' curling as very much their own, and not Great Britain's, we are having to learn to live with the difference. Arthur Aughey emphasises that the English continue to look two ways when it comes to the national question:

> On the one hand, for all the recent concern about an identity crisis, England's sense of nationhood remains deeply ingrained. On the other hand, local allegiance is also deeply ingrained but in a manner which rarely means identification with a region – however it may be defined.
> (Aughey 2001: 168)

New Labour has attempted to address the subject with proposals towards various English regional assemblies. Some regionalists counterpose these to English nationalism, associating the latter with centralisation at the expense of the periphery, while both unionists and some English nationalists fear regionalism as a counterweight to English statehood in some kind of federal mix. It should not be beyond the wit and wisdom of politics to combine statehood for the English with localised democracy, but to date few have bothered to rise to the challenge. In place of political expression Englishness primarily finds a cultural expression, hence the centrality of sport in general, and football in particular in its articulation.

Iain Macwhirter points to the dangers when an English cultural nationalism exists without any obvious political expression:

> We are told that the emergence of the flag of St George on the football terraces is a sign of awakening English consciousness . . . England may well begin to ask questions about where she stands politically in the new order. Better to start the process now, than to allow grievances to develop which could turn the constitution into a sport for hooligans.
>
> (Macwhirter 1998: 54)

Hooliganism is easy enough to denounce, if not eradicate. But it is slack juxtaposition to suggest that flag-waving necessarily needs to carry a national health warning. Coming from Scotland, land of the Tartan Army, self-styled 'friendliest fans' in world football, it might have been hoped Macwhirter would know better. It is reckless to decry English patriotism as an essentialised negative. Instead what is practised under patriotism's guise must be examined, accounted for, and where appropriate opposed. We cannot ignore what is written in England's history books, but nor should that history be used as an excuse for inaction. Engagement requires the seeking out of the variegated components of a historical narrative, and seeking out alternative narratives too. Can this search reveal the elements to construct an inclusive, internationalist nationalism?

Not on its own it won't, though without that pre-history a movement of the present will lose that essential ingredient, authenticity. It is a movement that can no longer be discounted as the concern of faddists and fascists. David Cox writing in the left-liberal *New Statesman* offered a powerful counterblast to those who would wish celebrations of Englishness would just fade away:

> Until recently a distaste for displays of nationhood was one of the few indisputable constituents of the English national character. Flag-waving was for lesser breeds: Englishness was at once too impregnable to need expression and too ineffable to allow it. Well, no longer.
>
> (Cox 2002: 14)

Two months before England kicked off their World Cup campaign in June,

Cox catalogued the numerous items of evidence of a heightened consciousness that being English is different to the previous cosy assumptions of Britishness.

World Cup 2002 for the English, home and away, revealed the potential of a celebratory, carnivalesque nationalism that will remain a vital resource of hope for many years, and seasons, to come. It wasn't the case everywhere: there were reports of racial attacks associated with large crowds of white males gathering to drink and watch matches around England (King 2002: 5). But thankfully, this was very much the exception rather than the rule. Darcus Howe was one among many writers to comment on the broad multiracial base of support for England at home, 'People from the Caribbean usually support Brazil, primarily because the players look like us (Brazil is a nation of manumitted slaves), but also because they play the game like West Indians play cricket. Yet this loyalty was transferred almost wholesale to England' (Howe 2002: 8). Jim Pines argues powerfully that the identification with the national football team, projected by the flying or wearing of the St George's Cross represents a moment of national inclusion, rather than exclusion as it is too often derided. He cites this process as first developing around World Cup 1998. Pines suggests

the St George's Cross is by no means a neutral emblem of nationhood, but it does not carry the same uncomfortable connotations generally associated with the Union Jack. Thus, the England flag was able to function – at least during the period of the 1998 World Cup – as a veritable emblem of multicultural inclusiveness and by doing so it succeeded in conveying a relatively progressive image of a multicultural England.

(Pines 2001: 58)

The process Pines describes was repeated on a much vaster scale around World Cup 2002 and this was among a variety of positive factors which meant instead of agonising over another tournament spoilt by the ever-worsening meaning of what it means to be English, we could sit back and celebrate the potential of our national identity. Or, as Miranda Sawyer put it: 'The real reason why the World Cup proved so popular – across genders, throughout the country – was that it was just a massive excuse for a party: and let's face it, we all love a bit of a do' (Sawyer 2002: 37).

Even after England's pitiful second-half performance against Brazil, England's World Cup exit continued to be marked by the kind of celebratory commentary of which Sawyer's is typical. Let us savour that moment of opportunity, while recognising that these 21 days in June should not be read as a completed outcome in the remaking of Englishness. The episode is partial, subject to particular circumstances. The fans who dressed in kimonos with a St George daubed across their face are as unrepresentative of the bulk of England fans as those who throw a punch or chuck a bottle as soon as they hit town. But the very obvious presence of a fancy-dress nationalism in Japan created the

conditions for a great mix of positive emotions and actions which it was possible to associate with being English, and wanting the team to win too. As
musician Fatboy Slim succinctly put it in the *Guardian* on the day England
played Argentina, 'This is the first time I've felt proud to be English'.

Flying the flag and football are so closely connected that it is remarkably
difficult to think of another occasion when there might be a similar outpouring of public national identity. The exception may well be monarchic
pageantry, although many commentators remarked that the Queen's Golden
Jubilee, which came to a climax during the World Cup, was a time when the
Union Jack was waved in great numbers rather than St George. The monarch is
today certainly the pre-eminent symbol of pan-Britishness. Standing alone
Queen Elizabeth leaves the rest of the architecture of her once united kingdom
exposed. As Tom Nairn put it,

> When the underpinnings of the British state-idea decay, there is aston-
> ishingly little left. And anyone can see these have largely disappeared.
> The external command-structure, the symbolism of regality, the old
> 'parliamentary-class' and the rigid prestige of the institution itself have
> either disappeared or diminished. Their iron has turned to rust.
>
> (Nairn 2000: 177)

Nairn returned once more to this theme of the inexorable decline, if not yet
break up, of Britishness in the book he wrote after the 2001 General Election.
'Blair's new Labour scuttled back into the bunker of Greatness whenever the
dust on the ornaments was disturbed. Only with the coming collapse of the
bunker itself is some successor likely to take reform more seriously' (Nairn
2002: 162).

The writers Julia Bell and Jackie Gay have pinpointed the broader cultural
consequences of a process that can begin with David Beckham leading his
team out on to the pitch and conclude with the constitutional break-up of
Britain.

> England's history is shameful and glorious, its people are black, gay and
> disabled as well as white Anglo-Saxon, its landscapes are devastated and
> breathtaking – sometimes at the same time. These are the contradic-
> tions we live with on this packed island, they are what we must make
> our future from. Devolvement of power allegedly places more
> responsibility for our government in our own hands, but before we
> know what we want, we have to know who we are.
>
> (Bell and Gay 2001: xii)

It is a process which if it is to have a progressive, rather than a regressive,
outcome must explore the potential for a positive English patriotism. Without
that exploration the outcome we can be assured will only be regressive. The

gallery notes that accompanied Ravi Deepres' photography exhibition *Patriots* sum up the potential place for football in this exploration: 'Football's emotive environment has a huge capacity for discussion of national, group, and individual identity' (Sealy 2003). The environment is unruly, highly mediated, and hugely memorable. But most of all it is a crowded arena of contested meanings of Englishness. Home and away, on and of the pitch, this is a contest the English cannot afford to ignore.

AFTERWORD
'Strolling spectators' and 'practical Londoners': remembering the imperial past

Bill Schwarz

To the delight of most of London's inhabitants – the only exception appears
to be the city's cabbies – the north end of Trafalgar Square, in front of the
National Gallery, has at last been closed to traffic. In this small enclave the
urban tempo has quietened. When I first paid a visit, in the uncharacteristically
burning sunshine of a July evening, city life was moving as if in slow-motion. It
was one of those rare London moments when no one seemed hassled. People
enjoyed the last moments of the sun, drinking chic coffees at the newly laid-
out tables. Two young Britons – the very image of the conventional English
football fan – stripped down to their boxers, and splashed and wrestled in the
fountain, tumbling over in laughter when one of them, more than once,
revealed his white buttocks. A couple of David Blunkett's newly styled community police officers observed from afar, clearly not regarding this as an occasion which required their attention. Tourists, too, looked on, perhaps quizzical
or amused, but unabashed. Some braved a more demure paddle – skirting,
when necessary, the antics of the near-naked British revellers.

This was not a moment when history impinged – or at least not immediately, or not formally. It's likely that conversation was animated more by the
choice of coffees than by the historical significance of Admirals Beatty, Jellicoe
or Cunningham, whose bronze busts adorn the north wall. Trafalgar Square is
history in monumental mode, though marking only the mere beginnings of
what was once planned as the wholesale reconstruction of the centre of the
capital, befitting the world's greatest imperial power. This is the imperial past
enshrined for the present, dominated by the towering figure of Lord Nelson, so
high in the firmament that his own mortality has (we may think) been tran-
scended. The living are destined to walk in his shadow: literally so. But few of
us, natives to London or visitors, crane our necks for very long, looking to his
image in the heavens. Few Britons, I expect, exult in the military victories
associated with his name. To do so, today, would seem crazed or disturbed. One

could imagine it of an admirer of the late Enoch Powell, perhaps, or maybe – fearing the consequences of a national forgetfulness – it is an issue one could conceive preoccupying the purple-inked correspondence of Prince Charles, admonishing spiritless bureaucrats in the Department of Media, Culture and Sport for some perceived slight on the heroes of the nation's past. Nor, in the same vein, is it likely that those French who visit, even those of Gaullist sensibilities, grieve over a national defeat of two centuries back. These are monuments which provide the *mise-en-scène* for the more present-orientated practices of everyday city life: drinking an espresso in the evening sun, or stopping to watch an impromptu urban pantomime.

This is simply to note that we should not forget the virtues of forgetting. Perhaps, though, to employ the first person plural in this context represents a sleight of hand. It is unlikely that those passing the time in a city square on a summer evening had to strive for forgetfulness, banishing from their minds events of previous historical times. The problem is more particular. For historians especially, or for those persuaded by the benefits of thinking historically, it can be uncomfortable to be reminded of the necessity of forgetting. A passion for history turns on overcoming forgetfulness, on discovering new ways of imagining time in which past, present and future can interconnect and interact. Yet even for those most dedicated to bringing the past into the present, the idea of total recall – of attacking forgetfulness at every juncture – can be no more than a fantasy. The idea of total history, in this regard, is an impossibility. To remember everything, for an individual or for a larger social collective, would indeed be to succumb to a painful, disabling and speedy insanity. Memory can only work in conjunction with forgetting. They, memory and forgetting, are not so much different mental operations as aspects of a single process. For good or ill, memory is organised by what has been forgotten, and how it has been forgotten.

Intellectually, proponents of forgetfulness have been rather fewer than those advocating the importance of remembering, though there are signs that in contemporary academic preoccupations this balance may be shifting. For the purposes of this volume, though, it is helpful to return to two earlier thinkers who were sensitive, at least in part, to the value of forgetting. The first is Nietzsche, who in his influential programmatic statement of 1873, 'On the uses and disadvantages of history for life', determined to confront the effects of a modern consciousness overly formed, as he saw it, by the past.

His essay began from the premise, familiar to those tuned into our own contemporary debates on memory and memorialisation, that 'we are suffering from a consuming fever of history', and that the first requirement of critical thought was to recognise that this was so. There existed such 'oversaturation' of the past in the present that historical thought itself was becoming ever more difficult to achieve. Modern man had become reduced to 'a strolling spectator' in the labyrinthine re-creations and representations of the past, to such an extent that he 'has arrived at a condition in which even great wars and revolutions are able to influence him for hardly more than a moment'. It was precisely the weight of the past on the present which Nietzsche believed to be 'harmful and ultimately destructive'. What he took to be at issue was the 'degree of historical sense' which operated in the modern world.

> To determine this degree, and therewith the boundary at which the past has to be forgotten if it is not to become the gravedigger of the present, one would have to know exactly how great the *plastic power* of a man, a people, a culture is: I mean by plastic power the capacity to develop out of oneself in one's own way, to transform and incorporate into oneself what is past and foreign, to heal wounds, to replace what has been lost, to recreate broken moulds.

In order to address this issue, Nietzsche identified three different modes in which historical time can be imagined and organised. The first he explicitly called 'monumental', which − he argued − was driven by the conviction that greatness existed in the past, and thus could exist again in the future. Yet he claimed that to think in these terms, although giving every appearance of respecting the historical past, in fact contravened a cardinal presupposition of historical inquiry: that the past is not the same as the present. Monumental history makes 'the dissimilar look similar' − and he cited, as commemorations particularly prone to this error, the practices customarily enacted in 'religious or military anniversaries'. In fact, the monumentalisation of history allowed it only to be 'free poetic invention', a 'mythical fiction', or a 'fanaticism'. History in monumental mode lets 'the dead bury the living'.

Second, he identified antiquarian history, whose dominant impulse derived from piety toward the past. 'By tending with care that which has existed from of old, he [the antiquarian] wants to preserve for those who shall come into existence after him the conditions under which he himself came into existence . . .' 'The trivial, circumscribed, decaying and obsolete', Nietzsche went on to observe, 'acquire their own dignity and inviolability through the fact the preserving and revering soul of the antiquarian man has emigrated into them and there made its home'.

Third, is what Nietzsche designated as critical history, which for him was history in the positive mode, 'for life' − though on this he has least to say. The purpose of thinking critically about history, he suggested, was 'to break up and dissolve a part of the past' (Nietzsche 1991: 60–83).

I will come back to Nietzsche. But before I do, there occurs an important passage in Freud which directly connects to this same theme. This appears in his first (of five) lectures on psychoanalysis delivered at Clark University, in the United States, in September 1909. Toward the end of the lecture he said this:

> I should like to formulate what we have learned so far as follows: *our hysterical patients suffer from reminiscences*. Their symptoms are residues

and mnemic symbols of particular experiences. We may perhaps obtain a deeper understanding of this kind of symbolism if we compare them with other mnemic symbols in other fields. The monuments and memorials with which large cities are adorned are also mnemic symbols. If you take a walk through the streets of London, you will find, in front of one of the great railway termini, a richly carved Gothic column – Charing Cross. One of the old Plantagenet kings of the thirteenth century ordered the body of his beloved Queen Eleanor to be carried to Westminster; and at every stage at which the coffin rested he erected a Gothic cross. Charing Cross is the last of the monuments that commemorate the funeral cortege. At another point in the same town, you will find a towering, and more modern, column which is simply known as 'The Monument'. It was designed as a memorial of the Great Fire, which broke out in that neighbourhood in 1666 and destroyed a large part of the city. These monuments, then, resemble hysterical symptoms in being mnemic symbols; up to that point the comparison seems justifiable. But what should we think of a Londoner who paused to-day in deep melancholy before the memorial of Queen Eleanor's funeral instead of going about his business . . .? Or again what should we think of a Londoner who shed tears before the Monument that commemorates the reduction of his beloved metropolis to ashes . . .? Every single hysteric and neurotic behaves like these two unpractical Londoners. Not only do they remember painful experiences of the remote past, but they still cling to them emotionally; they cannot get free of the past and for its sake they neglect what is real and immediate.

(Freud 1978: 16–17)

In their respective idioms, both these commentaries suggest that the past can consume the present, and that in such situations relations between past and present are feverish, neurotic or destructive. There are domains, or moments, of modern life which need to be kept free from the burdens of the past. Freud's idea of 'practical Londoners' is telling: he conceives of them, as a requirement of their *being practical*, needing to 'free' themselves of the past in order to get on with the 'real and immediate'. In Nietzsche's terms, this freeing of the past is necessary 'for life'. Or in the scenario of the summertime *flâneur*, it is a condition for enjoying the modest, fleeting pleasures of modern living – the espresso in the sun, the elusive human movement of the city street.

Yet neither Nietzsche nor Freud presents an argument against history, or against historical memory. On the contrary, Nietzsche's 'strolling spectator' is a figure only apparently immersed in history. In the vocabulary of our own times, he lives entirely in the world of simulated images, of incessantly commodified representation, which suppresses anything resembling historical knowledge. Even 'great wars and revolutions' pass him by. For Nietzsche, monumentalism and antiquarianism were the enemies of history, at least in

219

their unadulterated manifestations. He appreciated the degree to which men and women are constituted by their pasts, and that the dream that they might effect a categorical emancipation from these pasts was exactly that: a dream, or an illusion. 'Every man and nation' needs 'a certain kind of knowledge of the past' – though one which doesn't deprive a vigorous future of its roots (Nietzsche 1991: 75–7). And for Freud as well, memory could take many forms, therapeutic as well as destructive. In the proper conditions, forgetting functions as an *aide-mémoire*.

So what of the scene in Trafalgar Square composed of 'practical Londoners', in a rare moment of urban tranquillity? To the naked eye, all appeared untouched by the monuments of the imperial past which organise the space itself. Equally, no sign could be discerned of those counter-histories which also populate the location of Trafalgar Square. The ghosts of many demonstrations for popular rights, and of many angry denunciations of colonial wrongs, have left no visible trace. (For a study which excavates, with skill and insight, both this history and the many others which converge on Trafalgar Square, see Mace 1976.) Despite much talk, Nelson Mandela – the other Nelson – awaits his more modest monumental moment outside South Africa House, on the east side of the square. Should this matter? What are the virtues of remembering?

How, more particularly, do these issues affect the questions which arise out of post-colonial inquiry? Post-colonialism comes in many different varieties, the outcome of competing theoretical temperaments: this requires us to proceed with care. But minimally the modish prefix ('post') indicates that the issue of temporality is decisive – suggesting that post-colonialism seeks to imagine a new temporality in which the connections between the colonial world of the past to the post-colonial world of the present and future can be illuminated. Evidence of these concerns can be found in formal historiography, in museum-curating, in fiction and popular memoirs, and in all manner of innovatory practices in the visual arts. In this endeavour, the boundaries between historiographical convention and 'memory-text' are becoming increasingly convoluted. While there exists a powerful current of thought which insists that our own times conspire to make memory a cognitive impossibility, there is simultaneously an extraordinary outpouring of different types of memory-text. The best of these rearrange given notions of temporality, thereby creating new passages between past and present. The inspirations behind these attempts to bring the past into the present are varied. In the metropolitan countries, however – in the old imperial centres, and certainly in Britain – a common purpose in bringing these pasts into the present is to demonstrate the continuation of colonial mentalities in the post-colonial world. In this the issue of race is uppermost. If a single imperative drives the political agenda of post-colonialism, it turns on the belief that contemporary racial thought is the immediate legacy of empire. Remembering empire becomes a means for us – in the present – to know race. But how does this injunction to remember square with the everyday forgetfulness of 'strolling spectators' and 'practical Londoners'?

Empire, in the context of popular memory, is a very large abstraction; it is, for the most part, too large a category to be good to think with. Empire, in its full compass, comprised many centuries of events over many continents. As well as conquest and exploitation, there comes within its story the full gamut of human life. To endeavour to bring all this past into consciousness in the present would indeed bring with it many impracticalities, to use Freud's term. Or to adapt Nietzsche, it would give rise to a 'fanaticism'. But fanaticism, in this sense, is a judgement which derives not from the content of ideas expressed, but rather from the manner of their expression. Imagine a posse of proselytising historians – armed with bulging briefcases of appropriate documents and with easily digestible tracts for the innocent novice – interposing themselves in Trafalgar Square, insistently explaining to those enjoying the summer evening the importance of the imperial past. We could, perhaps, give this scenario a sectarian flavour. We could imagine one group declaring that the imperial legacy continues to generate many evils in the present, and another adopting the contrary view, determining to demonstrate the good which empire bestowed. There is nothing fanatical in supposing that knowledge of the imperial past is in itself valuable. I happen to think this about all knowledge of the past. Fanaticism occurs as a result of the dispositions of knowledge. It occurs when proselytisers organise themselves as outcasts from what Nietzsche designated as 'life', and Freud as the 'real and immediate'; when a consuming sense of the past prevails; when the past is absolute to such a pitch that nothing can – ever – be forgotten. Or as Nietzsche put this, in uncharacteristically modulated terms, the decisive issue is the 'degree of historical sense' which operates in the present.

To think in such terms – in terms of the 'degree' to which the past is active in the present – serves to undermine any abstract notion of historical time. It directs us toward the weight of *that* past in *this* present, or of *those* pasts in *these* presents. It draws our attention to the valency of historical time: to the fact that different pasts reverberate to different effect in different moments of the present. It breaks into a commonsense notion that the past is simply an inert lump of time ('what happened'), or that the past is 'homogenous', as Walter Benjamin described this view. Not least, it alerts us to the possibility that human intervention – the power of the human imagination – can activate different pasts to become meaningful in the present. I think, loosely, this is what Nietzsche was proposing when he indicated the potential for a historical practice which he deemed 'critical'.

All explorations of the historical past need to negotiate between the requirements of the past and the requirements of the present; between the dead and the living; between remembering and forgetting. Perhaps it is little surprise that historians tend to err toward the first element in each of these pairings – which may represent less an occupational hazard than a temperamental predisposition which drew them into historical enquiry in the first place. But whatever the proclivities of the historian, these polarities mark out the moral dilemmas of encountering the past. For the most part, in professional history, the position adopted by the historian remains unstated or implicit. In the profusion of memory-texts outside the academy, in many popular reconstructions of the past, and in public life more generally, they are often more heavily accentuated. At one extreme – the extreme which accentuates the requirements of the dead over the living – a mode of historical time is employed which can properly be called sacred. This is a historical time which is absolute, and shares much with what Nietzsche identified as monumental and antiquarian histories. In this conception, the ties to previous generations are of such profound and fundamental significance that they dictate the moral conduct of the present. In this respect, sacred time received exemplary philosophical expression in the writings of Edmund Burke, where human wisdom *was* the generational lineage connecting the present to the past. At the other extreme – the extreme which accentuates the requirements of the living over the dead – we see something of the mirror-image of the sacred, in which the present exists in a domain entirely free from all that came before it. In turn, this might be thought of as a Jacobin conception of historical time, in which the calendar itself is revolutionised, inaugurating Year One. This too is a mode of historical time which is absolute, resolutely repudiating any belief in the necessity of a dialogical understanding of the relations between past and present. Absolute historical time is in essence monologic. Nietzsche's commitments to a 'critical' imagining of history were motivated exactly in order to open up the possibilities for a more deeply dialogical encounter between past and present, dead and living, remembering and forgetting.

In the public arena manifestations of absolute historical time are not infrequent. If for example we think back to the Thatcherite moment of the 1980s it is apparent that Mrs Thatcher herself possessed a truly schizophrenic conception of the past, speaking in the tongue of Edmund Burke whilst conducting policy as if she were the reincarnation of Maximilien Robespierre. After she secured the military defeat of Argentina in 1982 her idea of the past became classically, unambiguously monumental, supposing a revivified national – and imperial – spirit to be just around the corner. Those Tories who have followed her as leader of the Conservative Party readily intone a bizarrely sacramental history, while their party declines apace, as if incantation will hold back the liquidation that engulfs them. Labour on the other hand – New Labour – gives every indication of wishing to be cut adrift from history. In the Blairite lexicon, the past signifies what is old and obstructive, an impediment to the riches that the future will bring. 'There has never been a time', Blair declared to a Washington audience, 'when . . . a study of history provides so little instruction for our present day' (*Guardian*, 30 July 2003). How much this has been plotted intellectually is difficult to tell. It could simply be a consequence of a willed indifference to any idea which falls beyond the remit of the ruthless pragmatism which has increasingly come to characterise current

Labour administrations. The effect, though, is to create a phantom, one-dimensional institution of public life, in which politics itself is accorded the role of uninvited guest.

However this situation is more complex than at first appears, and much revolves around what can be called ethnic time. Ethnicity, it appears, is a consequence of modernity: it supplies a powerful, if imaginary, sense of history, origins and location. It serves to reassure the subjects of modern life that not only are they 'from' somewhere, but that this somewhere has an identifiable, flesh-and-blood location. This too can work as a form of absolutism; it is potentially the most intoxicating of all contemporary forms of a lived, embodied consciousness of the past. At its most ferocious it fires faith in racial particularism. It can deploy an entire melodrama of blood-lines, as if *the same blood* has been transmitted from generation to generation, from time immemorial. Distant ancestors from the past make up the imagined 'us' to the exclusion of the living others of the present. Ethnic time, or the time of 'old' ethnicities, works by an unappeased, exclusive memory: the dead can't be forgotten; the living, possessed by the past, are exiled from the 'real and immediate'. (For the distinction between 'old' and 'new' ethnicities, see Hall 1996.)

This is a mode of thought and life in which the old has a premium. In this respect one would have supposed that such sentiments would have been far removed from the day-to-day concerns of New Labour. The Labour administrations of Mr Blair have not been noticeable in addressing racial issues. Both racism and anti-racism occupy that never-never land of 'the old' which Labour strives to transcend. A society which encourages opportunity based on merit, individual competence in the market, and reward for social respectability: these, it seems, will bring about the withering away not only of racial difference, but so too of its troublesome, obsolescent counterpart, anti-racism. After all just look at the United States, where Colin Powell and Condoleezza Rice are testament to the blessings of a racially blind meritocracy. In the closing formulation of his address to Congress, Blair put this in heroic terms: 'Tell the world why you are proud of America. Tell them when the Star-Spangled Banner starts Americans get to their feet . . . Not because some state official told them to. But because, whatever race, colour, class or creed they are, being American means being free' (Blair 2003). Yet patriotic fervour of this intensity can easily transmute into an ethnic recidivism which bears all the hallmarks not just of the old, but of the ancient.

Shortly after winning the election in 1997, Blair and his then Home Secretary, Jack Straw, commissioned an inquiry into the issue of race and ethnicity in Britain. Drafted under the auspices of the Runnymede Trust and chaired by Bhikhu Parekh, it was finally published in October 2000. Amongst its comprehensive conclusions appeared the following observation:

Britishness, as much as Englishness, has systematic, largely unspoken,

racial connotations. Whiteness nowhere features as an explicit condition of being British, but it is widely understood that Englishness, and
therefore by extension Britishness, is racially coded . . . Race is deeply
entwined with political culture and with the idea of nation, and
underpinned by a distinctively British kind of reticence – to take race
and racism seriously, or even to talk about them at all, is bad form,
something not done in polite company.

(Runnymede Trust 2000: 38)

'Unspoken racial connotations . . .': it's hardly an insurgent formulation. Yet
the controversy it induced was staggering. It wasn't simply that the tabloid
press, or its usual suspects, went wild; the reaction from the broadsheet papers
was little different. Andrew Roberts, a historian of spectacularly right-wing
sensibilities, made the running in the *Sunday Telegraph*, arguing that the idea of
Britain was not a contingent historical contrivance, but an 'inherent' and
'organic' manifestation of a deep underlying nationhood, in which a distinct
historic destiny was (and is) inscribed. He identified the unlikely figure of the
historian, Linda Colley, as the malevolent intellectual inspiration for the Commission – repeating an unguarded attack which had first been aired in *The
Times* a little while before, and which Conservatives were to rehearse in the
future (Roberts 2000; *The Times* 2000; *The Guardian*, 5 May 2001). This was
ethnic time in full flood. That a figure of the political eccentricity of Roberts
should pursue such a line is not surprising; that others, of more liberal conviction, should organise their argument in similar mode is worrying indeed. Thus
Will Hutton, for example, who symbolises a certain intransigent radicalism in
the broadsheet press, and who is sympathetic to much of what the report
proposed, bridled at its reading of Britishness. To emphasise the 'racial connotations' of Britain, he claimed, served not to open public debate, but to close it
down – leading him, and he supposed many others, to rally to '*The Sun's* 12
reasons to be proud of being British' (Hutton 2000). This theme was picked up
by others. Jack Straw, who originally launched the inquiry, was representative
of this response. On publication, he back-tracked fast. He was quoted by the
the *Sunday Telegraph* (15 October 2000) as believing that the Report had come
from those 'who had turned their backs on the concept of patriotism'. To this
he added the assertion – seeing no need for further embellishment – 'I am
proud to be British'. There may be many reasons why people choose to
embrace patriotism or to feel pride in their country. But surely a thoughtful,
responsible pride must also coexist with recognition of the moments of barbar-
ism, with an understanding of the ills which have arisen from conduct perpetrated in the name of one's country? How else can pride be manifest?
Should it not also require confronting – where this occurs – the continuing
destructive consequences, in the 'real and immediate', of past deeds? A recognition, minimally, of liability in the present? Would it not be wise for those who
choose to claim a proud connection to the good past to recognise, equally, the

shameful? To suppose otherwise is indeed to subscribe to Nietzsche's idea of fanaticism.

That a fanatical recuperation of the past, along these lines, should emanate from the pragmatic ultras of New Labour is revealing. It marks, I think, an instance of what Freud described as 'acting out'. In his paper 'Remembering, repeating and working through' he suggested that a certain kind of personality 'does not remember anything of what he has forgotten and repressed, but acts it out. He reproduces it not as a memory but as an action; he repeats it, without, of course, knowing that he is repeating it' (Freud 1958: 150). 'Acting out', as opposed to 'working through', represents an unconscious repetition of previous mental habits. It speaks itself, as if it came from nowhere. As Adam Phillips indicates, to act out is to live in the past, but not to live in history (Phillips 2004). In this sense it is a paradigmatic form of ethnic time – the time of ethnic absolutism. 'Working through', on the other hand, allows a requisite degree of forgetfulness, and in so doing creates the possibilities for engaging productively with past and present, such that neither one subsumes the other. By thinking critically of the past, as Nietzsche would have it, and by centring the realities of the present, it is possible to imagine what ethnic time prohibits: the chance to think historically.

In Britain, opportunities for thinking historically in the public sphere are at best uneven; more especially, as I have implied, day-to-day politics seems entirely devoid of any comprehension of the deeper historical past. One significant counter-tendency, though, particularly given to the *public* imperatives of 'working through', is the burgeoning movement across the globe for those in the present who seek redress for past crimes – for crimes committed either against their own selves in earlier years, or against family and ethnic forebears further back in historical time (see Thompson 2002). These various movements now address a myriad of past injustices, drawing into public speech horrors which were hitherto unspeakable, or which – if spoken – went systematically unheard in public life. Colonialism, slavery and racial injustice have been prominent in these attempts to bring the past into the present. As yet, the British state has barely been touched by any one of these movements, while politicians give every indication that the last thing they want is to be embroiled in old historical controversies which (they assume) will bring few electoral returns. Those pleas for public redress which have occurred have been relatively random, reminding us that bids for reparation are subject to political and media power, and that their influence in the present may conform only very unequally to the scale of past injustice. The Queen has formally apologised to the Maoris for the dispossession of their lands in the colonial period. She apologised, too, in India for the Amritsar massacre of 1919, though there is reason to think the apology compromised by unwise comments uttered about the massacre by her husband. Tony Blair apologised for the Irish famine. But when he was in South Africa in January 1999, in the face of significant public pressure, he refused to make any apology for the concentration camps for Boer civilians instituted by the British during the South African War – a refusal repeated later in the year by the Duke of Kent, who was representing the Queen at the official commemoration of the War. A small number of Kikuyu in Kenya are seeking legal redress for abuse they received at the hands of the British military and colonial authorities during the Mau Mau rebellion in the early 1950s, and – arising from the period after independence – rural Kenyan women are lobbying for recognition of the sexual crimes committed against them by British forces stationed in Kenya, and for compensation. The controversies which followed the Bloody Sunday shootings in Derry in 1972 have been shunted off to a strictly juridical domain, with no government wishing directly to confront the question of liability. In January 2001 around New Cross in south-east London the Metropolitan Police posted hundreds of 'Appeal for assistance' notices in connection with the house-fire of 20 years before, when 14 young black people died. This was a tragedy intensified on two counts: first, the conviction held by many that the deaths were caused by a racially motivated arson attack; second, the widespread perception that in the public life of the nation these deaths of blacks just didn't seem to count, or didn't count in the same way as the deaths of white teenagers. These factors turned the event into something more than just another unsolved crime. To its critics, the British state was implicated not as a result of a sin of commission (unleashing violence on its citizens) but of a sin of omission (failing to protect its citizens and indict the wrong-doers). Twenty years on, these 14 young faces stare out from street-posters, ghosts from an unfinished and turbulent past: one can't help but imagine the lives they never had. But in so far as these memories remain a public issue in our own times, they principally do so, intermittently, as a police or administrative matter.

All these issues came to public attention as a result of campaigns seeking recognition and reparation, in a bid to resolve injustices from the past that had been carried forward into the present. They represent very different historical experiences, united only by the fact that there were those in the present who endeavoured to keep these memories alive, and who called upon the British state to accept public liability. In different ways, they all, I think, connect to 'life', at least for those engaged in the remembrance, without necessary recourse to overarching categories like empire or colonialism. Some of these episodes were indisputably imperial, like the killings at Amritsar or the counter-insurgency in Kenya. All bear the undercurrent, or more, of racial violence. Those events closer to our own times represent particular responses to particular wrongs to particular named individuals: *that* past in *this* present. In each case, the process of bringing the past into the present works by different mechanisms, in different institutional settings, which impose different discursive criteria on the manner in which the truth of the past can be established (see Radstone 2003). Prominent in the narratives produced in these situations has been the emphasis on their therapeutic capacities: on the belief that the souls of those who have suffered in the past, or of those descendants who carry their

pain in the present, can only be stilled once their story has been told, legitimated, and recognised by others. Alongside this, although working by different
institutional and discursive procedures, is recourse to the rule of law. Different
again, campaigns to address the wrongs of the past invariably also call upon
formal historical knowledge. Therapeutic, juridical and historiographical procedures all have different ends, work to different effect, and depend on what
may well be conflicting categories of historical truth (see Wood 1999: ch. 5).
On occasion, the conflict between the historical record, and other – popular or
remembered – recuperations of the past can ignite anew further controversies
in the present, prolonging rather than stilling painful memories. (For a compelling
instance, which requires us to take heed, see Hobsbawm 1997: ch. 21.)

Given the extent of the differences in play no general conclusion about this
form of remembrance is possible. To hear Mr Blair apologise for the Irish
famine, with no larger historical understanding apparent of Ireland and of its
connections to Britain, and with no palpable consequence in the political present, seems no more than nominal, a safe opportunity for the Prime Minister to
display his well-paraded moral earnestness. In other circumstances, the making
of an apology on the part of an oppressor can trigger a new consciousness of
the past, and can open up new historical possibilities. Importantly, as Wole
Soyinka insists, it can also shape *the future*:

> Memory – of what has been, of acts of commission or omission, of a
> responsibility abdicated – affects the future conduct of power in any
> form. Failure to adopt some imaginative recognition of such a prin-
> ciple merely results in the enthronement of a political culture that
> appears to know no boundaries – the culture of impunity.
>
> (Soyinka 1999: 81–2)

Whether this can ever 'heal wounds', 'replace what has been lost', or 're-
create broken moulds', as Nietzsche hoped, must remain an open matter. (An
important historiographical argument to the contrary can be found in Wood
2000.) Everything depends on the conjunctural balance of political forces, in
the present, of which public atonement is only ever a part.

The efficacy of apology-making, and of the kindred practice of establishing
truth commissions, has been questioned from many different quarters. Conventional critiques draw attention to the extent to which moral issues subsume
politics, and to the privileging of the therapeutic over the historiographical
process. The historical time of apology-making and truth commissions is
clearly (in the terms described above) sacramental – a point made explicitly by
Marina Warner (Warner 2000). In extreme situations – and truth-commissions
are convened to manage historical extremities – what is intended to free people
from the past can end up doing exactly the opposite. There can be no guarantees. The Truth and Reconciliation Commission (TRC) in South Africa,
which remains the most celebrated public attempt in contemporary times to

harmonise the present with the terror of the past, drew upon a powerful sense of the claim which the past has over those in the present. The idiom in which this was most frequently expressed was sacramental or, more particularly, Christian. Forgiveness, atonement, redemption: these were the watchwords of the TRC. Their living embodiment occurred in the figure of Archbishop Desmond Tutu, who chaired the commission – and, more indirectly, in the political example of the new nation's leader, Nelson Mandela. Desmond Tutu's determination to take inside himself the pain of the apartheid past was extraordinary to witness, turning around expectations. (On Tutu, see Derrida 2001: 42–4.) This was sacramental history which worked – in Nietzsche's terms – by what he designated as 'critical procedures': by incorporating 'into oneself what is past and foreign'. The institutional organisation of the TRC undoubtedly shaped the words which were spoken: as in any social situation, generic forms emerged and those speaking quickly learned what was expected of them. Yet at the same time, what was impressive about the TRC was that when people were asked to tell their stories, as so often in such cases, many unpredictable things happened. There occurred a cacophony of voices which never quite conformed to official expectation (see Krog 1998).

The TRC was launched to investigate the violence of the apartheid years. Its terms did not include the longer historical issue of racial segregation in southern Africa. If they had, then the actions of the British state would have come under scrutiny. But this is symptomatic. There are many parts of the world in which – in the *longue durée* – British intervention in the past has been a factor in contemporary catastrophes: not only in South Africa, but in Iraq, Palestine, Kashmir, Zimbabwe, and so on. In these political emergencies, however, the perspective of the *longue durée* is not easily accommodated, or liability easily unravelled. At the same time, in Britain, these crises, and others like them in earlier times, are not readily connected in the popular mind to a specifically British past, or not in any concrete or historical sense. They too quickly comprise that elusive domain of a history which happened 'elsewhere', or 'overseas', some far away region of the globe from which *we* – Britons – remain disconnected. There is little sign in Britain of a cacophony of voices engaged in public discussion about the history and legacies of empire. Where debate does occur it is, as a result, strangely stilted.

The depth of this silence is significant, and it opens out certain paradoxes. We can see this clearly in the case of Australia. In its founding as a nation, Australia was powerfully encoded as a white man's country – with an intensity as great of that of the Union of South Africa, born in the same decade. Much of the history of Australia in the later part of the twentieth century turned on the disintegration of the white settler nation, and on the uneven, protracted emergence of a less racially exclusive society. For the displacement of the anglophone settler to begin, the unspeakability of the internal, violent history between settler and Aborigine needed to be recognised by the white population, internalised and overcome. Whites had to recognise themselves as white, and to learn both the privileges which this had brought and the claims which *that* past had on *this* present. In a nation which took pride in its democratic commitments, in both political and civil society, these were hard lessons to learn. Deep in the imaginings of the nation, the inner forms of the older settler society continued to be acted out; the *frenzied* capacities of whiteness, which from the beginning had underwritten the democratic ideal of the settler, continued to be repeated. Yet the extraordinarily complex political and symbolic work of confronting this collective past and of imagining new possibilities for the future – despite evidence of manifold intellectual dissension, and of many political setbacks too – has in its way been exemplary, especially from a British perspective. This is a cultural transformation which has worked on many fronts, in which (broadly) juridical, historiographical and therapeutic interventions have operated, if not harmoniously, at least in recognition of the overall, distinctive contribution of each. The result has been manifest in the upheaval of the received settler conceptions of the relation between past and present. A new plurality of voices has been triggered, signalling the possibilities for new temporalities to emerge from which, in turn, present and future will assume a different shape and disposition.

Predictably, such a transformation generated its own backlash. Perhaps the height of this reaction, in public, occurred toward the end of 1996, following Pauline Hanson's maiden speech in parliament. Hanson had won the Queensland seat of Oxley as an independent, engineering a huge swing in what previously had been a Labour stronghold. In her electoral campaign she had been vociferous in denouncing government assistance to Aborigines, and in her victory speech she vowed to represent everyone in her constituency, no matter what their race, except for Aborigines and Torres Strait Islanders. Much of her own justification for arriving at such positions rested on her stated conviction that *she* was speaking what zealots of political correctness had endeavoured to make unspeakable: the rights of white settlers. In the controversies which followed, those who supported her in the Liberal Party – from which she had been expelled during the Oxley campaign – adopted this same line: that she was exercising her right of free speech to raise a legitimate issue of public concern. This was certainly the position of the Liberal prime minister, John Howard, who himself, some 8 years earlier, had found himself in a situation similar to Hanson's. In a parliamentary debate on 30 October 1996, when the Hanson phenomenon was alive in the public imagination, Howard addressed the problem of race and nation. He emphasised the right of Australians 'to feel extremely proud about our past', due to the fact that there 'are few nations in the world that can boast such a record of democracy, such a record of fair treatment and such a record of harmonious blending together of people from different racial backgrounds than Australia'. He welcomed the prospect of 'reconciliation' between white Australians and Aboriginal and Torres Strait Islander people, indicating his 'regret' for the treatment of indigenous peoples in the past. He then continued:

But I could also say that I profoundly reject with some vigour what others have described, and I have adopted the description, as the black armband view of Australian history. I believe the balance sheet of Australian history is a very generous and benign one. I believe that, like any other nation, we have black marks upon our history but amongst the nations of the world we have a remarkably positive history.

I think there is a yearning in the Australian community right across the political divide for its leaders to enunciate more pride and sense of achievement in what has gone before us. I think we have been too apologetic about our history in the past.

. . . I have said before, and I am happy to repeat it, that I do believe that in recent times there has been a tendency towards excessive political correctness in political debate in this country

(Howard 1996a; for an incisive interpretation, see Brett 1997)

The notion of 'black armband' history had been coined in 1993 by Geoffrey Blainey; Howard's use of it propelled it into the public limelight. He returned to the idea again a month later, in a set-piece public lecture: 'The "black armband" view of our past reflects a belief that most Australian history since 1788 has been little more than a disgraceful history of imperialism, exploitation, racism, sexism and other forms of discrimination' (Howard 1996b). Notwithstanding the sectarian ill-will which lies behind these statements, I think that – politically, tactically – they have served his cause effectively. For to accuse others of imagining history as one relentless story of oppression works to divest himself of his own fanatical conception of the past, to turn the tables, and to brand his opponents as the new fanatics.

The irony here is inescapable. Those engaged in recasting the history of Australia, in order to take account of the silences that have enveloped the violence of the nation's ethnic past, have done so in the hope of freeing themselves, and others, from the damage of a fanatical, monologic, history. And yet they become the stigmatised.

These confrontations in Australia throw interesting light on the circumstances in Britain, especially on the discussions among professional historians. My sense is that it is common for historical enquiry which aims to confront the racially exploitative dimensions of empire to be disparaged – as being too simple; too present-minded; too fixated on race; in a word, too fanatical. I haven't heard mainstream historians in the UK employ the notion of 'black armband' history, as such, though sentiments recognisably the same are routinely spoken. More particularly, among historians, this has become a reflex reaction against the idea of the post-colonial, as if all that post-colonial perspectives can deliver is a litany of weak-minded political condemnation, using the categories of the present in order to condemn those of the past. This has become something of a stock currency, reproducing the sentiment without engaging in the argument. Even historians of brilliance succumb to this.

Anthony Pagden, for example, is happy to depict post-colonialism simply as the inversion of 'the old schoolroom narrative', supposing that 'the post-colonial vision' sees only 'rapacious merchant adventurers and overbearing racists stripping and slaughtering defenceless indigenous peoples' (Pagden 2002). True enough, there is plenty of bad and indifferent history-writing, post-colonial or otherwise. But why the denunciation of what he calls 'the post-colonial vision', *tout court*? There are I expect two explanations, both of which touch on real issues.

The first has to do with temporality itself. The collective intellectual endeavour which goes under the name of post-colonialism represents a great variety of conceptual positions. Some of these are valuable for historical explanation, and some aren't. As I see it, and as I have suggested throughout this chapter, one of the most promising insights of post-colonial theory is that which encourages a re-imagining of the question of historical time. It demands that we explore the complexities of the passages which connect the colonial past to the post-colonial present; it demands, in other words, that we explicitly deploy a sense of history which can comprehend the-past-in-the-present. Yet arguably this is also the least developed aspect of current post-colonial research. Excellent historical work has shown how the racial and colonial imperatives of the past organised entire systems of thought which not so long ago appeared, if not entirely innocent, at least free from any deep-seated or colonial imprimatur (including the 'unspoken racial connotations' attached to the imagined collectivity of Britain, for example). Less fully achieved, however, is a more deeply historical, theorised understanding of the ways in which these inherited cognitive systems are reproduced (or not) in the present. Without being more attentive to the complex links between past and present it can seem as if too much is being assumed or short-circuited. To a degree, this reflects an underdeveloped feature of current work; if one feels less generously motivated, one might also say it supplies a pretext to sceptical, or hostile, critics.

The second returns us to the question of fanaticism, complicating the scenario I've sketched so far. There is no reason to be defensive either about a sober historical audit of empire and colonialism which concludes that systematic exploitation lay at the heart of the imperial story, or one which links this historiographical interpretation to a moral or political critique. After all, it is necessary to spell out these positions, which in themselves are hardly remarkable, only in so far as contrary views prevail. Historiographically, this is little different from John and Barbara Hammond, at the beginning of the last century, setting out to persuade professional historians of the full force of the human costs of the industrial revolution. No one should suppose that to think in these terms must preclude all the *other* facets of human activity – the unanticipated, wondrous, bizarre – which occurred under the aegis of empire, or indeed to underestimate the passion for ethical conduct which accompanied imperial rule. Nor is this to impose the ideas of the present on those of the past, or to opt for simplicity rather than historical complexity. But it is true that the present does hold a privileged position, in that the shifting shape of the present asks new questions of the past. This is so of all historical enquiry; in those versions influenced by post-colonial approaches, this is merely made explicit. Few, if any, past civilisations in human history have been free from systematic violence. Why, then, a particular concern with Britain's imperial past? Because – or only because – of the belief that the inner forms of *that* past continue silently to be reproduced in *this* present, and that this matters for the 'real and immediate'. Or as Adorno argued in a different context, because 'the past one wishes to evade is still so intensely alive' (Adorno 1986: 115). In the first instance, this turns on a political reading of the present more than it does the historical reconstruction of the past. If sceptics don't find this political reading persuasive, then in all likelihood they will find the history it generates contrived: it will appear as history in black-armband mode – as fanatical.

Here indeed is an irresolvable dilemma between 'life', on the one hand, and 'fanaticism', on the other. The concept of 'life', in the Nietzschean sense, has much going for it, not least for historians who are always susceptible to privileging the past over the present. Yet 'life' is also one of those deceptive concepts (in the same way as Marx describes population) which appears to be grounded and concrete – what could be truer to life than chilling in Trafalgar Square? – but which carries within it many unseen historical determinations (Marx 1973). The difficulty about thinking of the colonial past in the post-colonial present is that this is a situation, especially in its racial co-ordinates, where much remains unspoken or unspeakable. Much is invisible. It is a situation that contains a complex history in which particular aspects of the past are not easily confronted for what they are. Bringing these histories into the light of day requires revealing the conditions of their unspeakability, or understanding what Parekh courteously calls 'a distinctively British kind of reticence'.

Reflex declamations of pride in one's nation represent only another form of unspeakability. 'A thing which has not been understood', wrote Freud, 'inevitably reappears; like an unlaid ghost, it cannot rest until the mystery has been solved and the spell broken' (Freud 1955: 122). To speak the unspeakable – 'for life' – requires what may be construed as a fanatical moment, otherwise the unspeakable dimensions of life continue to remain unspoken, 'like an unlaid ghost'. Nietzsche was explicit in his conviction that critical history needed to draw into itself elements from both monumental and antiquarian modes of thought. Perhaps 'a degree' of fanaticism – as the counter rather than as the adjunct to absolute historical time – is a necessary virtue?

Historians, as the practitioners of formal written history, are rightly concerned to maintain the integrity of the voices of the historical past. As we know well enough from our own times, it is no longer only in 'religious or military anniversaries' that the past mimics the present. But what of 'mnemic' systems other than those of formal history?[1] What of the organisation of public memory?

The scene at Trafalgar Square – to return to the opening image – was *underdetermined* by its historical past, as if suspended from historical time. In this lies its allure. The surrounding monuments to empire, so far as the casual observer could tell, played no active part in the summer tableau. Yet for all the pleasures of the moment, those actors in this transitory scene were not simply hedonistic urban nomads, passing through the present untouched by the weight of history. If the tableau is set in motion, then the temporal dimensions of before and after take on greater effect: the relaxed participants begin to find themselves moving into situations in which they cease to be 'strolling spectators' and a sharper degree of historical determination prevails. But even the monumental *mise-en-scene* might prove more complex than I have implied.

It has become too easy, I think, to assume that history in monumental mode is only history in calcified form, either heroising a dodgy past, or falling into deserved oblivion. This, though, derives from a familiar formalism. It is true, only a melodramatically 'unpractical Londoner', hurrying on his or her way to catch the train at Charing Cross, would stop to weep in front of the statue of Queen Eleanor. It's true, too, that there are few people on the planet so touched by the memory of Lord Nelson that they stretch their necks to look 167 feet into the heavens, just to get a glimpse of a bronze figure three times the height of the real-life human being it commemorates. But it might prompt others, of a curious disposition, to ask why mid-nineteenth-century Britons would have pressed for such a memorial – to which there are predictably profane, though still important, answers.

History in monumental mode seeks to enclose the past, and elevate the dead over the living; yet like any mnemic system, it has its unruly moments. Monumental history is not always able to free itself from the constraints of the present. On the south of Trafalgar Square is a statue of Charles I, which occupies the exact spot that marks the symbolic centre of London.[2] During the period of the republic, parliament, suitably attuned to the cash-nexus, sold the statue and ordered that it be melted down. Instead, in a wonderful gesture anticipating an entire genre of magical realism, royalist sympathisers furtively buried the effigy, and resurrected it after the monarchy was restored. It now stands facing the place where Charles met his death on the executioner's block in Whitehall, the figure commemorated in bronze (according to one venerable guidebook) looking 'singularly well-dined, almost debonair' (Piper 1964: 94). Closer to our own times we might consider, perhaps, the fate of the marble statue of Lady Thatcher, commissioned for the lobby of the House of Lords. When first on show, Paul Kelleher, an events organiser from Isleworth, aimed a blow at the statue's nose with a cricket bat which he had hidden in his raincoat. In mitigation he explained that he was hoping to make the world a safer place for his young son; he, in turn, was informed by the magistrate that there was

a right and proper way to protest and also a wrong way to do so. The way you acted to knock the head off a valuable statue of a politician

233

who left power over 10 years ago and whose party is no longer the party of government, was very much the wrong way.

(*Guardian*, 20 February 2003)

Kelleher was jailed for 3 months. Clearly, the iconoclastic assailant in this case recognised the mnemic power of the image he had decapitated, endeavouring to bring the memory of Lady Thatcher back from monumental time to historical time. As the magistrate correctly indicated, there are other – admittedly less spectacular – ways of doing this which don't require the use of a cricket bat. For example, I've written elsewhere about the statue of Field-Marshall Jan Smuts, the anglophile prime minister of South Africa in the early decades of the Union, which now stands in Parliament Square in London (Schwarz 1999). From the years of the First World War until his death in 1950, Smuts was a political-media celebrity of huge renown in Britain. Yet after his death so quickly did his memory recede from popular life that, by the time the statue was erected in 1956, he had already entered virtual oblivion – a transformation connected to the larger demise of British confidence in its empire. The transition from celebrated mortal time to a forgetful monumental time was in this instance peculiarly rapid. My purpose in returning to Smuts, however, was to break this forgetfulness, revive his memory, and pull him back into history – not least because he was a decisive figure in organising, at a key period, the 'racial connotations' of what it meant to be British.

Much depends on historical context. Ribbon-cutting and a few mumbled platitudes by a dignitary at an unveiling do much to speed a memory on its way to monumental oblivion; sentiments, though, which truly connect to life create the contrary effect – as Lincoln's epochal, transfigurative words, for example, demonstrated at Gettysburg, in which he imagined a new compact for the American people between the living and the dead. (Above all, see Wills 1992.) Or conversely, unexpected feelings can be triggered when historical monuments to an old, discredited regime are systematically dismantled. This occurred in Budapest at the end of the Communist years, when the city's memorials to the Communist heroes of the past were transported to a park on the outskirts. Some of the capital's citizens supported this policy; others wanted the statues and plaques to remain where they were; others again wished them all destroyed. Many, though, had become habituated to these monuments, or to particular ones of them, regarding them less as icons to the Communist past than as familiar, affective landmarks in the everyday urban present. They became invested, in other words, with new meanings (Nadkarni 2003). In this sense, a city's monuments do indeed work as a collective mnemic structure, spatialising the historical past in the urban landscape of the present. For long periods, these memorials may remain unseen, lying dormant in the urban imagination. But as in any other mnemic system, in new circumstances they can become active again. This happened, in fact, during the replanning of Trafalgar Square. Quite unexpectedly, the merits of the two generals

234

commemorated in the square, Major General Sir Henry Havelock and General Sir Charles Napier, became a matter of public controversy. The leader of the Greater London Authority, Ken Livingstone, subscribing to a characteristically Jacobin viewpoint, believed them both rightfully forgotten, and implied that their memorials – along with many others in the city – could usefully be scrapped. In reaction, Bernard Jenkin, the Conservative shadow minister for London, condemned this as 'Britain bashing', whilst a colonel in Havelock's old regiment, relying on a sacramental interpretation, complained that if Livingstone's recommendations were to be carried out it would be tantamount to 'consigning our history to oblivion' (*Guardian*, 20 October 2000). More surprising, though, was the range of – informed – opinion which seriously debated the appropriateness of commemorating in the twenty-first century these ancient military heroes of empire. The setting of Trafalgar Square proves to be less inert, as a historical force, than it might appear to the naked eye.

If we follow Freud's suggestion that monumental history is a mnemic system, with certain affinities to other social forms in which memory is organised, then it necessarily has a degree of openness, dynamism and unpredictability. If, at the same time, monumental time spatialises the historical past then the histories it represents are significant in the present. This spatialisation of the past serves as a resource for the present: at times dormant, at other times – potentially at least – active, in ways that can never be anticipated. For this reason, I can see in principle no objection to having the official imperial past remembered in the streets of the capital; sooner this than banish every figure in stone or bronze who does not rate sufficient immediate recognition quotient. Over time, certain memorials will be ravaged by the elements, be replaced or removed by official intervention, or even, perhaps, become the object of popular ire. Like any mnemic system, monumental history exists in a temporal dimension that requires evolution and transformation. But if the official empire is recalled in this way, then so too *other* memories of empire need to be recorded in public form. A bust of Nehru outside India House, and of Mandela on the South Bank, doesn't quite do it.

The injunction to remember the empire, or any aspect of the historical past, has necessarily to be a limited one. More important than recalling this or that episode is to devise a means by which we can imagine the complex temporalities in which past, present and future are organised. But one of the difficulties which arises is that the vocabulary we possess to grasp the-past-in-the-present has traditionally been profoundly sacramental – composed of metaphors of souls or spirits, redemption or atonement – while a more forcefully present-minded consciousness, described here as Jacobin, relies on a starker, more rectilinear and secular sense of the world. While conventional historiographies do not easily accommodate themselves to history in sacramental mode, for perfectly persuasive intellectual reasons, in the Jacobin imagination, on the other hand, questions of the power of the historical pasts, and of their continuation into the present, can barely be formulated. The current interest in the operations of memory represents, among other things, an attempt to overcome this dichotomy. Or from another perspective, Benjamin's reflections on differing conceptions of historical time, in his 'Theses on the philosophy of history', remain extraordinarily valuable for our own historical epoch. 'There is a secret agreement between past generations and the present one', he wrote. 'Our coming was expected on earth. Like every generation that preceded us, we have been endowed with a *weak* Messianic power, a power to which the past has a claim. That claim cannot be settled cheaply' (Benjamin 1973: 256).

Notes

1 The standard English-language translation from Freud uses the term 'mnemic', rather than the conventional 'mnemonic'. I'll rely on the former.
2 Not only does Trafalgar Square condense a particular version of historical time. It organises too, in sharp relief, national and imperial space. The determination to fix the centre of the capital represents one aspect of this. Another concerns measurement itself: embedded in the north wall are bronze replicas of imperial standards of length.

BIBLIOGRAPHY

Act Together (2003) *Our Life in Pieces: Objects and Stories from Iraqis in Exile*, Booklet accompanying exhibition at the Diorama Gallery, London, 8–23 March.

Adorno, T. (1986) 'What does coming to terms with the past mean?', in G. Hartman (ed.) *Bitburg in Moral and Political Perspective*, Bloomington: Indiana University Press.

Agyeman, J. and P. Kinsman (1997) 'Analysing Macro- and Micro-environments from a Multicultural Perspective', in E. Hooper-Greenhill (ed.) *Cultural Diversity: Developing Museum Audiences in Britain*, Leicester: Leicester University Press.

Aitchison, C. (1996) 'Monumentally Male', Trouble and Strife no. 34.

Alexander, Z. and A. Dewjee (eds) (1999) *The Wonderful Adventures of Mrs Mary Seacole in Many Lands*, Bristol: Falling Wall Press.

Alibhai-Brown, Y. (2000a) *After Multiculturalism*, London: Foreign Policy Centre.

Alibhai-Brown, Y. (2000b) *Who Do We Think We Are? Imagining the New Britain*, London: Allen Lane.

Allen, N. (1998) 'Maori Vision and the Imperialist Gaze', in T. Barringer and T. Flynn (eds) (1998) *Colonialism and the Object: Empire, Material Culture and the Museum*, London: Routledge.

Anderson, B. (1998) *Imagined Communities: Reflections on the Origins and Spread of Nationalism*, London: Verso.

Anderson, J. (1881) *Scotland in Early Christian Times* (Second Series) *The Rhind Lectures in Archaeology for 1880*, Edinburgh: David Douglas.

Appadurai, A. (1998) *Modernity at Large*, Minneapolis: University of Minnesota Press.

Araeen, R. (1989) *The Other Story: Afro-Asian Artists in Post-War Britain*, London: South Bank Centre.

Archives and Museum of Black Heritage (AMBH) Leaflet (2001).

Arthur, P. (1980) *Political Realities: Government and Politics of Northern Ireland*, London: Longman.

Arts Council of England (2000) *Whose Heritage? The Impact of Cultural Diversity on Britain's Living Heritage*, Report of National Conference at G-Mex, Manchester 1–3 November 1999, London: Arts Council of England.

Ascherson, N. (2003) (Revised Edition) *Stone Voices: The Search for Scotland*, London: Granta Books.

Ash, M. (1991) *This Noble Harbour: A History of the Cromarty Firth*, Invergordon: Comarty Firth Port Authority.

Ashcroft, B., G. Griffiths and H. Tiffin. (1989) *The Empire Writes Back*, London: Routledge.

Askari, K. and J. Yumibe (2002) 'Cinema as "Vernacular Modernism" Conference, University of Chicago 2002', *Screen*, vol. 48 no. 4.

Attfield, J. (2000) *Wild Things: The Material Culture of Everyday Life*, Oxford: Berg.

Aughey, A. (2001) *Nationalism, Devolution and the Challenge to the United Kingdom State*, London: Pluto Press.

Back, L., T. Crabbe and J. Solomos (2001) *The Changing Face of Football: Racism, Identity and Multiculture in the English Game*, Oxford: Berg.

Barber, B. (1996) *Jihad vs. McWorld – How Globalism and Tribalism are Reshaping the World*, New York: Ballantine Books.

Barkan, E. and R. Bush (eds) (2002) *Claiming the Stones, Naming the Bones: Cultural Property and the Negotiation of National and Ethnic Identity*, Los Angeles: Getty Publications.

Barr, A. (1996) *Learning for Change: Community Education and Community Development*, London: Community Development Foundation / The Scottish Community Development Centre.

Barraclough, G. (1955) *History in a Changing World*, Oxford: Basil Blackwell.

Barringer, T. (1998) 'The South Kensington Museum and the Colonial Project' in T. Barringer and T. Flynn (eds) *Colonialism and the Object: Empire, Material Culture and the Museum*, London and New York: Routledge.

Barringer, T. and T. Flynn (eds) (1998) *Colonialism and the Object: Empire, Material Culture and the Museum*, London and New York: Routledge.

Barry, B. (2001) 'Muddles of Multiculturalism', *New Left Review* 8, March/April, second series, pp. 49–71.

Barth, F. (1969) 'Introduction', in F. Barth (ed.) *Ethnic Groups and Boundaries: The Social Organisation of Difference*, London: George Allen and Unwin.

Barthes, R. (1982) *Camera Lucida*, London: Flamingo.

Basu, P. (2002) *Homecomings: Genealogy, Heritage-Tourism and Identity in the Scottish Highland Diaspora*, Unpublished PhD thesis, University College London.

Bauman, Z. (1989) *Modernity and the Holocaust*, Cambridge: Polity.

Bayley, S. (2003) 'Tear it Down and Start Again', *The Independent*, 8 August.

Beck-Gernsheim, E. (1999) *Juden, Deutsche und andere Erinnerungslandschaften*, Frankfurt: Suhrkamp.

Belich, J. (1997) *Making Peoples*, London: Penguin.

Bell, J. and J. Gay (eds) (2001) 'Introduction' to *England Calling: 24 Stories for the 21st Century*, London: Weidenfeld and Nicolson.

Benjamin, A. (2002) 'Mixed metaphor' in the *Guardian (Society* section), 14 March 2002 p. 5.

Benjamin, W. (1973) *Illuminations*, London: Fontana.

Benjamin, W. (1985) 'A Berlin Chronicle', in *One Way Street and Other Writings*, London: Verso.

Bennett, T. (1995) *The Birth of the Museum: History, Theory, Politics*, London and New York: Routledge.

Bennett, T. (1998) *Culture: A Reformer's Science*, London: Sage.

Berry, D. (1994) *Wales and Cinema: The Last Hundred Years*, Cardiff: University of Wales Press.

Bhabha, H. (ed.) (1991) *Nation and Narration*, London: Routledge.

Bhabha, H. (1994) *The Location of Culture*, London: Routledge.

Bianchini, F. (1987) 'GLC R.I.P.: Cultural Policies in London, 1981–1986, *New Formations* no.1, Spring, pp.103–7.

Billig, M. (1995) *Banal Nationalism*, London: Sage.

Bird, J. (1996) 'Art History and Hegemony', in J. Bird *et al.*, *The Black Reader in Visual Culture*, London: Routledge.

Blair, T. (2001) 'Holocaust Memorial Day: Reflection', *Perspectives*, Summer, pp. 4–5.

Blair, T. (2003) 'Speech to United States Congress', www.number-10.gov.uk, 18 July.

Bloody Sunday Trust, 2003. www.bloodysundaytrust.org/historycentre (accessed 1 April 2003).

Board of Education (1929) *Handbook of Suggestions for Teachers*, London: Board of Education.

Bodnar, J. (1992) *Remaking America. Public Memory, Commemoration and Patriotism in the Twentieth Century*, Princeton, NJ: Princeton University Press.

Boniface, P. and P. J. Fowler (1993) *Heritage and Tourism in 'The Global Village'*, London: Routledge.

Boswell, D. and J. Evans (eds) (1999) *Representing the Nation: A Reader: Histories, Heritage and Museums*, London: Routledge.

Bragg, B. (2002a) 'My Favourite World Cup Moment' in *Observer Sport Monthly*, July.

Bragg, B. (2002b) 'Keep the Flag Flying' in *What's On UK*, July.

Brah, A. (1992) 'Difference, Diversity and Differentiation', in J. Donald and A. Rattansi (eds) *Race, Culture, Difference*, London: Sage.

Brah, A. and A. E. Coombes (eds) (2000) *Hybridity and its Discontents: Politics, Science, Culture*, London: Routledge.

Branston, G. (2000) *Cinema and Cultural Modernity*, Maidenhead: Open University Press.

Brett, G. (1991) 'Unofficial Versions', in S. Hiller (ed.) *The Myth of Primitivism – Perspectives on Art*, London: Routledge.

Brett, J. (1997) 'John Howard, Pauline Hanson and the Politics of Grievance', in G. Gray and C. Winter (eds) (1997) *The Resurgence of Racism: Howard, Hanson and the Race Debate*, Melbourne: Monash Publications in History.

British Library Website www.bl.ac.uk (Accessed April 2004).

Brocklehurst, H. and R. Phillips (eds) (2004) *History, Nationhood and the Question of Britain*, Basingstoke: Palgrave Macmillan.

Burston, W. H. (1963) *Principles of History Teaching*, London: Methuen.

Butts, D. (2002) 'Maori and Museums: The Politics of Indigenous Recognition', in R. Sandell, *Museums, Society and Inequality*, London: Routledge.

Caretta, V. (ed.) (1996) *Unchained Voices: An Anthology of Black Authors in the English-Speaking World of the Eighteenth Century*, Lexington: University Press of Kentucky.

Carlucci, A. and P. Barber (2001) *Lie of the Land: The Secret Life of Maps*, London: The British Library.

Carver, M. (1999) *Surviving in Symbols: A Visit to the Pictish Nation*, Edinburgh: Canongate Books.

Cesarani, D. (1997) 'Lacking in Convictions: British War Crimes Policy and National Memory of the Second World War', in M. Evans and K. Lunn (eds) *War and Memory in the Twentieth Century*, Oxford: Berg.

Chandran, R. (2000) 'An Insult to all Our Countrymen', *Daily Mail*, 11 October, p. 7.

Clarke, D. (1996) 'Presenting a National Perspective of Prehistory and Early History in the Museum of Scotland', in J. Atkinson, I. Banks and J. O'Sullivan (eds) *Nationalism and Archaeology*, Glasgow: Cruithne Press.

Clendinnen, I. (1999) *Reading the Holocaust*, Cambridge: Cambridge University Press.

Clifford, J. (1988) *The Predicament of Culture: Twentieth Century Ethnography, Literature and Art*, Cambridge: Harvard University Press.

Clifford, J. (1997) *Routes: Travel and Translation in the late Twentieth Century*, Cambridge, MA: Harvard University Press.

Cohen, A. P. (1985) *The Symbolic Construction of Community*, London: Routledge.

Cole, P. (2000) *Philosophies of Exclusion: Liberal Political Theory and Immigration*, Edinburgh: Edinburgh University Press.

Colley, L. (1992) *Britons: Forging the Nation 1707–1837*, London: Pimlico.

Cooke, S. and F. McLean (2002) '"Our Common Inheritance"? Narratives of Self and Other in the Museum of Scotland', in D. Harvey, R. Jones, N. McInroy and C. Milligan (eds) *Celtic Geographies: Old Culture New Times*, London: Routledge.

Coombes, A. E. (1991) 'Ethnography and the Formation of National and Cultural Identities', in S. Hiller (ed.) *The Myth of Primitivism – Perspectives on Art*, London: Routledge.

Coombes, A. E. (1994) *Reinventing Africa: Museums, Material Culture and Popular Imagination*, London: Yale University Press.

Corner, J. and S. Harvey (eds) (1991) *Enterprise and Heritage: Crosscurrents of National Culture*, London: Routledge.

Cox, A. with Singh, A. (1997) 'Walsall Museum and Art Gallery and the Sikh Community: A Case Study' in E. Hooper-Greenhill (ed.) *Cultural Diversity: Developing Museum Audiences in Britain*, Leicester: Leicester University Press.

Cox, D. (2002) 'At Last the Silent People Speak' in *New Statesman*, London, 22 April.

Critchley, S. (2001) 'Preface' to Jacques Derrida, *On Cosmopolitanism and Forgiveness*, London: Routledge.

Crooke, E. (2000) *Politics, Archaeology and the Creation of a National Museum in Ireland: An Expression of National Life*, Dublin: Irish Academic Press.

Crooke, E. (2001) 'Confronting a Troubled History: Which Past in Northern Ireland's Museums', *International Journal of Heritage Studies*, vol. 7 no. 2, pp. 119–36.

Cultural Action Group (2001) *'Not For the Likes of You': Barriers to Attendance Across the Cultural Sector*, London: Cultural Action Group.

Dabydeen, D. (1987) *Hogarth's Blacks: Images of Blacks in Eighteenth Century English Art*, Manchester: Manchester University Press.

Davies, E. (1950) *The Heritage of History*, Edinburgh: McDougall.

Davies, J. (1982) 'Aristocratic Town-Makers and the Coal Metropolis: The Marquises of Bute and the Growth of Cardiff 1776–1947', in D. Cannadine (ed.) *Patricians, Power and Politics in Nineteenth Century Towns*, Leicester: Leicester University Press.

Davies. N. (1999a) *The Isles: A History*, Basingstoke: Macmillan.

Davies, N. (1999b) 'But We Never Stand Quite Alone', *The Guardian*, 13 November.

DCMS (2000) *Centres for Social Change: Museums, Galleries and Archives for All*, London: HMSO.

DCMS (2001a) *Building on PAT 10*, London: HMSO.

DCMS (2001b) *Count Me In: The Dimensions of Social Inclusion through Culture, Media and Sport*, London: HMSO.

DCMS (2002) *People and Places: Social Inclusion Policy for the Built and Historic Environment*, London: HMSO.

Defoe, D. (1994) *Robinson Crusoe*, Harmondsworth: Penguin.

Delin, A. (2002) 'Buried in the Footnotes: The Absence of Disabled People in the Collective Imagery of Our Past', in R. Sandell (ed.) *Museums, Society, Inequality*, London: Routledge.

Deliss, C. (1996) 'Free Fall – Free Frame: Africa, Exhibitions and Artists', in R. Greenberg, B. Ferguson and S. Nairne (eds) *Thinking About Exhibitions*, London: Routledge.

Dennis, F. and N. Khan (eds) (2000) *Voices of the Crossing: The Impact of Britain on Writers from Asia, the Caribbean and Africa*, London: Serpent's Tail.

Derrida, J. (1982) *Margins of Philosophy*, Brighton: Harvester.

Derrida, J. (2001) *On Cosmopolitanism and Forgiveness*, London: Routledge.

Dickinson, A., P. P. L Gordon and J. Slater (eds) (1995) *International Yearbook of History Education*, vol. 1, London: The Woburn Press.

Dicks, B. (1999) 'The View of Our Town from the Hill: Communities on Display as Local Heritage' in *International Journal of Cultural Studies* vol. 2 no. 3.

Dodd, J. and R. Sandell. (eds) (2001) *Including Museums*, University of Leicester: Research Centre for Museums and Galleries.

Down County Museum (2003) *The Bicentenary of the 1803 Rebellion: Events Pamphlet*, Down County Museum.

Down District Council (1997) *Down County Museum Plan 1997–2001*, Down District Council.

Duberman, M. B. (1989) *Paul Robeson*, London: Pan Books.

Duncan C. and A. Wallach (1980) 'The Universal Survey Museum', *Art History*, vol. 3 no. 4, December pp. 448–65.

Durie, M. (1998) *Te Mana, Te Kawanatanga: The Politics of Maori Self-Determination*, Auckland: Oxford University Press.

Dyer, G. (2003) *Yoga For People Who Can't Be Bothered to Do It*, London: Abacus.

Dyer, M. (1986) *Heritage Education Handbook*, London: Heritage Education Trust.

Dyer, R. (1986) 'Paul Robeson: Crossing Over' in *Heavenly Bodies*, London: bfi and Macmillan.

Dyer, R. (1997) *White*, London: Routledge.

Edwards, P. and D. Dabydeen (eds) (1991) *Black Writers in Britain 1760–1890*, Edinburgh: Edinburgh University Press.

English Heritage (2000) *Power of Place: The Future of the Historic Environment*, London: English Heritage.

Falk, J. H. and L. Dierking (2000) *Learning from Museums: Visitor Experiences and the Making of Meaning*, California: Altamira Press.

Fanon, F. (1990) *The Wretched of the Earth*, Harmondsworth: Penguin.

Ferguson, N. (2003) *Empire: How Britain Made the Modern World*, London: Allen Lane.

Ferguson, W. (1998) *The Identity of the Scottish Nation: An Historic Quest*, Edinburgh: Edinburgh University Press.

Field, S. (ed.) (2001) *Lost Communities, Living Memories*, Cape Town: David Philip Publishers.

Finkelstein, N. (2000) *The Holocaust Industry: Reflections on the Exploitation of Jewish Suffering*, London: Verso.

Fitzduff, M. (1993) *Approaches to Community Relations Work*, Belfast: CRC Pamphlet no. 1 (3rd edition).

Flanzbaum, H. (ed.) (1999) *The Americanization of the Holocaust*, Baltimore and London: The Johns Hopkins University Press.

Foster, S. M. (2001) *Place, Space and Odyssey: Exploring the Future of Early Medieval Sculpture*, Inverness: Groam House Trust.

Foucault, M. (1977) *Discipline and Punish*, London: Tavistock.

Foucault, M. (1986) *The Order of Things: An Archeology of the Human Sciences*, London & New York: Tavistock Publications.

Foucault, M. (1991) *The Order of Things: An Archeology of the Human Sciences*, London: Routledge.

Frei, N. (1999) *Vergangenheitspolitik: Die Anfänge der Bundesrepublik und die NS-Vergangenheit*, Munich: DTV.

Freud, S. (1955) 'Analysis of a Phobia in a Five-year-old Boy', *Two Case Histories, Standard Edition of the Complete Psychological Works of Sigmund Freud, vol. 10*, London: Hogarth Press.

Freud, S. (1958) 'Remembering, Repeating and Working Through', *The Case of Schreber; Papers on Technique, and other works, Standard Edition of the Complete Psychological Works of Sigmund Freud, vol. 12*, London: Hogarth Press.

Freud, S. (1975) 'On Transience', *The Standard Edition of the Complete Works of Sigmund Freud, vol. 14*, London: Hogarth Press.

Freud, S. (1978) *Five Lectures on Psychoanalysis; Leonardo da Vinci, and other works. Standard Edition of the Complete Psychological Works of Sigmund Freud, vol. 11*, London: Hogarth Press.

Freud, S. (1985) 'Our Attitude Toward Death', *Freud Pelican Library 12*, Harmondsworth: Penguin.

Freud, S. (1990) 'Totem and Taboo', *Freud Pelican Library 13*, Harmondsworth: Penguin.

Fryer, P. (1984) *Staying Power: The History of Black People in Britain*, London: Pluto Press.

Fukuyama, F. (1989) 'The end of history?', *National Interest* 16, Summer, pp. 3–18.

Fukuyama, F. (1992) *The End of History and the Last Man*, Harmondsworth: Penguin.

Fulbrook, M. (1999) *German National Identity after the Holocaust*, Cambridge: Polity.

Furedi, F. (2001) 'The "second generation" of Holocaust survivors', http://www.spiked-online.com/articles/00000000545B.htm (accessed April 2002).

Futuresonic (2003) Press release for *Migrations* exhibition at Gallery Oldham, 19 July–27 September.

Geraghty, C. (2000) *British Cinema in the Fifties: Gender, Genre and the 'New Look'*, London: Routledge.

Gerzina, G. (1999) *Black England: Life Before Emancipation*, London: Allison and Busby.

Gibson, F. (2000) 'Reminiscence and Museums', *Museum Ireland*, no. 10 pp. 26–35.

Gillis, J. R. (ed.) (1994) *Commemorations: The Politics of National Identity*, Princeton, NJ: Princeton University Press.

Gilroy, P. (1987) *There Ain't no Black in the Union Jack: The Cultural Politics of Race and Nation*, London: Hutchinson.

Gilroy, P. (2000) *Between Camps: Nations, Cultures and the Allure of Race*, Harmondsworth: Penguin.

Gilroy, P. (2002) *Neither Jews nor Germans: where is liberalism taking us?*, in *www.opendemocracy.net* (accessed September 2002).

Glancey, J. (2002) 'By George!' in *The Guardian*, 20 June.

Goldberg, M. (1995) *Why Should Jews Survive? Looking Past the Holocaust Toward a Jewish Future*, New York: Oxford University Press.

Golden Jubilee Unit (2002) *Celebrations*, Belfast: Golden Jubilee Unit.

Graham, B., G. J. Ashworth and J. E. Tunbridge (2000) *A Geography of Heritage: Power, Culture and Economy*, London: Arnold.

Gray, J. (2002) 'Community as Place-Making: Ram Auctions in the Scottish Borderland', in V. Amit (ed.) *Realizing Community: Concepts, Social Relationships and Sentiments*, London: Routledge.

Green, A. (1986) 'The Analyst, Symbolization and Absence', *On Private Madness* London: Hogarth Press.

Greenspan, H. (1999) 'Imagining survivors. Testimony and the Rise of Holocaust consciousness', in H. Flanzbaum (ed.) *The Americanization of the Holocaust*, Baltimore: Johns Hopkins University Press.

Gundara, J. S. and I. Duffield (eds) (1992) *Essays on the History of Blacks in Britain: From Roman Times to the Mid-Twentieth Century*, Aldershot: Avebury.

Gupta, A. and J. Ferguson (1997). 'Beyond 'Culture': Space, Identity and the Politics of Difference', in A. Gupta and J. Ferguson (eds) *Culture, Power, Place: Explorations in Critical Anthropology*, Durham, NC: Duke University Press.

Habermas, J. (1999) *The Inclusion of the Other: Studies in Political Theory*, Cambridge: Polity.

Hall, C. (ed.) (2000) *Cultures of Empire: A Reader*, Manchester: Manchester University Press.

Hall, S. (1992a) 'New Ethnicities', in J. Donald and A. Rattansi (eds) *Race, Culture, Difference*, London: Sage.

Hall, S. (1992b), 'Our Mongrel Selves', in *New Statesman*, London.

Hall, S. (1996) 'New ethnicities' in D. Morley and K. Chen (eds) (1996) *Stuart Hall: Critical Dialogues in Cultural Studies*, London: Routledge.

Hall, S. (1999a) 'Culture, Community, Nation', in D. Boswell and J. Evans, *Representing the Nation, A Reader: Histories, Heritage and Museums*, London and New York: Routledge.

Hall, S. (1999b) 'Race against Time: Ethnicity, Race and Nation', Barry Amiel and Norman Melburn Trust Lecture, London, 1 July.

Hall, S. (1999c) 'Whose Heritage? Un-settling "The Heritage", Re-imagining the Post-nation', *Whose Heritage?* Conference, G-Mex, Manchester; reprinted in this volume.

Hall, S. (2000a) 'A Question of Identity', *The Observer*, 15 October, p. 27.

Hall, S. (2000b) 'Conclusion: The Multicultural Question', in B. Hesse (ed.) *Un/settled Multiculturalisms: Diasporas, Entanglements, Transruptions*, London and New York: Zed Books.

Hallam, E. and B. V. Street (eds) (2000) *Cultural Encounters: Representing Otherness*, London: Routledge.

Handelman, D. (1998) *Models and Mirrors: Towards an Anthropology of Public Events*, Oxford: Berghahn.

Handler, R. (1988) *Nationalism and the Politics of Culture in Quebec*, Madison: University of Wisconsin Press.

Hansen, M. (2000) 'The Mass Production of the Senses: Classical Cinema as Vernacular Modernism', in C. Gledhill and L. Williams (eds) *Reinventing Film Studies*, London: Arnold.

Hartman, G. (ed.) (1994) *Holocaust Remembrance: The Shapes of Memory*, Oxford: Blackwell.

Harvey, D. C., R. Jones, N. McInroy and C. Milligan (eds) (2002) *Celtic Geographies: Old Culture, New Times*, London: Routledge.

Hassan, S. 'The Modernist Experience in African Art: Visual Expressions of Self- and Cross-Cultural Aesthetics' (1999) in O. Oguibe and O. Enwezor (eds) *Reading The Contemporary: African Art From Theory To The Market-Place*, London: Institute of International Visual Arts (InIVA).

Heathcote Amory, E. and G. Rayner (2000) 'Racism Slur on the Word "British"', *Daily Mail*, 11 October, pp. 6–7.

Heinen, A. (2000) 'Towards a European "Experience Space"?', in S. Macdonald (ed.) *Approaches to European Historical Consciousness. Reflections and Provocations*, Hamburg: Körber.

Held, D., A. McGrew, D. Goldblatt and J. Perraton (1999) *Global Transformations*, Cambridge: Polity.

Her Majesty's Inspectorate (1988) *History from 5 to 16: Curriculum Matters 11*, London: HMSO.

Herzfeld, M. (1997) *Cultural Intimacy: Social Poetics in the Nation-state*, London: Routledge.

Hesse, B. (ed.) (2000) *Un/settled Multiculturalisms: Diasporas, Entanglements, Transruptions*, London and New York: Zed Books.

Hesse, B. (2002) 'Forgotten Like A Bad Dream: Atlantic Slavery and Ethics of Postcolonial Memory', in D. T. Goldberg and A. Quayson (eds) *Relocating Postcolonialism*, Oxford: Blackwell.

Hewison, R. (1987) *The Heritage Industry: Britain in a Climate of Decline*, London: Methuen.

Hewison, R. (1995) *Culture and Consensus: England, Art and Politics since 1940* London: Methuen.

Heywood, F. (2003) 'Bittersweet Legacy', *Museums Journal*, vol. 103 no. 10 pp. 28–31.

Higson, A. (2001) 'Heritage Cinema and Television', in D. Morley and K. Robins (eds) *British Cultural Studies: Geography, Nationality and Identity*, Oxford: Oxford University Press.

Hiller, S. (ed.) (1991) *The Myth of Primitivism: Perspectives on Art*, London: Routledge.

History Today, 'Imagining History' Editorial, vol. 38, June 1988.

Hitchens, P. (2002) 'Why I Can't Wait for It All to Be Over for England' in *The Mail on Sunday*, London, 2 June.

Hobsbawm, E. (1992), *Nations and Nationalism since 1780: Programme, Myth and Reality*, Cambridge: Canto.

Hobsbawm, E. (1997) *On History*, London: Abacus.

Hobsbawm, E. and T. Ranger (eds) (1983) *The Invention of Tradition*, Cambridge: Cambridge University Press.

Holt, O. (2002) 'Back To Business as Normal' in the *Daily Mirror*, London, 14 October.

Home Office (1999) *Government Proposal for a Holocaust Remembrance Day*, London: Home Office Communications Directorate.

Hooper-Greenhill, E. (ed.) (1997) *Cultural Diversity: Developing Museum Audiences in Britain*, Leicester: Leicester University Press.

Hooper-Greenhill, E. (1997) 'Towards plural perspectives', in E. Hooper-Greenhill (ed.)

Cultural Diversity: Developing Museum Audiences in Britain, Leicester: Leicester University Press.

Hooper-Greenhill, E. (2000) *Museums and the Interpretation of Visual Culture*, London: Routledge.

Hooper-Greenhill, E. (2002) *Evaluating the Impact on Learning of the Museum Visit*, Paper delivered at Museums and Audiences Seminar, Tate Liverpool, Museum and Society Study Group, 31 October 2002.

Horne, D. (1984) *The Great Museum: The Re-Presentation of History*, London: Pluto Press.

Hoskins, A. (2003) 'Signs of the Holocaust: Exhibiting Memory in a Mediated Age', *Media, Culture and Society*, vol. 25, no. 1 pp. 7–22.

Howard, J. (1996a) 'Racial tolerance', *[Australian] Commonwealth Parliamentary Debates*, 30 October.

Howard, J. (1996b) 'Sir Robert Menzies Lecture', *The Australian*, 19 November.

Howe, D. (2002), 'Blacks Usually Support Brazil' in *New Statesman*, London, 1 July.

Hoyles, M. (1991) *The Story of Gardening*, London: Journeyman.

Huntington, S. (1993) 'The Clash of Civilizations?', *Foreign Affairs* vol. 72. no. 3, pp. 22–49.

Huntington, S. (1996) *The Clash of Civilizations and the Remaking of World Order*, New York: Simon and Schuster.

Huntington, S. (1997) 'The West and the Rest', *Prospect*, February, pp. 34– 9.

Hutcheon, L. (1994) 'The Post Always Rings Twice: The Postmodern and the Postcolonial', *Textual Practice*, vol 8, Summer 1994, pp. 205–38.

Hutchinson, J. and A. D. Smith (eds) (1996) *Ethnicity*, Oxford: Oxford University Press.

Hutton, W. (2000) 'Never mind facts, let's have a scandal', *Observer*, 15 October, p. 30.

Huyssen, A. (1995) *Twilight Memories: Marking Time in a Culture of Amnesia*, New York: Routledge.

Interculture, *Vision 2003: New Freedoms* conference, Harewood House Leeds, 11–13 June.

James, C. L. R. 'Popular Art and the Cultural Tradition' in Third Text, no. 10, Spring 1990, pp. 3–10.

James, H. (2002) *Investigation of the Setting and Context of the Hilton of Cadboll Cross-slab, Recovery of the Stump and Fragments of Sculpture*, unpublished report, Glasgow University Archaeological Research Division.

James, S. (1999) *The Atlantic Celts: Ancient People or Modern Invention?*, London: The British Museum Press.

Jeismann, M. (ed.) (1999) *Mahnmal Mitte: Eine Kontroverse*, Köln: DuMont.

Jenkins, R. (1997) *Rethinking Ethnicity*, London: Sage.

Jermyn, H. and P. Desai (2000) *Arts: What's in a Word? Ethnic Minorities and the Arts*, London: Arts Council of England.

Johnson, P. (2000) 'In praise of being British', *Daily Mail*, 11 October, pp. 12–13.

Johnston, P. (2000a) 'Straw wants to rewrite our history: British is a racist word, says report', *Daily Telegraph*, 10 October, p. 1.

Johnston, P. (2000b) 'Thinkers who want to consign our island story to history', *Daily Telegraph*, 10 October, p. 6.

Johnston, P. (2000c) 'Straw beats a very British retreat over race report', *Daily Telegraph*, 14 October, p. 1.

Jones, S. (1997) *The Archeology of Ethnicity: A Theoretical Perspective*, London: Routledge.

245

Jones, S. (2003) *Early Medieval Sculpture and the Production of Meaning, Value and Place: the case of Hilton of Caboll*, unpublished report for Historic Scotland, Edinburgh.

Jones, S. (2004) ' "They made it a living thing didn't they . . . ": Hilton of Cadboll and the Production of Identity, Place, and Belonging', in S. Foster and M. Cross (eds) *Able Minds and Practised Hands: Scotland's Early Medieval Sculpture in the Twenty-First Century*, Edinburgh: Society for Medieval Archaeology.

Jones, S. (in preparation) *Fragments from the Margins: Heritage, Place and Belonging in the Modern State.*

Jordan, G. and C. Weedon (1995) *Cultural Politics: Class, Gender, Race and the Postmodern World*, Oxford: Blackwell.

Jordan, G. and C. Weedon (2002) 'When the Subalterns Speak, What Do They Say? Radical Cultural Politics in Cardiff Docklands', in P. Gilroy, L. Grossberg and A. McRobbie (eds) *Without Guarantees: In Honour of Stuart Hall*, London: Verso.

Jordanova, L. (2000) *History in Practice*, London: Arnold.

Kaeppler, A. L. (1994) 'Paradise Regained: The Role of Pacific Museums in Forging National Identity', in F. Kaplan (ed.) (1996) *Museums and the Making of 'Ourselves': The Role of Objects in National Identity*, London: Leicester University Press.

Kaplan, F. (ed.) (1996) *Museums and the Making of 'Ourselves': The Role of Objects in National Identity*, London: Leicester University Press.

Karp, I, and S. Lavine (eds) (1991) *Exhibiting Cultures: The Poetics and Politics of Museum Display*, Washington, DC: Smithsonian Institute.

Kaufman, N. (2003) 'The Sugar Songs', Paper given at *Vision 2003: New Freedoms* conference, Harewood House, Leeds, 11–13 June.

Kavanagh, G. (2000) *Memory and the Museum*, Leicester: Leicester University Press.

Kelly, L. and P. Gordon. (2002) 'Developing a Community of Practice: Museums and Reconciliation in Australia', in R. Sandell (ed.) *Museums, Society and Inequality*, London: Routledge.

Kempny, M. (2002) 'Cultural Islands in the Globalizing World: Community-Cum-Locality of the Cieszyn Lutherans', in V. Amit (ed.) *Realizing Community: Concepts, Social Relationships and Sentiments*, London: Routledge.

Khan, N. (1976) *The Arts Britain Ignores: The Arts of Ethnic Minorities in Britain*, London: Community Relations Commission.

Khan, N. (2000) *Responding to Cultural Diversity: Guidance for Museums and Galleries*, London: Museums and Galleries Commission.

Khan, N. (2002) *Towards a Greater Diversity: Results and Legacy of the Arts Council of England's Cultural Diversity Action Plan*, London: Arts Council of England.

Khan, N. (ed.) (2003) *Reinventing Britain: Cultural Diversity Up Front and on Show*, London: *The Guardian*/decibel.

Kidd, C. (2002) 'The ideological uses of the Picts, 1707–c.1990', in E. J. Cowan and R. J. Finlay (eds) *Scottish History: The Power of the Past*, Edinburgh: Edinburgh University Press.

King, S. (2002) 'Racial Violence Mars World Cup Progress' in *Searchlight*, London, July 2002.

Kipling, R. (1975) *Puck of Pook's Hill*, Inverness: Piccolo.

Kipling, R. (1991) *Something of Myself*, London: Canto.

Kirkdale Archaeology (1998) *Hilton of Cadboll Chapel, 3 August 1998*, unpublished report for Historic Scotland.

Kirkdale Archaeology (2001) *Hilton of Cadboll Chapel Site Archaeological Excavation, 7 March 2001*, Unpublished Report for Historic Scotland.

Kirshenblatt-Gimblett, B. (1998) *Destination Culture: Heritage, Tourism and Museums*, Berkeley: University of California Press.

Kirshenblatt-Gimblett, B. (1991) 'Objects of Ethnography', in I. Karp and S. Lavine (eds) *Exhibiting Cultures: The Poetics and Politics of Museum Display*, Washington, DC: Smithsonian Institute.

Koppel, G. (2001) 'To stage a nation's remembrance', *Perspectives*, Summer, pp. 6–8.

Krog, A. (1998) *Country of My Skull*, London: Cape.

Kuhn, A. (2002) *An Everyday Magic: Cinema and Cultural Memory*, London: I.B.Tauris.

Kushner, T. (1992) 'Heritage and Ethnicity: An Introduction', in T. Kushner (ed.) *The Jewish Heritage in British History: Englishness and Jewishness*, London: Frank Cass, pp. 1–28.

Kushner, T. (1994) *The Holocaust and the Liberal Imagination: A Social and Cultural History*, Oxford: Blackwell.

Kushner, T. (1997) ' "I want to go on living after my death": the memory of Anne Frank', in M. Evans and K. Lunn (eds) *War and Memory in the Twentieth Century*, Oxford: Berg.

Kushner, T. (1998) 'Remembering to Forget: Racism and Anti-Racism in Post-War Britain', in B. Cheyette and L. Marcus (eds) *Modernity, Culture and 'the Jew'*, Cambridge: Polity.

Lacey, J. (1999) 'Seeing Through Happiness: Hollywood Musicals and the Construction of the American Dream in Liverpool in the 1950s' in A. Kuhn and S. Street (eds) *Journal of Popular British Cinema*, vol. 2.

Lackmann, T. (2000) *Jewrassic Park: Wie baut man (k)ein Jüdisches Museum in Berlin*, Berlin and Vienna: Philo.

Lang, B. (1999) *The Future of the Holocaust. Between History and Memory*, Ithaca: Cornell University Press.

Lang, C. and S. Wilkinson (2000) *Social Inclusion Fact Sheet*, London: Museums and Galleries Commission.

Le Goff, J. and P. Nora (eds) (1985) *Constructing the Past: Essays in Historical Methodology*, Cambridge University Press.

Leonard, M. (1997) *Britain TM: Renewing our identity*, London: Demos.

Leonard, M. (2002) 'Living Together after 11 September and the Rise of the Right' in P. Griffith and M. Leonard (eds) *Reclaiming Britishness*, London: The Foreign Policy Centre.

Lindfors, B. (1999) *Africans on Stage: Studies in Ethnological Show Business*, Bloomington: Indiana University Press.

Littler, J. (2000) 'Creative Accounting: Consumer Culture, the "Creative Economy" and the Cultural Policies of New Labour' in T. Bewes and J. Gilbert (eds) *Cultural Capitalism: Politics after New Labour*, London: Lawrence and Wishart.

Littler, J. and R. Naidoo (2004) 'White Past, Multicultural Present: Heritage and National Stories' in H. Brocklehurst and R. Phillips (eds) *History, Nationhood and the Question of Britain*, Basingstoke: Palgrave Macmillan.

Longley E. (2001) 'Multiculturalism and Northern Ireland: Making Differences Fruitful', in *Multi-culturalism: The View from the Two Irelands*, Cork: Cork University Press.

Lowenthal, D. (1998) *The Heritage Crusade and the Spoils of History*, Cambridge: Cambridge University Press.

McCalman, I. (ed and introduction) (1991) *The Horrors of Slavery and Other Writings by Robert Wedderburn*, Edinburgh: Edinburgh University Press.

McCrone, D., A. Morris and R. Kiely (1995) *Scotland – the Brand: The Making of Scottish Heritage*. Edinburgh: Polygon.

McCrone, D. (2002) 'Nationalism, identity and history', in E. J. Cowan and R. J. Finlay (eds) *Scottish History: The Power of the Past*, Edinburgh: Edinburgh University Press.

Macdonald, J. and A. Gordon (1971) *Down to the Sea: An Account of Life in the Fishing Villages of Hilton, Balintore and Shandwick*, Fort William: Ross and Cromarty Heritage Society (3rd edn, n.d.).

Macdonald, S. (1997) *Reimagining Culture: Histories, Identities and Gaelic Resistance*, Oxford: Berg.

Macdonald, S. (2003) 'Trafficking in History: Multitemporal Practices', *Anthropological Journal on European Cultures*, vol. 11, pp. 93–116.

Mace, R. (1976) *Trafalgar Square*, London: Lawrence and Wishart.

McEnchroe Williams, M. (2001) 'Constructing the Market Cross at Tuam: The Role of Cultural Patriotism in the Study of Irish High Crosses', in C. Hourihane (ed.) *From Ireland Coming: Irish Art From the Early Christian to the Late Gothic Period and its European Context*, Princeton, NJ: Princeton University Press.

McGarr, P. (2002) 'Show Red Card to Nationalism' in *Socialist Worker*, London, 22 June.

McGuigan, J. (1996) *Culture and the Public Sphere*, London: Routledge.

McManus, G. (1992) 'The Te Maori Exhibition and the Future of Museology in New Zealand', in S. Pearce (ed.) *Museums and Europe*, London: The Athlone Press.

MacPherson, W. (1999) *The Stephen Lawrence Inquiry: Report of An Inquiry by Sir William MacPherson of Cluny*, London: HMSO.

Macwhirter, I. (1998) 'The Bulldogs that didn't Bark' in *Renewal*, vol. 6 no. 4 pp. 47–54.

Malik, K. (1996) *The Meaning of Race: Race, History and Culture in Western Society*, Basingstoke: Macmillan.

Mandler, P. (1997) *The Rise and Fall of the Stately Home*, New Haven: Yale University Press.

Martin, S. I. (1996) *Incomparable World*, London: Quartet Books.

Martin, S. I. (2000) *Britain's Slave Trade*, London: Channel 4 Books.

Matustík, M. J. B. (1998) 'Ludic, Corporate and Imperial Multiculturalism: Imposters of Democracy and Cartographers of the New World Order', in C. Willet (ed.) *Theorizing Multiculturalism*, Oxford: Blackwell.

Marx, K. (1973) 'The 1857 Introduction', *The Grundrisse*, Harmondsworth: Penguin.

Merriman, N. (1993) *The Peopling of London: Fifteen Thousand Years of Settlement from Overseas*, London: Museum of London.

Merriman, N. (1997) 'The Peopling of London Project' in E. Hooper-Greenhill (ed.) (1997) *Cultural Diversity: Developing Museum Audiences in Britain*, Leicester University Press.

Mewitt, P. G. (1986) 'Boundaries and Discourses in a Lewis Crafting Community', in A. P. Cohen (ed.) *Symbolising Boundaries: Identity and Diversity in British cultures*, Manchester: Manchester University Press, pp. 71–87.

Michman, D. (ed.) (2002) *Remembering the Holocaust in Germany, 1945–2000: German Strategies and Jewish Responses*, New York: Peter Lang.

Ministry of Education (1952) *Teaching History*, Pamphlet no. 23, London: Ministry of Education.

Miskell, P. (1997) 'Film Exhibition in Wales: A Study of Circuits and Cinemas c.1918–1951' in *Llafu: Journal of Welsh Labour History*, vol. 7 no. 2.

Morgan, R. (1994) *Cardiff: Half-and-half a Capital*, Cardiff: Gomer Press.

Moriarty, C. (1997) 'Private Grief and Public Remembrance: British First World War Memorials', in M. Evans and K. Lunn (eds) *War and Memory in the Twentieth Century*, Oxford: Berg.

Morley, D. (2000) *Home Territories: Media, Mobility and Identity*, London: Routledge.

Morley, D. and K. Robins (eds) (2001) *British Cultural Studies: Geography, Nationality and Identity*, Oxford: Oxford University Press.

Mouffe, C. (2000) *The Democratic Paradox*, London: Verso.

Nadel, J. (1984) 'Stigma and Separation: Pariah Status and Community Persistence in a Scottish Fishing Village, *Ethnology* vol. 23 no. 2, pp. 101–15.

Nadel-Klein, J. (1991) 'Reweaving the Fringe: Localism, Tradition and Representation in British Ethnography', *American Ethnologist* vol. 18 no. 3, pp. 500–15.

Nadel-Klein, J. (2003) *Fishing for Heritage: Modernity and Loss along the Scottish Coast*, Oxford: Berg.

Nadkarni, M. (2003) 'The Death of Socialism and the Afterlife of its Monuments: Making and Marketing the Past in Budapest's Statue Park Museum' in K. Hodgkin and S. Radstone (eds), *Contested Pasts: The Politics of Memory*, London: Routledge.

Naidoo, R. (1998) 'All in the Same Boat?' *Soundings* Issue 10 pp. 272–79.

Nairn, T. (2000) *After Britain: New Labour and the Return of Scotland*, London: Granta Books.

Nairn, T. (2002) *Pariah: Misfortunes of the British Kingdom*, London: Verso.

Nancy, J. (1993) *The Birth to Presence*, Stanford, CA: Stanford University Press.

Nandy, A. (1983) *The Intimate Enemy*, Oxford: New Delhi.

National Curriculum (1999) London: HMSO, Department of Education.

National Curriculum History Working Group (1990) *Final Report*, London: Department of Education and Science and the Welsh Office, April.

Newman, J. (2002) *Windrush Forbears: Black People in Lambeth 1700–1900*, Lambeth: Lambeth Archives.

Nietzsche, F. (1991) 'On the Uses and Disadvantages of History for Life', in *Untimely Meditations*, Cambridge: Cambridge University Press.

Niven, B. (2002) *Facing the Nazi Past: United Germany and the Legacy of the Third Reich*, London: Routledge.

Nooteboom, C. (2002) *All Souls' Day*, London: Picador.

Norgrove, K. (2001) *Taking Part: An Audit of Social Inclusion Work in Archives*, Sheffield: National Council on Archives.

Norquay, G. and G. Smyth (2002) 'Introduction: Crossing the Margins', in G. Norquay and G. Smyth (eds) *Across the Margins: Cultural Identity and Change in the Atlantic Archipelago*, Manchester: Manchester University Press.

Novick, P. (2000) *The Holocaust and Collective Memory: The American Experience*, London: Bloomsbury.

O'Toole, F. (2000) 'Art has not reflected our grief', *Irish Times*, 1 August 2000.

Oliver, W. H. (1984) *The Oxford History of New Zealand*, Oxford: Clarendon Press.

Ollins, W. (1999) *Trading Identities: Why Countries and Companies are Taking on Each Others' Roles*, London: Foreign Policy Centre.

Pagden, A. (2002) 'Oak in a Flowerpot', *London Review of Books*, 14 November.

Parekh, B. (1997) 'National culture and multiculturalism', in K. Thompson (ed.) *Media and Cultural Regulation*, London: Sage.

Parekh, B. (1999) 'Political theory and the Multicultural Society', *Radical Philosophy* no. 95, May/June, pp. 27–32.

Parekh, B. (2000a) *Rethinking Multiculturalism: Cultural Diversity and Political Theory*, Basingstoke: Macmillan.

Parekh, B. (2000b) 'Why it is vital to change what it means to be British', *The Daily Telegraph*, 18 October, p. 26.

Parekh, B. (2000c) 'Integrating Minorities', London: ICA Diversity Lecture.

Parekh, B. (2000d) 'A Britain We All Belong To', *The Guardian*, 11 October, p. 19.

Parkhill, T. (2003) ' "That's Their History": Can a Museum's Historical Presentation Inform the Reconciliation Process in a Divided Society?', Paper delivered at the *Heritages Seminar Series, Academy for Irish Cultural Heritages*, University of Ulster, 7 February.

Parsons, T. (2002) 'Our Flag's Reclaimed', *Daily Mirror*, London, 24 June.

Paul Robeson Cymru Committee/Bevan Foundation (2001) *Let Paul Robeson Sing*.

Pearce, S. (ed.) (1992) *Museums and Europe*, London: The Athlone Press.

Phillips, A. (2004) 'Close-ups' *History Workshop Journal*, no. 57.

Phillips, J. (1996) 'Our History, Our Selves: The Historian and National Identity', *New Zealand Journal of History*, vol. 30, no. 2, pp. 107–22.

Phillips, M. (2002) 'Rebirth of England' in the *Sun*, London, 21 June.

Phillips, R. (1997) 'Thesis and Antithesis in Tate's Views on History, Culture and Nationhood', *Teaching History*, no. 86.

Phillips, R. (1998) *History Teaching, Nationhood and State: A Study in Educational Politics*, London: Cassell.

Phillips, T. and M. Phillips (1998) *Windrush: The Irresistible Rise of Multi-Racial Britain*, London: Harper Collins.

Pines, J. (2001) 'Rituals and Representations of Black "Britishness" ' in D. Morley and K. Robins (eds) (2001) *British Cultural Studies: Geography, Nationality and Identity*, Oxford: Oxford University Press.

Piper, D. (1964) *The Companion Guide to London*, London: Collins.

Pocock, J. G. A. (1975) 'British History: A Plea For a New Subject', *Journal of Modern History*, no. 47 pp. 601–21.

Pollock, V. (2000) 'Local Identities at Armagh and Fermanagh County Museums', *Museum Ireland*, no.10, pp. 68–74.

Poovaya-Smith, N. (1997) 'Academic and Public Domains: When is a Dagger a Sword?' in E. Hooper-Greenhill (ed.) (1997) *Cultural Diversity: Developing Museum Audiences in Britain*, Leicester: Leicester University Press.

Poovaya-Smith, N. (2003) 'The Suga Babes', Paper given at *Vision 2003: New Freedoms* conference, Harewood House, Leeds, 11–13 June.

Porter, R. (ed.) (1992) *Myths of the English*, Cambridge: Polity Press.

Private Eye (2000) no. 1013, 20 October, p. 19.

Public Services Quality Group (1999) *National Survey of Visitors to British Archives*, London: Public Record Office.

Radstone, S. (2003) 'The Limits of Memory', Paper presented to the Memory

Colloquium, Raphael Samuel History Centre, University of East London, June.

Ramdin, R. (1987) *The Making of the Black Working Class in Britain*, Hants: Gower.

Ramdin, R. (1999) *Reimaging Britain: 500 years of Black and Asian History*, London: Pluto Press.

Ramirez, M. C. (1996) 'Brokering Identities: Art Curators and the Politics of Cultural Representation', in R. Greenberg, B. Ferguson and S. Nairne (eds) *Thinking About Exhibitions*, London: Routledge.

Ransom, D. (2001) *The No-Nonsense Guide to Fair Trade*, London: Verso.

Rassool, C. and S. Prosalendis (eds) (2001) *Recalling Community in Cape Town: Creating and Curating the District Six Museum*, Cape Town: District Six Museum.

Reichel, P. (2001) *Vergangenheitsbewältigung in Deutschland. Die Auseinandersetzung mit der NS-Diktatur von 1945 bis heute*, Munich: Beck.

Richards, E. (2000) *The Highland Clearances*, Edinburgh: Birlinn.

Richards, J. (1997) *Films and British National Identity*, Manchester: Manchester University Press.

Richardson, B. (ed.) (1997) *A Grand Design: The Art of the Victoria and Albert Museum*, New York: Harry N. Abrams Press.

Ridgwell, S. (1995) 'South Wales and the Cinema in the 1930s', in *Welsh History Review*, vol. 17 no. 4. pp. 590–615.

Ritchie, A. (1989) *Picts: An Introduction to the Life of the Picts and the Carved Stones in the Care of Historic Scotland*, Edinburgh: Historic Scotland.

Roberts, A. (2000) 'We know in our hearts what Britain means', *Sunday Telegraph*, 15 October.

Robins, K. (1991) 'Tradition and Translation: National Culture in its Global Context', in J. Corner and S. Harvey (eds) *Enterprise and Heritage: Crosscurrents of National Culture*, London: Routledge.

Rojek, C. (1993) *Ways of Escape: Modern Transformations in Leisure and Travel*, London: Macmillan.

Rosenberg, G. (1997) 'Das jüdische Dilemma: Identitäten zwischen Diaspora und Zionismus', *Lettre International*, vol. 39, no. 4. pp. 46–53.

Rowlands, M. (1999) 'Remembering to Forget: Sublimation as Sacrifice in War Memorials', in A. Forty and S. Küchler (eds) *The Art of Forgetting*, Oxford: Berg.

Runnymede Trust (2000) *The Future of Multi-Ethnic Britain: The Parekh Report*, London: Profile Books.

Rushdie, S. (1988) *The Satanic Verses*, London: Vintage.

Rutherford, J. (1997) *Forever England: Reflections on Masculinity and Empire*, London: Lawrence and Wishart.

Said, E. (1983) *The World, The Text and the Critic*, Cambridge, MA: Harvard University Press.

Salmond, A. (1992) *Two Worlds – First Meetings Between Maori and Europeans 1642–1772*, Auckland: Viking Press.

Samuel, R. (1990) 'The Return of History', *London Review of Books*, 14 June 1990; reprinted in R. Samuel (1998) *Island Stories: Unravelling Britain: Theatres of Memory, Volume II*, London: Verso.

Samuel, R. (1994) *Theatres of Memory. Volume 1: Past and Present in Contemporary Culture*, London: Verso.

Samuel, R. (1998) *Island Stories: Unravelling Britain: Theatres of Memory, Volume II,* London: Verso.

Sandell, R. (2002) 'Museums and the Combating of Social Inequality: Roles, Responsibilities, Resistance', in R. Sandell (ed.) *Museums, Society, Inequality,* London: Routledge.

Sandell, R. (ed.) (2002) *Museums, Society, Inequality,* London: Routledge.

Sawyer, M. (2002) 'Women like Beckham', in *Observer Sport Monthly,* London.

Schaefer, S. (2002) 'We Can Fly the Flag with Pride' in *Tribune,* London, 5 July.

Schama, S. (2000) *A History of Britain: At the Edge of the World?,* London: BBC Worldwide.

Schneer, J. A. (2001) *London 1900: The Imperial Metropolis,* New Haven, CT: Yale University Press.

Schwarz, B. (1999) 'Reveries of race: The Closing of the Imperial Moment', in B. Conekin, F. Mort and C. Waters (eds) *Moments of Modernity? Reconstructing Britain, 1945–1964,* London: Rivers Oram.

Scott, D. (1999) *Refashioning Futures: Criticism After Post-Coloniality,* Princeton, NJ: Princeton University Press.

Scottish Executive (1999) *Treasure Trove in Scotland: Information on Treasure Trove Procedures, Criteria for Allocation and the Allocation Process,* Edinburgh: Scottish Executive.

Seaford, H. (2001) 'The Future of Multi-Ethnic Britain: An Opportunity Missed', *Political Quarterly* vol. 72 no. 1, pp. 107–13.

Sealy, M. (2003) *Programme Notes to an Exhibition,* Hatton Gallery, Newcastle.

Shaikh, H. (2001) 'Exploring Cultural Diversity', in J. Dodd and R. Sandell (eds) *Including Museums,* University of Leicester: Research Centre for Museums and Galleries.

Shemilt, D. (1980) *History 13–16: Evaluation Study,* Edinburgh: Holmes McDougall.

Sheridan, K. (1998) 'A Farewell to Arms', *Irish Times,* 13 June 1998.

Sherwood, M. (1991) 'Racism and Resistance: Cardiff in the 1930s and 1940s' in *Llafur: Journal of Welsh Labour History,* vol. 5 no. 4. pp. 51–70.

Simpson, M. G. (2001) *Making Representations: Museums in the Post-Colonial Era,* 2nd edn, London and New York: Routledge.

Sinclair, N. M. C. (1997) *The Tiger Bay Story,* Cardiff: Butetown History and Arts Project.

Slater, J. (1995) *Teaching History in the New Europe,* London: Cassell.

Smith, D. (1984) *Wales! Wales?,* London: George Allen and Unwin.

Smout, T. C. (1969) *A History of the Scottish People 1560–1830,* London: Fontana Press.

Sollers, W. (1986) *Beyond Ethnicity,* Oxford: Oxford University Press.

Soyinka, W. (1999) *The Burden of Memory: The Muse of Forgiveness,* New York: Oxford University Press.

Speers, T. (2001) *Welcome or Over-Reaction? Refugees and Asylum Seekers in the Welsh Media,* Wales Media Forum, School of Journalism, Media and Cultural Studies, Cardiff University.

Stacey, J. (1994) 'Hollywood Memories', *Screen,* vol. 35 no. 4. pp. 317–35.

Starkey, D. (2001) 'The English Historian's Role and the Place of History in English National Life', *The Historian,* no. 71, Autumn.

Starkey, D. *et al.* (1987) *The English Court: From the Wars of the Roses to the Civil War,* London: Longman.

Stead, P. (1986) 'Wales in the Movies', in T. Curtis (ed.) *Wales: The Imagined Nation: Essays on Cultural and National Identity*, Bridgend: Poetry Wales Press.

Straw, J. (2000) 'Blame the Left not the British', *Observer*, 15 October, p. 27.

Szekeres, V. (2002) 'Representing Diversity and Challenging Racism: The Migration Museum' in R. Sandell (ed.) *Museums, Society, Inequality*, London: Routledge.

Tal, K. (1998) 'Duppies in the Machine', http://www.freshmonsters.com/kalital/Text/Articles/Duppies.html (accessed 10 September 2003).

Tamarapa, A. (1996). 'Museum Kaitiaki: Maori Perspectives on the Presentation and Management of Maori Treasures and Relationships with Museums' in J. Davis, M. Segger and L. Irvine *Curatorship: Indigenous Perspectives in Post-Colonial Societies*, Toronto: Canadian Museum of Civilisation.

Te Maori Management Committee (1988) *Te Maori, Final Report of the Te Maori Managment Committee*, Wellington: Government Printer.

The Times (2000) 'Editorial: The Strip of History', 17 June.

Thomas, B. (1997) *Fleapits and Picture Palaces*, Cardiff: National Museum of Wales.

Thomas, L. M. (1999) 'Suffering as a Moral Beacon: Blacks and Jews', in H. Flanzbaum (ed.) *The Americanization of the Holocaust*, Baltimore: Johns Hopkins University Press.

Thomas, N. (1991) *Entangled Objects: Exchange, Material Culture and Colonialism in the Pacific*, London: Harvard University Press.

Thomas, N. (1994) *Colonialism's Culture: Anthropology, Travel and Government*, Cambridge: Polity.

Thomas, N. (1995) 'Kiss the Baby Goodbye: Kowhaiwhai and Aesthetics in Aotearoa New Zealand', *Critical Inquiry*, Autumn, 1995, pp. 90–121.

Thompson, J. (2002) *Taking Responsibility for the Past: Reparation and Historical Injustice*, Cambridge: Polity Press.

Thompson, P. (2000) *The Voice of the Past*, Oxford: Oxford University Press.

Tulloch, C. (2001) *Exhibitions Policy of the Archives and Museum of Black Heritage*, London: AMBH.

Turner, V. (1967) *The Forest of Symbols*, Ithaca, NY: Cornell University Press.

Ulster People's College (2002) *Prospectus*, Belfast: Ulster People's College.

Urry, J. (1990) *The Tourist Gaze: Leisure and Travel in Contemporary Society*, London: Sage.

Vergo, P. (ed.) (1989) *The New Museology*, London: Reaktion.

Victoria and Albert Museum (V&A) (2002) *Connections and Disconnections: Museums, Cultural Heritage and Diverse Communities*, leaflet.

Vincendeau, G. (ed.) (2001) *Film/Literature/Heritage: A Sight and Sound Reader*, London: bfi publishing.

Visram, R. (1986) *Ayahs, Lascars and Princes: Indians in Britain 1700–1947*, London: Pluto Press.

Walker, S. (1997) 'Black Cultural Museums in Britain: What Questions Do They Answer?', in E. Hooper-Greenhill (ed.) *Cultural Diversity: Developing Museum Audiences in Britain*, Leicester: Leicester University Press.

Wallace, A. (2001) 'Collections Management and Inclusion', in J. Dodd and R. Sandell (eds) *Including Museums*, University of Leicester: Research Centre for Museums and Galleries.

Walsh, K. (1992) *The Representation of the Past: Museums and Heritage in the Post-modern World*, London: Routledge.

Walvin, J. (1992) 'From the Fringes: The Emergence of British Black Historical Studies', in J. S. Gundara and I. Duffield (eds) *Essays on the History of Blacks in Britain: From Roman Times to the Mid-Twentieth Century*, Aldershot: Avebury.

Walvin, J. (2003) 'The Academic Research on Harewood', paper given at *Vision 2003: New Freedoms* conference, Harewood House Leeds, 11–13 June.

Ware, V. (1991) *Beyond the Pale: White Women, Racism and History*, London: Verso.

Ware, V. and L. Back (2002) *Out of Whiteness: Color, Politics and Culture*, Chicago: University of Chicago Press.

Warner, M. (1996) *Monuments and Maidens: The Allegory of the Female Form*, London: Vintage.

Warner, M. (2000) 'Sorry: the present state of apology', www.opendemocracy, 7 November.

Warner, R. (ed.) (2000) *Icons of Identity*, Belfast: Ulster Museum.

Welsh Language Unit (2003) *Iaith Pawb: A National Action Plan for a Bilingual Wales* Cardiff: Welsh Assembly.

Williams, C. (2003) 'Strange Encounters: Our Assumptions about Race', *Planet* no. 158 April/May 2003 pp. 19–24.

Williams, G. A. (1985) *When Was Wales?*, Harmondsworth: Penguin.

Williams, R. (1963) *The Long Revolution*, Harmondsworth: Pelican.

Williams, R. (1992) 'Homespun Philosophy', in the *New Statesman*, London.

Willis, P. (1980) 'Notes on Method', in S. Hall, D. Hobson, A. Lowe and P. Willis (eds) *Culture, Media, Language*, London: Hutchinson and CCCS.

Wills, G. (1992) *Lincoln at Gettysburg: The Words that Remade America*, New York: Simon and Schuster.

Wilson, A. (1978, 4th edn 1988) *Finding a Voice: Asian Women in Britain*, London: Virago Press.

Wilson, E. (1989) *The Myth of British Monarchy*, London: The Journeyman Press.

Withers, C. W. J. (1996) 'Place, Memory, Monument: Memorializing the Past in Contemporary Highland Scotland', *Ecumene* vol. 3 no. 3, pp. 325–44.

Wolf, E. (1982) *Europe and the People Without History*, Berkeley: University of California Press.

Wood, M. (2000) *Blind Memory: Visual Representations of Slavery in England and America, 1780–1865*, Manchester: Manchester University Press.

Wood, N. (1999) *Vectors of Memory: Legacies of Trauma in Postwar Europe*, Oxford: Berg.

Wood, S. (1998) 'Issues of National Identity and the School Curriculum in Scotland', in J. Arnold, K. Davies and S. Ditchfield (eds) *History and Heritage: Consuming the Past in Contemporary Culture*, Dorset: Donhead.

Worpole, K. (2001) 'Cartels and Lotteries: Heritage and Cultural Policy in Britain', in D. Morley and K. Robins (eds) *British Cultural Studies: Geography, Nationality and Identity*, Oxford: Oxford University Press.

Wright, P. (1985) *On Living in an Old Country: The National Past in Contemporary Britain*, London: Verso.

Wright, T. (2000) 'Introduction: England, whose England?', in S. Chen and T. Wright (eds) *The English Question*, London: The Fabian Society.

Young, J. E. (1993) *The Texture of Memory: Holocaust Memorials and Meanings*, New Haven, CT: Yale University Press.

Young, J. E. (2000) *At Memory's Edge: After-Images of the Holocaust in Contemporary Art and Literature*, New Haven, CT and London: Yale University Press.

Young, L. (1996) *Fear of the Dark: 'Race', Gender and Sexuality in the Cinema*, London: Routledge.

Young, R. J. C. (1995) *Colonial Desire: Hybridity in Theory, Culture and Race*, London: Routledge.

Young, R. J. C. (2001) *Postcolonialism: An Historical Introduction*, Oxford: Blackwell.

Yuval-Davis, N. and M. Silverman (2002) 'Memorializing the Holocaust in Britain', in *Ethnicities*, vol. 2 no. 1 pp.107–23.

INDEX

Note: References to annotated text are indicated as '25 (n21)'; references to Notes as '261 n21.'